A Theological Examination of Symbolism in Ezekiel with Emphasis on the Shepherd Metaphor

Joel K. T. Biwul

MONOGRAPHS

© 2013 by Joel K. T. Biwul

Published 2013 by Langham Monographs
an imprint of Langham Creative Projects

Langham Partnership
PO Box 296, Carlisle, Cumbria CA3 9WZ, UK
www.langham.org

ISBNs:
978-1-783689-96-5 Print
978-1-783689-95-8 Mobi
978-1-783689-94-1 ePub

Joel Biwul has asserted his right under the Copyright, Designs and Patents Act, 1988 to be identified as the Author of this work.

All rights reserved. No part of this publication may be reproduced, stored in a retrieval system or transmitted, in any form or by any means, electronic, mechanical, photocopying, recording or otherwise, without the prior written permission of the publisher or the Copyright Licensing Agency.

Scriptures taken from the Holy Bible, New International Version®, NIV®. Copyright © 1973, 1978, 1984, 2011 by Biblica, Inc.™

British Library Cataloguing in Publication Data
Biwul, Joel K. T., author.
  A theological examination of symbolism in Ezekiel with emphasis on the shepherd metaphor.
  1. Bible. Ezekiel--Criticism, interpretation, etc.
  2. Bible. Ezekiel--Language, style. 3. Metaphor in the Bible. 4. Ezekiel (Biblical prophet)--Prophecies.
  5. Ezekiel (Biblical prophet)--Symbolism. 6. Prophecy--Judaism. 7. Shepherds in the Bible. 8. Jews--History--Babylonian captivity, 598-515 B.C.
  I. Title
  224.4'064-dc23

ISBN-13: 9781783689965

Cover & Book Design: projectluz.com

Langham Partnership actively supports theological dialogue and a scholars right to publish but does not necessarily endorse the views and opinions set forth, and works referenced within this publication or guarantee its technical and grammatical correctness. Langham Partnership does not accept any responsibility or liability to persons or property as a consequence of the reading, use or interpretation of its published content.

In memory of my dear paternal uncle, Nda Miskaham Daniel Danehep Gurumdi Dalang (died 28 August, 1980).

Contents

List of Abbreviations xi

Abstract xiii

Acknowledgements xv

CHAPTER ONE 1
Introduction
   1.1 Introduction to the Study 1
   1.2 Statement of the Research Problem 4
   1.3 The Problem with Ezekiel 7
   1.4 Purpose and Significance of the Study 12
   1.5 Research Methodology and Procedure 15
   1.6 Ezekiel in the Prophetic Tradition 18
   1.7 Definition of Terms and Concepts 23
   1.8 Conclusion 30

CHAPTER TWO 31
Ezekiel's Use of Symbolism and the Shepherd Metaphor
   2.1 Introduction 31
   2.2 The Context for Ezekiel's Use of Symbolism 32
      2.2.1 The Reasons for Ezekiel's Use of Symbolism 37
      2.2.2 The Categories and Meaning of Ezekiel's Symbolism 46
   2.3 Ezekiel's Use of the Shepherd Metaphor 74
      2.3.1 Reasons for His Use of the Shepherd Metaphor 78
      2.3.2 His Methodology in Using the Shepherd Metaphor 86
   2.4 The Etymology and Semantics of the Shepherd Metaphor 89
      2.4.1 Its Etymology 89
      2.4.2 Its Semantic Domains 92
   2.5 Conclusion 95

CHAPTER THREE 97
The Historical and Literary Contexts for the Shepherd Metaphor in Ezekiel 34
   3.1 Introduction 97
   3.2 The Historical Context for the Use of the Shepherd Metaphor in Ezekiel 98
      3.2.1 The Shepherd Metaphor in Ancient Nomadic Life 100
      3.2.2 Ancient Near Eastern Usage of the Shepherd Metaphor ... 112

3.3 The Literary Context for the Shepherd Metaphor in Ezekiel 120
3.4 The Shepherd Metaphor in Pre-Classical Prophetic Texts 121
    3.4.1 Its Treatment in Isaiah's and Micah's Texts......................123
    3.4.2 Its Treatment in Jeremiah's Text...128
3.5 Conclusion 130

CHAPTER FOUR 131
Ezekiel's Shepherd Metaphor and the Norms of Deuteronomic Theology
4.1 Introduction 131
4.2 The Significance of Deuteronomic Theology to Israel...............133
    4.2.1 Israel as a Nation Characterised by the Covenant Motif...136
    4.2.2 Israel as a Nation Characterised by the Blessing Motif....140
4.3 The Implications of Deuteronomic Theology for Exilic Israel....143
    4.3.1 Exile Questions the Reality of Yahweh's Covenant 145
    4.3.2 Exile Questions the Reality of Yahweh's Status 148
    4.3.3 Exile Questions the Traditional Belief in
          Israel's Existence 151
4.4 Ezekiel's Eschatological Response to the Exiles 154
    4.4.1 Exile Has a Punitive Purpose Preparatory for
          Eschatological Shepherding..156
    4.4.2 Exile Has a Preservative Purpose to Achieve
          Eschatological Shepherding..159
    4.4.3 Exile Has a Restorative Motif to Achieve
          Eschatological Worship 164
4.5 Ezekiel Critiques Judah Against the Norms of Deuteronomic
    Theology 168
    4.5.1 The People Critiqued for False Reliance on
          Zion Theology 173
    4.5.2 Royal Leadership Critiqued for Official Abuses...............176
    4.5.3 Religious Leadership Critiqued for Incompetence...........182
    4.5.4 Ezekiel's Watchman Motif as a Model for
          True Shepherding..188
4.6 Conclusion 192

CHAPTER FIVE... 193
A Case for Eschatological Shepherding in Ezekiel 34
5.1 Introduction 193
5.2 The Literary and Structural Context for Ezekiel 34 195
    5.2.1 Ezekiel Chapters 13, 17 and 19 as a Literary Context
          for the Shepherd Metaphor. 198
    5.2.2 The Literary Structure of Ezekiel 34................................201

  5.3 Indictment of Imperfect Human Shepherds, vv. 1-16 203
    5.3.1 "Woe" Oracle Indicting Israel's Bad Shepherd's, vv. 1-6 ... 204
    5.3.2 Judgement Oracle Against Israel's Bad Shepherds,
    vv. 7-10 208
    5.3.3 Oracle of Yahweh's Eschatological Rescue Mission,
    vv. 11-16 210
  5.4 Indictment and Sifting of Israel's Imperfect Flock, vv. 17-22 212
    5.4.1 Yahweh's Indictment and Judgement of the Evil Sheep,
    vv. 17-21 213
    5.4.2 Yahweh's Justice for the Helpless Sheep, v. 22 217
  5.5 The Declaration of a Perfect Eschatological Society for
  Shepherding, vv. 23-31 219
    5.5.1 An Eschatological Experience of a Davidic Tradition
    of Shepherding, vv. 23-24 220
    5.5.2 Yahweh's Covenant of a Tranquil Society for
    Eschatological Shepherding, vv. 25-31 224
  5.6 The Eschatological Role of Ezekiel's Recognition Formula 226
  5.7 Conclusion 228

CHAPTER SIX 231
Ezekiel's Theology of an Eschatological Shepherd and the New Society
  6.1 Introduction 231
  6.2 Ezekiel's Theology of Eschatological Shepherding Is Yahwistic
  in Outlook 233
    6.2.1 His Shepherding Theology Has a Visionary Undertone ... 235
    6.2.2 Yahweh's Shepherding Exhibits His Covenant Fidelity 239
  6.3 Eschatological Shepherding Requires a Return to Yahweh 244
    6.3.1 Eschatological Shepherding Demonstrates
    Yahweh's Grace 245
    6.3.2 Eschatological Shepherding Demands Honour for
    Yahweh's Name 248
  6.4 Ezekiel's Theological Basis for Disqualifying Israel's Shepherds
  from Eschatological Shepherding 252
    6.4.1 A Contrast of Yahweh's Shepherding Attributes with
    Israel's Imperfect Human Shepherds 253
    6.4.2 Theological Indictment of Israel's Worthless Shepherds ... 260
  6.5 Ezekiel's Theology of "I AM YAHWEH" for Eschatological
  Shepherding 266
  6.6 Conclusion 269

CHAPTER SEVEN 271
Summary and Conclusions
    7.1 Summary of the Study 271
    7.2 Some Observations from the Study...274
        7.2.1 Its Implications for Contemporary
            Ecclesiastical Leadership...277
        7.2.2 Its Implications for Contemporary Political Leadership 282
    7.3 Recommendations for Further Research..................................290

Bibliography... 293

List of Abbreviations

AB	The Anchor Bible
ABD	The Anchor Bible Dictionary
ANE	Ancient Near East
AJBS	African Journal of Biblical Studies
ANET	Ancient Near Eastern Text edited by James B. Pritchard
BDB	Francis Brown, S. R. Driver, and Charles A. Briggs
BST	The Bible Speaks Today
BS	Bibliotheca Sacra
BA	The Biblical Archaeologist
BW	The Biblical World
CAN	Christian Association of Nigeria
CBR	Currents in Biblical Research
CBQ	The Catholic Biblical Quarterly
EBS	Encountering Biblical Studies Series
ECWA	The Evangelical Church Winning All
GR	Geographical Review
HTR	Harvard Theological Review
IVP	Inter-Varity Press
IBT	Interpreting Biblical Texts
ISBE	The International Standard Bible Encyclopaedia
JETS	Jos ECWA Theological Seminary
JSOTSup	Journal for the Study of the Old Testament Supplement Series
JHS	The Journal of Hebrew Scriptures
JCAS	Journal for Criminal Animal Studies
JFSR	Journal of Feminist Studies in Religion
JR	The Journal Religion

JBL	Journal of Biblical Literature
JSOT	Journal for the Study of the Old Testament
LTQ	Lexington Theological Quarterly
MLA	Modern Language Association
MSJ	The Master's Seminary Journal
MCB	Mercer Commentary on the Bible Series
NICOT	New International Commentary on the Old Testament
NAC	The New American Commentary Series
NAC	The NIV Application Commentary Series
NIDOTTE	The New International Dictionary of Old Testament Theology and Exegesis
NIDNTT	The New International Dictionary of New Testament Theology
NEA	Near Eastern Archaeology
OTS	Old Testament Studies Series
RQ	Restoration Quarterly
SBL	Society of Biblical Literature
SJT	Scottish Journal of Theology
SCM	Scripture Christian Mission Press
TOTC	Tyndale Old Testament Commentaries series
TB	Tyndale Bulletin
TDNT	Theological Dictionary of the New Testament
TDOT	Theological Dictionary of the Old Testament
VT	Vetus Testamentum
WBC	Word Biblical Commentary

Abstract

The use of symbolic and metaphoric expressions is normative in the literary convention of Jewish prophetism. Ezekiel stands in this prophetic tradition in his use of symbolic sign-acts and particularly the shepherd metaphor in chapter 34. Our topic, "A Theological Examination of Symbolism in Ezekiel with Emphasis on the Shepherd Metaphor," seeks to discover, first, the reason(s) why symbolic sign-acts are used in Ezekiel far more than any other Jewish prophet. As one called into the prophetic function in Babylonia, we seek second, to know why the prophet used the shepherd metaphor while addressing his fellow Babylonian exiles. In this quest, we noted that apprehension had dominated the heart and spirit of the Babylonian exiles. This was precipitated by the fact that they were struggling hard to come to terms with recent events in their history vis-à-vis the traditional belief in Jerusalem as inviolable. As a consequence, they had turned to accusing Yahweh for allowing such a disaster to befall his covenant people, city, and his shrine, the Temple. In a careful response to such scenario, we argued that as an active participant in the agony of the Babylonian exile, Ezekiel used symbolic sign-acts basically as an antidote to defuse the apprehension of his fellow exiles against his prophetic word. Ezekiel's goal in this respect was to gain attention so he is able to explain the causation for their being in exile, and why Jerusalem's impending demise was inevitable so that perhaps they would resort to a productive therapeutic action.

As we particularly argued for the theological-eschatological perspective of the shepherd metaphor in Ezekiel 34, we insisted that Ezekiel used the shepherd metaphor against the massive failure in Israelite society, caused by Israel's bad and imperfect human shepherds who failed to be true under-shepherds of Yahweh's flock. We indicated that such failure became unavoidable because Israel's shepherds resorted to seeking their own glory instead of glory for Yahweh's name as his responsible under-shepherds. As a result, the flock suffered in the hands of both internal and external human predators. On this basis, we pointed out that Ezekiel used the shepherd metaphor against the norms of Deuteronomistic theology with an indictive approach vis-à-vis the acts of covenantal infidelity on the part of Israel as a people in covenant relationship with Yahweh. Furthermore, we submitted that massive abuse of human rights also existed in Israelite society controlled by the self-seeking aristocratic upper class pictured as the goats and rams, that is, the robust sheep, for lack of true shepherds.

In particular, we noted that it is against the backdrop of a failed Israelite state as well as the exhibition of the negative shepherding attitudes of Israel's bad and imperfect human shepherds that Ezekiel employed the shepherd metaphor with a theological-eschatological perspective to give hope to the oppressed in such society. He did this both as a remedy and as a recipe for an anticipated perfect and tranquil society to be made conducive for Yahweh's eschatological shepherding of his bastardised and weary flock.

Acknowledgements

History is crucial to human existence. A number of individuals form part of my life's history and success story. On the basis of the principle of courtesy therefore, I wish to place on record the following: First, I am most thankful to my late uncle, Nda Miskaham Daniel Danehep Gurumdi Dalang, who sacrificed his health for my education. He was the one who taught me the essence of Christian values and commitment to faith. From him I learned the biblical principles of patience, honesty, prudence, generosity, and commitment. He taught me by his lifestyle what it means to be compassionate and to sacrifice one's pleasure for the comfort of others. But for his immense labour and sacrifice, it is unlikely that I would have come this far in my academic pursuit. To this rare gem, to this man of very rare religious piety, to a hero and mentor par excellence, I owe my all in life, in ministry, and in scholarship.

Second, I am most thankful to my late father who taught me the essence of hard work, of defending my fundamental human rights, of standing for truth and justice, and of fighting in defence of the oppressed and downtrodden of society. Both my father and mother taught me the principles of boldness, firmness and self-confidence. These two, though dead (mother died January 27, 2005 and father died December 12, 2007), are my hero and heroine in their individual rights.

Third, words fail to express how deeply grateful I am to Rev. Associate Professor Jotham Maza Kangdim of the University of Jos, Nigeria, who guided this research. His believing in my academic capability and encouraging comments kept me on course. Similarly, I remain deeply grateful to Professors Margaret Sinclair Odell and Daniel Isaac Block for their critical comments. Odell's were particularly quite challenging and motivating. I also owe a debt of gratitude to Professor Samuel Waje Kunhiyop of

Jos ECWA Theological Seminary (JETS), Jos, Nigeria, now the General Secretary of The Evangelical Church Winning All (ECWA), for encouraging me to undertake my doctoral training within the African context, particularly in Nigeria, even when I had planned to have such training elsewhere. The counsel of Professors Yusuf Turaki of JETS and Zamani Buki Kafang of ECWA Theological Seminary, Kagoro, Nigeria, at the initial stage in my proposal is deeply appreciated. The friendship I enjoyed from Professor Hendricks L. Bosman of Stellenbosch University, Cape Town, South Africa, during my research visit to Stellenbosch, is greatly acknowledged. The confidence that Dr. Jim Crouch of JETS had in my academic ability was no less very motivating and propelling. I am thankful to Rev. Dr. Samuel Olarewaju for challenging me to pursue a PhD against all odds.

Fourth, I lack words to express my deep gratitude to Dr. Ronald Rice for accepting to edit this work at very short notice, almost under duress. His queries were very helpful. Also, I remain grateful to the Board of Governors of JETS who granted me study leave to pursue this study. The encouragement of the Provost of JETS, Rev. Associate Professor Bulus Y. Galadima, is appreciated. I do equally acknowledge the financial contribution of the Overseas Council International (OCI) towards my studies. Besides, the financial support that I enjoyed from some local churches and individual friends significantly aided my research expenses. The financial support of ECWA Goodnews, Maitama in Abuja, and the love of their pastors, Rev. Michael Ijah and Pastor Ogidi Joshua Dickson, are worthy of mention. I also deeply acknowledge the wise suggestions of Pastor Baba Bulus Wambai towards fund raising as well as the true friendship and support I enjoyed from Pastor and Mrs. Jane and Nathan Chiroma during my research trip to Cape Town, SA. I acknowledge severally the material and financial contributions of Rev. Col. Simon Kachiro Bargo, Engr. Babachir David Lawal, Mr. and Mrs. Isaac Yamma, Mr. and Mrs. Abigail and John Paul Tyndale Hunt, Mrs. Grace S. Got, Mr. Yiljap Abraham, Mrs. Oklah Joshua Lidani, Mrs. Halima John Isandu, Dr. Miss. Halima Rabeh, Mr. Maren Damina Makut, and host of other friends.

Lastly, I deeply acknowledge the huge support enjoyed from my family members during the period of my torturous studies, particularly, the concern of my three children (Dorcas Andih, Seth Ahmetmu, and

Grayom Aputgurum). Also, the ideological concept of "Providential" and "Consolatory Theology" of Dr. Matthew Michael (Rabbi Mikhail) and "Bakomi Theology" of the Rev. Dr. Bitrus Alkali Sarma, when we all were passing under the seemingly unending yoke of JETS PhD work, were quite encouraging, reassuring and relieving of my stress and pains of academic rigours. I do appreciate the friendship of my friends and fellow JETS doctoral students, Rev. Stephen O. Baba and Pastor Ishaku Kubgak. The tireless effort of Dr. Randee O. Ijatuyi-Morphe, the Chair of the doctoral programme, and that of the PhD Committee in directing the programme and to graduate the first class is duly acknowledged. Particularly, the passion with which Professor George E. Janvier, the PhD Programme Director, administered the programme was quite stimulating and propelling to me. I sincerely appreciate the friendship of Peter Williams, the warden, and Elizabeth the librarian, both of Tyndale House, Cambridge, for granting me access to their research library. The same appreciation is extended to the management and staff of the Theology Library of Stellenbosch University, Cape Town, SA. The laughter, teasing, smiles and encouraging words of Mrs. Amina Barje Maigadi, the Secretary to the PhD Director, are highly appreciated. I am particularly also thankful for the prayers and encouraging words of my students and the entire JETS community.

CHAPTER ONE

Introduction

1.1 Introduction to the Study

It is obvious from the final form of his book that Ezekiel uses symbolism and the shepherd metaphor in his prophetic speeches. The main emphasis of the shepherd metaphor in the Old Testament expresses "the care of shepherds for their sheep."[1] By using this metaphor, it appears Ezekiel is here suggesting that Israel's shepherds have acted contrary to such necessary shepherding character. The shepherds who should tend the flock and "use their positions of authority to serve the people . . . instead used their power for dishonest gain . . . to satisfy their own needs."[2] Such shepherding dislocation forces Yahweh, the true Shepherd of his covenant community, to raise a lament oracle against the selfish attitude of Israel's shepherds whom he has placed over his flock. Yahweh declares, "Woe, shepherds of Israel who only feed themselves! Should shepherds not feed the flock?" (Ezek 34:2).

As a result of the shepherds' covenant infidelity and their brute behaviour to Yahweh's flock, the calamity of the demise of Jerusalem became its obvious consequence. The grievous effect of this disaster for Israel is the loss of the city of Zion, Jerusalem, and the temple with its priesthood. Consequently, Ezekiel leans on the hope principle derived from the

---

1. Ronald M. Hals, *Ezekiel* (Grand Rapids, Mich.: Eerdmans, 1989), 249.
2. Bill T. Arnold and Bryan E. Beyer, *Encountering the Old Testament*: EBS Series, 2d ed. (Grand Rapids, Mich.: Baker, 2008), 421.

shepherding *hesed* of Yahweh[3] to point his audience to Yahweh's programme of future restoration for Judah. This eschatological hope principle becomes evident in Ezekiel because it is grounded in his recall of Yahweh's shepherding *hesed* in the first exodus. It is even more evident, because of the presence of many shepherding clusters used for Yahweh in the Old Testament.

The Old Testament is clustered with the shepherd metaphor because Yahweh, from whom Israel's history has its roots, is Israel's Shepherd and Israel is his flock. On this basis, the Psalter uses the shepherd motif often to describe Israel as Yahweh's people, the sheep of his pastures.[4] With this understanding, descriptive terms such as Defender (Pss 82:3; 119:154; Isa 1:17; 51:22), Provider (Pss 111:5, 9; Isa 43:20), Protector (Pss 5:11; 32:7; 91:14; 116:6), Shield (Pss 7:10; 28:7; 33:20; 115:9; 144:2; cf. Prov 18:10), Rock (Pss 18:2; 19:14; 89:26; Isa 26:4), Refuge (Pss 9:9; 46:1; 91:2; 62:8; 119:114; 144:2), Saviour (Pss 25:5; 27:9; 65:5; 79:9; Isa 17:10; 45:15; 48:17; 59:20; Mic 7:7), and so on are assigned to Yahweh in the Psalter and in the prophets. Even prior to its occurrence in the Pentateuch, the shepherd metaphor already had its origin from its ancient Near Eastern (ANE) usage. Against this background, Israel's patriarchs[5] developed and assigned

---

3. Yahweh, as Shepherd of his flock, expressed his *hesed* to Israel in several ways. See Pss 33:12; 28:9; 65:9; 68:35. Israel recognized this fact and therefore had always looked to him for his shepherding care. See Pss 79:13; 77:20; 95:7.

4. King David affirmed, "The LORD is my shepherd, I shall not be in want" (Ps 23:1 NIV). The emphatic expression of the Davidic statement that "The LORD is my shepherd" יהוה רעי is directly applied to Israel, for that is how the people understood Yahweh who kept his covenant relationship with them despite their covenant infidelity. Also see Pss 29:11; 95:7; 100:1-5; 144:15.

5. As Timothy Laniak points out, it is very "apparent that pastoralism was a widely visible and significant sector of all Near Eastern societies from the very beginning of human civilization. Sheep and goats were central to sacrificial cults, their products were necessary for daily sustenance and clothing, and ownership of large flocks marked wealth and status…Abraham was a wealthy semi-nomadic pastoralist who moved with all of his family and belongings from Ur." Timothy S. Laniak, *Shepherds after My Heart: Pastoral Traditions and Leadership in the Bible* (Downers Grove, Ill.: Inter-Varsity, 2006), 42-3.

this pastoral image to Yahweh[6] as their Shepherd.[7] This gives the prophet Ezekiel the warrant to rebuke Israel for covenant infidelity and indicting the nation's shepherds in particular, for failing to possess a shepherd character[8] like Yahweh does and exhibits towards Israel as his flock.

The interest to study the theological-eschatological perspectives of the shepherd metaphor in Ezekiel's corpus (Ezek 34) was motivated by two factors. First, the writer's pastoral background knits him to Ezekiel's theological message of indictment of the bad shepherds of Israel. Ezekiel's personal experience and participation in the agony of the Babylonian captivity, though a priest and prophet, caught the writer's attention regarding the effects of leadership failure and greed on both the righteous and unrighteous of the citizenry. Like David Petersen observes, although Ezekiel was "born into a priestly family, probably Zadokite, and had followed the ritual requirements that allow one to work as a priest, [yet, he was] taken into exile along with other prominent Judahites."[9] The implication of Ezekiel's exile experience, no doubt, suggests that when leadership fails to live up to

---

6. Yahweh is the principal Shepherd who delegates this shepherding responsibility to human under-shepherds who were to justify their responsibility by the faithful discharge of the duties of their office. He demanded undivided loyalty from these leaders. Pastoral language is employed by the prophets to show Yahweh's covenant relationship with Israel warranting his jealousy for his ownership of the people and demanding unitary and unwavering worship from the nation.

7. For instance, Jacob referred to God as shepherd in his blessing speech to Joseph's two sons, Manasseh and Ephraim (Gen 32:22-30). He said, "May the God before whom my fathers Abraham and Isaac walked, the God who has been my shepherd all my life to this day" (Gen 48:15-16 NIV; cf. Gen 28:10-22). He also described God as "the shepherd, the Rock of Israel" when pronouncing Joseph's blessings (Gen 49:24). Also, from his shepherding experience, Moses alludes to God as a shepherd of his people in his prayer, "May the LORD, the God of the spirits of all mankind, appoint a man over this community to go out and come in before them, one who will lead them out and bring them in, so the LORD's people will not be like sheep without a shepherd" (Num 27:16-17 NIV). God himself ascribed the shepherd metaphor to the judges of Israel in his response to David's desire to erect a house for him. He spoke through prophet Nathan, "Wherever I have moved with all the Israelites, did I ever say to any of their rulers whom I commanded to shepherd my people Israel...?" (2 Sam 7:7 NIV; cf. 2 Sam 5:2).

8. Prophets Isaiah (40:11), Zechariah (11:5-11) and Micah (3:1-8) employed the shepherd metaphor with an eschatological tone pointing to the Messiah. Jeremiah (23:1-4; 30:17) and Ezekiel (34:1-28) employed it with accusing tone to refer to the wayward shepherds of Israel. Ezekiel combines both the tone of indictment and eschatology.

9. David L. Petersen, "Ezekiel," in *The Harper Collins Study Bible*, ed., Wayne A. Meeks (New York: Harper Collins, 1993), 1222.

its socio-political, socio-economic, ethical, and theological obligations to society, both the righteous and the wicked suffer the consequence.

Secondly, the writer observes that a cursory survey of the attitude of contemporary political and religious leadership of Africa in general and of Nigeria in particular, towards the citizenry finds close connection with the message of Ezekiel to Israel's shepherds of his day. That Ezekiel indicted the royal and religious leaders[10] of his day for failure in their shepherding obligations to society and for their negative attitude in shepherding the flock, suggests some socio-political and theological implications for contemporary leadership. As Petersen rightly submits that the book of Ezekiel "presents several distinctive theological formulations,"[11] we think that the concept of shepherding as presented by Ezekiel has an emerging theology that is also relevant to contemporary leadership functions.

1.2 Statement of the Research Problem

The book of Ezekiel, from the first to the last chapter, despite its reflection on seeming divine abandonment, clearly indicates that it is heavily dominated by the divine shepherding motif, with particular stress on the theological-eschatological perspectives. It also indicates that Ezekiel's use of such dominant theological-eschatological motif arises against the backdrop of massive failure in both gentile and Israelite societies. But it appears this critical motif only stands in the footnotes of works on Ezekiel. A careful reading of the document of this prophet reveals that Ezekiel stands out in his treatment of numerous symbolic signs and metaphors,[12] prominent

---

10. The kings of the united and divided Kingdoms of Israel occupied both royal and political leadership status. Included on the list of political leadership also are the princes and passively, the aristocrats. While we try to consistently maintain the term 'royal leaders' or 'royal leadership' in this work, we also occasionally use 'political leadership' in reference to the same category of leadership where the context for such usage warrants. But the term 'religious leaders' or 'religious leadership' is used consistently in reference to the priests and prophets.

11. Petersen, "Ezekiel," 1223.

12. Prophet Ezekiel employs symbolic signs and metaphoric speech devices to strike a faster and clearer note in the hearing ability of his audience. He uses, for example, the fire metaphor (Ezek 15:4-5; 21:3; 22:20; 24:10) and wood of the vine metaphor (Ezek

among which is the divine shepherding motif. While admitting the use of metaphors by other prophets, Karin Schöpflin points out that they use more of imageries in contrast to Ezekiel's use of metaphoric speeches.

> The scholar argues: Elaborate metaphorical passages or even narratives are one striking characteristic of the book of Ezekiel. Of course, we find a metaphorical way of speaking in other Writing Prophets as well; but as a rule their single verses or small clusters of verses made up of metaphorical speech are neither compositions as extensive as they are in Ezekiel nor do they focus on very few basic metaphors that are in part repeatedly modified. With other Writing Prophets, imagery is much more varied throughout a book.[13]

If symbolism and metaphors, as Karin Schöpflin argues, are predominant and more obvious in Ezekiel's work than in any other Israelite prophet, why is due attention not paid to his treatment of the theological-eschatological aspects of the divine shepherding motif by scholars? This absence is the reason for our study.

The study attempts to deal with the following questions: Why does Ezekiel who is an exilic prophet and himself an active participant in the pains of the Babylonian exiles, use symbolic sign-acts in his prophetic speeches? Particularly, why does he use the shepherd metaphor at this critical moment in Judah's history? How does Ezekiel use the shepherd metaphor to evaluate and critique the Judean environment? What are the emerging theological-eschatological imports of Ezekiel's symbolism and the shepherd metaphor for exilic Israel? What is the warrant for Ezekiel's

---

15; 21:2-4) in his woe oracles against Jerusalem; the sword metaphor (Ezek 21:8); the dross metaphor in reference to Jerusalem's sin (Ezek 22:17-22); the cookery metaphor (Ezek 24:3-14); marriage metaphor to accuse Israel of her covenant infidelity (Ezek 16); the pornographic metaphor to depict the sin of Israel and Judah in respect of political alliances with foreign nations (Ezek 23); the watchman metaphor/parable (Ezek 33); the eagle, cedar and vine metaphor (Ezek 13, 17, 19); and the lion metaphor (Ezek 19).

13. Karin Schöpflin, "The Composition of Metaphorical Oracles within the Book of Ezekiel," *VT* 1 (2005): 102. She adds that in Ezekiel, "metaphors seem to be employed in an almost systematic fashion, and the arrangement of the metaphorical passages within the book appears to be a deliberate composition."

use of Deuteronomic theology in evaluating the Judean environment in the face of a seemingly failed Israelite state? What are the extant historical and literary contexts aiding Ezekiel's use of the shepherd metaphor? What theological framework of eschatological shepherding does Ezekiel construct with which to evaluate and critique royal and religious leadership in Israel? These probing questions[14] are crucial as a compass is to the pilot and radar to the captain because they serve as the guiding beacons for our inquiry.

This inquiry presupposes that Ezekiel employs symbolic sign-acts as a rhetoric device in order to get concrete attention from his stubborn and apprehensive audience, to whom he is to be "a sign." In particular, he uses the shepherd metaphor for royal leaders[15] in Israel who are his primary object of critique, and secondly to critique religious leaders for their failure to possess a shepherd character in shepherding Yahweh's flock under their care. In this connection, Ezekiel explains, in response to his audience's apprehension and argumentation regarding divine abandonment, that although Israel's leaders fail to be good shepherds, there is still hope for the nation because Yahweh, the true leader and Shepherd of Israel, will lead Israel through purposeful shepherding of his flock. He is the One who declares that אני יהוה ("I am Yahweh"), רעה ישראל (the "shepherd of Israel"), and he does not fail as Israel's leaders have. On this ground, the study further presupposes that coming from a priestly tradition, Ezekiel applies his critique of the people and leadership in Israel within the context of Deuteronomic

---

14. It is said that "a researcher's most valuable ability is the knack of being puzzled by ordinary things;" for it is in this puzzled state the researcher is able to "Cultivate the ability to see what's odd in the commonplace." Kate L. Turabian, *A Manual for Writers of Research Papers, Theses, and Dissertations,* 7th ed., rev. Wayne C. Booth, Gregory G. Colomb, Joseph M. Williams, and the University of Chicago Press Editorial Staff (London: The University of Chicago Press, 2007), 13. Engaging in research is like embarking on a journey that, though the traveller has some idea from the start about why he is travelling, where he is travelling to, and how he will get to his destination, yet, he is not too certain what may happen along the way and how exactly his destination would look like when he finally arrives. Of a necessity, questions are quite helpful for the travelling student on the academic journey. The obvious reason being that "If the writer asks no question worth pondering, he can offer no focused answer worth reading, (and) Readers of research reports don't want just information; they want the answer to a question worth asking." Wayne C. Booth, Gregory G. Colomb, and Joseph M. Williams, *The Craft of Research,* 2d ed. (London: The University of Chicago Press, 2003), 45.

15. Paul M. Joyce, *Ezekiel: A Commentary* (paperback ed.; N. Y.: T & T Clark, 2009), 196.

theology, emphasizing on the point of Israel's covenant infidelity in contrast to Yahweh's faithfulness.

1.3 The Problem with Ezekiel

The book of Ezekiel has been a neglected book and a fallow ground in biblical studies. We have observed, vis-à-vis previous studies,[16] that prophetic students, until very recently, had given more space to the treatment of other major prophets in the Jewish Scripture like Isaiah, Jeremiah, Daniel, Amos, Hosea, and Malachi than to prophet Ezekiel and his book. For instance, Walther Zimmerli asserts that, ". . . it is not surprising that critical work on the book of Ezekiel only began very hesitatingly and late."[17] This detour in scholarship is understandable because reasons always serve to explain actions.

Iain M. Duguid asserts for instance, that the book of Ezekiel "has always been hard to understand"[18] and David L. Petersen explains the reason as being that the book has a unique character that appears deterring, probably because the prophet's priestly and prophetic roles are often viewed as incontrovertibly opposed.[19] Jim Mayo equally observes that,

> The book of the prophet Ezekiel has been one of the most troublesome of canonical works to both Jewish and Christian exegetes. The rabbinic tradition records that Ezekiel would have been kept from the Jewish canon except for the efforts of Chananiah, a rabbi of the first century A.D.[20]

---

16. Only few brief comments regarding the shepherd metaphor or motif in Ezekiel are found scattered here and there in the commentaries on Ezekiel where the subject appears. Few monographs and scholarly articles similarly have made such attempts. However, no major work has appeared as yet on the subject of the theological-eschatological perspectives of the shepherd metaphor in Ezekiel.
17. Walther Zimmerli, *Ezekiel 1: A Commentary on the Book of the Prophet Ezekiel, Chapters 1–24* (eds. Frank Moore Cross and Klaus Baltzer with the assistance of Leonard Jay Greenspoon; trans. Ronald Ernest Clements; Philadelphia: Fortress, 1979), 3.
18. Iain M. Duguid, *Ezekiel and the Leaders of Israel* (Leiden: Brill, 1994), 1.
19. Petersen, "Ezekiel," 1222.
20. Jim Mayo, "Covenant Theology in Ezekiel," *RQ 1* (1973): 1.

who was able to harmonise the book to the satisfaction of the rabbis. To this difficulty, Andrew Blackwood had noted, "It is easy to understand why the prophecy is not widely read and appreciated, for the book is filled with material that is difficult to appreciate."[21] Or as Stephen Cook puts it, the prophecies in the book of Ezekiel are "among the most fascinating and puzzling writings in the Bible [because] the prophet expresses his thought through a variety of literary forms – signs, visions, allegories, denunciations, and legal arguments, among others . . . [using] bizarre or extreme imagery and elaborates it to an almost excessive point."[22] We cite two cases to echo the point thus: Mary E. Shields claims, "By any account, Ezekiel 16 is a problematic passage and the most extreme case among the prophetic oracles of accusation that use marital and sexual imagery."[23] Also, Linda Day states,

> For modern readers, Ezekiel 16 is one of the more difficult texts in the Hebrew Bible with which to deal. Textually problematic, it contains numerous words of obscure origin and uncertain meaning. Yet even more so is it ethically problematic. . . . The erotic imagery and vocabulary scandalize, bordering on the pornographic.[24]

So, from the preceding, sufficient reasons are not lacking for the scholarly neglect and bypass of Ezekiel. Explaining further the reasons for this eclipse of Ezekiel, particularly by the Christian community, Daniel Isaac Block points out that, "For many Christians Ezekiel is too strange and his

---

21. Andrew W. Blackwood, Jr., *Ezekiel: Prophecy of Hope* (Grand Rapids, Mich.: Baker, 1965), 11.
22. Stephen L. Cook, "Ezekiel," in *The New Oxford Annotated Bible: The Revised Standard Version with the Apocrypha* (3d ed.; eds., Michael D. Coogan et al. Oxford: Oxford University Press, 2001), 1180.
23. Mary E. Shields, "Multiple Exposures: Body Rhetoric and Gender Characterization in Ezekiel 16," *JFSR* 1 (1998): 5.
24. Linda Day, "Rhetoric and Domestic Violence in Ezekiel 16," *Interpretation* 3 (2000): 205.

book too complex and bizarre to deserve serious attention. So the prophet remains a mystery."²⁵ Joseph Blenkinsopp expatiates this point further:

> There is no doubt that Ezekiel is a difficult book, and not just because of its length. The language is rich, overloaded, and frequently hyperbolic, and the images are often strange, remote from mundane experience, and sometimes wilfully repellent. The vocabulary is frequently obscure and the text imperfectly transmitted, as one may gauge by the number of textual notes in modern versions such as the RSV. The intensity and even ferocity of negative emotion – anger, disdain, indignation – in the first half of the book (chps. 1-24) may also be found disturbing.²⁶

In fact, even in recent times, Ezekiel still remains a difficult book. For example, in their preface to the book they edited, Paul M. Joyce and Andrew Mein²⁷ admit the lingering difficulty in Ezekiel study. While comparing the book of Ezekiel with that of Isaiah and Jeremiah for instance, Walter Brueggemann concedes that, ". . . Christian readers of the book of Ezekiel are likely to find the articulations of the book at least unfamiliar, if not peculiar and difficult to follow. There is no doubt that the book of Ezekiel is cast in a mode that is foreign to most contemporary readers, certainly most contemporary Christian readers."²⁸ As Brueggemann points out, the

---

25. Daniel Isaac Block, *The Book of Ezekiel Chapters 1-24* (Grand Rapids, Mich.: Eerdmans, 1997), xi.
26. Joseph Blenkinsopp, *Ezekiel: Interpretation* (Louisville, Ky.: John Knox Press, 1990), 3.
27. These credible scholars in Ezekiel claim that, "There can be few, if any, books of the Bible that have generated a more diverse and challenging reception history than the book of Ezekiel. Ezekiel himself often comes across as a problematic figure, and the book that bears his name has long been considered the most difficult of all the prophetic books to understand." However, despite this lingering difficulty, they uphold the significant contributions of this difficult prophet. Paul M. Joyce and Andrew Mein, eds, "Preface," in *After Ezekiel: Essays on the Reception of a Difficult Prophet* (London: T & T Clark, 2011), vii.
28. Walter Brueggemann, *An Introduction to the Old Testament: The Canon and Christian Imagination* (Louisville, Ky.: Westminster John Knox, 2003), 191.

book of this prophet casts common themes in uncommon modes because it "voices a quite distinctive sense of Israel's faith in crisis."²⁹

From the preceding reasons that explain less interest in Ezekiel because of the book's nature, it is valid to observe that Ezekiel has been a neglected document in the field of biblical scholarship vis-à-vis the quantum of attention given to other prophetic documents. Allan MacRae agrees with our observation when he concludes that Ezekiel has become "one of the Bible's most neglected books" because scholars have failed to appreciate the situation in which Ezekiel was involved and for the poor impression about its first chapter perceived as "being extraordinarily symbolical and quite remote from normal human experience."³⁰ With this given, it should not come as a surprise to interested students of Ezekiel that biblical scholars have neglected and bypassed the shepherd metaphor in the book of Ezekiel, particularly its theological-eschatological imports.

One observes that even the older and newer students of Ezekiel who care to give attention to his book hurriedly gloss over his treatment of the shepherd metaphor to channel their academic energy to other themes in the text.³¹ For instance, William Irwin's article, which appeared in 1953, traces issues treated in Ezekiel's research between 1943 and 1953. The issues handled by the scholars whose works he surveyed on Ezekiel all border more on the question of authorship, date, locale, and methodology than on the shepherd metaphor. This, in our opinion, buttresses his own admission and submissions that ". . . the book of Ezekiel now stands well to the fore among the problems of contemporary Old Testament scholarship

---

29. Brueggemann, *An Introduction*, 191.

30. Allan A. MacRae, "The Key to Ezekiel's First Thirty Chapters," *BS* (1965): 227. It is quite obvious that it would be with great reluctance for one to venture into a project that is too difficult, strange, complex and mysterious. This is so for the fear that such effort is not only time-wasting, but its result, at the end of the day, may also be worthless.

31. Such scholars do so either for their lack of interest in the shepherding import of the book or for Ezekiel's ambiguities. Petersen notes for instance that, "He speaks, falls down, acts God's word, travels between Mesopotamia and Syro-Palestine in a visionary state, sees strange visions, and proclaims dangerous message." Petersen, "Ezekiel," 1222. Or, as Ellison observes, "the rush of modern life, which makes it difficult for so many to give long hours of study to an individual Old Testament book" like Ezekiel, causes this glossary approach. Henry Leupold Ellison, *Ezekiel: The Man and His Message* (Grand Rapids, Mich.: Eerdmans, 1956), 11.

... a consensus on even larger issues has not yet emerged."[32] Also, David Freedman's article, which appeared one year after, is not helpful either. He only glosses over the shepherd metaphor with brief comments on chapters 22 and 34.[33] Quite notably are the two German volumes of Walther Zimmerli's commentaries on Ezekiel, which came out in 1969, and the English translations published in 1979 and 1983. These volumes have been acclaimed and celebrated by scholars as groundbreaking work in Ezekiel studies in recent time. Surprisingly, however, his 77-page introduction gives no significant space to the shepherd metaphor until he gets to chapter 34. Even then, his concern is more on its literary form.[34]

Furthermore, very recently, Katheryn P. Darr's article on research in Ezekiel appeared in 1994. In identifying early and present trends in studies in Ezekiel, her survey indicates that the shepherd metaphor is waylaid and kept behind bars to allow for issues assumedly more critical to the book by scholars. Even Darr herself only admits in passing that, "Ezekiel's oracles are treasure troves for students of metaphor."[35] Similarly, Risa L. Kohn's article which is a follow-up to Darr's appeared in 2003. Although she admits that, "The twentieth century was most eventful for the scholarly study of the book of Ezekiel,"[36] yet, her treatment of the trends in the older and newer works in Ezekiel scholarship so far shows no significant treatment of the theological-eschatological perspectives of the shepherd metaphor in regards to the aspect of the divine shepherding motif in the roll call of the key themes in the book.

---

32. William A. Irvin, "Ezekiel Research Since 1943," *VT* 1. (1953):54-66.
33. David Noel Freedman, "The Book of Ezekiel," *Interpretation* 4 (1954):446-471.
34. See his two volumes thus: *Ezekiel 1: A Commentary on the Book of the Prophet Ezekiel, Chapters 1 – 24* (eds., Frank Moore Cross and Klaus Baltzer with the assistance of Leonard Jay Greenspoon; trans. Ronald Ernest Clements (Philadelphia: Fortress, 1979), 1-77, and *Ezekiel 2: A Commentary on the Book of the Prophet Ezekiel, Chapters 25 – 48* (ed., Paul D. Hanson with Leonard Jay Greenspoon; trans. James D. Martin, Philadelphia: Fortress, 1983), 203-223. The German volumes appeared in 1969 by Neukirchener Verlag des Erziehungsvereins.
35. Katheryn Pfisterer Darr, "Ezekiel Among the Critics," *CBR* 2 (1994):9-24.
36. Risa Levitt Kohn, "Ezekiel at the Turn of the Century," *CBR* 1, (2003): 9. As Kohn's article reveals, most students of Ezekiel rather give attention, broadly, to the issue of the literary, psychology, gender metaphor, corporate and individual responsibility, temple, restoration, and visions in this great prophetic corpus at the detriment of the prophet's treatment of the shepherd metaphor. See pp. 9-23.

We will risk misunderstanding if we allow the unique situation of a particular prophet slip from our grasp. When we grapple with the exilic period and context of Ezekiel and his book, and when we interpret the text against this background, the difficulty that confronts the reader will be minimised. Joyce rightly asserts in this direction when he says, "The ministry of the prophet Ezekiel and the tradition to which his work gave rise cannot be understood except against the background of the particular circumstances to which they were a response."[37] It is our contention that Ezekiel's shepherd metaphor, which has been neglected[38] over the years by scholars, is as critical as the other themes in the book, if not more. As such, Ezekiel's shepherd metaphor is to be given adequate attention, particularly so, given the exilic context within which he used the metaphor. We think therefore that to ask why Ezekiel focused on the shepherd metaphor, especially the divine shepherding motif, is a question not only worth contemplating but worth pursuing.

1.4 Purpose and Significance of the Study

Two major contributions of this research to scholarship are obvious. First, the theological-eschatological perspectives of the shepherd motif, rooted in Ezekiel's recognition formula, "You will know" and "They will know," is critical. Because of this, the obvious neglect and bypass by scholars on Ezekiel's theological-eschatological treatment of the shepherd metaphor specific to the divine shepherding motif needs to be addressed. So far, no

---

37. Joyce, *Ezekiel: A Commentary*, 3. Joyce supports his thesis with the explanation that, "Our own time and place as readers profoundly affect our experience of and interpretation of a biblical text, but the time and place of Ezekiel's original ministry remain vital issues. When and where something happened is often the key to why it may have happened."

38. Petersen exhorts, not only for the shepherding theme but for the entire corpus of Ezekiel, that despite the observable ambiguities in the book, "designing readers of Ezekiel have the opportunity to encounter one of ancient Israel's most vigorous religious thinkers, a thinker concerned with both classical priestly concerns–purity and holiness–and prophetic issues–righteousness and religious propriety." Petersen, "Ezekiel," 1222. The theme of shepherding brings to light, as seen all over the book, Yahweh's shepherding attributes in sharp contrast to those exhibited by the political and religious leaders of Israel and Judah.

significant scholarly works have appeared in this direction in Ezekiel research. Since available works on the book of Ezekiel reveal that a number of variables account for the general bypass[39] by scholars on the book, this attitude by scholars makes the book look like an accident of history in the prophetic tradition. We therefore intend particularly to help Ezekiel's readers understand the intentionality of the shepherd metaphor (Ezek 34) in the prophet. The focus of this intentionality is rooted in the context of human leadership failures as it relates to the divine shepherding motif.

Second, this study clearly points out why Ezekiel gives space to the treatment of symbolic sign-acts far more than any other Old Testament prophet. We argue that his uniquely exilic context is crucial in this respect because there are undergirding factors responsible for Ezekiel's use of symbolism. The prophet's symbolism functions as a literary device in his prophetic speeches to communicate the prophetic word. Against this context, his readers should appreciate not only the struggles the prophet himself went through, but even the issues that look bizarre and deterring in the book.

In view of the preceding, the study argues for Yahweh's covenantal commitment to Israel in Ezekiel's shepherd metaphor. This draws attention to the theological-eschatological import of Ezekiel's shepherd metaphor vis-à-vis persistent failures in human shepherding context. This thrust is reflected in his treatment of the "covenant formula" motif. The study also points out that the shepherd metaphor in Ezekiel is the prophet's major theological critique of the failure of human leadership in Israel.

We do think that our contribution finds leaning on Ralph Klein's observation that, "The continued, even renewed excitement about this good and problematical prophet and the flurry of new angles of investigation promise a prominent role for scholarship on Ezekiel in the twenty-first century."[40] By this effort, we are hopeful that wider interest in the study of

---

39. To emphasise this point, Jesús Asurmendi asserts that, "The book of Ezekiel has never been very fashionable" to scholarship because Ezekiel's book is a prophetic field many scholars shy away from, either by design or by default. Jesús Asurmendi Ruiz, "Ezekiel," in *The International Bible Commentary: A Catholic and Ecumenical Commentary for the Twenty-First Century* (ed., William R. Farmer; Collegeville, Minn.: The Liturgical Press, 1998), 1050.

40. Ralph W. Klein, "Introduction: Ezekiel at the Dawn of the Twenty-First Century,"

Ezekiel is motivated because he is not only an exciting personality but has also left behind in his prophetic work an inexhaustible gold mine for biblical research. The priestly and exilic prophetic backgrounds (Ezek 1:1-3; 2:1-5) make Ezekiel the most colourful and important of all the prophets of Israel who preceded and succeeded him. As a Judean priest who received his prophetic commission in Babylonia, Ezekiel is the only one who assumed both priestly and prophetic ministry as a Babylonian exile to his fellow exiles. In this connection, Henry McKeating contends that his dual ministry "can hardly be overstressed" because Ezekiel is not only "placed at the great crisis point of Israel's history"[41] but he is also one who "was born into a turbulent world."[42]

His work is suggested to serve as the lead for the birth and development of Judaism.[43] The prophet assures the exiles of the "abiding presence of God among them"[44] despite the catastrophe that had just befallen Jerusalem. It is Ezekiel who stands in the gap of the events of history (the Babylonian exile) at a very crucial and deciding moment for Israel's existence. John Skinner aptly captures the point: "Ezekiel had lived through a period of unprecedented public calamity, and one fraught with the most momentous consequences for the future of religion."[45] If this research is able to raise more issues than answers in the attempt to address the theological-eschatological motif of Ezekiel's shepherd metaphor, and if it is able to refocus the

---

in *The Book of Ezekiel: Theological and Anthropological Perspectives* (eds., Margaret Sinclair Odell and John T. Strong; Atlanta, Ga.: SBL, 2000), 11.

41. Henry McKeating. *Ezekiel*. JSOT (Sheffield: Sheffield Academic Press, 1993), 11.

42. Block, *The Book of Ezekiel Chapters 1-24*, 1.

43. Brueggemann divides Ezekiel's book into two broad themes—Yahweh's judgement (chs. 1-24) and Yahweh's restoration (chs. 25-48). The first part is considered "harbingers" to the second in which "…the theological shape of Ezekiel's voice…establishes what became a normative pattern of discernment in emerging Judaism that shaped the final form of the text in these voices of prophetic anticipation." Brueggemann, *An Introduction*, 196.

44. Bruce M. Metzger and Roland E. Murphy, eds., *The New Oxford Annotated Bible* (N.Y.: Oxford University Press, 1994), 1057. Some think Jeremiah has a priestly lineage like Ezekiel. For instance, Donald Wiseman states, "His association with Anathoth (1:1; cf. 1 Kgs 2:26-27) has led many to assume that he was of a priestly family." Donald Wiseman, "Jeremiah," in *The International Bible Commentary* (2d ed., ed. Frederick Fyvie Bruce; Grand Rapids, Mich.: Zondervan, 1986), 765.

45. John Skinner, "The Book of Ezekiel," in *The Expositor's Bible: A Complete Exposition of the Bible in Six Volumes, Vol. IV* (ed. W. Robertson Nicoll; Grand Rapids, Mich.: Eerdmans, 1943), 221.

attention of scholarship in the area of prophetic study to give more space to Ezekiel research, its goal will have been achieved.

1.5 Research Methodology and Procedure

The overriding methodology employed in this study is theological.[46] However, on a minimal scale, it is also a multidimensional methodological framework[47] in the sense that embedded within its main theological grid is the historical[48] and comparative[49] approaches. Although it is composed as a

---

46. The whole of Scripture as sacred text–Jewish and Christian–has an emerging theology. This is to be easily seen in the different categorisation of the various parts of the sacred text as well as its individual books. The theological approach used in the present research therefore attempts to locate Ezekiel's theological presupposition and understanding of the concept of shepherding as tied to his perception of Yahweh as Shepherd of his covenant people.

47. The history of biblical hermeneutics reveals that since the beginning of biblical scholarship, quite a number of methodologies and interpretive approaches with which to understand the biblical text have appeared. Richard Soulen and R. Soulen have reported some of these methods and approaches as follows: "Textual Criticism, Historical Criticism, Literary Criticism, Form Criticism, Tradition Criticism, Redaction Criticism, Rhetorical Criticism, Structuralism, Postcritical Biblical Interpretation, Afrocentric Biblical Interpretation, Ideological Criticism, Reader-Response Criticism, Feminist Biblical Interpretation, Advocacy Criticism, and others." Richard N. Soulen and R. Kendall, *Handbook of Biblical Criticism* (3d ed.; Louisville, Ky.: Westminster John Knox, 2001), xi.

48. The historical approach taken in this study attempts to locate Ezekiel and his work within a clearly defined historical timeframe, without which it is difficult to adequately comprehend his prophetic utterances. As scholars have observed, the interpreter of the Hebrew text "must go beneath the surface of what the text says and probe more deeply into what it meant in its ancient Israelite context, for this is the key to understanding what it means theologically for the people of God of all ages. To appreciate fully the meaning of a text, one must understand the historical context from which it derives and the cultural realities that it reflects and assumes." Robert B. Chisholm Jr., *From Exegesis to Exposition: A Practical Guide to Using Biblical Hebrew* (Grand Rapids, Mich.: Baker, 1998), 149. We need also mention that a literary approach is minimally used in this work in an attempt to locate the main text under study (Ezekiel 34) within its literary boundary and structure in the whole book. Even then, our approach takes seriously the historical and cultural contexts of the text into account. Our judgement assumes that "the text is rooted in a historical-cultural context that is inextricably linked to its meaning." See Chisholm as above, p. 151.

49. The comparative approach is necessitated by the evaluation of the behaviour of contemporary ecclesiastical and political leadership in Africa against Ezekiel's use of the shepherd metaphor as a yardstick to critique the leadership of his day. Ezekiel's critique of leadership failure and negative attitude along with that of his close contemporary,

literary material that is segmented into literary units, the book of Ezekiel is also a historical prophetic document because the events enumerated by the prophet not only emerge from a historical background but are themselves historic in their own right. Employing the historical method therefore lays a basic framework for the theological examination of the subject being pursued. This plays out in our discussion of chapter three. The comparative method on the other hand is reflected in our discussion of the implications of the study to contemporary ecclesiastical and political leadership experience in chapter seven. Since we are here dealing with a biblical text that demands appropriate understanding of its theology within its specific historical context, the hermeneutical approach with which we engage our discourse is biblical-theological. This approach to biblical theology takes the final form of the canon of Ezekiel as a unified whole.[50] It trails the line of the historical, literal-grammatical approach to biblical hermeneutics. To be clear, by its narrowed definition and limitation, the interpretive method employed in this work is viewed as that which:

> . . . seeks to understand the ancient text in light of its historical origins, the time and place in which it was written, its sources, if any, the events, dates, persons, places, things, customs, etc., mentioned or implied in the text. [It also proceeds with the understanding that] Its primary goal is to ascertain the text's primitive or original meaning in its original historical context (its "literal sense," or more precisely, its *sensus literalis historicus*).[51]

Jeremiah, has some points of commonality. It is on this basis that we think it expedient to employ the comparative method.

50. In his introductory comments to the work he edited, Johan Lust admits the presence of divergent methods to the study of this prophet. He wonders, "Faced with this somewhat bewildering diversity of opinions, one wonders what the methodological presuppositions are of their proponents." Johan Lust, "Introduction: Ezekiel and His Book," in *Ezekiel and His Book: Textual and Literary Criticism and their Interpretation* (ed. Johan Lust; Leuven: Leuven University Press, 1986), 2-3.

51. Soulen and Kendall, *Handbook of Biblical Criticism*, 3d ed., 79.

As a matter of procedure, the organisation of the research is developed topically in seven chapters. The first chapter presents the introductory elements of the entire work. It unveils the research problem and its hypothesis, the purpose and significance, the methodology and the procedure of how the study unfolds, and lastly, a definition of some key terms and concepts that weave through the entire study. The second chapter undertakes a contextual inquiry into the use of symbolism and the shepherd metaphor in the book of Ezekiel. It basically explores the reasons for the prophet's much use of symbolism and their categorisation. It also explores Ezekiel's reasons for using the shepherd metaphor as well as the methodology he employs in addressing the exiles as his primary audience.

The study proceeds to the third chapter by seeking to understand the historical and literary contexts for the shepherd metaphor in Ezekiel chapter 34. It discusses the historical roots of the shepherd metaphor in its ancient Near Eastern and Israelite traditions. Here, we look into the crucial roles of sheep and shepherds by considering the shepherd metaphor in some late Babylonian, late Assyrian, and in some Israelite pre-classical prophetic texts. This effort grows out of the conviction that Ezekiel draws his shepherd metaphor from an already existing nomadic life-experience that is not foreign to his audience who had known the nature of sheep and the role of a shepherd. Chapter four examines how Ezekiel uses the shepherd metaphor to evaluate and critique the Judean environment against the norms of Deuteronomic theology. It traces the significance of this theology to Israel as well as its implications for exilic Israel to show the prophet's eschatological response to the concerns of his fellow exiles regarding the existence of Yahweh's people and the city of Jerusalem.

Chapter five undertakes a significant theological and hermeneutical discourse of Ezekiel 34. It considers Ezekiel's oracular speeches with both its indicting and restorative tone in his treatment of the shepherd motif. Here, we discuss largely the prophet's declaration of a perfect eschatological society for divine shepherding with specific stress on his use of the recognition formula. Chapter six discusses Ezekiel's theological construct for an anticipated eschatological shepherding. It sets Ezekiel's shepherding theological frame against Yahwistic motivation. With this, he is able to evaluate and critique the imperfection of human shepherding in Israelite society.

Lastly, chapter seven draws the entire study to a close by summarising the discussions in the previous chapters, and making some observations from the study. From such observations, the study draws some critical implications for contemporary ecclesiastical and political leadership experience in Africa and in Nigeria in particular.

1.6 Ezekiel in the Prophetic Tradition

Ezekiel the prophet, and subsequently the prophetic book, emerges against the backdrop of his call and commission to the prophetic function in Israel,[52] not in the land of Israel as traditionally expected; but in a foreign land against what is considered normative of Jewish understanding of Yahweh's holiness and self-revelation. Prophetic function in Israel as a community of faith in covenant relationship with Yahweh is inseparably attached, not only to its religious expression, but also to its socio-political, socio-economic and socio-ethical functions in society as well. James Merrill Ward notes in this direction that, "An essential element in the relations between YHWH and Israel is prophecy, for without it, YHWH is not known or acknowledged."[53]

This is indicative that prophetic voice echoes divine voice in Israel's sacred history established at Sinai.[54] As Christopher Seitz points out,

---

52. While Ezekiel the son of Buzi is still an exile in Babylonia, Yahweh calls and commissions him to the prophetic office (Ezek 1-3). Yahweh's call comes to him through a vision (Ezek 1). He is commissioned by the eating of a scroll to speak to a rebellious people (Ezek 2:1-3:15). His is a commission to serve as a watchman (Ezek 3:16-27; 33:1-20). The hand of the LORD and the Spirit play vital roles in his call and commission.

53. James Merrill Ward, *Thus Says the Lord: The Message of the Prophets* (Nashville, Tenn.: Abingdon, 1991), *191*.

54. Although it is obvious that the origin of Israel began with the Abrahamic covenant, its defining political and religious historical existence cannot move past Sinai, not even before it. To this claim, Benjamin D. Sommer asserts: "The event that transpired at Mount Sinai some three months after the Exodus represents the central event of Jewish history. More than the redemption from slavery, more than the gift of the Land of Israel, more than the selection of Abraham and Sarah, the experience at Sinai created the intermingling of religion and ethnicity that we now call Judaism." Benjamin D. Sommer, "Revelation at Sinai in the Hebrew Bible and in Jewish Theology," *JR* 3 (1999):425.

> The theological conviction undergirding literary configuration is that God is acting consistently and comprehensibly across time. Prophets see his hand at work and hear him speak. Through this medium, and because the speech is that of the author of time, God continues to speak and inspire hearing.[55]

This assertion no doubt, places prophetic function in Israelite society at a very crucial focal point; so strategic as to the entrance of its city gates and to the watchman's tower as not to miss its view.

In Jewish context, prophetic literature[56] falls within the domain of Jewish literary activity as the Jews[57] evolved into nationhood along with their culture, customs, values, norms, worldview, and literature unique to their national identity. A comparative examination of the Ebla documents and particularly the Mari texts on prophetism elsewhere reveals that, "None of these, however, rivals the work of Israel's[58] prophets in length, literary

---

55. Christopher R. Seitz, *Prophecy and Hermeneutics: Toward a New Introduction to the Prophets* (Grand Rapids, Mich.: Baker, 2007), 8.

56. Literary and non-literary prophets existed in Israel's prophetic tradition. Elijah was the first formal official prophet in Israel after Samuel who himself came after Moses (1 Kgs 17:1-24; 18:16-48; 19:1-9; 2 Kgs 1; 2:11-12; cf. Jas 5:17). Also, Elisha his successor (1 Kgs 19:16-21; 2 Kgs 2:1-25; 3; 4:1-44; 5; 6:1-23) who also played a political advisory role (2 Kgs 6:24-8:6; 9:1-3; 13:14-19; 8:7-15; 13:20), Nathan who was a prophet and chronicler of Israel's history (1 Chr 29:29; 2 Chr 9:29; 1 Chr 17; 2 Sam 7; 11-12:13; 1 Kgs 1), Micaiah (1 Kgs 22:1-28), and a few others were some non-literary prophets whose prophetic activities most likely laid the foundation for the work of the literary prophets who succeeded them. The literary prophets are those whose works are documented in the Hebrew and Christian Scriptures–seventeen in number in the case of the latter document while the former includes the books of Joshua–Kings as the Former Prophets.

57. It is quite clear from Jewish Scripture that the Jewish nation had its historical root in Yahweh's call of its patriarch Abraham, particularly when Yahweh fulfilled his *promise* of a 'great nation' to him in the birth of Isaac, the promised seed (Gen 12:1-3; 15:1-5, 17- 21; 17:1-8; 21:1-5).

58. James Merrill Ward admits the difficulty in defining "Israel" given the changes that this ethnographic group experienced. As a result, he argues that a definition of "Israel" "during the pre-exilic, monarchical era was different from its definition during the exilic and postexilic eras." Ward, *Thus Says the Lord*, 13-14. In between the time when Jacob's descendants were liberated from Egyptian captivity and took their position in Canaan (Gen 12:3; Exo 12:29-38; Josh 1-24), they officially became a Jewish nation designated as "Israel." Israel was one united state under the monarchical rule of Saul, David, and Solomon. But a change in paradigm occurred soon after Rehoboam succeeded his father, Solomon, when the united Israelite state divided into two. The North, under the

quality, ethical orientation, or power."[59] The basic reason for the development of prophetic function and literary activity in Israel is the failure of the nation to adhere to the provisions and requirements of the Sinaitic covenant enshrined in the Decalogue[60] and in the Deuteronomic Code. Both leaders and people strayed from Yahweh's covenant requirements because they soon forgot Yahweh's "powerful presence"[61] in their deliverance from the Egyptian oppression and in their battle with the Canaanites during the war of conquest. The inability of Israel to keep the law and its requirements therefore plunged the nation into serious crises necessitating the prophets to call the people to order and change the paradigm. To this effect, Walter Kaiser says prophets hand down threatening words and messages of judgement. "Constantly they warned God's people of the judgment that hung over them should they fail to repent and turn from the wicked course they had set their minds to following."[62] Commenting further on the factors warranting prophetic function in Israel, C. Hassell Bullock rightly notes, "Had there been no crisis, there would have been little need for the prophets. When the list of literary prophets is posted, it will be noted that they are clustered around critical historical events or eras."[63]

---

leadership of Jeroboam, was called "Israel" with its capital in Samaria and the South, under the leadership of Rehoboam, was called "Judah" with its capital in Jerusalem (1 Kgs 12:1-24; 2 Chr 10:1-11:17). Daniel Block uses the term "Israel" as a theological and ethnic designation for the so-called people of Yahweh, whether they be the original twelve tribes, the kingdom of Judah, or the remnant of exiles. Block, *The Book of Ezekiel Chapters 1-24*, 4. In this study, we use the term "Israel" consistently to refer to the one united chosen covenant people. However, where explicit separation is required by the context of usage, the Northern kingdom and the Southern kingdom or Judah are used.

59. Leon J. Wood, *A Survey of Israel's History*, (rev. and enl. ed. by David O'Brien; Grand Rapids, Mich.: Zondervan, 1986), 4.

60. See Exod 20:1-17; cf. Deut 5:6-21. The term 'Decalogue' has its origin in the Greek often used as a synonym for the Ten Commandments. The crux of the Sinaitic covenant was the required monotheism that was to reflect in the people's worldview, attitude, character, ethics and lifestyle. This was principled on Yahweh's command, "I am the LORD your God, who brought you out of Egypt, out of the land of slavery. You shall have no other gods before me," vv. 2-3.

61. Raymond B. Dillard and Tremper Longman III, *An Introduction to the Old Testament* (Leicester: Apollos, 1995), 67.

62. Walter C. Kaiser, Jr., *Preaching and Teaching from the Old Testament: A Guide for the Church* (Grand Rapids, Mich.: Baker, 2003), 101.

63. C. Hassell Bullock, *An Introduction to the Old Testament Prophetic Books* (Chicago, Ill.: Moody, 1986), 11. Marvin A. Sweeney also observes that "Although many think of

With the official prophetic office firmly established, the prophets "called the Hebrews to remember . . . [the] covenant obligations . . . to return to God and his word . . . [They] called God's people to return to their heritage, a heritage rooted in God and his word."[64] This suggests that the prophets had a context of ministry. As the superscription or other narrative introduction at the head of every prophetic work serves to identify the specific prophet as its subject, its literary content also serves "to provide a historical, social, theological, ideological, or literary context by which the reader might understand the prophet's sayings and actions."[65] Abraham Heschel states that the prophet's task in this connection therefore, serving also as "poet, preacher, patriot, statesman, social critic, [and] moralist . . . is to convey a divine view . . . He speaks from the perspective of God as perceived from the perspective of his own situation [speaking and acting] as if the sky were about to collapse because Israel has become unfaithful to God."[66]

Additionally, Israel's prophets are to be construed neither as diplomats nor as politicians. They are Yahweh's representatives on a crucial errand and with a message critical to the society of their day. Functioning in this capacity, they have no time to waste or any moral ground to compromise the message. The message is divine and it is theirs only to deliver it as it is given. To this aspect of the prophetic function, Heschel holds that by virtue of his commission and most daunting vocation, "The prophet was an individual

---

prophets as persons who predict the future, prophets are concerned primarily with the events and circumstances of their own times and with influencing people within their own societies." Sweeney, *The Prophetic Literature*, 23.

64. Arnold and Beyer, *Encountering the Old Testament*, 2d ed., 347. Arnold and Beyer note in addition that Israel's drift and spiritual decline was as a result of their falling prey to the temptation of surrounding nations. In their words, "Israel and Judah's world contained many temptations to compromise spirituality and morality…At Sinai, the people had affirmed God's covenant, but latter generations had changed their attitude. They slowly drifted away from the God who had made them what they were, and as they did, they became less and less like what God wanted them to be," p. 347.

65. Sweeney, *The Prophetic Literature*, 33.

66. Abraham Joshua Heschel, *The Prophets: Two Volumes in One* (Peabody, Mass.: Hendrickson, 2007), viii, 4. We must take notice that given the nature of their calling and the urgency of their context of ministry, the prophetic message was daunting and uncompromising, offering both condemnation and consolation in a judicial, cause-effect fashion. This makes the presence of the messenger, recognition, signature formulae and others a normative characteristic of their prophetic oracles.

who said No to his society, condemning its habits and assumptions, its complacency, waywardness, and syncretism."[67] The prophets outrightly condemned "the Hebrew's own shortcomings."[68] This prophetic posture stands on the ground of critique. As O. Palmer Robertson describes it, "The prophets of Israel had the responsibility of denouncing their contemporaries for their sins and calling them to a life of faith and holiness. It was the solemn duty of the prophet to critique the life of God's people, while also issuing words of hope."[69]

In this connection, assuming their role as Yahweh's messengers and mouthpiece, Israel's prophets employed verbal and non-verbal literary devices[70] to communicate the divine message to their contemporary society. These literary devices evoked succinct images in the mind of the audience as they "communicated graphically"[71] the received messages. It is within this literary tradition that Ezekiel uses symbolic sign-acts and the shepherd metaphor to put his message of condemnation and consolation across to his audience.[72] The shepherd metaphor becomes a dominant theme among

---

67. Heschel, *The Prophets*, xiii.

68. Kenneth Anderson Kitchen, *On the Reliability of the Old Testament* (Grand Rapids, Mich.: Eerdmans, 2003), 395. Kitchen adds, the crest of prophetic condemnations of Israel was, "above all else, their disloyalty to their ancient covenant with YHWH as their sole god and sovereign, by adding other cults to his, or even going over to other cults in his stead, and indulging in forbidden practices. With this go the prophetic condemnations of social injustice in Israel/Judah's conduct of daily life, which also constituted breach of the social justice dimension of the basic covenant, held since Sinai." See above.

69. O. Palmer Robertson, *The Christ of the Prophets* (Phillipsburg, New Jersey: P&R, 2004), 121.

70. The literary product that Israel's prophets produced has a mixture of prose and poetry. They used literary devices such as symbolism, imageries (metaphors and similes), parables, figure of speech, and the like. Since these prophets used communicative patterns and devices that the literary conventions of their day warranted, their employment of symbolic and metaphoric expressions became unavoidable.

71. Ralph H. Alexander, "Ezekiel," in *The Expositor's Bible Commentary Vol. 6* (ed. Frank E. Gaebelein; Grand Rapids, Mich.: Zondervan, 1986), 745. These divinely received messages communicated by the prophets to their audiences, using human language conventions, were either those of blessings, comfort, direction, warning, condemnation, or judgement.

72. Ezekiel accused the people of their attitude of covenant infidelity–their acts of religious idolatry and incessant disobedience against Yahweh. He blamed the various levels of leadership also for their acts of abuse of their rights, shepherding irresponsibility, self-centredness and greed. He rebuked the aristocrats for usury and the priests and prophets for professional incompetence and inefficiency, warning all categories of the

prophetic speeches and oracles[73] primarily because Yahweh presents himself to Israel as her Shepherd and the nation as the sheep of his pasture[74] in keeping with the terms of his covenant with the nation.[75] Hence, the frequent phrase עַמִּי, "my people"[76] in divine speeches in prophetic literature is both an explicit and implicit reminder to Israel in this regard.[77]

1.7 Definition of Terms and Concepts

In pursuance of better understanding of our discourse, certain key terms and concepts that either weave through the whole or part of this work deserve definition. These are symbolism, metaphor, shepherd/shepherding, Deuteronomic theology, exile, eschatology, Davidic tradition, and Yahwism. First, the term "symbolism" is understood as a system of communicative devices that paint images by using concrete objects, events

---

Judaneans both in exile and back at home of imminent divine judgement on Judah and her inhabitants via the demise of the city and the Temple with its priesthood. This, notwithstanding, he promised the restoration of Israel after she had passed through the refiner's fire.

73. While it is incorrect to assert that the entire prophetic corpus of the Hebrew Bible is coloured with the shepherd metaphor, it is quite correct to affirm that such a metaphor existed in Israel and that it became a major motif in the writings of some of her prophets. See Isa 40:11; Zech 11:5-11; Jer 23:1-4; 30:17; Micah 3:1-8; Ezek 34.

74. See Pss 28:9; 80:1; Jer 31:10; Pss 100:3; 78:52. Yahweh revealed himself to Moses as "I am the God of your father, the God of Abraham, the God of Isaac and the God of Jacob" (Exod 3:6). Cf. Gen 24:12 for the prayer of Abraham's chief servant using a similar phrase. In essence, God watches over his promise and the people of the promise so none of his promises would fail (see Josh 23:3, 14; cf. 21:44-45).

75. God keeps his covenant forever. This element of covenant fidelity reveals itself in the Noahic (Gen 9:11-17), Abrahamic (Gen 17:1-14), Mosaic (Exod 19:5-6; cf. Judg 2:1-3), and Davidic (2 Sam 7; 1 Chr 17; cf. 2 Sam 5:1-7) covenants. Cf. the content and explanation of the Shema in this regard (Deut 6:4-19). God, in view of the terms, intent, and nature of the covenant, remained committed and bound by his oath to Abraham, even though Israel had broken the contract made through Moses. His covenant faithfulness is not contingent on Israel's obedience as it is on the principle of his moral character.

76. This phrase occurs 125 times in 120 verses in the prophetic corpus. Out of these, 22 occur in the book of Ezekiel (Ezek 13:9, 10, 19, 21, 23; 14:8, 9; 21:17; 25:14; 31:12; 33:31; 34:30; 36:12; 37:12, 13; 38:14, 16; 39:7; 44:23; 45:8, 9; 46:18).

77. See Isa 1:3; 52:6; Jer 2:32; 30:3; Ezek 13:23; 37:13; Hos 2:23; Zech 8:7. See also Isa 40:11; Jer 23:1-4; 31:10; Ezek 34; Zech 11:9, 17; 13:7; Mic 3:1-8).

or actions, mostly visualised, whose literal meaning comes to light only when interpreted.[78] As Leland Ryken notes, "A symbol is a concrete image or event that represents meanings in addition to itself."[79] In other words, "A symbol is an image that stands for something in addition to its literal meaning."[80] Basic to the import of symbolism is its representative[81] connotation to convey meaning. This is clear in the case of Ezekiel who, through the use of symbolic objects and dramatic sign-acts, "explained to the exiles that the fall of Jerusalem was inevitable."[82] Symbolic expressions are mostly associated with apocalypses and apocalyptic literature in biblical literature as this plays out largely in the book of Daniel, Ezekiel, and Revelation.

Second, closely connected to symbolism is the term "metaphor." Metaphor is derived from the Greek words *meta*, meaning "over" and *pherein*, meaning "to carry." A combination of the Greek preposition and verb suggests a meaning of "carrying over." From this background, Ryken submits that in using metaphor in this Greek sense, "we need to *carry over* meaning from one subject to another . . . [because] metaphor assert[s] a correspondence between two things . . . [that is, it] asserts that one thing is another."[83] Metaphor asserts a correspondence because, as Grant Osborne observes, it is an aspect of figurative speech that "deals with direct comparisons between items."[84] Metaphor, in Carol Newsom's understanding,

---

78. For additional explanation on this, see the work by John B. Gabel and Charles B. Wheeler, *The Bible As Literature: An Introduction* (N.Y.: Oxford University Press, 1986), 27.

79. Leland Ryken, *Words of Delight: A Literary Introduction to the Bible* (2d ed.; Grand Rapids, Mich.: Baker, 1992; repr., 2001), 442.

80. For further information, see Leland Ryken, James C. Wilhoit, and Tremper Longman III, eds., *Dictionary of Biblical Imagery* (Downers Grove, Ill.: Inter-Varsity, 1998), xiv. Some scholars see metaphor, simile and symbol as similar terms that could be used interchangeably. It is stated, "*Metaphor* and *simile* function much like symbol, and nothing much is lost if these terms are used interchangeably," See Ryken, et al above, p. xiv.

81. Symbolism as a language of representation, "it is often a material object representing something immaterial." J. Robertson McQuilkin, *Understanding and Applying the Bible* (Chicago, Ill.: Moody, 1983), 221.

82. Willem A. VanGemeren, *Interpreting the Prophetic Word: An Introduction to the Prophetic Literature of the Old Testament* (Grand Rapids, Mich.: Zondervan, 1990), 325.

83. Ryken, *Words of Delight*, 442, 166.

84. Grant R. Osborne, *The Hermeneutical Spiral: A Comprehensive Introduction to Biblical Interpretation* (Downers Grove, Ill.: Inter-Varsity, 1991), 103. It is thought that when

acts as a filter to bring "into prominence human characteristics"[85] that correspond with the object of comparison. Ezekiel addresses leaders in Israelite society as "shepherds" because it has a corresponding image to their status and functions.

Third, the concept of "shepherd" and "shepherding" emerge from the domain of animal husbandry with the embedded quality of tending, caring, and protecting. To this responsibility, Jay Edward Adams conceives of the shepherd as "the one who provides full and complete care for all of his sheep."[86] The quality of "care" expresses itself in the area of provision, protection and direction. Against the background of Israel's experience of Yahweh as a shepherd, Peter C. Craigie and Marvin E. Tate say of the metaphor of shepherding in Psalm 23 that the terminology of the shepherd metaphor "associates it with the Exodus from Egypt and the Hebrew's travels in the wilderness, when God's provision and protection had been known like that of a shepherd."[87] This caring quality is also emphasised in the teaching of Jesus. To this, George R. Beasley-Murray comments, "The use of the imagery of shepherd and sheep in the synoptic teaching of Jesus . . . depicts the care of God for the lost."[88] Although the shepherd concept is defined mostly on the basis of function, the underlying understanding is that the concept "shepherd" and "shepherding" both capture the intuitive caring oversight responsibility of the one who shepherds. The

---

conceptualised as a language of characterisation, metaphor is perceived as a linguistic device, that is, a "word that is literal in the contexts within which it is usually found [and] taken out of those contexts and used in a context of some other kind." Gabel and Wheeler, *The Bible As Literature*, 24.

85. Newsom, "A Maker of Metaphor," 152. In a sense, metaphor brings "two objects [that] have something in common [within the context of] an area of shared meaning" because its basic import is the replacement or exchange of an "abstract idea [with] something specific and concrete [by which] the everyday experience of the [target] audience furnishes the source from which meaning is drawn." Gabel and Wheeler, *The Bible As Literature*, 24, 26. Metaphor functions beyond the contextual understanding of its comparative meaning of objects and events as a simile would to the understanding of its bolder assertive strategy of comparison.

86. Jay Edward Adams, *Shepherding God's Flock: A Handbook on Pastoral Ministry, Counselling, and Leadership* (Grand Rapids, Mich.: Zondervan, 1980; repr., 1986), 5.

87. Peter C. Craigie and Marvin E. Tate, *Psalm 1-50: WBC Vol. 19* (2d ed. Columbia: Thomas Nelson, 2004), 206.

88. George R. Beasley-Murray, *John: WBC Vol. 36* (2d ed. (Dallas: Thomas Nelson, 1999), 168.

true human shepherd, the good human shepherd, is the person[89] saddled with a caring leadership responsibility who faithfully executes these shepherding functions.

Fourth is the concept of Deuteronomic theology. By way of contrast, Deuteronomic history, on the one hand, refers to the content of the "Former Prophets" (from Joshua-Kings) in the Jewish Scripture. Deuteronomic theology, on the other hand, refers to the theology that emerges from the content of Deuteronomy,[90] heavily covenantal and Yahwistic in import. Deuteronomic theology grows out of the content of the Torah as a careful reflection on the Decalogue, requiring careful remembrance and strict obedience. Such theology derives from Deuteronomy and dominates the corpus of Joshua-Kings.[91]

Fifth, the term "exile" is not only a biblical concept but most importantly, a theological motif that runs through both the Old and New Testaments. The idea denotes captivity – that of a person or community taken captive by a stronger party (an individual or group), and stripped of all rights and privileges. Conceived this way, exile is both a taking away from and a deprivation of possessions and freedom. As Martin G. Klingbeil puts it, exile is "a departure from the individual's or people's known environment, their homeland, the shattering of the harmonious relationship between humanity and land, the rupturing of social ties, including

---

89. Put in modern perspective, William Oglesby rightly conceives the concept of "shepherd" and "shepherding" as "A pastoral care metaphor which attempts to integrate the notions of healing, sustaining, and guiding, as well as other characteristics of the ancient shepherd." William B. Oglesby Jr., "Shepherd/Shepherding," in *Dictionary of Pastoral Care and Counseling* (ed. Rodney J. Hunter; 2d ed., ed. Nancy J. Ramsay; Nashville: Abingdon, 2005), 1164. In a similar fashion, Wayne Kraiss observes that to describe the pastor as shepherd is most appropriate because he or she has God's flock under his or her care requiring the exercise of oversight function. As such, "The shepherd protects, comforts, and feeds the flock." Wayne Kraiss, "The Pastor as Shepherd," in *The Pentecostal Pastor: A Mandate for the 21st Century* (eds. Thomas E. Trask, Wayde I. Goodall, and Zenas J. Bicket; Springfield, Miss.: Gospel Publishing House, 1997; repr., 2000), 203.

90. Regarding the content and purpose of the book of Deuteronomy, Duane L. Christensen states, "The book expounds the implications of the historic agreement at Mount Sinai between God and Israel by which the latter became the chosen people. The author's purpose was to maintain the loyalty toward God that Israel professed when the Sinai covenant was ratified, so that the people would never doubt the high moral and spiritual standards demanded by God of his people." Duane L. Christensen, *WBC Volume 6A: Deuteronomy 1:1-21:9* (2d ed., Nashville: Thomas Nelson, 2001), lvii.

91. Brueggemann, *An Introduction*, 15.

humiliation, often violence and always loss of possession."[92] So, when we approach the concept of "exile," we should do so with the understanding that its "essential ingredient" is basically in reference to "a person who has been banished from a native place and is now living or wandering in foreign parts."[93]

When such understanding is used in reference to Israel, Klein notes that exile meant for them "death, deportation, destruction, and devastation" because "Exilic Israel . . . was a defeated nation that had lost its independence, its land, its monarchy, and its temple."[94] Israel thought of herself and her status in this manner on the basis of the general philosophy of exile. As put by Kitchen, exile is the "removal from their homeland – of people (s) rebellious against their would-be overlords."[95] Against this philosophical backdrop, exile meant for Israel not only desolation but dissolution. The reason for this is as explained by VanGemeren:

> The fall of Jerusalem meant the desolation of the temple, alienation from the Lord, the break of the people from the land of promise, and the removal of the Davidic monarchy . . . [because] In exile the people experienced alienation from God, the temple, Jerusalem, the king, the priesthood, the land, and all other covenant benefits.[96]

---

92. Martin G. Klingbeil, "Exile," in *Dictionary of the Old Testament: Pentateuch* (eds. T. Desmond Alexander and David Weston Baker; Downers Grove, Ill.: Inter-Varsity, 2003), 248.
93. Ryken, Wilhoit, and Longman III, eds., *Dictionary of Biblical Imagery*, 250.
94. Ralph W. Klein, *Israel in Exile: A Theological Interpretation* (Philadelphia: Fortress, 1979), 2, 3. The historical account of "exile" as presented in the canon is being challenged by modern scholarship to the effect that "the actual reality of deportation was less decisive and radical than the biblical record attests," (cf. 2 Kgs 24-25; Ps 137; Jer 52; 2 Chr 36:22-23). While we recognise the challenge based on ideology, it would appear to us that the historical narrative still remains appealing. However, we align our thinking with Brueggemann: "It is enough that some generative elements in the community of emerging Judaism, after the destruction of Jerusalem in 587 BC, presented themselves as "exiles" who had to live and practice faith in a landless environment without the conventional supports of city, temple, or monarchy. Indeed, if the exile is not taken at full value as "historical," then it is yet another spectacular case of "imaginative remembering," an act that is never completely disinterested." Brueggemann, *An Introduction*, 22.
95. Kitchen, *On the Reliability*, 65.
96. Willem A. VanGemeren, *Interpreting the Prophetic Word: An Introduction to the*

Sixth, the idea of Old Testament and in particular, prophetic eschatology has the understanding of a future expectation, a forward-looking to a future perfection beyond the experience of the present imperfect human society. The undergirding import of biblical eschatology, Old or New Testament is always a personal figure whether divine or human. The "Day of the LORD" either for judgement or salvation features prominently in prophetic eschatology. In Ezekiel, his understanding of eschatology is restoration of an exiled Israel to its land. As David L. Baker points out, "the exilic prophets introduce optimism as they point to a new beginning, a new creation and a new salvation."[97]

Seventh, the concept of the Davidic tradition was and still is most cherished in Jewish tradition. The term "tradition" in its general sense, Groves says, "refers to valued stories that are preserved and passed on by one generation in a community to the next . . . [and the] process involves reinterpretation and application of those stories by the succeeding generations." In other words, tradition is "both preserved stories/narratives and the interpretation (application) of those stories."[98] In biblical and theological circles, "tradition" presupposes a clearly defined and established framework or model upon which all else stands and revolves.[99] Based on the preceding understanding, the concept of the Davidic tradition designates Yahweh's choice and establishment of the Davidic dynasty, that is, ". . . David's

---

Prophetic Literature of the Old Testament (Grand Rapids, Mich.: Zondervan, 1990), 57, 142.

97. David L. Baker, *Two Testaments, One Bible: The Theological Relationship Between the Old and New Testaments* (3d ed.; Downers Grove, Ill.: Inter-Varsity, 2010), 27. He notes particularly that time, people, place and person are major features in prophetic eschatology.

98. J. Alan Groves, "Zion Traditions," in *Dictionary of the Old Testament: Historical Books* (eds. Bill T. Arnold and Hugh Godfrey Maturin Williamson; Downers Grove, Ill.: Inter-Varsity, 2005), 1019-1020.

99. For instance, Osborne notes the argument of some modern scholars in this connection that the prophets in Israel "were not innovative theologians but rather revivalists, seeking to bring the people back to Yahweh and the traditional truths of the Jewish faith…[theirs was a] prophetic cry for Israel to return to her ancestral worship of Yahweh." Osborne, *The Hermeneutical Spiral*, 208. Also, in connection to dogma, Osborne defines "tradition" as referring "to that set of beliefs and practices which has developed throughout the history of a movement and which directs and shapes the current form of the group." See Osborne above, p. 291.

lineage as the ruling line over God's chosen people."[100] For the sake of this enduring choice coupled with David's own disposition, it is said, "David, despite his moral lapses, high-handed policies, and failure to order his own household, gave Israel some of its finest moments.[101]

Lastly, "Yahwism," the religion of Yahweh, as a theological concept, has direct link to Israel's cult worship. This theological concept is located only within the religious circle of Israel. Its idea originates, as Daniel Block states, in "Yahweh's relationship with Israel" through his election of Abraham. This relationship extends to his "descendants through two defining events: his rescue of Israel from slavery in Egypt . . . and his establishment of Israel as his covenant people at Sinai."[102] In as much as Yahweh's relationship with Israel is traceable to his election of Abraham, the official establishment and development of the concept of "Yahwism" has its root in the Sinaitic covenant where Israel first encountered Yahweh, and where the official religion of Israel is inaugurated under the Mosaic Law, the Torah. The Torah then becomes its operational religious guide, for it "defines Israel

---

100. Michael A. Grisanti, "The Davidic Covenant," *MSJ* 2 (1999): 233-250. The Davidic tradition is connected to the concept of Zion tradition and Zion theology. Groves conceives of the latter as the "theology and traditions concerning the rule of Yahweh on earth by means of the election of the house of David...and Zion/Jerusalem, the place from which he would rule." J. Alan Groves, "Zion Traditions," in *Dictionary of the Old Testament: Historical Books* (eds. Bill T. Arnold and Hugh Godfrey Maturin Williamson; Downers Grove, Ill.: Inter-Varsity, 2005), 1019. The concept of "Zion" and "Zion theology" stands as a symbolic and metaphoric reference for the "historical city of Jerusalem, the Canaanite city captured by David, who made it his political and religious capital." Ryken, Wilhoit, and Longman III, eds., *Dictionary of Biblical Imagery*, 980. This concept carries with it essentially the idea of "Jerusalem as the king's city and the capital of the kingdom; and Jerusalem as the city of God and locus of the sanctuary." Moshe Weinfeld, "Zion and Jerusalem as Religious and Political Capital: Ideology and Utopia," in *The Poet and the Historian: Essays in Literary and Historical Biblical* Criticism (ed. Richard Elliott Friedman; Chico, Calif.: Scholars Press, 1983), 94. In essence, this concept, as noted by J. J. M. Roberts, quoted by Groves, "concern[s] how Yahweh exercised his kingship over all creation through a human (Davidic) king in Zion/Jerusalem." Groves, "Zion Traditions," in *Dictionary of the Old Testament*, 1019.

101. In fact, it is stated that all "future kings were measured by their likeness to him.... [so much so that] recent archaeological evidence indicates that foreigners used the phrase "house of David" for the Judean kings who reigned in Jerusalem." William Sanford Lasor, David Allan Hubbard, and Frederic William Bush, *Old Testament Survey: The Message, Form, and Background of the Old Testament* (2d ed.; Grand Rapids, Mich.: Eerdmans, 1996), 192.

102. Block, "God," in *Dictionary of the Old Testament*, 349-50.

above all in religious terms."[103] "Yahwism," therefore, is a theological concept used to refer exclusively to the religion of Yahweh with particular focus on the theocentric-monotheistic worship of Yahweh, primarily entered into by Israel at Sinai.

1.8 Conclusion

Being the preliminary introduction to the entire study, chapter one assumes the statement of the research problem to be the lack of adequate attention given by scholars to the theological-eschatological import of Ezekiel's treatment of the shepherd metaphor. Even for the fact that the name Ezekiel "does not occur elsewhere in the Old Testament" apart from its "two occurrences in the prophecy"[104] should signal the motivation for scholars to have studied this prophet; much more, his treatment of the shepherd metaphor and its emerging theology.

---

103. Daniel E. Fleming, "Religion," in *Dictionary of the Old Testament: Pentateuch* (eds. T. Desmond Alexander and David Weston Baker, Downers Grove, Ill.: Inter-Varsity, 2003), 672.
104. Roland Kenneth Harrison, *Introduction to the Old Testament* (Grand Rapids, Mich.: Eerdmans, 1969; repr., 1979), 822.

CHAPTER TWO

Ezekiel's Use of Symbolism and the Shepherd Metaphor

2.1 Introduction

Ezekiel's use of symbolism receives more scholarly attention than his use of the shepherd metaphor because "Symbolism figures prominently in [his] writing."[1] Consequently, subsequent works[2] on his treatment of the theological-eschatological import of the shepherd metaphor appears impoverished. Embedded within this chapter is a cursory interaction with what preceding students of Ezekiel have already done regarding his contextual and purposeful use of symbolism and the shepherd metaphor. Against the background of Ezekiel's painful exilic experience and his exilic audience, we attempt to probe in this chapter why he uses symbolic sign-acts and the shepherd metaphor in his prophetic oracles and speeches, bearing in mind here that his time was a critical moment in Judah's history.

---

1. VanGemeren, *Interpreting the Prophetic Word*, 326.
2. It would appear an impossibility to state that one is breaking fallow ground in scholarship in whatever field of studies in as much as other scholars have already ventured into such field(s). More so, the endeavour of subsequent scholars is only a building on an already laid foundation, as they stand on the shoulders of giants in the field. This notwithstanding, no major work on the theological-eschatological perspectives of Ezekiel's use of the shepherd metaphor has so far appeared in scholarship. It is this gap that the present research effort attempts to bridge.

The prophet's use of symbolic sign-acts is described as his participation in "God's series of instructive dramas"[3] played out before his disenfranchised and apprehensive audience. Every one of the symbolic sign-acts that he uses and performs has a specific message. Hence, the apparent categories of the symbolic sign-acts in Ezekiel are examined to extract their theological messages. Also, the etymological entries and the various semantic domains of the shepherd metaphor are studied in an effort to achieve understanding of the various nuances of the shepherd metaphor. This is to enhance a broad-based understanding of the concept upon which Ezekiel anchors his shepherding theology.

2.2 *The Context for Ezekiel's Use of Symbolism*

Symbolism generally serves a literary purpose in Ezekiel's prophetic document. Ryken, Wilhoit and Longman hold that symbolism are images evoked in the mind of the reader for "characters and events that really exist or will really occur,"[4] though the images themselves are not literal. This suggests that symbolism take on physical realities with literal and sometimes spiritual overtones. Building on this concept of image evocation but in a slightly different mode, Robert B. Chisholm explains that "A symbol represents something or someone by association, resemblance, or convention . . . Language can also be symbolic, especially terms and phrases that refer to symbolic material objects."[5] The literary import of symbolisation indicates both an evocation and representation to decode meaning.

The ancient Near Eastern (ANE) and Jewish prophetic traditions of religious symbolism serve as two major backgrounds to Ezekiel's use of symbolism. The ANE environment serves to a large extend, as a background for Jewish cultural and religious expressions. This would normally also affect Jewish prophetic symbolism. To this ANE foreground, Hess notes, "The background to the religious practices of Israel during the monarchy

---

3. Lamar Eugene Cooper, *Ezekiel, The New American Commentary Vol. 17* (America: Broadman & Holman, 1994), 149.
4. Ryken, Wilhoit, and Longman III, eds. *Dictionary of Biblical Imagery*, 718.
5. Chisholm, Jr., *From Exegesis to Exposition*, 173.

of the first millennium BC lies in previous millennia. In particular, it should be located in the West Semitic world of which Israel was a part, as defined by language and religion."⁶ Such connection is obvious because, as Othmar Keel reports, the findings of recent archaeological research leave modern biblical scholars with the conclusion to now "see the Bible imbedded in a broad stream of ancient traditions [within which] OT conventionalities and originalities emerge."⁷ Jewish prophetic symbolism though quite unique in its own right, is to be understood against its ANE background.

The world of ANE is everywhere painted with religious colouration to the effect that it is hard to draw any clear dichotomy between the sacred and the secular. As John H. Walton observes, their conceptualised worldview sees the heavenly and earthly events as intertwined, with deity too integrated into it as the one that controls cosmic order. Given such worldview, "All experience was religious experience, all law was spiritual in nature, all duties were duties to the gods, all events had deity as their cause."⁸ Such religious conceptualisation of its cosmic environment makes it quite clear that symbolic language and religious symbols must have featured in the religious texts of ancient Near Eastern peoples prior to their use by Israel's prophets. It has been discovered within the traditions of the ancient Near East that symbols by iconographic representations were used to achieve "stress or emphasis."⁹

The role of religious symbols elsewhere centres around cosmology, built on nature such as rain, the moon, stones, vegetation, or other forms,

---

6. Richard S. Hess, *Israelite Religions: An Archaeological and Biblical Survey* (Grand Rapids, Mich.: Baker, 2007), 81-82.

7. Othmar Keel, *The Symbolism of the Biblical World: Ancient Near Eastern Iconography and the Book of Psalms*, trans. Timothy J. Hallett (N.Y.: Seabury, 1978; repr., Winona Lake, Ind.: Eisenbrauns,1997), 7-8.

8. John H. Walton, *Ancient Near Eastern Thought and the Old Testament: Introducing the Conceptual World of the Hebrew Bible* (Grand Rapids, Mich.: Baker, 2006), 87. Walton explains that the cosmos operates under the supervision of the collective community of religious deities. As such, "Every aspect of what we call the natural world was associated with some deity in the ancient Near East. The result is that the term "natural world" would be meaningless or nonsensical to them. There was nothing about the world that was natural. There was no purely natural cause and effect, no natural laws, no natural occurrences–everything was imbued with the supernatural." See p. 97.

9. Keel, *The Symbolism of the Biblical World*, 7-8.

principally as these are believed to contain power.[10] For example, water is considered by the primitive Semitic peoples to serve a religious function. Sprinkling or bathing in running water not only serves a therapeutic role but assumedly purifies and protects from harm.[11] This is clear indication that signs and portents[12] had existed in the religious world of ANE. Furthermore, in the practice of the divination of the Palestine Semites, Wood reports that even the bubbling of water, rustling of the leaves of trees or their re-echoing the sound of an approaching army, and movements from sacred animals and birds potent some religious symbolism[13] with specific messages when properly decoded. While these representative symbols are not acted, yet, they convey concrete and unambiguous meanings. Also, there existed a prevailing belief in Mesopotamia to the effect that the gods spoke to the citizens through signs of all sort. Kenton Sparks states that in the omen of *oblativa* and *impetrita*, "strange and unusual events were viewed as signs from the gods . . . unusual historical events, strange animal behaviours, and unexpected meteorological or astronomical phenomena"[14] also convey the same meaning. Similarly, in an acted symbolism, it is discovered from the Old Babylonian Mari prophetic text that a prophet "publicly skinned and ate a raw lamb, dramatically illustrating his claim that an epidemic would strike Mari's livestock"[15] unless a positive response was quickly enacted.

---

10. Hess, *Israelite Religions*, 32. See also Mircea Eliade, *Patterns in Comparative Religion* (trans. R. Sheed; N.Y.: Sheed & Ward, 1958).

11. W. Carleton Wood, "The Religion of Canaan: From the Earliest Times to the Hebrew Conquest," *JBL* 1/2 (1916): 18-22. The divine life that animates a spring also animates the tree by its bank. Here, not only springs, trees, but mountains all have religious connotations, and in some sense, carry religious symbols for their worshippers.

12. Moshe Weinfeld, "Ancient near Eastern Patterns in Prophetic Literature," *VT* 2 (1977):179-80.

13. Wood, "The Religion of Canaan, 44-46.

14. Kenton L. Sparks, *Ancient Texts for the Study of the Hebrew Bible: A Guide to the Background Literature* (Peabody, Mass.: Hendrickson, 2005; repr., 2006), 217. Here, Sparks explains that *Oblavita* and *impetrita* are religious signs found in Neo-Assyrian religious divination, understood to have reflected an earlier and later Mesopotamian religious practice. These are religious signs that indicate the gods have spoken.

15. Sparks, *Ancient Texts*, 225.

Religious symbols in ANE located in rituals, divination, and other forms of religious expressions, were appropriately decoded by religious specialists[16] who served as their interpreters. Israelite prophets were also construed as religious specialists who acted out and interpreted their symbolism. In both religious expressions, symbolism function as communicative mode used to achieve specific results. But contrary to ANE belief in magical power whose peculiar effects resided in the power of human actions, prophetic symbolic sign-acts in Israel were rather "deliberately performed in order to serve as a proclamation of the mighty will of God"[17] soon to actualise. For example, Blenkinsopp understands the presence and performance of symbolism in prophetic activity as "mimes or speech acts," or more appropriately, as "mimetic prophecy."[18] When we interpret this understanding against the Israelite prophetic writing, we see that prophetic symbols and symbolic sign-acts are representative signs that the prophets employ to communicate[19] the divine message. Specific to the Israelite context, Frederick Fyvie Bruce submits that the prophetic symbolic actions "performed by the prophets of Israel were an integral element in the self-fulfilling word of God which they were given to communicate and helped to ensure the accomplishment of what they symbolized."[20]

Being a literary society, the religious Scripture of Israel is clustered with symbolism. Particularly, its prophetic literature[21] in which the use of symbolic sign-acts arose against specific contexts[22] has specific theological mes-

---

16. The act of intermediation required religious specialists to mediate between the spirit world and society. In the Mesopotamian religious environment, specialists such as diviners were well educated scholars considered as privileged classes of society while prophets were not scholars, generally less educated and illiterates. Sparks, *Ancient Texts*, 217, 225.

17. Walther Eichrodt, *Ezekiel* (Philadelphia: The Westminster Press, 1970), 82.

18. Blenkinsopp, *Ezekiel*, 33–34.

19. The images of representation in Ezekiel's symbolism are complex. By implication, "It is easy to get lost in Ezekiel's images and forget his larger concern; it is easy as well to pick out striking passages and ignore the context of the book as a whole." Michael D. Coogan, ed., *The New Oxford Annotated Bible* (3d ed.; (N.Y.: Oxford University Press, 2001), 1180.

20. Bruce, "Ezekiel," in *The International Bible Commentary* (2d ed.; ed., F. F. Bruce, England: Marshall Morgan & Scott, 1986), 814.

21. Petersen observes that the term "prophetic literature," though not easily defined, generally refers to "literature that attests to or grows out of the activity of Israel's prophets." Petersen, *The Prophetic Literature*, 4.

22. Symbolism, imageries and figurative speeches are closely related within the domain

sages inherent in them. In addition to its ANE context, Ezekiel leans on the Jewish prophetic tradition of symbolic expression to develop his extended symbolic sign-acts because symbolism is a notable characteristic of the prophetic literary tradition in Jewish society. Jeremiah,[23] for instance, uses more symbolism than any other prophet, except in the case of Ezekiel. C. Hassell Bullock reports that in addition to his use of speech as a primary mode of communication and writing, he also uses acted signs. In the latter, some "were performed or observed in private and some publicly, always accompanied by interpretation."[24]

Even prior to Jeremiah's use of symbolic acts, eighth century prophets such as Hosea and Isaiah had already used them, though at a very minimal scale compared to Jeremiah's and much more Ezekiel's. Yahweh instructs Hosea to marry a woman of harlotry, an action that is representative of Israel's theological contamination (Hos 1:2-3). That the Levitical law forbade priests from marrying any woman of harlotry implies that prophets too, as religious functionaries, were not allowed to marry women of such background (Lev 21:7). But Hosea's divinely arranged marriage is symbolic of the Yahweh-Israel covenant relationship, expressing the infidelity of the latter vis-à-vis the fidelity of the former. Bullock asserts that in a graphic

---

of poetic mode of communication. Since the "goal of interpretation is to discern what the figure points to because the thing figured is to have a literal fulfilment in history," care is required. McQuilkin, *Understanding and Applying the Bible*, 220. Being an aspect of apocalyptic literature, symbolism hold certain definite messages for its readers. The meaning and messages of such symbolic representations are best understood against the context of their day. For example, apocalyptic symbols and symbolic language could represent message(s) of hope for the oppressed; for such type of literature usually arose against the background of persecution, suffering, and pain. Secondly, it could send a message of warning to the oppressor in view of eminent judgement, usually from the divine. Or thirdly, it could be a call for commitment, particularly to the wavering who are unsure of their loyalty, whether it is to the Pharaoh, Emperor, or to God their Creator and owner of their lives.

23. Like Ezekiel, Jeremiah was often instructed to use symbolism to highlight and heighten his message. Examples include a ruined and useless belt (13:1-11), a smashed clay jar (19:1-12), a yoke of straps and crossbars (ch. 27), large stones in a brick pavement (43:8-13), etc. Of symbolic value also are his refraining from marriage (16:1-4), his being barred from entering a funeral house (16:5-9), and his restraint from buying a field from his hometown, Anathoth (32:6-15).

24. Bullock, *An Introduction*, 190. He notes that in contrast to Jeremiah, Ezekiel uses "four different modes to convey his message" such as oracles, visions, symbolic actions, and prophetic discourse, see discussion on p. 231.

and animated manner, Isaiah and Micah also use symbols in their prophetism. Both prophets share the symbol of walking barefoot and naked. Isaiah is instructed to walk naked and barefoot for years (Isa 20). Some scholars suggest that this symbolic sign-act serves as a "sign of the Assyrian defeat of Egypt and Cush."[25] Also, in a lament fashioned over the transgression of the covenant people, Micah is to weep and wail and to walk barefoot and naked (Mic 1:8). These forerunners serve as a ready platform for Ezekiel's unique engagement of symbolic sign-acts in his prophetic tradition.

2.2.1 The Reasons for Ezekiel's Use of Symbolism

The effort to unravel reasons why Ezekiel, being one among the Babylonian exiles, employs symbolism in his literary activity, and particularly his unique mode of usage, unique personality, and unique context of ministry, deserves close attention.[26] It is observed that Ezekiel employs so many symbols in his oracular speeches that "they seem to become the rule with Ezekiel."[27] A cursory survey reveals that he uses no less than fourteen major symbols: The symbol of eating the scroll (2:8-3:3), his dumbness (3:26-27), the clay tablet on which he drew the picture or model of the city of Jerusalem, laying siege to it (4:1-3), his lying on his left side for 390 days, then on his right side for 40 days (4:4-8), his eating rationed food and drinking rationed water (4:9-17), the shaving of his head and beard with a sharp sword (5:1-4), the striking of his hands and the sword as well as stamping of his feet (6:11; 21:14-17), the packing of his personal effects in the day-time and departing the city through a hole dug in the wall at

---

25. Bullock, *An Introduction*, 88.

26. The personality and ministry of Ezekiel uniquely stands out within the prophetic tradition in a number of ways. Bullock observes, for instance, that "with the prophet Ezekiel we clearly have a merging of the two thought strands, or classical roles, in Israelite history [that is]…In Ezekiel prophet and priest converge;…[for] the two offices contribute their essential strengths through him to bring the coming kingdom of God into sharp focus." Bullock, *An Introduction*, 227. Cooper rightly asserts that "Ezekiel was the first prophet both to live and to prophesy in exile." Cooper, *Ezekiel*, 24. This uniqueness plays out clearly in his use of the phrase "in the midst of the exiles" or "I was among the exiles" (1:1). Furthermore, his much personal participation and deep involvement in the pains, hurts, and judgement of Israel through his symbolic acts, no doubt, clearly sets him apart as unique.

27. J. Alberto Soggin, *Introduction to the Old Testament* (2d ed.; trans. John Bowden, London: SCM Press, 1980), 303.

dusk with exile baggage on his shoulder (12:3-16), his eating psychology of trembling and shuddering (12:18-19), his groaning instead of crying (21:6-7), his setting up of a road sign (21:19-23), his inability to mourn the death of his wife (24:15-27), his vision of the valley of dry bones (37:1-14), and the joining of two sticks to become one entity (37:15-28).

These symbolic actions are to be understood as performances before the Babylonian exiles with a specific focus on Jerusalem as both land and city had become the centre of attention. The import of such prophetic symbolic acts became more graphic to the exiles because of Ezekiel's personal involvement, thus possessing clear portents for the exiles as these symbolic sign-acts strikingly illustrate "the union of the Divine and human in the prophetic message."[28] Ezekiel's knitted involvement means that, as Bullock explains, "In these actions message and messenger were combined into one inseparable mode of communication."[29] As such, Clements points out, "Accordingly, not only his mind and lips but his body, hands, and his entire being were to become vehicles of the divine message"[30] to the exiles who stood by and watched how the drama played out. In the ranks of Old Testament prophetic writings as stated earlier, Ezekiel ranks equal to none as his artistic and stylistic "combination of vision, symbolic action, ornate symbolism, and logical discourse stands without parallel."[31] What then is the essence of prophetic symbolism in the prophetic word that Ezekiel ranks top in its usage? Specifically, what are the precipitating factors that made Ezekiel employ symbolic sign-acts in communicating the divine word to the Babylonian exiles? To this question, we now turn our attention.

By employing symbolism, Margaret Sinclair Odell asserts that Ezekiel is placed "in a long line of prophets who conveyed their messages through gestures as well as through words."[32] Accordingly, while "'sign-acts" were a regular part of the way prophets went about their business,'"[33] Ezekiel's

---

28. Ellison, *Ezekiel: The Man and His Message*, 28.
29. Bullock, *An Introduction*, 232.
30. Ronald Ernest Clements, *Ezekiel* (Louisville, Ky.: Westminster John Knox, 1996), 23.
31. Petersen, *The Prophetic Literature*, 137.
32. Margaret Sinclair Odell, *Ezekiel: Smyth and Helwys Bible Commentary* (Macon, Ga.: Smyth & Helwys, 2005), 55.
33. Duguid, *Ezekiel*, 92.

usage far outweighs that of any prophet. Walter Kaiser sustains this when he asserts, "His ministry was filled with some of the most exotic of all symbolic actions performed by the prophets."[34] Further to the claim, it is also stated that "unlike the symbolic acts of earlier prophets, which were brief, pointed, and designed to have an immediate impact on the audience, Ezekiel's symbolic acts are literary representations of the originals."[35] The preceding thoughts are all indications that Ezekiel's usage of prophetic symbolic sign-acts was uniquely staged-managed. The undergirding import lies in his particular context of ministry, his particular audience, and in the particular issues that confronted Judah in this period. This particularism indicates that "of all the prophets, Ezekiel was probably the most colourful" in his use of symbolism. Notably, "He used pantomime, would cry and wail and slap his thighs, ate a scroll, and did many other unusual things to burn his messages into the minds of the people."[36]

Further to his purpose and methodology, VanGemeren suggests that "More likely, he chose this vehicle as the most effective means of communicating God's word to those who, hardened in their sin, waited optimistically for their release from exile and their return to Judah."[37] As people who "had come from the upper classes of Judean society[,] They were a privileged group that had not often heeded prophetic warnings in the past [and] were hostile to Ezekiel's message and dismissed his words as entertaining prattle."[38] Therefore, "the author's message for Israel"[39] was conveyed through symbolic modes because, as Zimmerli submits, "the purpose of the prophet's sign-actions is to set forth in a visible action the event announced by Yahweh as something already begun."[40] The unbelieving who

---

34. Walter C. Kaiser, Jr., *Toward an Old Testament Theology* (paperback ed.; Grand Rapids, Mich.: Zondervan, 1991), 236.
35. Robert R. Wilson, "Ezekiel," in *The Harper Collins Bible Commentary* (2d ed.; ed. John Luther Mays, N.Y.: Harper Collins, 2000), 594-5.
36. Spiros Zodhiates, ed., *Hebrew–Greek Key Word Study Bible* (Chattanooga, Tenn.: AMG, 1990), 1082.
37. VanGemeren, *Interpreting the Prophetic Word*, 326.
38. Tremper Longman III and Raymond B. Dillard, *An Introduction to the Old Testament* (2d ed.; England: Inter-Varsity, 2007), 354.
39. Sidney Greidanus, *Preaching Christ from the Old Testament: A Contemporary Hermeneutical Method* (Grand Rapids, Mich.: Eerdmans, 1999), 257.
40. Zimmerli, *Ezekiel 1*, 29.

had hoped for a soon return to Judah needed to come to terms with this reality. In this connection, the import of prophetic symbol or sign-act "guarantees, establishes, or serves to indicate the fact that God acts" in a manner and with force that "makes [the unbelieving also] become an actor"[41] in the message. Commenting further on this purpose of prophetic symbolic modes, Blenkinsopp notes that "such sign acts should not be regarded as merely illustrative . . . Their purpose was to enhance the force of the spoken word, to make possible the more intense kind of identification with it that successful theatre can achieve."[42] In essence, in case the hearing sense of Ezekiel's audience had failed, the sight would take over with an appeal to the psyche to internalise and act on the performed prophetic message.

Our discussion of the reasons why Ezekiel took on symbolic sign-acts uniquely characteristic to him as a communicative mode must also of necessity, reflect on the context and psychology of his audience. VanGemeren draws attention to the fact that we must first recall that "Ezekiel lived an extraordinary life during a puzzling period of Israel's history."[43] As Bullock observes, given the context of his time, "The fall of Jerusalem was a turning point in the ministry of Ezekiel,"[44] or, as put by Blenkinsopp, "The central point or fulcrum on which the prophecy turns is the fall of Jerusalem."[45] One of the reasons therefore that made Ezekiel employ symbolism and the shepherd metaphor was to respond to the various objections and apprehensions raised by the Judeans following the captivity. John Taylor presents some of the different objections thus:

> Some felt that the punishment due to them for their disobedience had been exhausted by the events of 597 BC and there remained nothing to do but wait for repatriation. Others took the fatalistic line and regarded themselves as the unfortunate heirs to their fathers' sins for which an unjust God was now punishing them. Most felt a measure of security in that, as

---

41. Eichrodt, *Ezekiel*, 82.
42. Blenkinsopp, *Ezekiel*, 34.
43. VanGemeren, *Interpreting the Prophetic Word*, 325.
44. Bullock, *An Introduction*, 246.
45. Blenkinsopp, *Ezekiel*, 6.

they were Yahweh's own people, He could never punish them too drastically without losing face in the eyes of the heathen. A few felt that Yahweh had lost face and had been shown to be impotent before the gods of Babylon.[46]

Should Jerusalem cease to exist, it goes without question that Temple worship would also cease. Of more consequence, as the exiles thought, is the fact that the cessation of Jerusalem equally implies the cessation of national Israel. "This, then," Blenkinsopp observes, "was the situation that faced the survivors and with which Ezekiel, as one of them, was attempting to come to terms," because such a crisis moment "could threaten to undermine the religious assumptions on which their lives are based."[47] Clearly then, as Roland K. Harrison acknowledges, Ezekiel's message was communicated to a "demoralized and unhappy remnant in exile."[48] While still coming to terms with this dream-like situation that constitutes a stumbling block to the prophetic messages, Ezekiel, "through these symbolic acts . . . explained to the exiles that the fall of Jerusalem was inevitable,"[49] so they could face up to the challenge of facing this soon-coming unimaginable and unbelievable event in Judah's history.

However, prior to the destruction of Jerusalem, scepticism regarding prophetic predictions and apprehension regarding Yahweh's laxness in tolerating the invasion of Jerusalem, and the false confidence in Jerusalem's inviolability and invulnerability as Yahweh's city, had existed in the minds of the Babylonian exiles and the Judean remnants back in Palestine. Blenkinsopp explains the situation,

> Conflict within prophetic circles, amply in evidence in Jeremiah and Ezekiel, and a growing public skepticism and disillusionment with respect to prophets in general, testify to the crisis that prophecy was undergoing at that time. What

---

46. John Bunn Taylor, *Ezekiel: An Introduction and Commentary* (London: Tyndale, 1969),42.
47. Blenkinsopp, *Ezekiel*, 12.
48. Harrison, *Introduction to the Old Testament*, 852.
49. VanGemeren, *Interpreting the Prophetic Word*, 325.

was worse, disillusionment with prophecy inevitably induced loss of confidence in the reality, power, and justice of the God in whose name the prophets spoke.[50]

With this given, consequent upon the effects of false prophetism, Blenkinsopp argues further that scholarship be fair to the dilemma of the disoriented and disillusioned exiles whose fate Ezekiel himself recognises and comes up "with original and creative, even disconcerting, forms of prophetic ministry"[51] in an attempt to resolve the flux. In defence of his thesis, Blenkinsopp argues still that:

> . . . prophecy was at that time as much part of the problem as it was of the solution to the problem. At the most obvious level, optimistic prophecy which apparently flourished in the Babylonian diaspora (see, e.g., Jer 28-29) was soon to be shown up as illusory and fatally misleading. These are the prophets who proclaimed "peace, peace" when there was no peace . . . Intercession was an essential function of prophecy . . . their refusal or failure to intercede had left the people to their own devices or even that their predictions of doom had contributed to the situation they predicted . . . An important corollary is that, given the nature of the prophetic claim, the collapse of confidence in prophecy at that time involved necessarily a crisis of faith in the God in whose name the prophet spoke.[52]

As a consequence of the preceding scenario, Ezekiel's primary audience, the Babylonian exiles, are not only seen to be adamant but resistant to the prophet and the divine message. William J. Dumbrell observes that since the prophet's audience are rebels, "They may have reacted violently to the message [of judgement and warning to repent], feeling that they had

---

50. Blenkinsopp, *Ezekiel*, 13.
51. Blenkinsopp, *Ezekiel*, 26.
52. Blenkinsopp, *Ezekiel*, 26.

already been sufficiently punished and that they did not need to repent."[53] One means of counteracting this self-defence mechanism to get them to listen to Yahweh's warning and to take heed lies in Ezekiel's use of symbolism. As Allen also observes, Ezekiel uses a lot of allegories and sign acts in "an attempt to represent in a "theatrical" form the plain truth of the coming fall of Jerusalem and the end of the nation of Judah." He states that the key factor that necessitates this is the preoccupation of the exiles with the hope of imminent return which makes them unwilling to listen to the prophet. Therefore, "To break through this natural resistance, the prophet resorted to picture after picture" acting out the demise of Judah in dramatic form "to reinforce the oracles of judgment."[54] In essence, if Yahweh's message through Ezekiel is to be understood and acted upon, the prevailing feeling and attitude of scepticism, apprehension, fatalism, and even the false belief in Jerusalem's inviolability that had built resistance in the minds of the exiles had to be defused. Lamar Eugene Cooper states to this effect that "Ezekiel was instructed to present his messages in symbolic actions before the people. These symbolic actions were God's way of communicating truth without words"[55] to them. In this connection also, Iain M. Duguid observes that sign-acts are "affective aids" aimed at people's hearts and wills, not their eyes. They are "designed not merely to help people see the truth, but to feel the truth" as they are "given not so much to clarify the message of the prophet as to drive it home to the people's hearts."[56]

Accordingly, Ezekiel employed symbolism to get attention and arouse the curiosity of his audience as an easy channel through which to communicate the message of Yahweh. In Ezekiel's tradition, Walther Eichrodt notes that symbolic sign-acts play out as "the enigmatic way in which God acts . . . as a means of arousing or disturbing the indifferent"[57] to achieve cogitation on the part of the exiles. As much as "Word and action support

---

53. William J. Dumbrell, *The Faith of Israel* (2d ed.; Leicester: Apollos, 2002), 155.
54. Leslie C. Allen, "Ezekiel" in *Old Testament Survey: The Message, Form and Background of the Old Testament* (2d ed.; eds. William Sanford Lasor, David Allan Hubbard, and Frederic William Bush, Grand Rapids, Mich.: Eerdmans, 1996), 360.
55. Cooper, *Ezekiel*, 91.
56. Duguid, *Ezekiel*, 93.
57. Eichrodt, *Ezekiel*, 82.

one another to create effective communication,"[58] this approach is needful. Internal evidence substantiates this effect in the question the primary audience asks Ezekiel, "Won't you tell us what these things have to do with us?" (12:9; 21:7; 24:19; 37:18). Allen states in this respect that "If actions speak louder than words, here they were a megaphone for the prophetic words."[59] Or, to put it differently, these unique prophetic actions serve as a cathedral's signalling bell to draw the attention of its worshippers to sacramental function.

Ezekiel's tradition presents a unique pattern of symbolic sign-acts because the prophet himself is told to function as "a sign." While earlier prophets used symbolism as "a means of expressing their message," Ezekiel engaged in symbolic actions "so as to give a sign to the people of Israel"[60] of what was awaiting Judah. It appears all the symbols which spice Ezekiel's writing serve as confirmation of the inevitability of divine judgement upon Yahweh's people via captivity. He acted out this truth because he himself was commissioned to be "a sign" to his audience (Ezek 12:6; 24:27). All his symbolic sign-acts point to the evident fall of Jerusalem alongside its adverse effects on his audience. Ezekiel's review of Israel's religious history "exposed the depravity of a moral situation in which no attempt whatever had been made to meet the requirements of God"[61] by both people and leadership. As such, "The symbolic actions introduce dramatically the judgments God was to bring against Israel and Judah."[62] Given the "especially difficult communication task" that Ezekiel faced when preaching the fact of Jerusalem's "destruction to a people who believed it inviolable," acting out this truth through symbolic acts before a "potentially hostile audience"[63] was obviously a necessary method. This recalls the fact that

---

58. Duguid, *Ezekiel*, 93.
59. Allen, *Ezekiel 1-19*, 66.
60. Eichrodt, *Ezekiel*, 81. Samuel J. Schultz and Gary V. Smith state in this vein that, "Although most of the people in exile did not believe God would ever allow Jerusalem to be destroyed, Ezekiel used symbolic acts and messages of destruction to convince them that God would destroy the nation because of its terrible sins." Schultz and Smith, *Exploring the Old Testament*, 191.
61. Harrison, *Introduction the Old Testament*, 852.
62. Cooper, *Ezekiel*, 92.
63. Duguid, *Ezekiel*, 94.

if the scepticism and the apprehension of his audience was to be defused successfully and productively, and if their false belief in the inviolability of Jerusalem was also to be productively corrected, Ezekiel had to change, in a radically unique way, this conventional paradigm or belief pattern by moving against the prevailing currents to act symbolically.

Therefore, being "a sign," the tradition of Ezekiel's unique symbolic sign-acts not only reveals a confirmatory element but also a participatory one as well. He uses a strategy which suggests his direct participation in the pains of what is soon to befall Judah. His restraint from weeping for the loss of his wife is a clear case in point here (Ezek 24:15-17). Such a rhetorical strategy is to achieve a deep personal feeling in the prophet's audience. In this line of thought, Block submits that Ezekiel's "rhetorical agenda" and "rhetorical strategies" are both "visual and oral," meant to "transform his audience's perspectives of their relationship with Yahweh and ultimately to change their behaviour," for his prophetic endeavours are "all designed to penetrate the hardened minds of his readers."[64] With such a soul-piercing strategy, Odell could be right to think that Ezekiel's symbols are perhaps the "most graphic warning"[65] to the exiles. The effects of pain which Ezekiel's participatory device caused him and that which his message would cause in the exiles finds close connection with Habakkuk's similar experience at the receipt of Yahweh's message concerning the mode of judgement that was to come upon his people (Hab 1:5, 12-13; 2:2-4). The exiles' unbelief and built-up resistance could not change Yahweh's planned action which was to function as a means of honouring his name, just as Habakkuk's amazement and complaint could not restrain Yahweh from acting in judgement against his people.

Having seen some reasons why Ezekiel used symbolism to get his prophetic message across to the original audience in a graphic way, these

---

64. Block, *The Book of Ezekiel Chapters 1-24*, 15. After all, "symbolic acts serve a dual function: they prepare Ezekiel for his role as sentinel, and they disclose the fate of Jerusalem." But with a persistent wave of unbelief still flowing in the minds of the exiles against the prophet's activity, some kind of further warning needed to be handed down as a caution to their sinful behaviour. Odell, *Ezekiel*, 56.

65. Odell, *Ezekiel*, 55.

symbolism can possibly be designated into categories for ease of comprehending their theological messages. To this issue therefore, we now turn our focus.

2.2.2 The Categories and Meaning of Ezekiel's Symbolism

The prophetic tradition of Israelite society has both socio-ethical and socio-theological imports in addition to other functions. Ward asserts that its function in society is a "message for Israel" as well as "the word of life for Israel."[66] The prophets are considered by Bullock as people who "found their legitimacy and valid credentials . . . in Yahweh's call . . . [and] their fundamental concern was national destiny"[67] as they faithfully declared Yahweh's message. In order to enhance its effectiveness within the community as they "spoke with the authority of the One who sent"[68] them, Israel's prophets employed various literary strategies.[69] Such literary strategies set Israelite prophetic tradition as unique because their "prophetic literature entails far more than words that prophets spoke."[70] Jesús Asurmendi Ruiz affirms when he notes that "although prophets are primarily word-bearers, many among them use symbolic actions as a means of expressing their message,"[71] of which some dramatise their oracles through signs.[72]

---

66. Ward, *Thus Says the Lord*, 13. This expression goes to show the basic function of religious symbolism in Israel. Israelite prophetic symbolism serve as one of the major means of communicating the divine message. As Petersen states, prophetic symbolic action is descriptive of prophetic behaviour designed to convey a message. As such, in prophetic symbolism, "Action, rather than words, provides the key element." Petersen, *The Prophetic Literature*, 20. Accordingly, its primary essence on the part of the prophet is not just "a mere accompaniment of his discourse" but it is more "an independent means of preaching" to achieve "the effective delivery of the message." Eichrodt, *Ezekiel*, 81. Such communicatory mode also has a confirmatory purpose to a prophetic word or vision. Sweeney, *The Prophetic Literature*, 35.

67. Bullock, *An Introduction*, 16-17.

68. VanGemeren, *Interpreting the Prophetic Word*, 75.

69. Because Israel's prophets "lived in a cultural milieu in which oral and literary forms were the accepted ways of communication," they "employed distinct forms of prophetic speech and rhetorical devices." VanGemeren, *Interpreting the Prophetic Word*, 76.

70. Petersen, *The Prophetic Literature*, 1. For further discussion on the literary strategies employed by Israel's prophets, see pp. 18-32.

71. Ruiz, "Ezekiel,", 1058.

72. Pre-classical prophets in Israelite tradition had used symbolic acts. Hosea was instructed to marry an adulterous woman (1:2-9; 3:1-5), Isaiah was instructed to walk naked through the streets of Jerusalem (20:1-6), Jeremiah appeared inside a Jerusalem

The exilic and crisis context of Ezekiel's ministry accounts for the numerous use of symbolism in his prophetic oracular speech discourse far more than any other. Ellen Davis explains the need to give "special attention" to Ezekiel's sign-acts because on the one hand, scholars negatively cite them as "flagrant indications of psychic abnormality and thus contribute to many misapprehensions of Ezekiel's prophetic function." On the other hand, some scholars also positively see them "as one of the most important aspects of Ezekiel's self-representation."[73] Apart from those instructions with symbolic[74] undertone that the prophet was to do, Ezekiel's symbolic sign-acts can conveniently be assigned to no less than four categories,[75] as

---

court with a yoke on his neck (27:1-12), and many of these similar symbolic sign-acts appear in Ezekiel.

73. Ellen F. Davis, *Swallowing the Scroll: Textuality and the Dynamics of Discourse in Ezekiel's Prophecy* (JSOTS 78, Sheffield: Almond, 1989), 67.

74. Ezekiel was given some instructions on certain things he was to do. These connote some symbolic elements. For example, he was instructed to cut and dispose of his hair and beard but to preserve a remnant of hair (Ezek 5:1-4). The use of a "piercing military weapon" on the head and beard connotes "extreme sharpness" as portrayed by the meaning of the harshness of this symbolic act. The actions of "burning," "striking" with the sword, and of "scattering" to the wind a third each of his hair (Ezek 5:5-17) emphasises "the totality of the impending judgment." Block, *The Book of Ezekiel Chapters 1-24*, 192, 194. Also, Ezekiel was to pack his personal effects, dig through the wall and leave the city with his face covered (Ezek 12:1-16). An "exile pack" is said to contain just enough that an exile is able to "carry along on the long journey." Duguid, *Ezekiel*, 161. As an "exile's knapsack" or "container of exile," it held bare necessities for survival during the long exile trek. Block says its usage here may suggest that perhaps either Ezekiel still had his exile bag with its content or his fellow exiles had theirs in storage. Block, *The Book of Ezekiel Chapters 1-24*, 369. Greenberg conceives the "exile's pack" as "vessels of exile," and explains its content as holding only the "barest necessities" like a skin, a mat, and a bowl. On the long exile journey, the skin is useful for holding flour, water, and perhaps it is used as a pillow; the mat is useful for sitting and lying; and the bowl is useful for eating and drinking. Moshe Greenberg, *Ezekiel 1-20: AB Vol. 22B* (Garden City, N.Y.: Doubleday, 1983), 209. Giving the pack a symbolic rather than literal understanding, Margaret S. Odell says the exile's pack may signify the degrading of circumstances of leaders forced out of their city. Odell, *Ezekiel*, 137.

75. The categorisation of biblical symbolism into numerical, material, animal, place, people, and events all take representative symbolic overtones with comprehensible meaning. McQuilkin says for instance, that forty is used "to symbolize testing, six to symbolize man, and seven to show completeness or perfection." McQuilkin, *Understanding and Applying the Bible*, 221-222. Similarly, symbolic objects, colours, numbers, and so on connote definite meanings given the prevailing context of its time. For instance, "White is the color of purity; red, of either evil or warfare; black, of death. The numbers three, seven, ten and twelve signify perfection, completeness, fulfillment, victory." Ryken, Wilhoit, and Longman III, 37.

follows: dietary, gestures, objects, and speech symbols. Every one of these symbolic sign-acts has a definite theological message that was conveyed to Ezekiel's original audience.

2.2.2.1 *Dietary Symbolism*

Ezekiel's symbolic acts of eating the scroll (2:8-3:3), of eating rationed food prepared on animal dung and human excrement, of drinking rationed water (4:9-17), and lastly, of eating in a horrifying psychological atmosphere of insecurity (12:17-20), all come under the canopy of dietary symbolism. As part of the preparatory ground in the prophet's inauguration, Ezekiel was clearly told he was to minister to a "rebellious nation" that had been in revolt against Yahweh since the days of their fathers (2:3-5; 3:5-7). This is a clear presupposition that our prophet is commissioned to assume a hazardous and an uphill task with no less several implications. His appears to be an already failed mission since his audience would not listen to his prophetic message. To this seemingly failed mission, Duguid points out, "If responsiveness is to be the measure of success, Ezekiel's mission is declared a failure before it even begins"[76] as his audience would not listen to him nor give thought to his message.

The eating of the scroll by Ezekiel (2:8-3:3) is to signal a shift in behavioural paradigm. Duguid sees in this symbolic -act a behavioural contrast between the normal and abnormal behaviour. He states, "The prophet himself is to provide an alternative model of behaviour"[77] contrary to that of Israel, as he was not to be like them in heart and attitude (Ezek 2:8). The resistant attitude of Israel is figuratively described as briers, thorns, and scorpions (2:6). While the people are rebellious and stubborn, Ezekiel is to be submissive and obedient; while the people are obstinate, Ezekiel is to act in line with the dictates of Yahweh (2:3-8). Presupposing that a disobedient environment has a way of contaminating whoever comes in contact with it, Block sees an infective element in Ezekiel's eating of the scroll. He explains, "The prophet is warned not to let himself be infected by the Israelite disease – insubordination to the covenant Lord, which was

---

76. Duguid, *Ezekiel*, 68.
77. Duguid, *Ezekiel*, 68.

expressed fundamentally in refusing to listen to Yahweh."[78] The prophet's total obedience was to serve as antidote against such persistent pathogenic tendency. As such, Yahweh's command to eat the whole scroll should be understood as serving as a test of Ezekiel's obedience to the covenant. Greenberg writes that the prophet's obedience is to be in contrast to the people's disobedience.[79] Expressing her support to Greenberg, Odell argues, "Even if Yahweh suspects the entire house of Israel of violating the covenant, Ezekiel's act of swallowing the scroll establishes his innocence in this regard."[80]

If our prophet is to function truly as "a sign" to his audience, this interpretation is to be taken as correct because its understanding is set against Israel's attitude of callousness, rebelliousness, stubbornness, and obstinateness against which Ezekiel was to prophesy. The prophet's coerced submission by eating the scroll as a test of his obedience to Yahweh invariably serves, in Moshe's words, "as a stocking of the prophet with a content by which to counter the defiant words of the people."[81] Unconditional submission and obedience to covenant Yahweh on the part of Ezekiel in contrast to Israel's rebellious attitude is the undergirding theological message of the symbolic act of swallowing the scroll. The scroll Ezekiel was commanded to eat had written on both sides words of lament, mourning and woe. This is descriptive of the awkward mind-set and attitude of the people of Israel, a situation that Ezekiel's radical ministry was to evoke change (2:10). In order to evoke the needed effects of the message, Allen submits Ezekiel is not only to "stand" in readiness to speak Yahweh's message of inevitable judgement, but he must also "listen" to that message.[82] This indicates that Ezekiel's eating of the scroll is a symbolic sign that would counter the "inveterate rebelliousness of Israel"[83] preparatory "for a prophetic ministry to

---

78. Block, *The Book of Ezekiel Chapters 1-24*, 123.
79. Greenberg, *Ezekiel 1-20*, 73.
80. Odell, *Ezekiel*, 44.
81. Greenberg, *Ezekiel 1-20*, 73.
82. Allen, *Ezekiel 1-19*, 40.
83. Greenberg, *Ezekiel 1-20*, 73.

God's people [that would] . . . invoke hostility and rejection,"[84] one of the reasons for which he was to be a "sign" to them.

Another dietary act that Ezekiel was instructed to perform in the full view of the exiles resides in his eating rationed food baked on human excrement[85] and his drinking rationed water (4:9-17). Yahweh expressly instructed the prophet to "Take wheat and barley, beans and lentils, millet and spelt" and put them in a storage jar. With these cereals, he was to make bread for himself, and also from which he was to "Weigh out twenty shekels of food to eat each day and eat it at set times" for 390 days, the period he was confined, lying on one side. Additionally, his drinking water is equally to be measured commensurate to his food – a sixth of a hin[86] – that would be drunk also at set times (4:9-11).

The next paragraph (4:16-17) explains the implication of this symbolic act preceding the literal scarcity and starvation in Judah during the final siege of the city. Block[87] notes that the combination of these cereals captures the scarcity of the "siege diet," making it so difficult to find enough of any to bake even a single loaf. During the Babylonian siege leading to the final demise of Jerusalem in 587 BC, Greenberg explains that in scrambling for such siege food, Jerusalem's residents would find "no one kind [of these cereals] being available in amounts sufficient to bake a loaf of it."[88] This scarcity would cause Jerusalem's residents to starve to death. Therefore, they would not only scramble for food but would scrap the bottom of its storage barrel or baking dough during the Babylonian siege. Consequentially, Clements asserts that this sign-act "was a declaration that once again, and against all expectation, Jerusalem would be placed under

---

84. Allen, *Ezekiel 1-19*, 41.

85. If the nature and quantity of the food and water the prophet was to take posed no problem to him (even though such meal stands in aberration to the combination of a normal usual delicacy in Israel), its mode of preparation surely is worrisome. By all standards, Ezekiel is not to eat what is considered defiled for a Jew, much more for a priest. But his meals were to be baked on defiled fuel (4:15). The prophet's protest attests to the fact of its defilement (4:14). See Peter's similar experience in Acts 10:13, 14.

86. A hin is an ancient Hebrew unit of liquid measure equal to about 1.5 U.S. gallons (5.7 litres). Ezekiel was to drink only 1/6 of it, that is, about 0.2 kilogram.

87. Block, *The Book of Ezekiel Chapters 1-24*, 184.

88. Greenberg, *Ezekiel 1-20*, 106.

siege and would suffer terrible deprivation, and its inhabitants would then be brought to ruin and disaster, with great loss of life."[89]

From the foregoing discussion, it is clear that the city of Jerusalem is the focus of this symbolic act and the exiles are its immediate audience. The consensus of scholars is that the principle of a "ration meal" points to the severe scarcity of even the commonest food in Jerusalem to be experienced by its residents. As is noted, "Barley bread was the staple of lower income groups, [and] wheat products the food of the privileged."[90] Yet, none will be available in the day of Jerusalem's calamity. The impression one gets from this symbolic act is that its physical effect is limited only to the city of Jerusalem.

As 4:13 indicates, Blenkinsopp and Duguid think that this symbolic act has a dual meaning, first, for the residents of Jerusalem, and second, for the Babylonian exiles. Duguid argues that the command of the prophet's meal restrictions, correctly interpreted to mean "the rations are small and poor quality,"[91] symbolises the siege diet of Jerusalem's inhabitants. Its preparation in a defiled manner, which the prophet protests, also symbolises the defiled food the Israelites would eat in a defile exilic land. Blenkinsopp also submits that in as much as the ration meal is to "mime the lot of the besieged by baking bread out of whatever scraps of cereal can be found"[92] when the siege on Jerusalem becomes intense, this is later expanded in verses 12-15 to refer to the condition of the deportees who face the "difficulty of observing the laws of ritual purity outside the land of Israel."[93] While we do not discount the validity of this interpretation, the prophets' protest may well be pointing to the Babylonian defiling of Jerusalem during the period of the siege (4:14).

On theological ground, this symbolic act also has ritual implications for the exiles and the Jerusalem remnants. Ezekiel's protestation as a parallel to Simon Peter's[94] (4:14-15) seems to affirm the function of ritual laws in the

---

89. Clements, *Ezekiel*, 22.
90. Greenberg, *Ezekiel 1-20*, 107.
91. Duguid, *Ezekiel*, 91.
92. Blenkinsopp, *Ezekiel*, 37.
93. Blenkinsopp, *Ezekiel*, 37.
94. See Acts 10:9-15; cf. Jewish cult ritual regulations in Deut 14:21; Lev 7:18; 17:15;

Jewish community as Yahweh's chosen covenant people. As Blenkinsopp rightly observes, all the ritual laws given to Israel to observe, by and large, came "to have confessional status, as one of several means of affirming the distinctive character and uniqueness of this particular community."[95] But the soon coming demise of the city of Jerusalem would change this understanding as those left in it were also to be dispersed among the nations. The force of the prophet's protest to Yahweh's source of fuel points in this direction. Block explains that Yahweh's sympathetic conceding to the prophet's personal sensitivities drives home the point that,

> . . . just as cooking food over a fire fueled by excrement renders the food unclean, so preparing food in a foreign land yields defiled food. Ezekiel's intention in this deliberate contravention of traditional dietary laws would be to shock his audience into taking seriously the threat of Jerusalem's collapse . . . Since the prophet's immediate audience consisted of people already in exile, it reinforced the shame of their own lot.[96]

Greenberg notes, "Lands outside the land of Israel were [considered] 'unclean,' . . . probably on account of the idolatrous practices that went on in them." Thus this dietary symbolic act, undoubtedly, suggests that the "Exiles were therefore necessarily in a state of uncleanness" by their presence in a land outside that of Israel; hence, by further consequence, even "the food they prepared and ate"[97] is defiled. By implication, the exiles were defiled and therefore lacked cultic standing before Yahweh their undefiled God. This is a truth the exiles needed to come to terms with should they concern themselves only with the fate of Jerusalem.

19:5-8. To show Jewish abhorrence for ritually unclean food (animal or cereal), Simon Kistemaker says of the case of Peter that his "ingrained cultural objections are so strong that he forcefully refuses to obey God's command to kill and eat." Simon J. Kistemaker, *New Testament Commentary: Exposition of the Acts of the Apostles* (Grand Rapids, Mich.: Baker, 1990; repr., 2004), 379.

95. Blenkinsopp, *Ezekiel*, 38.
96. Block, *The Book of Ezekiel Chapters 1-24*, 187.
97. Greenberg, *Ezekiel 1-20*, 107.

The sum total of Ezekiel's dramatisation before the "obstinate and stubborn" exile community was to achieve the point of recognition and exoneration. At the fulfilment of every one of Ezekiel's prophetic words, then the rebellious house of Israel would know that a prophet had been among them (2:5). Particularly, "when the predicted disasters befall Israel, [then] they will recognize that God had previously warned them of what was to happen."[98] This way, they would have only themselves to blame, neither Yahweh nor his messenger, should they fail to act on the prophetic message.

2.2.2.2 Gestures Symbolism

Some of the symbolic signs performed by Ezekiel are gestural. Five symbolic signs form the gestures[99] category. These are Ezekiel's lying on his sides (4:4-8); his striking the hands and stamping the feet (6:11-14); his eating psychology of trembling and shuddering (12:18-19); his smiting the thigh and beating the breast (21:12); and his clapping of the hands and striking of the sword (21:14-17). These gestural symbolic signs point to the city of Jerusalem as its target. They are considered gestural signs principally because the prophet's bodily parts set in purposeful motion, nonverbally communicated meaning to the sight and psyche of his audience. Ellen explains its purpose further when he submits that though less developed than the sign-actions, Ezekiel's "expressive gestures . . . are a feature of the innovative form of his prophecy . . . [used in] facilitating the audience's imaginative engagement."[100]

In the first instance, Ezekiel, bound with ropes as a metaphor for divinely imposed restraint,[101] is to lie on his left side for 390 days to "bear" the sins of the house of Israel and then to lie on his right side for 40 days

---

98. Duguid, *Ezekiel*, 68.

99. The idea of gesture here refers to those symbolic signs that concern the direct involvement of the prophet's bodily movement. Such bodily movement is meant to express meaning, emotion, or to communicate an instruction. In Ezekiel's tradition, it is clear that actions, more than words, communicate graphic meaning to his obstinate and resistant audience.

100. Davis, *Swallowing the Scroll*, 70.

101. Greenberg, *Ezekiel 1-20*, 106. In Greenberg's point of view, the 390 days and 40 days culminating in iniquities are not the same. He argues that the first is to be understood as Israel's sin during the monarchy while the second as punishment by exile. See the discussion on pp. 105, 118-119.

to also "bear" the sins of the house of Judah (4:4-8).[102] The quest for the interpretation of the idea of "bearing the sin of" the house of Israel in the 390 days and that of the house of Judah in the 40 days, alongside the meaning of the prophet's lying on his left side for Israel and right side for Judah, attracts divergent opinions. For instance, Odell[103] argues that the 390 days represents the long history of Israel's guilt that began in 982 BC while the 40 days signifies Judah's punishment for the long accumulated guilt. Odell is right in recognising a dual meaning of sin and punishment. Yet, we view it rather as a rehearsal of two separate histories of the two kingdoms whose continued covenantal disobedience now attracts Yahweh's national purging and cleansing. We also share Odell's view that the sum total of 430 days (a little above 1. 2 years) has a representative import as it has a historic flashback. However, we query if she is correct in suggesting that the aspect of "bearing sin" is to be taken to mean Ezekiel's initiation into a liminal[104] state indicating his being stripped of his priestly identity and active function as such. A representation should always be seen to be more figurative than literal. After all, the prophet, as in other similar cases, only demonstrates by action as one under divine impulsion what is to happen to Judah, and not himself. Walter Eichrodt's view seems plausible on this issue. He states, "It is much more probable that we ought to think of the years of guilt as standing for liability, and that we should see in the binding of the prophet a symbol of punishment which in that case can only be interpreted as consisting in the imprisonment of the exile."[105]

The prophet's imposed sleeping position is to "bear guilt" for the sin of Israel and Judah. Eichrodt[106] introduces a typological as well as a representative view here where, as a type of Yahweh, the prophet suffers the disgrace

---

102. The possibility exists that the representative 390 years by 390 days may represent the period from the time of Solomon's unfaithfulness to the fall of Jerusalem and the representative 40 years by 40 days may represent the long reign of wicked Manasseh before his repentance. See 2 Kgs 4:5; cf. 2 Kgs 21:11-15; 23:26-27; 24:3-4; 2 Chr 33:12-13.

103. Odell, *Ezekiel*, 63-64.

104. The idea of liminality or a liminal state suggests a process of change or transformation from one state to the other. It means a total disengagement and loss of a former state to take on the new state. For how this relates to Ezekiel's transition from priestly to prophetic role, see a comprehensive discussion in Odell, *Ezekiel*, 40-1.

105. Eichrodt, *Ezekiel*, 84.

106. Eichrodt, *Ezekiel*, 85.

and burden of shame consequent upon the oppressive guilt of the covenant people. We think that this "bearing" is to be understood as a representative participation of the prophet in the agony of exile rather than as typological or even a substitutionary "bearing" of sin as Odell[107] suggests. A scapegoat principle indicates removal of guilt; a typological principle indicates forgiveness; and a substitutionary principle indicates a transference of guilt upon a priestly functionary similar to that of the scapegoat. But since the events of siege and exile dramatised by the prophet are not averted as one would expect from any of these principled interpretations, a representative principle is to be favoured. We think also that the "binding" aspect of the prophet with ropes so he is unable to alternate his lying position until the completion of the specified period is a figurative representation of the intensity of the unalterable and inescapable siege and demise of Jerusalem (4:8). It may also well be that the captivity of Judah's last king and many of its citizens is in view; for these were led helplessly to Babylon as captors.

Seen in this perspective, a shift in the prophet's role occurs to take on a priestly import. Hitherto, Ezekiel has been Yahweh's representative with the prophetic word. But now, as Block submits, he "plays the role of the priest, carrying the burden of his people's sins on his shoulder."[108] Block particularly argues that the prophet's lying on his sides for different specified number of days signifies that "Ezekiel fulfilled a normal priestly function, and in so doing he offered a nonverbal dramatization of Yahweh's indictment of his people"[109] for which exile is inevitable. Doubtless, as Cooper concedes, the prophet's forced sleeping position on "the right and left sides symbolically pointed to Israel and Judah"[110] as the latter is used interchangeably by Ezekiel in the term "house of Israel."[111] In as much as the number of days refers both to Israel's period for bearing punishment and also for a generation, it is also possible that "the time limit set by Yahweh on Ezekiel's prone position suggests a limit to his patience."[112]

---

107. Odell, *Ezekiel*, 62.
108. Block, *The Book of Ezekiel Chapters 1-24*, 175.
109. Block, *The Book of Ezekiel Chapters 1-24*, 179.
110. Cooper, *Ezekiel*, 94.
111. Block, *The Book of Ezekiel Chapters 1-24*, 176.
112. Block, *The Book of Ezekiel Chapters 1-24*, 179.

Similarly, in the second instance of this gestural symbolic sign, Ezekiel is instructed to "strike your hands together and stamp your feet and cry out "'Alas!;'" "prophesy and strike your hands together" (6:11-14; 21:14-17). As is the case with the other gesture symbolism, the use of the metaphor of hand, foot and voice convey imbedded meanings connoting a warlike situation. We find here an expression of intense abhorrence for a detestable act that has been committed. Duguid opines that given the division of this chapter into two parts (Ezek 6), "each of which begins with a hostile gesture on the part of the prophet,"[113] it no doubt signals Yahweh's judgment. Greenberg lends support to this thought when he notes that the performed gestures by the prophet, followed by the outcry, "is to represent God's satisfaction at venting his rage upon Israel"[114] for her persistent syncretism. This symbol "combines dramatic and vocal elements" directed at "the mountains and high places . . . associated with pagan worship"[115] in disregard to God's commands.

The gestural act of striking the hands and stamping the feet, Cooper explains, both function "as signs of excitement and emotion used to decry the abominations and idolatrous practices of the Jewish people."[116] This fits well with the outcry "alas," acting as a word of lamentation and judgement. The reason for the use of this prophetic gesture is not so much the mixing of Yahwism and Baalism in Israel much less Israel's preference for the latter[117] as the language of Ezekiel 6:13-14 indicates. Yet, the people saw no wrong in it, much less their need to abandon it for Yahweh's worship. They held tenaciously to a syncretic attitude and practice described by Duguid as "old habits died hard."[118] The context of this text suggests that Yahweh is not charging Israel against the norms of Deuteronomic theology, although the entirety of the Ezekiel writing suggests that, but more against their failure

---

113. Duguid, *Ezekiel*, 106.
114. Greenberg, *Ezekiel 1-20*, 135.
115. Cooper, *Ezekiel*, 106.
116. Cooper, *Ezekiel*, 109.
117. As Ellison explains, this emotion-driven lamentation comes because "…the sin that was bringing destruction on Jerusalem was above all a religious one, the worship of Jehovah as though He had been but a nature god." Ellison, *Ezekiel*, 36.
118. Duguid, *Ezekiel*, 107.

to keep the covenant terms of the Decalogue which the nation swore to uphold. Duguid explains this precarious situation further by submitting that judgement is coming upon the land not,

> . . . because the Israelites had mistreated one another. Nor was judgment coming because they had taken advantage of the poor or been unfaithful to their wives, or even because they had robbed each other and filled the land with violence, but essentially because they held to a false religion. For them, what they believed would literally be a matter of life and death.[119]

Consequently, Blenkinsopp points out that this gesture symbolism is emotion-driven in relation to the coming judgement, revealing the "passionate involvement of Yahweh as participant in Israel's history" on account of his envy for his land that is "desecrated by false cults."[120] As an effect, Clements states that what follows finally is that Jerusalem's "pitiable victims of this act of bravado can only moan and grieve in horror at their helplessness"[121] when divine judgement is finally executed.

Progressively, a third subunit of the gesture symbolism plays out in Yahweh's command to Ezekiel to tremble as he ate his food and to shudder in fear as he drank water (12:18-20). The word used for "tremble" has the import of an earthquake-like tremble. Noting the word order – the combination of "quake" and "tremble," Greenberg[122] explains that it specifies the "emotion to be converged" by facial expression. Acting out this symbol before the exiles, Greenberg explains, indicates that Ezekiel is to "enact the symptoms of the terror that would seize the population in the face of the Babylonian onslaught."[123]

Some, however, take Ezekiel's role in the performance of this symbolic sign as his identifying with Jerusalem's condition, its inhabitants being the direct recipients of this horrific anxiety. In this sense, the prophetic action

---

119. Duguid, *Ezekiel*, 113.
120. Blenkinsopp, *Ezekiel*, 41.
121. Clements, *Ezekiel*, 94.
122. Greenberg, *Ezekiel 1-20*, 222.
123. Greenberg, *Ezekiel 1-20*, 225.

shifts from its traditional representative import to take a priestly identity. For instance, Block points out that although Ezekiel plays a representative role in previous symbolic signs, "This time his identification with the victims is unequivocal. Like the performance of a professional actor, Ezekiel's dramatization would have been passionate."[124] He grounds his argument on the point of Ezekiel's priesthood having the Jerusalemites as his fellow Israelites. Blenkinsopp also shares this view. He argues that being told to simulate the practical condition in Jerusalem, Ezekiel's "trembling arises not from self-absorption but from intense identification with the suffering of the prophet's fellow Judeans who were to be overwhelmed by the disaster"[125] coming upon Jerusalem that nothing was capable to avert it.

We however feel that it would appeal more to reason to think that this acted symbolic sign by Ezekiel depicts, not the point of identification here but a forecast of the emotional expression of the fear, anxiety, horror, and insecurity of the Judeans during Jerusalem's long siege and its uncompromising final deportation to Babylon. Quite certainly, this symbol points to the psychological experience of the Jerusalem inhabitants following the siege and final destruction of the city. Given the magnitude of the devastation and destruction to be unleashed upon Jerusalem however, such an event would leave lingering effects even on the few remnants that would remain in the land. As the mood of Ezekiel indicates, the cause of this trembling is not as a result of cold or fever, anger, joy, grief, or some kind of bad health. Rather, as Bunn notes, the prophetic gesture exhibits the "fearfulness and terror . . . being symbolic of the frightening violence and destruction which are to come upon the . . . peasant population of Judah [descriptive of] the sufferings that the population will have to undergo"[126] prior to and even long after the event had occurred. Ezekiel's dramatisation before the exiles was to affirm what would soon happen to the land of Judah and to the city of Jerusalem.

The fourth and fifth instances of the gestures symbolic signs employ the metaphor of hand and sword (21:12-18). In view of the coming

---

124. Block, *The Book of Ezekiel Chapters 1-24*, 383.
125. Blenkinsopp, *Ezekiel*, 67.
126. John Bunn Taylor, *Ezekiel: An Introduction and Commentary*, TOTC (Leicester, England: Inter-Varsity, 1969), 117.

slaughtering sword of the enemy, Ezekiel received the divine command to "beat your breast" (21:12d), "strike your hands together," and to "Let the sword strike twice, even three times" (21:14). The action of "striking" and "sword" all converge at the use of the hand in carrying out the action. While recognising the difficulty of its interpretation, Odell admits that the general sense of the oracle of 21:8-17 is clear – a prepared battle sword is placed in the hand of the slayer, and is ready to attack.[127] Odell is quite right because her interpretation is grounded in the understanding of the act of "beating the breast," which Blenkinsopp explains is the reaction to bad news, a gesture of grief and frustration.[128] Also, the "striking" of the hands that cling to the sword which Allen explains are vivid emphasis of the "severity and inevitability of the coming crisis" that the sharpened sword is destined to destroy "Yahweh's people and the members of their government"[129] as victims (Ezek 21:9-11, 15).

Such gestural symbolic acts signify a whole sweep of war and judgement. The sword that strikes twice, then thrice, as an instrument of Yahweh's judgement through an agent acting in his stead,[130] no doubt emphasises the extend of the judgment[131] to come upon Jerusalem. Clements explains that the "prophet's poetic imagination brings home the full terror of war"[132] to be unleashed on Yahweh's city by his agent. This vengeful action plays out in Yahweh striking his hands together against his covenant people. Cooper states that this action by Yahweh is clear indication that "his determination to dispense judgment until his fury was spent" is inescapable because the judgement would be "swift, severe, indiscriminate, and final."[133] As Block rightly observes, when "Yahweh's sword" descends in judgement on his

---

127. Odell identifies this difficulty by pointing out an apparent contradiction. She queries that the Yahweh who speaks with evident pain that his people will fall on the sword, is also the Yahweh who claps with glee at the destruction of his city and people. Odell, *Ezekiel*, 267, 268.
128. Blenkinsopp, *Ezekiel*, 93.
129. Allen, *Ezekiel 1-19*, 26.
130. Blenkinsopp, *Ezekiel*, 93.
131. Cooper, *Ezekiel*, 212.
132. Clements, *Ezekiel*, 96.
133. Cooper, *Ezekiel*, 213.

Covenant People, it would be "as the fulfilment of the covenant curses"[134] the people had long been warned by Moses to expect should they fail to keep covenant terms and remain loyal to Yahweh their suzerain lord.

2.2.2.3 Objects Symbolism

Prophet Ezekiel also received instruction from Yahweh to employ the use of objects as symbols in conveying the prophetic message to the exiles. These objects symbols are: the city of Jerusalem drawn on a clay tablet (4:1-3), the setting up of a road sign (21:19-23), the joining together of two sticks to become a unitary entity (37:15-28), and the vision of the valley of dry bones (37:1-14). The first three have psychomotor effect while the last is optical in nature.

First, Ezekiel is instructed to set a "sign to the house of Israel" by drawing the city of Jerusalem on a clay tablet (4:1-3), after which he would set "siege works against it." Pearson points out that this act reveals "Setting forth the coming siege of Jerusalem, with its attendant hardships and the captivity following thereupon."[135] Additionally, Blenkinsopp explains that the mimic siege of the city of Jerusalem "with imitation ramparts, entrenchments and other apparatus of a siege [in which Ezekiel] himself acts the besieger [serves as a clear sign] to warn the exiles not to place their hopes in the survival of Jerusalem"[136] because the city was unavoidably going to fall into the hands of Nebuchadnezzar in due course. Ezekiel is therefore asked to apply this symbol to the model city because the Judeans had seen Jerusalem as a well fortified city "so as to withstand the assault"[137] of any invading enemy. The point is to disclaim and dismiss any human confidence in the security and strength of the city on the day of its calamity. And by now, the message of this symbolic sign should have been obvious to

---

134. Block, *The Book of Ezekiel Chapters 1-24*, 676.
135. Anton T. Pearson, "Ezekiel," in *The Wycliffe Bible Commentary* (eds. Charles F. Pfeiffer and Everett F. Harrison, Chicago, Ill.: Moody, 1962), 713. The principle of setting a siege to a city in ancient war tactics was "to starve out the enemies and wear them down by halting their flow of food, supplies, and weapons." Charles H. Dyer, "Ezekiel," in *The Bible Knowledge Commentary: Old Testament* (eds. John F. Walvoord and Roy B. Zuck, America: SP Publications, 1985; repr., 1987), 1235.
136. Bruce, "Ezekiel," in *The International Bible Commentary*, 814.
137. Greenberg, *Ezekiel 21-37*, 427.

the exiles; in spite of the fortification of Jerusalem's walls, the Babylonians would destroy it because the hand of Yahweh was already against the city.

Block explains this obvious demise when he states that in a "series of disturbing but rhetorically powerful sign-acts [Ezekiel] is to address head-on the inevitable fate of Jerusalem."[138] Ellison submits that even without interpretation on Ezekiel's part, the message of the symbol is "obviously intended to be clearly understood by any chance visitor."[139] Though the exiles raised a protest, their protest was to no avail. Christopher Wright paints such protest thus: "Had not Yahweh guaranteed to protect his own city? Had he not placed his own eternal name in the temple itself?" Also, their false hope in past events leads to the next protest: "Yahweh would soon come to the rescue as he had before and scatter those enemy camps." But on the contrary, the message of this symbol "clearly [speaks] of hostility and attack"[140] against Jerusalem that would not be averted. The point is clear and simple, if Ezekiel's audience had taken him for a ride and his sign-acts taken for granted, then certainly not this one. Herein lies a clear example of the intended effect of symbolism in prophetic tradition. Ellison posits that prophets engaged symbolism "when they could no longer obtain a hearing for the spoken word." So, in Ezekiel's case, "Such actions not merely tickled men's curiosity, but filled them with a sense of awe as they superstitiously believed that the prophet was doing things that would bring evil on men."[141]

The divine instruction to the prophet to "erect siege works against it, build a ramp up to it, set up camps against it and put battering rams around it. Then take an iron pan, place it as an iron wall between you and the city and turn your face toward it," signifies the intensity and severity of the future event awaiting Jerusalem. It is clear that this event is irreversible and the city's destruction is unavoidable. As Blenkinsopp points out, "the besieging army is acting as agent of divine judgment"[142] and Yahweh is now the enemy, not any invading nation as was the case previously. To

---

138. Block, *The Book of Ezekiel Chapters 1-24*, 164.
139. Ellison, *Ezekiel*, 33.
140. Christopher J. H. Wright, *The Message of Ezekiel*, BST (Leicester, England: Inter-Varsity, 2002), 76.
141. Ellison, *Ezekiel*, 32.
142. Blenkinsopp, *Ezekiel*, 34.

this, Clements asserts, "Jerusalem will again face a terrible siege; it will again be overthrown; and a great many of its citizens will be plunged into the horrors of death by either the sword or famine."[143] Accordingly, since "The fate of the population was equally crucial, hence the need for the exilic portrayals. The prophet's aim was to destroy the people's false bases of security and to dash all hope among his compatriots of an early return to the homeland."[144]

Second, another object symbol Ezekiel was instructed to perform in this connection is the setting up of a road sign/signpost that would direct the sword of the invading King Nebuchadnezzar of Babylon against Jerusalem (21:19-23). Drawn either on sand, brick/clay, or tile, our prophet was to indicate at the junction between the road leading to Rabbah of the Ammonites and the road leading to Judah and fortified Jerusalem for the sword of the slayer. Block notes that the use of "hand" in the Hebrew construction "for signpost suggests a road sign on which is carved the form of a hand with fingers pointing in the direction specified."[145] If Block is correct, then this would easily aid the direction for Nebuchadnezzar to carryout his agenda.

With the help of this road signpost, all of Nebuchadnezzar's divination "methods would point to Jerusalem as the goal against which the invaders"[146] would easily lay siege. This aided the invading king in deciding at the crossroad which of the rebelling vassals was to first "feel the weight of his chastisement"[147] and be quelled. The combination of a signpost and divination omen (21:21) was needful because at the time, Jerusalem, the capital city of Judah, and Rabbah, the capital city of Ammon, "had rebelled against their Babylonian overlord about the same time."[148] Such a vassal's

---

143. Clements, *Ezekiel*, 20.
144. Block, *The Book of Ezekiel Chapters 1-24*, 169.
145. Block, *The Book of Ezekiel Chapters 1-24*, 684.
146. Pearson, "Ezekiel," 736.
147. Ellison, *Ezekiel*, 86.
148. When Jerusalem rebelled against Babylon in 588 BC., she was one of three cities or countries seeking independence. The others were Tyre and Ammon. Nebuchadnezzar led his force north and west from Babylon along the Euphrates River. On reaching Riblah, north of Damascus in Syria, he had to decide which nation to attack first. On deciding not to take Tyre as his first target, he was left to decide either to head down the coastal

rebellious attitude would no doubt be met with the decisive military action of the suzerain lord.[149]

Were we to interpret Ezekiel's placing of the road sign at the crossroad against modern political ideological and environmental norms, our prophet would have been heavily criticised as being a political traitor, because his action would have been taken for his conniving with political enemies. But conversely, Ezekiel stands at this point in the tradition of a radical pragmatist in opposition to the pretentious norms of Israel. He insistently and relentlessly "declare[d] with boldness the complete collapse of the nation"[150] by the use of a signpost. Clements points out further that Ezekiel ". . . brings home the full terror of war . . . [he] has not spared his hearers a sense of pain and hurt . . . It is not for him to hide the truth about war from his hearers by refusing to show the corpses . . . He wants people to face the truth, and he does so by taking down the screen of social censorship."[151] In this connection, Robertson asserts that despite the opposing attitude of his kinsmen, "Ezekiel remained faithful in standing against the tide of popular sentiment by declaring God's word concerning the certainty of the fall of the city."[152]

Third, Ezekiel was commanded to produce yet another object symbol by joining two sticks together (37:15-28). Yahweh instructed Ezekiel,

> Son of man, take a stick of wood and write on it, 'Belonging to Judah and the Israelites associated with him.' Then take another stick of wood, and write on it, 'Ephraim's stick,

---

highway and attack Judah, or to head down the Transjordanian highway and attack Ammon. The signpost was a significant aid to this decision when Nebuchadnezzar chose Jerusalem as his first target of military operation. Bruce, "Ezekiel," 828.

149. The road sign suggests "God supernaturally guiding Nebuchadnezzar to Jerusalem to overthrow the city." Dyer, "Ezekiel," 1268. A combination of the road sign and idolatrous consultation of omens by Nebuchadnezzar, serves technically and most importantly theologically, to explain Yahweh's sovereignty as creator and controller of events in human history. This presupposition appears obvious as Bruce points out, for "Even pagan divination is overruled by the true God for the accomplishment of His purpose" to further confirm the inevitable ruin of Jerusalem. Bruce, "Ezekiel," 828.

150. O. Palmer Robertson, *The Christ of the Prophets* (Phillipsburg, New Jersey: P&R, 2004), 289.

151. Clements, *Ezekiel*, 96.

152. Robertson, *The Christ of the Prophets*, 292.

belonging to Joseph and all the house of Israel associated with him.' Join them together into one stick so that they will become one in your hand (37:16-17 NIV).

The symbol of the two sticks is clearly a representation of the Northern and Southern Kingdoms of the once one united now wasting away in exile and in national political and religious ruins. Taylor notes that these two sticks, each on which is to be written specific but slightly distinct words, "represent the two kingdoms of former days, before Samaria fell to the Assyrians under Sargon II (722/1 BC) and Israel, the northern kingdom, lost her identity."[153]

It appears the distant future restoration of a once again united Israel is in view here. It seems obvious that the prophet's "symbolic act of joining two sticks" signifies the future restoration and reintegration of the people of Israel into one united nation. Pearson points out that this means that "just as the sticks were united into one, so Israel and Judah are to be reunited into one kingdom"[154] in the restored state. This monologue unifying principle is implied by the mention of "Israel" on each stick. On this point Cooper observes that "using the term in its full sense"[155] suggests that the "two kingdoms were always [meant to be] recognized as an ethnic [and] theological unity."[156] Essentially, the prophet foretold "the future union of the two kingdoms under one head . . . a David-like ideal ruler"[157] who would lead the gathered and restored nation of Israel. Duguid notes in this regard that the merging of the two sticks into a single, united entity, not only suggests that the events of recent history would be reversed, but also the events of much earlier history would be undone – "The divided kingdom will once again be undivided."[158]

Here lies the heavy emphasis on the theological-eschatological Israel, a resurrected people of God in a new pastureland. This symbol builds on

---

153. Taylor, *Ezekiel*, 238.
154. Pearson, "Ezekiel," 754.
155. Ellison, *Ezekiel*, 132.
156. Cooper, *Ezekiel*, 326.
157. Pearson, "Ezekiel,", 754.
158. Duguid, *Ezekiel*, 435.

the principle of hope for a restored Israel in that it comes on the feet of the vision of the valley of dry bones as "an extension of Ezekiel's message of national resurrection."[159] Here, "both Judah and Israel have been resurrected together"[160] into its former glory of one united entity of a covenant nation. Clements explains that it points to "the new Israel that is to be born," for "the first [of the two sticks] concerns the unity of Israel as God's people (vv. 15-23), and the second reaffirms the unity of the nation under a single Davidic ruler (vv. 24-28)."[161]

Lastly, the final object symbol in this category combines both sight and action in its accomplishment. This is Ezekiel's vision of an odourless, lifeless, and hopeless valley of dry bones, and his engagement under Yahweh's command to bring about life in them (37:1-14). In the visionary account, the prophet saw "bones that were very dry" (37:2), and was asked if there remains any slightest possibility of life to enter into them. Following his careful response "O Sovereign LORD, you alone know," Ezekiel was then commanded to prophesy life into the dry bones. The prophet's response is motivated more by faith in Yahweh's sovereign power and omniscience than by a rational human thought in view of the present condition of exilic Israel.[162] Beasley-Murray observes that given the condition of Israel then, as a matter of fact, "nothing but a stupendous act of God could effect a restoration." On this premise, he submits that the object of dry bones clearly "is a prediction of the reintegration of Israel's political life"[163] to be effected only by God himself. Accordingly, to the prophet's amazement, while still standing in the valley of dry bones, he watched as Yahweh caused

---

159. Cooper, *Ezekiel*, 326. Significantly, this development would imprint hope on the minds of the despondent exiles who had already lost any hope in the existence of Jerusalem in view of the insistence by Ezekiel on its imminent destruction. The symbol of joining the two sticks clearly overturns the prevailing modern notion about "the ten lost tribes of Israel."

160. Ellison, *Ezekiel*, 132.

161. Clements, *Ezekiel*, 167.

162. National Israel was no more except a shadow of the land now lying in ruins. For at that time, "she was '"dead"' as a nation–deprived of her land, her king, and her temple. She had been divided and dispersed for so long that unification and restoration seemed impossible." Dyer, "Ezekiel," 1298.

163. George R. Beasley-Murray, "Ezekiel" in *The New Bible Commentary* (2d ed.; eds. Donald Guthrie et al (Grand Rapids, Mich.: Eerdmans, 1970; repr., 1981), 681.

"the bones becoming skeletons, the skeletons corpses, and the corpses once again a living army."[164] Although Odell posits that, "in the poetic literature, the metaphor of bones represents the totality of the human person,"[165] a representative rather than a literalistic approach to hermeneutics is to be applied to this visionary object symbol of dry bones. As Ellison adequately underscores the point, this vision must be "understood in any other sense than that the bones represent '"the whole house of Israel.""[166] Ezekiel affirmed to the exiles that despite the present seemingly irredeemable circumstance of Israel, such that "any hope of national revival is as much out of the question for them as for any of the other ethnic groups which lost their identity as a result of deportation, [yet], the sovereign act of God will revive them and restore them to their own land."[167]

The object symbol in the vision of the valley of dry bones suggests the dawn of a new era for Israel. The feeling one has from this prophetic vision or what Odell understands as a trance[168] experience brings hope and a breath of life for the exiles. Not only Judah but both Judah and Israel, as a covenant nation in her former state, will be restored and unified. Life will soon blossom in the land that now lies in ruins and disdain. As Odell rightly points out, Ezekiel sees in this vision "the end result of the rebellion of the whole house of Israel, as well as the completion of Yahweh's judgment,"[169] meaning, it is Yahweh himself who "brings the people up out of their graves and brings them into the land"[170] of their possession that their sin hitherto had caused its dispossession. That Yahweh would do this so Israel would continually be the envy of other nations is purely an act of

---

164. John A. Goldingay, "Ezekiel," in *Eerdmans Commentary on the Bible* (eds. James D. G. Dunn et al; Grand Rapids, Mich.: Eerdmans, 2003), 657.
165. Odell, *Ezekiel*, 453.
166. Ellison, *Ezekiel*, 128.
167. Bruce, "Ezekiel," 838.
168. In support of her submission, Odell points out that "Because this unit begins with the formula that introduces each of Ezekiel's other visions, '"the hand of the LORD was upon me"' (cf.1:3; 3:22; 8:1; 40:1), it is often interpreted as a vision. However, since the narrative does not employ Ezekiel's terms for a visionary experience, it is better understood as a narrative concerning a trance or seizure during which Ezekiel performs a symbolic act." Odell, *Ezekiel*, 454.
169. Odell, *Ezekiel*, 454.
170. Odell, *Ezekiel*, 455.

his grace. This action would cause Israel to know that he is Yahweh, a covenant keeping God. Religious and political Israel is non-existent without him as the nation stands or falls on the fact that Yahweh. Yahweh, who created all humans but specifically chose Israel for his possession in order to achieve his progressive salvific plan, is the One who holds religious and political Israel in the hollow of his hands.

Observably, the symbolism of the joining of the two sticks to become one and the vision of the valley of dry bones are both affirmed by the import of the Christological statement in John 15:5 and the Pauline statement in Acts 17:28 to the effect that apart from God, the nothingness, hollowness, emptiness, helplessness, hopelessness and vulnerability of humanity comes to the fore. To this effect, Harrison notes, "By this proclamation of hope for the future the prophet showed that man is dead until quickened by the divine Spirit, and that society cannot flourish in the truest sense unless sustained by the presence of God."[171] The revival and restoration of religious and political national Israel is dependent on covenant Yahweh in this respect.

2.2.2.4 Speech Symbolism

Ezekiel performed at least three speech symbols under divine direction. First is his loss of speech (3:26-27), then his groaning instead of crying as a sign of intense pain (21:6-7), and lastly, his keeping silent instead of mourning the death of his wife (24:15-27). As the prophet was to be "a sign to the house of Israel," each of these speech symbols had a clear message for them. In the first symbolic act, Ezekiel would be unable to speak so he could rebuke the exiles after Yahweh had stuck his tongue to the roof of his mouth (3:26). Hence, he remained silent but was able to speak to his audience only when Yahweh enabled him to. The intention of Ezekiel's momentary loss of speech or dumbness was so that the exiles among whom he lived would learn lessons from such a dramatisation.

The understanding of the message of the prophet's dumbness seems problematic (3:26). Scholars have raised the query in view of its literary placement and the wider understanding of Ezekiel's entire ministry.

---

171. Harrison, *Introduction to the Old Testament*, 854.

Bruce raises the issue, "If his dumbness persisted without intermission" for the period from his inauguration until he received news of the fall of Jerusalem, then "he could hardly have fulfilled his commission to be a warning voice to the house of Israel."[172] Against this view, Bruce sees only a momentary silence on the part of the prophet. This way, he thinks the prophet's "dumbness was broken only when he was given a divine message to proclaim and returned when it was completed."[173] In this sense, it would suggest that the prophet's ministry at the moment is devoid of free will. Dumbrell argues in support that, "He does not act unless God, through the Spirit, has caused him to act. The prophet only speaks the divine word that has been put in his mouth (3:27), and he does not elaborate the message in any way."[174] Or as put differently by Taylor, "When he spoke, it was because God had something to say; when he was silent, it was because God was silent."[175] Further in support, Nicholas J. Tromp argues that as a man influenced by Yahweh both "by hand and by mouth," he was essentially powerless and "incompetent to independent action." He explains that this is because the "Spirit places him completely at God's disposal so that Ezekiel will be silent when God is silent and will speak to the people as soon as God speaks to him."[176]

The intended message of the prophet's symbolic act of dumbness for his audience is still fuzzy (3:26). As stated previously, Ezekiel's ministry is directed to a rebellious, stubborn, obstinate, and stiff-necked people.[177] Does

---

172. Bruce, "Ezekiel," 814.

173. Bruce, "Ezekiel," 814.

174. Dumbrell, *The Faith of Israel*, 154.

175. Taylor, *Ezekiel*, 74. Dyer had argued similarly that, being a watchman, Ezekiel had to proclaim "thus said the Lord." On this ground, his dumbness "was not continuous or permanent." He argues further that being a man under divine order, Ezekiel spoke only when God told him to; therefore, "when he was silent, it was because God had not spoken. When he spoke, it was because God had given him a message." Dyer, "Ezekiel," 1234.

176. Nicholas J. Tromp, "The Paradox of Ezekiel's Prophetic Mission: Towards a Semiotic Approach of Ezekiel 3, 22-27," in *Ezekiel and His Book: Textual and Literary Criticism and their Interpretation* (ed. Johan Lust; Leuven, Belgium: Leuven University Press, 1986), 200-213.

177. Dyer explains the situation of the rebels: "Rather than acknowledging God's judgment and confessing their sins, the Jewish exiles viewed their time in Babylon as a temporary setback that would be alleviated by their soon return to Jerusalem. They refused

the possibility exist that the sign of dumbness until the news of Jerusalem's fall reached the exiles is affirmative of Yahweh's execution of judgement on Israel? While Ellison understands Ezekiel's dumbness as "no actual inability to speak, but a refusal to speak on ordinary matters with those who had refused to hear God's messenger,"[178] Odell sees it as a liminal state where Ezekiel is unable to "act as mediator between the people and Yahweh and is thus no longer able either to reconcile the estranged parties or to avert the danger."[179] Neither of these thoughts adequately resolves the problem as we are still left wondering why the prophet should be dumb at all. Even Wright's point of view seems not quite helpful either. He states, "Just as all normal relations between himself and his family and neighbours would be broken off by such dumbness, so too was all 'conversation' between God and Israel,"[180] and this way, his prophetic role comes to a temporary halt.

The focus of Ezekiel's intended message looks beyond the present. His prophetic dumbness is to continue until God's judgement has reached its full course, having the destruction of 587 BC in view here. As Goldingay opines, this act is "more likely a sign of God's judgment on the rebellious house," pointing to the "constraint of siege" and the "confinement"[181] of the city in its final days. Apparently, "He was mute only to the extent that he could not associate with his fellowman in an ordinary way."[182] Poignantly, Brueggemann explains that this symbol is ". . . an unmistakable articulation of the depth of loss, alienation, and abandonment" which suggests that Ezekiel's ". . . awareness of the impending doom upon the city of Jerusalem has reduced him to silence, a traumatic personal embodiment of the public trauma to come upon Jerusalem in its final days"[183] to mark its demise (Ezek 24:25-27).

---

to admit their sin or to believe the threat of impending judgment on their disobedient nation." Dyer, "Ezekiel,", 1230.

178. Ellison, *Ezekiel*, 32.
179. Odell, *Ezekiel*, 58.
180. Wright, *The Message of Ezekiel*, 73.
181. Goldingay, "Ezekiel,", 627.
182. VanGemeren, *Interpreting the Prophetic Word*, 325.
183. Brueggemann, *An Introduction*, 196.

Second, Ezekiel is placed under divine order to perform yet another speech symbolic act. He was to groan before the exiles "with broken heart and bitter grief" (21:6-7). The import of groaning is significant to the meaning of this prophetic symbolic act. The act of groaning expresses the feeling of excessive pain that goes beyond the mere act of weeping. It is an aggravated graduating expression of deep sorrow and pain from crying to agonising, an emotional expression that is too heavy for words to covey. Groaning expresses the idea of a deeply sorrowful and mournful heart caused by deep hurt. It does express the deepest level of the experience of pain and grief that the exiles would feel when Jerusalem finally fell to the Babylonians. In this vein, Yahweh told Ezekiel to groan with broken heart and bitter grief (21:6-7) because his unsheathed sword would cut both the righteous and the wicked (21:2-5).

The theological pericope of Ezekiel 21:1-7 indicates that Yahweh's judgement on Israel for her sin is inevitably hanging on Jerusalem. The city, though well fortified and secured, would certainly fall to the sword of invading Nebuchadnezzar. This prophetic sign-act was to express and therefore convey to the hesitant exiles how they would receive with shock the news of the fall of Jerusalem, the city they had contested with Ezekiel the possibility of its destruction. This news of dismay would overturn the expectation of the exiles of a soon return to the city. This clearly plays out in Ezekiel's response to his audience's inquiry regarding his groaning. Despite their contest, Ezekiel was unambiguous when he explained that because of the news that was coming, "Every heart will melt and every hand go limp; every spirit will become faint and every knee become as weak as water. It is coming! It will surely take place" (21:7 NIV). This acted prophecy depicts, not only the behaviour of the Jerusalemites "under invasion and siege,"[184] but also indicates that the Babylonian exiles "would likewise be heartbroken"[185] when the "news of the catastrophe will be received."[186] More devastating was Ezekiel's insistence that Yahweh had

---

184. Bruce, "Ezekiel," 828.
185. Pearson, "Ezekiel," 735.
186. Beasley-Murray, "Ezekiel," 675.

already drawn the sword, "His instrument of judgment,"[187] never to return into its sheath until it accomplished the purpose of avenging his anger on his covenant people.

The sign-act of Ezekiel's groaning was to achieve the effect of generating curiosity in the exiles which would propel them to ask the prophet for its meaning (21:27). This was geared towards their repentance as they faced up to this forthcoming reality. Ezekiel therefore acted out, well ahead of the actual event, the exiles' response of grief and devastation at the awful realisation of their country's demise. To this point, Ellison submits that the symbol expresses a "sense of panic and emotional paralysis . . . [a] complete nervous and physical collapse [also of] deep emotional distress"[188] by the exiles upon the receipt of the news of their city and nation's demise. By implication therefore, this shocking as well as choking symbol was intended to serve as an emotional and psychological preparatory ground on the part of the exiles so they are able to face the situation when the news of Jerusalem's demise finally arrived (21:7).

Finally, the last in the series of speech symbols is an extra-ordinary and seemingly inhumane one as it affects the prophet directly. Here, Ezekiel is placed under an emotion-driven embargo. It is a burden too heavy for him to bear, for even the symbolic action "is not '"acted"' but lived."[189] He was restrained from mourning the death of the wife of his love who was to die, possibly by a plague[190] of some sort. (24:15-27). The helpless prophet is here placed under strict divine orders not to observe the cultural and cultic conventions of mourning the dead following the loss of his wife. Yahweh instructed,

> Son of man, with one blow I am about to take away from you the delight of your eyes. Yet do not lament or weep or shed any tears. Groan quietly; do not mourn for the dead. Keep your turban fastened and your sandals on your feet; do not

---

187. Taylor, *Ezekiel*, 161.
188. Ellison, *Ezekiel*, 162.
189. Ruiz, "Ezekiel," 1071.
190. Beasley-Murray, "Ezekiel," 676.

cover the lower part of your face or eat the customary food (24:16-17 NIV).

At this point, Ezekiel joins in the tradition of his earlier prophetic colleague, Hosea, in suffering Yahweh's unfairness[191] to the righteous in the line of duty. Here is a man who, from the onset, had faithfully and vigorously obeyed Yahweh in confronting the unresponsive exiles, and at other times, bearing their guilt and pain. Yet, he was to lose his wife as a further "sign" to the exiles.[192] The loss of Ezekiel's wife who is the 'delight of his eyes,' a term used for real endearment, of intense affection,[193] must certainly have been to him "a grief too great for tears"[194] and words to express its magnitude. The socio-ethical unfairness and seeming act of injustice that Yahweh displayed here in restraining faithful and dutiful Ezekiel from mourning the sudden loss of such a treasure, "his only precious possession ... ripped from him"[195] is unimaginable and inexplicable. In equating the gravity of the pain suffered from such loss, Wright notes, "We have here ... one of the most poignant moments in the rich story of Israel's prophets – comparable to, but possibly surpassing, the heartbreak of Hosea and the loneliness of Jeremiah."[196]

This speech symbolic act must have certainly conveyed a very graphic pictorial message to the prophet's audience, more than any that he had previously dramatised; a kind that burned in their hearts. Ezekiel's awkward, strange and abnormal psychology at the moment would be the centre of attraction that would force his audience to inquire of its meaning. As Ruiz notes, he behaved "in such a way as to cause people to wonder, and thereby

---

191. Ruiz States that, "As in the case of Hosea's marriage we have here an example of the radical personal involvement of prophets with their message." Ruiz, "Ezekiel," 1071. Cf. Ezekiel 24:15-27 with Hosea 1:1-3; 2:2-14.
192. See the personification of the woman and wife of virtue as described in Proverbs 31:10. A woman who is truly a wife, a good wife, a loving and caring wife, a selfless and people-centered woman is more precious than rubies. She is a source of peace, comfort, strength, and prosperity both for her family and society. Such women are difficult to find and too painful to lose.
193. Wright, *The Message of Ezekiel*, 215.
194. Taylor, *Ezekiel*, 162.
195. Wright, *The Message of Ezekiel*, 215.
196. Wright, *The Message of Ezekiel*, 214.

makes it possible for him to deliver his message."[197] Against such a graphic pictorial portrait, the prophet's action would naturally have symbolised "the death of the city"[198] which was the delight of Judah. As Ezekiel's wife was the delight of his eyes, so was the city of Jerusalem to Israel as its political nerve centre as well as the temple as the centre of its national cult where Yahweh had chosen as his residence[199] among his people. Schultz and Smith describe this sign as "ominous" because "God would also destroy His temple, the desire of the people's eyes, and they would be so devastated that they would not be able to mourn."[200] That such a national monument and treasure was to be destroyed, worst still, by a gentile nation, is a news too devastating and too difficult for the exiles to believe. It is the weight of this horrible news that would result in groaning on the part of the exiles. Ruiz explains that "the abstinence from mourning on the part of Ezekiel foreshadows what Judeans will have to go through at the time of the fall of the capital . . . at that time, it will be of no use to wail, but only to acknowledge"[201] the fact and live with its reality.

This particular symbolic act not only suggests Ezekiel's personal participation but overrides customary conventions in Israel. Indeed, this irreconcilable event, as Clements notes, "is the most extraordinary and . . . the most complex"[202] experience of Ezekiel's personal participation in the pains of his people. As Bruce observes, the loss on the part of the prophet is God's invitation to him to "now manifest his solidarity with his people under judgment." He explains the effects of this solidarity in the prophet's response to the inquiry of his fellow-exiles about his strange behaviour thus: "When Jerusalem's day of desolation comes, when the temple, the delight of its eyes, is destroyed and its children killed within it, the blow will be too unimaginably overwhelming to be expressed by any of the conventional

---

197. Ruiz, "Ezekiel," 1071. Through "his own heartbreaking experience the inner pain about to be felt by all those Israelites already in captivity…would normally produce an outpouring of grief and sadness." Dyer, "Ezekiel," 1274.
198. Ruiz, "Ezekiel," 1071.
199. See 2 Chronicles 7:11-16.
200. Samuel J. Schultz and Gary V. Smith, *Exploring the Old Testament* (Wheaton, Ill.: Crossway Books, 2001), 192.
201. Ruiz, "Ezekiel," 1071.
202. Clements, *Ezekiel*, 111.

tokens of grief."²⁰³ In addition to its implication on customary convention, Duguid explains that the absence of public weeping, or wailing, or mourning for the loss of the temple does not suggest "any absence of grief on their part, but because in the face of such a devastating, all-encompassing judgment, the usual social structures of mourning rites will be overwhelmed,"²⁰⁴ giving no allowance for its observance.

Such experience of loss and outburst of pain is to be expected of the Jewish people because, as Beasley-Murray explains, "Jerusalem and its sanctuary are as dear to them as a wife is to a husband."²⁰⁵ Stated differently, "The temple in Jerusalem was their pride and joy; it had become as precious to the Jerusalemites as the closest of relations."²⁰⁶ Therefore, Wright observes, the ripping from Ezekiel of the delight of his eyes, causing him a "heart-wrenching personal tragedy," is to be the last most graphic and compelling sign to the exiles; "the last thing he could give or do that would convince those capable of being convinced that Yahweh was serious in his intention to destroy Jerusalem and the temple."²⁰⁷

2.3 Ezekiel's Use of the Shepherd Metaphor

During the Babylonian raid of Jerusalem in 597 BC, a young Judean priest, Ezekiel, had fallen victim to deportation. He claims that, "In the thirteenth year, in the fourth month on the fifth day, while I was among the exiles by the Kebar River, the heavens were opened and I saw visions of God" (Ezek 1:1 NIV), implying that he was called into the prophetic function while a Babylonian captor. To seek to know why captor-prophet used metaphoric language in his prophetic speeches, and in particular, his use of the shepherd metaphor is quite engaging. It is apparently enigmatic that a Babylonian captor would employ the shepherd metaphor in such a critical period in Israel's history. Tamar Kamionkowski is right in submitting that,

---

203. Bruce, "Ezekiel," 830.
204. Duguid, *Ezekiel*, 315.
205. Beasley-Murray, "Ezekiel," 676.
206. Duguid, *Ezekiel* 315.
207. Wright, *The Message of Ezekiel*, 216.

"in order to fully grasp the richness of prophetic messages, one must carefully consider the phenomenon of metaphor."[208] As such, before we give attention to the shepherd metaphor in Ezekiel, we shall begin our discourse in this section with a brief survey of the concept of metaphor.[209] We think this is quite resourceful to our understanding why and how Ezekiel used the shepherd metaphor.

Generally, the term 'metaphor'[210] defies consensus definition because it is not easily defined. Janet Martin Soskice similarly observes that the subject is perceived, not only as "elusive, but [that] a definition of metaphor useful to one discipline often proves unsatisfactory to another,"[211] resulting in various descriptive terms being assigned to it by different disciplines. Eva Feder Kittay acknowledges the problem when she observes that, "although analyses of metaphor in the past few years have surpassed previous ones in subtlety and sophistication, we still lack an adequate understanding of metaphorical meaning."[212] Andrea Weiss affirms this fluidity further in the submission that "given the complexity of metaphors and the tremendous diversity of definitions and approaches, it is not surprising that developing a fool proof means of identifying a metaphor has proven to be an elusive endeavour."[213] These submissions indicate an enigmatic situation because

---

208. Tamar Kamionkowski, *Gender Reversal and Cosmic Chaos: A Study on the Book of Ezekiel*, JSOTSup. 368 (Sheffield: Sheffield Academic Press, 2003), 31.

209. "Metaphor" forms part of the figures of speech in literature. Its literary associates are simile, metonymy, synecdoche, hyperbole, apostrophe, allusion, personification, paradox, pun, irony, parallelism, repetition, and rhythm.

210. F. C. T. Moore draws attention to three commonly made assumptions about metaphor in an attempt to arrive at a definition. First, that it involves some deviation from ordinary and straightforward usage; second, that this deviation is semantic which involves meaning; and lastly, that the effect of such semantic deviation is to draw attention to similarities between what the metaphorical expression would ordinarily denote and that to which it is metaphorically applied. He argues from these assumptions that metaphor is not, or primarily not a semantic phenomena because it is not so much a change of meaning as an evocative exploitation of given meaning. F. C. T. Moore, "On Taking Metaphor Literally," in *Metaphor: Problems and Perspectives* (ed. David S. Miall; Sussex, Britain: The Harvester, 1982), 1-13.

211. Janet Martin Soskice, *Metaphor and Religious Language* (Oxford, N.Y.: Oxford University Press, 1985; repr., paperback ed., 1989), 15.

212. Eva Feder Kittay, *Metaphor: Its Cognitive Force and Linguistic Structure* (Oxford, N.Y.: Oxford University Press, 1987), 40.

213. Andrea L. Weiss, *Figurative Language in Biblical Prose Narrative: Metaphor in the Book of Samuel* (Leiden: Brill, 2006), 39.

one wonders why divergent views still exist despite metaphor's long history.²¹⁴ It appears difficult therefore to apply the same meaning of metaphor to all fields of disciplines. But does this fluidity imply that a chameleon-like description is applied to the function of metaphor? Why can not its one controlling meaning be applied to various fields of discipline?

Recognising the difficulty and the void of a satisfactory definition of metaphor that is suitable for all disciplines, Soskice proposes a minimal definition that seems fairly adequate. She says, a "metaphor is that figure of speech whereby we speak about one thing in terms which are seen to be suggestive of another."²¹⁵ Seen this way, she states, metaphor "as a figure of speech, is a form of language use"²¹⁶ because it functions within the speech²¹⁷ domain. This idea links the fabric of cognitive domain because of its literariness. To this, Nelly Stienstra submits, "Metaphor is now recognized as an important way for people to express ideas that are otherwise inexpressible."²¹⁸ Accordingly, Zoltán Kövecses sees metaphor as functioning within a "conceptual domain." He explains, "A conceptual metaphor consists of two conceptual domains, in which one domain is understood in terms of another."²¹⁹ Perhaps, this concept is better expressed in Kamionkowski's words when she observes that metaphor "has been acknowledged as a paradox because on some level a metaphor means what

---

214. Soskice has noted in response to the lingering problem that, "So readily did interest in metaphor obtrude itself upon even the earliest philosophical and grammatical analyses of language that one can say that the study of metaphor begins with the study of language itself." Soskice, *Metaphor and Religious Language*, 1.
215. Soskice, *Metaphor and Religious Language*, 15.
216. Soskice, *Metaphor and Religious Language*, 15.
217. Stein Olsen calls attention to the role of conventionalist and impositionalist theories in relation to the usage of metaphorical and figurative expression. This scholar submits that metaphor functions within the domain of speech communication; hence, attention is called to the need to understand literary metaphor. Stein Haugom Olsen, "Understanding Literary Metaphor," in *Metaphor: Problems and Perspective* (ed. David S. Miall; Sussex, Britain: The Harvester, 1982), 36-54.
218. Nelly Stienstra, *YHWH is the Husband of His People* (Kampen: Kok Pharos, 1993), 17.
219. Zoltán Kövecses, *Metaphor: A Practical Introduction* (Oxford, N.Y.: Oxford University Press, 2002), 4.

it does not really mean," yet, "metaphors create similarity," implying "a process of implication" rather than a "one-to-one corresponding identity."[220]

Metaphoric understanding is queried further. Why has the topic of metaphor "been the subject of such enduring, expanding interest in a range of fields"[221] in spite of its seeming fluidity? Cast differently, why do linguists, literarists, and rhetoricians employ metaphorical language in an effort to communicate meaning? Stienstra presupposes that this is so because "man's cognitive capacity is intrinsically and necessarily metaphorical with respect to abstract concepts." His thesis is predicated upon the assumption that "all our knowledge is primarily based on sensory perceptions, from which we may abstract in order to arrive at abstract concepts."[222] Therefore, he concludes on the basis of universal principle, that "there are certain basic universal metaphorical concepts, which all men will recognize simply because they are human."[223] By implication, as long as humans exist and as long as literary activity and human language still exist, the need and use of metaphor will continue just as humanity's need of air.

In literary domain, metaphor, conceived as a figurative language of expression, is employed for its dimensional[224] effects and functions. One of such functions in linguistic metaphor, for instance, is in its cognitive effect.[225] Construed from this perspective, Kittay comments that metaphor "provide[s] a perspective from which to gain an understanding of that which is metaphorically portrayed."[226] She explains that it is perspectival in the sense that "metaphor provides the linguistic realization for the cognitive activity by which a language speaker makes use of one linguistically articulated domain to gain an understanding of another experiential

---

220. Kamionkowski, *Gender Reversal and Cosmic Chaos*, 31, 34.
221. Weiss, *Figurative Language in Biblical Prose Narrative*, 1.
222. Stienstra, *YHWH is the Husband*, 17.
223. Stienstra, *YHWH is the Husband*, 40.
224. Metaphor has effects on both language and life. For the treatment of metaphor in its combination of language and social dimensions, see the collection of articles in this respect in *Confronting Metaphor in Use: An Applied Linguistic Approach* (eds. Mara Sophia Zanotto et al.; Amsterdam: John Benjamins, 2008).
225. For a work on linguistic analysis of metaphor in its cognitive nature, function and effects, see Gerard J. Steen, *Finding Metaphor in Grammar and Usage* (Amsterdam: John Benjamins, 2007).
226. Kittay, *Metaphor*, 13.

or conceptual domain, and similarly, by which a hearer grasps such an understanding."[227]

How then should we relate metaphoric understanding to biblical literature? As we make efforts to understand Ezekiel's use of the shepherd metaphor among other metaphors as his interpreters, we should keep in mind that in figurative speech, "the literal meaning of an expression is not identical to what the speaker intends us to understand," especially that "most figurative, rhetorical devices thrive on ambiguity,"[228] unless properly delineated. Specifically, we must note that in prophetic metaphorical statements, "context-embeddedness"[229] does exist, requiring that the interpreter associates the expression to its context. In other words, prophetic usage of "metaphors do not function in isolation"[230] as their appearance is tied to a context – be it rhetorical, literary, cultural, theological, and so on. As we make efforts to interpret Ezekiel's usage of the language of poetry and metaphoric expressions, we must endeavour to understand them within their literary, historical, and cultural contexts, all functioning within a religious foreground so we are able to achieve its appropriate meaning. Michael E. Travers well points out in this regard, "How, then, are figures of speech to be interpreted? They are to be interpreted like the rest of Scripture – in their appropriate contexts and for their theology."[231]

2.3.1 Reasons for His Use of the Shepherd Metaphor

Prophetic discourse oracles broadly consist of prose narratives and poetry. Its poetic aspects, though not all, are structured metaphorically as cognitive device to achieve rhetorical effect. For instance, Stienstra points out that Jeremiah, Hosea and few other Old Testament writers "made use of

---

227. Kittay, *Metaphor*, 14.
228. David H. Aaron, *Biblical Ambiguities: Metaphor, Semantics and Divine Imagery* (Leiden: Brill, 2001), 1.
229. Gerlinde Baumann, *Love and Violence: Marriage as Metaphor for the Relationship between YHWH and Israel in the Prophetic Books* (trans. Linda M. Maloney; Collegeville, Minn.: Liturgical, 2003), 33.
230. Sarah J. Dille, *Mixing Metaphor: God as Father and Mother in Deutero-Isaiah* (London: T&T Clark, 2004), 1.
231. Michael E. Travers, "The Use of Figures of Speech in the Bible," BS 164 (2007): 290. The major components of figures of speech (figures of similarity) whose presence are noticed in biblical literature include simile, metaphor, image, and symbol.

the marriage metaphor in order to drive home a number of truths that could not be expressed in another way."[232] To this David Aaron also submits that in view of human cognition, "metaphor, like other forms of figurative speech, is a rhetorical device, one which cannot operate unless the subject being described is, indeed, rather well understood."[233] This presupposes that the engagement of metaphoric expressions by Israel's prophets was not just to fit into the literary conventions of their day, although such would have been quite necessary, but it was particularly to express certain ideas and concepts about God that could be understood in no any other better way than through such a language mode. Thomas A. Golding asks in this line, "How does God, who is infinite beyond human experience and comprehension, explain Himself and His relationship to people in ways they can understand? The answer is through figurative or metaphorical language."[234] This finds connection with Apostle John's argument when he asserts, "For anyone who does not love his brother, whom he has seen, cannot love God, whom he has not seen" (1 John 4:20 NIV). In order for finite humans to comprehend and walk in obedience to the universal principles of the divine, which appear abstract, the employment of figurative and metaphorical language is unavoidable. It is on this ground that Golding states, "The human authors of Scripture employed . . . figures and motifs from human life in communicating aspects of God's nature to finite human beings."[235]

In view of the preceding, it is our intention at this point to find out why Ezekiel used the shepherd metaphor in his prophetic corpus. The assertion by Golding that "Shepherding is one of the most frequent and powerful images in the Bible"[236] as is the case in Ezekiel is an absolute fact. Regarding Ezekiel's tradition, Karin Schöpflin states that, "Elaborate metaphorical passages or even narratives are one striking characteristic of the book of

---

232. Stienstra, *YHWH is the Husband*, 21. While Jeremiah is deprived of the experience of marriage and raising a family, Hosea is to raise a family through a adulterous woman.
233. Aaron, *Biblical Ambiguities*, 11.
234. Thomas A. Golding, "The Imagery of Shepherding in the Bible, Part 1," *BS* 163 (2006):20.
235. Golding, "The Imagery of Shepherding in the Bible, Part 1," 20.
236. Golding, "The Imagery of Shepherding in the Bible, Part 1," 18.

Ezekiel."[237] Ezekiel was in exile, fully participating in the pains of being a fugitive as well as estrangement from all that being a Jew demands.[238] Given this context, why did he use the shepherd metaphor among his elaborate metaphoric pericopes? As one who was ministering in exile to the exiles, what motivating factors gingered Ezekiel's use of the shepherd metaphor that he devoted a whole chapter to its discourse in addition to its allusion within the book?

While tracing the development of the shepherd concept in Israel's history, J. Jeremias concedes that shepherd terms are used in Exodus-Deuteronomy, but doubts "whether there is any conscious feeling for the shepherd metaphor" as a vital concept, not until in the Psalter and in the "consoling prophecy of the Exile." Even then, he contends that "the content of the metaphor is more clearly developed in the latter than in any other place apart from Psalm 23."[239] Ezekiel's intention by using the shepherd metaphor was to make a public spectacle of Israel's political wheel without Yahweh. He did this by revealing the weakness and imperfection of Israel's human shepherds to allow for his projection of the ultimate strength of Yahweh as the only true Shepherd of national Israel. This way, as noted by Kamionkowski, Ezekiel's metaphors "convey theological and political messages."[240] Kamionkowski goes further to explain that on political ground, the exiles were in a pool of trauma following the deportation of Israel's population after the loss of her land, city, and Temple, and as such, "the nation of Judah was at an end and the future of the Davidic line was precarious at best."[241] Kamionkowski therefore contends that this

---

237. Karin Schöpflin, "The Composition of Metaphorical Oracles within the Book of Ezekiel," *VT* 1 (2005):101.

238. It is asserted that Ezekiel was "transplanted into unclean heathen soil" as a priest. Robertson, *The Christ of the Prophets*, 290. Ezekiel was a victim of circumstance–whisked as a Babylonian fugitive, away from his land, city, people, family, and from his priestly functions (if he had already assumed priestly function at this time), and as a sufferer with the suffering exiles. He alone, had to contend with the apprehensive, abhorrent, defensive, and elusive attitude of the Babylonian exiles, who found much difficulty in matching their knowledge of the personality and power of the God of their ancestors with recent events in the history of Judah.

239. J. Jeremias, "ποιμήν," *TDNT* VI (trans. Geoffrey W. Bromiley; ed. Gerhard Friedrich; Grand Rapids, Mich.: Eerdmans, 1968; repr., 1980), 487.

240. Kamionkowski, *Gender Reversal and Cosmic Chaos*, 58.

241. Kamionkowski, *Gender Reversal and Cosmic Chaos*, 59.

traumatic experience occurred not only with the loss of the "institutions of government, kingship, cult, family, agriculture and commerce," but significantly so because of its effects on "the theological belief"[242] of the people in the inviolability of Jerusalem, particularly that both Temple and its priests are now lost. Therefore, Ezekiel used the shepherd metaphor to call attention to poor governance in Israelite society as a major reason for Judah's experience of exile as "the shepherd metaphor was closely associated with the king's responsibility for the welfare of his people."[243] This is significant because the kings in Israel, "symbolized by herders, contracted by God to care for God's livestock, the people" whom he calls "my sheep,"[244] were to shepherd the people on behalf of Yahweh as his under-shepherds.[245] That leadership failure was largely responsible for the exile is clearly the prophet's point of argument as clearly presented by the shepherd metaphor.

Ezekiel's use of the shepherd metaphor, among the range of metaphors, also clearly indicates that the prophet's intention was to evoke the emotion of both national and individual guilt to call for repentance on the part of the exiles. As one who was "a sign" to the exiles, gaining their attention is crucial to the prophetic message. As Lawrence Boadt contends, "Elaborate imagery does not occur in Ezekiel solely for its beauty or its power to gain an audience's attention, but rather for its ability to convey his message."[246] While negatively, Ezekiel drew attention to the flaws of Israel's past and present human shepherds, positively, he provoked the exiles to repentance for the sins of both their national leaders as well as theirs; peradventure Yahweh would reduce his anger and rescind the planned destruction of Jerusalem. Ezekiel joined the people in his accusatory suit because, as

---

242. Kamionkowski, *Gender Reversal and Cosmic Chaos*, 60.
243. Odell, *Ezekiel*, 432.
244. Coogan et al, ed. *The New Annotated Bible*, 1229.
245. Figuratively, Yahweh is the Shepherd of Israel who delegated his shepherding responsibility to the monarchs. See Genesis 48:15; Isaiah 40:11; Hosea 4:16; Jeremiah 2:8; 3:15; 22:22; 2 Samuel 5:2; 7:7; Ezekiel 34:2, 3, 8, 10.
246. Lawrence Boadt, "Rhetorical Strategies in Ezekiel's Oracles of Judgment," in *Ezekiel and his Book: Textual and Literary Criticism and their Interpretation* (ed. Johan Lust; Leuven, Belgium: Leuven University Press, 1986), 190.

Peggy L. Day points out, among Israel's crimes is her "metaphoric adultery" (breach of covenant) as a promiscuous wife against Yahweh her husband.[247]

This expected remorseful response from the exiles to the import of the shepherd metaphor is captured clearly in Ezekiel's theology of generational responsibility in chapter 18. While Ezekiel did not deny that the failure of Israel's leaders and past generations was a contributory factor responsible for the condition of exilic Israel, he explained that the exiles also shared in the cause of their predicament because of their sin, a reality they must admit and face up to its repercussions. Based on this warrant, he refuted the "sour grapes" proverb popular in Israel at the time. By this proverb, Hill and Walton state, "The people of Judah had displaced blame by attributing their dire predicament to the sinful behaviour of previous generations . . . [thereby rejecting] the idea of each generation's responsibility and denied God's righteousness,"[248] particularly for his incapability of protecting Jerusalem. Ezekiel therefore argued that fundamentally, the sinfulness of leaders and people "effectively justifies God's decision to abandon his people to the natural consequences of their choices and to the curses of the Mosaic covenant."[249] And if there is to be any recourse at all as Clements points out, it is "Only when men and women recognize the cause of . . . divine wrath in their long history of national failings can [God's] anger be turned aside and a new beginning occur."[250]

The foregoing presupposes that the use of the shepherd metaphor by Ezekiel is intended to aid participation in the prophetic message. The prophet's audience were not to be passive listeners but active participants[251]

---

247. Peggy L. Day, "Adulterous Jerusalem's Imagined Demise: Death of a Metaphor in Ezekiel XVI," *VT* 3 (2000):286.

248. Andrew E. Hill and John H. Walton, *A Survey of the Old Testament* (2d ed.; Grand Rapids, Mich.: Zondervan, 2000), 448.

249. Laniak, *Shepherds after My own Heart*, 145.

250. Clements, *Ezekiel*, 20.

251. Kamionkowski draws attention to Ezekiel's use of metaphors in general as functioning in three broad categories: That the prophet uses metaphors as rhetorical technique to couch "his troubling message by means of another more familiar concept;" that he uses metaphors as a process of cognitive conceptual mapping of "an abstract system of emotions and concepts;" and lastly, that scholars understand Ezekiel's use of metaphors "through the insights of deconstructive reading" following recent literary theories and those put forward by "feminist cultural criticism." Kamionkowski, *Gender Reversal and Cosmic Chaos*, 57. An example of such feminist scholars is Margaret Hammer.

in the prophetic message. If the proposition that "metaphors construct meaning, order reality, serve to persuade, reveal cultural assumptions and reveal what cannot be said more directly"[252] is correct, then it follows that Ezekiel engaged the shepherd metaphor to enhance the "element of reader participation."[253] As a result, "far from being merely decorative, [Ezekiel's] metaphors have real cognitive content"[254] to enhance his audience's deep involvement. To this effect, Carol A. Newsom notes the convincing power of metaphor when she says, ". . . it does not allow its hearers to be passive but requires them to participate in the construction of the metaphorical meaning."[255] If the Babylonian exiles had given reason its right place, they would have been able to see issues from Ezekiel's perspective. This, perhaps, would have engaged a positive response to the prophetic message at its initial stage.

But a thick wall of resistance to the prophetic message was already built between the speaker and the listener. Persuasion as a rhetorical literary method would perhaps be useful at this point as a defusing strategy. It is quite possible therefore that Ezekiel engaged the shepherd metaphor as an "intentional, stylistic tool . . . [to express] the rhetorical power of narrative metaphor"[256] since even in biblical usage, "metaphor speaks the unspeakable"[257] as a form of and as a speech vehicle. This is necessary, as Kamionkowski argues, "If metaphor is one of our fundamental tools

---

Her work, written in three parts–Biblical perspectives, church history, and toward a birthing theology and ministry, traces the idea of birthing through Scripture, querying why the birthing metaphor of God is neglected by biblical scholars. In her argument, she asks why that when speaking of God in metaphoric terms like rock, king, etc, how often scholars overlook the birthing metaphor use of God who is a mother, a midwife. Arguing further, she states that the church should not refrain from talking or praying to God as a mother. She therefore calls attention to this crucial omission in scholarship. Margaret L. Hammer, *Giving Birth: Reclaiming Biblical Metaphor for Pastoral Practice* (Louisville, Kentucky: Westminster John Knox, 1994).

252. Kamionkowski, *Gender Reversal and Cosmic Chaos*, 56.
253. Julie Galambush, *Jerusalem in the Book of Ezekiel: The City as Yahweh's Wife* (SBLDS 130 Atlanta, Ga.: Scholars Press, 1992), 14.
254. Weiss, *Figurative Language*, 152.
255. Newsom, "A Maker of Metaphors, 152.
256. Galambush, *Jerusalem in the Book of Ezekiel*, 15.
257. Kamionkowski, *Gender Reversal and Cosmic Chaos*, 152.

of expression, it becomes an extraordinarily powerful instrument"[258] for Ezekiel to engage so as to explain and express the meaning of the exile's predicament. This approach, ordinarily, would appeal to the psyche of the exiles in order to gain a hearing. This is perhaps the purpose why earlier in Isaiah, Yahweh had invited Israel to allow reason to prevail.[259]

Yet, another significant reason for the prophet's use of the shepherd metaphor lies in the restorative motif. The disclosure of a future hope of restoration for Judah is a controlling theme in the last part of the book of Ezekiel as captured in chapters 40-48. It is quite obvious, given the conclusion of the Babylonian exiles that, "the worst had happened"[260] to Judah following the fall of Jerusalem, thus ending the Davidic dynasty. The covenant people had lost their land, therefore, a loss of their national identity; and by implication, a life of destitution had begun for national Israel. To this community, Ezekiel brings the message of hope in the "shepherd" metaphor as reflected in the recognition formula specific to salvific declaration (Ezek 34:27b, 31). This metaphor contrasts the failure of Israel's imperfect human shepherds with the faithfulness of Yahweh who is the only true

---

258. Kamionkowski, *Gender Reversal and Cosmic Chaos*, 37. Following this thought, Weiss observes, in discussing the effects of metaphor in discourse narratives, that it brings out three effects on the audience: "metaphors found in dialogue and narration produce interactional effects on the audience;" "metaphoric utterances paint a graphic, memorable image that engage the audience's imagination and attention;" and lastly, "metaphors also involve a certain conceptual economy, allowing the speaker to convey nuanced, multifaceted message through a single, vivid utterance." Weiss, *Figurative Language*, 126, 131.

259. Isaiah 1:18-20. Yahweh has always given his people the opportunity for a second chance, an opportunity of which they never took advantage. Ezekiel's use of the shepherd-sheep metaphor falls along this line. Odell rightly observes that, "Of all the metaphors in the Old Testament, the metaphor of God as the shepherd of the flock is perhaps the best known and most loved." Odell, *Ezekiel*, 430. Significantly, his use of this metaphor is to have the exiles reason that Yahweh is the only true Shepherd since human shepherds had failed, an admission that would have effectively caused the exiles' return to Yahweh. Being an active metaphor (a metaphor is considered dead when its effect or meaning is lost, unless brought back in some way when it is used), its use would have possibly gained attention to the prophet's message. Thus, the purpose of holding captive the imagination of his audience through the persuasive power of the shepherd metaphor is crucial to Ezekiel as he was addressing an audience whose minds, spirits, and hearts were being shaped by the reality of the events of the day. Being estranged from the city and therefore from the presence of Yahweh, they stood the risk of potentially losing both land and their treasured city, an event Ezekiel insisted was irreversible.

260. Kaiser, Jr., *Toward an Old Testament Theology*, 236.

Shepherd of his chosen people. Ezekiel anticipates the return of Yahweh's glory into the future temple on the basis of his faithfulness and honour for his name (Ezek 43:1-7). As Robertson submits, "Ezekiel's prophecies centre around the events of Israel's final exile and the anticipation of a future, glorious restoration . . . in the vision of the return of God's glory to the temple."[261] To this Kaiser maintains that, "the sustaining hope for a people who had lost every outward symbol of hope . . . [looking forward] to the new David, His throne, and His kingdom . . . was [the] only one place to go."[262]

Ezekiel rooted his shepherd metaphor in the theological element of this eschatological hope for the exiles and Judah. This approach is significant because, as Thomas M. Raitt asserts, "Prophetic faith interprets history from a theological perspective."[263] For Ezekiel, exilic experience has a positive side to Israel's national survival in view of its future restoration on the ground that Yahweh's shepherd character of compassion makes him a forgiving Yahweh. The future restoration of Israel indicates that it is predicated upon his compassionate and forgiving nature vis-à-vis his enduring covenant. The prophet put to the exiles that while "Israel's appointed shepherds failed so miserably in carrying out their responsibilities (Ezek 34:1-10), the Covenant Lord himself shall take on the task of shepherding his sheep."[264] The reality of this eschatological hope is anchored only on the divine covenant[265] principle, and as such, the benefit of such an experience is both for the present "exiles as well as for the generations that would follow."[266]

---

261. Robertson, *The Christ of the Prophets*, 291.
262. Kaiser, Jr., *Toward an Old Testament Theology*, 236.
263. Thomas A. Raitt, *A Theology of Exile: Judgment/Deliverance in Jeremiah and Ezekiel* (Philadelphia: Fortress, 1977), 1.
264. Robertson, *The Christ of the Prophets*, 300.
265. Robertson observes that "Ezekiel casts the return from exile in terms of the Abrahamic, Mosaic, Davidic, and new covenants.... [And the consummation of the] blessings of the[se] various covenants will be experienced when the Lord gathers his people from all the nations and brings them back to their own land," see p. 301 of his work above. See also Ezekiel 36:24; 37:21; 36:27-28; 37:24-25.
266. Robertson, *The Christ of the Prophets*, 301.

2.3.2 His Methodology in Using the Shepherd Metaphor

So far, we have seen that although the metaphor concept lacks a consensus definition that is applicable conveniently to all fields, it is a figure of speech used to convey meaning when given a literary understanding. Also, we have established so far some reasons why Ezekiel used the shepherd metaphor in his oracular discourse. In order to enhance our understanding of Ezekiel's theological development of shepherding therefore, we need to attend to the manner in which he employed this metaphor.

Our research concern is rooted in the fact that not much has been done on the theological-eschatological motif of the shepherd metaphor in the book of Ezekiel. In this direction, we think Kamionkowski is right when she asserts, "Biblical literature, particularly the prophetic material, is replete with metaphors. However, to date, examinations of the nature and function of metaphor, particularly in prophetic literature, are still relatively scarce."[267] Specific to Ezekiel, Galambush equally observes that, "to date, research on Ezekiel's use of metaphor is at an early stage."[268] If substantial literature is lacking on Ezekiel's treatment of metaphors as pointed out by these scholars, it is logical that this same reason also accounts for the impoverished literature on the theological-eschatological motif of Ezekiel's treatment of the shepherd metaphor in Ezekiel 34.[269]

---

267. Kamionkowski, *Gender Reversal and Cosmic Chaos*, 30.
268. Galambush, *Jerusalem in the Book of Ezekiel*, 20.
269. Although few major articles have appeared on Ezekiel's use of the shepherd metaphor, these have not significantly proved that the theological-eschatological import of Ezekiel 34 is substantially treated. Andrew Mein's treatment of the shepherd motif here is largely economical rather than eschatological since he focuses attention on what a sheep owner would lose from bad shepherding. See "Profitable and Unprofitable Shepherds: Economic and Theological Perspectives on Ezekiel 34," *JSOT* 4 (2007):493-504.
Although William H. Brownlee had admitted that the shepherd chapter of Ezekiel, like the shepherd Psalm, is one of the most beautiful chapters in the Old Testament, his focus is entirely literary and poetic rather than theological-eschatological. William H. Brownlee, "Ezekiel's Poetic Indictment of the Shepherds," *HTR* 4 (1958):191-203. John Paul Heil's treatment though has some theological and eschatological elements, only contrasts and compares Matthew's usage of the shepherd-sheep motif. See "Ezekiel 34 and the Narrative Strategy of the Shepherd and Sheep Metaphor in Matthew," *CBQ* 55 (1993):698-708. Coral A. Newsom's treatment of Ezekiel as a maker of metaphor ignores the shepherd metaphor completely. Carol A. Newsom, "A Maker of Metaphors – Ezekiel's Oracles Against Tyre," *Interpretation* 2 (1984):151-164. Karin Schöpflin's treatment only has a gloss on the shepherd metaphor. See "The Composition of Metaphorical Oracles Within the Book of Ezekiel," *VT* 1 (2005):101-120.

Despite this lacuna, we attempt at this point to examine how Ezekiel used the shepherd metaphor to achieve his purpose. As with other prophets, Ezekiel does not use the shepherd concept as a title for Israel's kings as was the case in the ancient Near East. Rather, as Wallis points out, he employs it as "a metaphor pondering the function of the king"[270] as a human shepherd. Ellison comments on this method: "whenever shepherd is used metaphorically it means king, except in the comparatively rare cases where the context makes it clear that the highest princes of the land are intended."[271] Similarly, Ezekiel applies an *extended* principle to enable him draw from the real natural and historical worlds. Petersen observes this characteristic method of Ezekiel thus: The prophet

> . . . will often establish a metaphor and then develop it . . . Sometimes that process seems allegorical, that is, various elements in the extended metaphor can be identified with elements in the real or historical world. In so doing, Ezekiel draws upon images from the worlds of fauna (lion, eagle, dragon) and flora (cedar, grapevine).[272]

This approach enabled the prophet to root the use of his metaphors in historic terms and in unveiling events – past, present, and future, to drive his point home. Petersen further notes in this connection when observing the nature of Ezekiel's poetry that it "often offers a version of events that might be conveyed in more historical terms, but the poetry draws out the implications of those events by depicting them using various images."[273] Ezekiel's historic purpose for the use of the shepherd metaphor was with the intention that the exiles, and indeed Israel, should admit that the present events in the people's experience is a repercussion of the nation's failure to faithfully and consistently play her role in her history. His accusation of

---

270. G. Wallis, "רָעָה," *TDOT* 8: 551.
271. Ellison, *Ezekiel*, 120.
272. Petersen, *The Prophetic Literature*, 152.
273. Petersen, *The Prophetic Literature*, 153.

the nation by way of his use of "sexual" metaphors in chapters 16 and 23 sustains this point of concern.

Educators and teachers usually employ the use of instructional technology for illustrative purposes. It is said that Ezekiel's use of metaphors has an illustrative purpose. Here, Ezekiel used the shepherd metaphor with an instructional import. Gerlinde Baumann notes in regards to Ezekiel's use of the marriage imagery for instance, that it is "to illustrate the relationship between YHWH and his people or city."[274] The author explains that this illustrative import is conveyed clearly in chapters 16 and 23 where Israel is imaged as Yahweh's ungrateful wife who neglects her husband's efforts and love for the love of a foreign lover. As a consequence, she becomes polluted, and, with a highly provoked husband, Ezekiel pronounces her doom with not the slightest opportunity for repentance, for her "destruction is already determined and carried out."[275] This illustrative principle finds connection with the use of the prophet's shepherd metaphor. The metaphor paints a picture of Yahweh, as is the case with the marriage imagery, as a faithful Shepherd of his sheep in contrast to the imperfect human shepherds as unfaithful to their shepherding tasks delegated by him. The metaphor illustrates the point of human unfaithfulness as contrasted with divine faithfulness to prove Yahweh's consistent care for his covenant sheep. The intended instructional element here is to point Israel back to total dependence on Yahweh who alone is perfect, very reliable and faithful.

A demonstrative element is also revealed in Ezekiel's critique and blame of Judah's rulers[276] that takes the shape of the shepherd metaphor. Petersen notes in his comment on Ezekiel 19:10-14 that "the prophet has worked with an image, the vine with its central stem, to demonstrate what has happened to Judah."[277] The demonstrative import of this metaphor is, as stated earlier, to show to the exiles the effects of leadership failure. Ezekiel demonstrated to his audience the fact that the godless leadership the covenant nation has had was largely responsible for the exile as well as the disil-

---

274. Baumann, *Love and Violence*, 135.
275. Baumann, *Love and Violence*, 135. See further discussion in this respect on pp. 135-145.
276. Laniak, *Shepherds after My own Heart*, 148.
277. Petersen, *The Prophetic Literature*, 153.

lusion of Jerusalem. This plays out in the indictment of Ezekiel 20, 22 and 34 where the prophet points out, "By their cruel treatment and senseless disregard of God's flock, the kings of Israel had become the accomplices of their enemies, preying on the very people they were called to protect."[278]

2.4 The Etymology and Semantics of the Shepherd Metaphor

2.4.1 Its Etymology

Our focus here is on the shepherd metaphor in Ezekiel. It is apparent that we need to give attention to the etymology of the concept of shepherding, that is, to the term "shepherd" in order to have better grasp on the Ezekielian usage of the shepherd metaphor. As broadly defined by James Barr, etymology is "the traditional term for several kinds of study, working upon words as the basic units and interested in the explication of them in relation to similar elements which are historically earlier, which are taken within the scope of the study as 'original,' which appear to be more basic as units of meaning."[279] Moisés Silva limits this definition to lexical semantics when he submits the opinion that etymological science refers to "that area of linguistic study that seeks to determine the origins of particular words."[280] This implies that lexical semantics has its basic focus on the historical study of distinct words. In this domain, Silva identifies four levels of etymological investigation: The first level is the one that identifies the component parts of a word; the second level is the one that determines specifically the earliest attested meaning from which possibly flows other derivatives; the third level is the one that deals with the prehistorical stages of a word, seeking the discovery of the meaning and or form a particular word had prior to its earliest attestation; and the last level is the one that

---

278. Laniak, *Shepherds after My own Heart*, 153.
279. James Barr, "Etymology and the Old Testament," in *Language and Meaning: Studies in Hebrew Language and Exegesis* (ed. A. J. van der Woude; OTS 19; Leiden: Brill, 1974), 1-28
280. Moisés Silva, *Biblical Words and Their Meaning: An Introduction to Lexical Semantics*, 2nd. ed. (Grand Rapids, Mich.: Zondervan, 1994), 38.

leads to a "reconstruction of the form and meaning of a word in the parent language by a careful examination of the cognate languages."[281] From this flows the understanding that etymological study concerns the origin, forms or nuances, occurrences, and function(s) of words and their meanings in their parent and cognate languages. The "cognate forms" of a word are understood as referring to the "group of words in different languages that are derived from a common ancestor;"[282] for example, Hebrew, Ugaritic, Akkadian, Arabic, Ethiopic, Phoenician, and Syriac languages share the same Semitic background.

How has the term "shepherd" or the concept of "shepherding" developed etymologically? The Hebrew verb רעה (rāʻâh)[283] from its root rʻh, translated "to shepherd," which in the Qal verbal form means to "graze, pasture, shepherd, shelter, and protect,"[284] or "to feed, to tend; to be a shepherd,"[285] grows out of a common Semitic lineage cognate root rʻy. Warren Baker and Eugene Carpenter state that "It means in general to care for, to protect, to graze, to feed the flocks and herds."[286] When used in its participial form רעה or רוֹעֶה (rōʻeh), it functions as a noun, meaning "shepherd, shepherders;" and shepherds "pasture, lead the sheep, flocks to eat"[287] as demanded of their vocation.

---

281. Silva, *Biblical Words and Their Meaning*, 38-40.

282. David Alan Black, *Linguistics for Students of New Testament Greek: A Survey of Basic Concepts and Applications* (Grand Rapids, Mich.: Baker Book House, 1988), 122.

283. This Hebrew word in its adjectival form רַע (raʻ) means something bad, evil. Baker and Carpenter suggest that depending on the context of usage, רעה has no less than ten shades of meaning, descriptive of people, events, and actions. That it also takes on the aspect of something disagreeable, unwholesome, or harmful, of place or lifestyle. Further, that literally, it can describe or depict something poor or low quality or even ugly in appearance. Still, they explain that רעה in its verb sense can also be used to indicate relationship and friendship to mean to associate with, to be a companion, to be a friend. That "it indicates a person who regularly associates with a group of persons, a companion, an associate, a friend, sharing common ideas and activities." Warren Baker and Eugene Carpenter, *The Complete Word Study Dictionary: Old Testament* (Chattanooga, Tennessee: AMG Publishers, 2003), 1062- 1066.

284. Ludwig Koehler and Walter Baumgartner, *The Hebrew and Aramaic Lexicon of the Old Testament* (2d. ed.; trans. Walter Baumgartner and Yohann Jakob Stamm; ed. M. E. J. Richardson Leiden: Brill, 1996), 1258. Cf. Genesis 30:31; 36; 37:2; Exodus 3:1; 1 Samuel 17:15.

285. Baker, *The Complete Word Study Dictionary*, 1065.

286. Baker, *The Complete Word Study Dictionary*, 1062-1063.

287. Baker, *The Complete Word Study Dictionary*, 1065.

Wallis[288] recognises that besides its Hebrew form, the word also occurs in a number of cognates. It occurs in Jewish Aramaic as *raʿeyaʾ,* in Phoenician as *rʿm* in its plural form, in Ugaritic as *rʿy* and *rʿym* in its plural form, and in Syriac as *rěʿāʾ*. It also occurs in Akkadian as *reʾû(m)*, meaning "to pasture, shepherd, protect, guard livestock;"[289] in Arabic as well as Old South Arabic as *raʿā* from *rʿy*; and in Ethiopic as *rěʿěya* and more rarely as *rěaya*. Louis Jonker notes that the noun roʿeh, the Qal participle, meaning shepherd, also has numerous cognates. It occurs in Phoenician in the plural as *rʿm*, in Egyptian Aramaic as *rʿy*, and in Ugaritic as *rʿy*. Also, the Akkadian form *reʾû(m)* in the masculine is maintained as in the verb form while its feminine form is *rěʾītu(m)*. Similarly, in Syriac, the masculine *rāʿyā* and feminine *rāʿītā* forms occur. The root *rʿy* occurs both in Coptic and Egyptian Aramaic. Again, it occurs in Mandean as *rʿia/rʿiia*, in Epigraphic South Arabic as *rʿy*, and in Arabic as *rāʿin*.[290] Koehler and Baumgartner note that the root *rʿy* may also be found in a personal name from Ebla, as in Ebla *ré-ì-na, ré-ì-malik/raʾī-malik* "malik is (my) shepherd."[291]

The Hebrew verb and noun for "shepherd" also have a number of frequent occurrences in the texts of the Hebrew Old Testament, Septuagint, and the Dead Sea Scrolls. The root *rʿh* occurs 168 times in its Qal in the Old Testament and 82 times in its masculine active substantive participle form rōʿeh. It occurs 8 times in the Dead Sea Scrolls in general agreement with the Old Testament usage. The various forms of the word also occur in the Septuagint. The verb occurs 38 times with poimaínein, to "graze, tend;" 22 times with bōskein, to "provide for;" 14 times with némein, to "put to pasture, feed;" and once each with tréphein, to "nourish, bring up;" diṓkein, to "lead;" lymaínein, to "graze bare, lay waste;" nomás, to "graze;" and hodēgeín, to "lead." Also, the Qal active participle is represented 65 times by poimḗn, 3 times by poimanṓn, and once each by némōn, bóskōn, and tḕ skeúē poinenikā.[292] The verb *rʿh* occurs 31 times in Ezekiel 34 and

---

288. Wallis, "רָעָה," TDOT 8:545.
289. Koehler and Baumgartner, *The Hebrew and Aramaic Lexicon*, 1258.
290. Louis Jonker, "רעה," *NIDOTTE* 3:1138-1143.
291. Koehler and Baumgartner, *The Hebrew and Aramaic Lexicon*, 1259.
292. Wallis, "רָעָה," TDOT 8:545.

10 times in Zechariah 11. Again, its derivatives mir'eh occurs 13 times, mar'ît 10 times, and rᵉ'î once.²⁹³

The basic meaning of the verb "shepherd" has the act of "grazing," and this could be used both transitively and intransitively. It could sometimes even be used adverbially. Wallis asserts, for instance, that, "when the verb is used transitively it refers to the work of the shepherd, who tends sheep and goats."²⁹⁴ Used in this sense, it has people as its subject, but with animals as subject, it assumes the intransitive function. From the foregoing, it can be easily seen that "shepherd" and its related concept of "shepherding" function primarily within the domain of animal husbandry and secondarily with poetic import to carry over its meaning to human domain.

2.4.2 Its Semantic Domains

With the help of the semantic field, the meaning (s) and function (s) of words become clearer. We would better comprehend "shepherd" in Ezekiel via its semantic domains. Generally, semantics concerns itself with linguistic meaning at various levels. As Silva points out, "Linguistic meaning can be studied at the level of individual words, or at the sentence level, or at the level of discourse."²⁹⁵ Directing attention to the role of words in semantics, Peter Cotterell holds that a word, by itself, "has no meaning at all;" and because words

> . . . are more or less effective symbols attached to referents, and each of such attachment is in some sense a unique use of the word, there is no '"central"' or '"fundamental"' or '"basic"' meaning of a word that lies behind every usage of it . . . Words are symbols available to an author to be given significance by being attached to a referent, an object, or an event.²⁹⁶

---

293. Jonker, "רעה," *NIDOTTE* 3:1139.
294. Wallis, "רָעָה," *TDOT* 8:545.
295. Silva, *Biblical Words and Their Meaning*, 11.
296. Peter Cotterell, "Linguistics, Meaning, Semantics, and Discourse Analysis," in *A Guide to Old Testament Theology and Exegesis* (ed. Willem A. VanGemeren; Grand Rapids, Mich.: Zondervan, 1999), 144, 146.

He admits that "within the semantic field of any particular lexeme there will be meanings that can be related to a common theme, and the recognition of that common theme might be helpful in elucidating the meaning of a particular usage of the lexeme." However, he cautions that "The nature of the common theme, however, must be allowed to conceal the possibility of some quite unpredictable departure from it into a quite different and unrelated semantic field."[297] In this connection, metaphoric expressions are to be situated within their textual contexts[298] to correctly decode meaning. And as Andrea L. Weiss notes, "A single lexeme, when situated in different linguistic contexts, can convey different meanings and nuances. Depending on the components of the surrounding text segments, the interpretation of the lexeme and its effects may vary."[299]

Our interest in semantics at this point is in an attempt to achieve an understanding of the lexical meaning of the word "shepherd" in Ezekiel. This delineates our focus to lexical semantics, a "branch of modern linguistics that focuses on the meaning of individual words,"[300] concentrating our effort on semantic change and semantic range.[301] As much as the exegetical task at this level "is to determine the discourse meaning of an utterance"[302] as is our intention in the case with Ezekiel 34, the exegete needs to be constantly "aware of the way in which words can shift meaning over time." He or she should be sensitive too that "different authors may use the same word in different ways." Similarly, he or she should take cognisance of the "distinctive meanings attached to certain words by certain authors."[303]

---

297. Cotterell, "Linguistics, Meaning, Semantics, and Discourse Analysis," 146.

298. Roger White submits that "a correct characterization of the nature of the sentence or phrase in which a metaphor is expressed leads directly to an understanding of the way metaphor works, and provides a basis from which all the traditional philosophical problems of metaphor become tractable." Roger M. White, *The Structure of Metaphor: The Way the Language of Metaphor Works* (Oxford, U. K.: Blackwell, 1996).

299. Weiss, *Figurative Language*, 1.

300. Silva, *Biblical Words and Their Meaning*, 10.

301. For discussion on this subject, see Black, *Linguistics for Students of New Testament Greek*, 120-140, Silva, *Biblical Words and Their Meaning*, 53-56, 75-94, and Donald Anderson Carson, *Exegetical Fallacies* (2d ed.; Grand Rapids, Mich.: Baker, 1996), 28-47.

302. Cotterell, "Linguistics, Meaning, Semantics, and Discourse Analysis," 144.

303. John H. Walton, "Principles for Productive Word Study," in *A Guide to Old Testament Theology and Exegesis* (ed. Willem A. VanGemeren; Grand Rapids, Mich.: Zondervan, 1999), 161-2.

In this sense, semantics basically concerns itself with historical meaning, tracking certain changes in the levels of meaning over time so as to arrive at its contextual meaning within a particular form of discourse material.

As we pointed earlier in our etymological consideration, the word "shepherd" serves both as verb and as noun participle. We also pointed out that the verb form רעה means to feed, graze, pasture, tend, and shepherd, while its noun participial form רעה means a shepherd,[304] that is, a person who tends, feeds, and pastures the flock,[305] because shepherds pasture, lead the sheep and flocks[306] to find food, water, and a secured rest. The literal and figurative subject of these forms are connected to the Hebrew word צאן, commonly translated both as "sheep" and "flock," the last being a mixture of sheep and goats. It is perceived as a "small cattle, sheep and goats, flock, flocks" but usually and commonly refers to "sheep and goats in one flock."[307] Jonker observes that this group of animals is most often associated with the verb *r'h*, occurring 274 times in the Old Testament.[308]

---

304. As to whether the related Hebrew word נקד (nōqēd), occurring only thrice in the Old Testament (2 Kgs 3:4 and Amos 1:1; 7:14), has the same sense as shepherd, or that it is to be used rather as a designate for an animal-keeper, sheep owner, or sheep-rarer, there is no consensus opinion. While Jonker favours the latter view (see Jonker, "רעה," 1139), I. Cornelius favours the former, arguing that its translation as "shepherd" is preferred "because there is nothing religious in the context" as used for King Mesha of Moab in 2 Kgs 3:4. I. Cornelius, "נקד," in *The New International Dictionary of Old Testament Theology and Exegesis Vol. 3*, ed., Willem A. VanGemeren (Grand Rapids, Michigan: Zondervan, 1997), 151. However, נקד is a masculine noun that refers to "a shepherd," literally referring "to a person who grazes sheep," but also extending to the concept of "total care involved in raising them." Baker and Carpenter, *The Complete Word Study Dictionary*, 751. Since the terms "sheep-breeder," "sheep-keeper," "sheep-rarer," "sheep-owner," even a "sheep care-taker," each individually possesses elements of shepherding, the idea of ownership is preferred here. King Mesha of Moab and prophet Amos were both sheep-owners; the one a monarch and the other a business man prior to his prophetic assignment. The former possessed them as part of his wealth to add value to his status as a monarch while the latter possessed them as a Tekoan merchant.

305. Jonker notes that "flock" is a collective term for sheep and goats. Jonker, "רעה," *NIDOTTE* 3:1139. Michael Moore and Michael Brown also note that the word צאן can refer to groups of sheep or goats, or to groups of sheep mixed with goats. See Michael S. Moore and Michael L. Brown, "צאן," in *The New International Dictionary of Old Testament Theology and Exegesis Vol. 3* (ed. Willem A. VanGemeren; Grand Rapids, Mich.: Zondervan, 1997), 727.

306. Baker, *The Complete Word Study Dictionary*, 1065.

307. Golding, "The Imagery of Shepherding in the Bible, Part 2," 162.

308. Jonker, "רעה," *NIDOTTE* 3:1139.

The Hebrew verb *rāʿah* and noun participle *rōʿēh* are used both literally and metaphorically/figuratively. "Shepherd" in its figurative sense, refers to an official responsible for the people, as a royal title, and as a designate for God.[309] When used in the literal sense, animals stand in the accusative position, for the transitive and intransitive use of the verb always has animals – cows, sheep, or flock as direct object.[310] However, when it is used in the metaphoric/figurative sense, human rulers and deities are in focus and people always stand in the accusative position as the flock.[311]

2.5 Conclusion

We have endeavoured to explicate the reasons why Ezekiel used symbolism and the shepherd metaphor in this chapter. We have argued that Ezekiel used symbolic sign-acts to defuse the apprehension of his audience so they would give attention to his prophetic message. We also argued that Ezekiel employed this approach as warning signs and as signals to the complacent and notorious exiles of a more devastating, unimaginable and unthinkable judgement yet to come upon Jerusalem. These warnings were needed to assist the exiles to face up to the news of Jerusalem's demise. We pointed out

---

309. Koehler and Baumgartner, *The Hebrew and Aramaic Lexicon*, 1260-1. Given the inseparable pastoral/nomadic life of the Mesopotamian region and Palestine, the literal meaning of "shepherd" is indelible. J. Jeremias states, "Throughout the biblical period tending flocks, with agriculture, was in Palestine the basis of the economy. The dryness of the ground made it necessary for the flocks of sheep and cattle to move about during the rainless summer and to stay for months at a time in isolated areas far from the dwelling of the owner," p. 486. Even from the time of Jesus up until today, shepherding activities still take place in Palestine.
310. Francis Brown, S. R. Driver, and Charles A. Briggs, *The Brown-Driver-Briggs Hebrew and English Lexicon* (Boston: Houghton, Mifflin and Company, 1906; repr., Peabody, Mass.: Hendrickson, 2005), 744-5.
311. Brown, Driver, and Briggs, *The Brown-Driver-Briggs Hebrew and English Lexicon*, 945. Following the "Exodus Event," Israel has always understood Yahweh as her Shepherd, able to provide and ever strong to protect and keep. In this connection, Jonker observes, "The tradition of God as Israel's Shepherd originated in Israel's life in the desert…[as such], The symbol of God as Shepherd was common for depicting the Exodus." Jonker, "רעה," *NIDOTTE* 3:1141. Ezekiel's usage of the shepherd metaphor would have aided the reflection of his audience on Yahweh's shepherding role during the Exodus Event as he also pointed them to the second exodus. This time, Yahweh would call his people out of Babylon.

that the demise of Jerusalem would be news so shocking as well as choking an experience that its effects on the exiles would be like what Jeremiah had painted poetically: "A voice is heard in Ramah, mourning and great weeping, Rachael weeping for her children and refusing to be comforted, because her children are no more" (Jer 31:15 NIV). The last symbolic act, reflected by the prophet's sudden loss of his wife, is the "last stroke that breaks the Carmel's back" for the exiles; for the imminent loss of Jerusalem and the Temple would naturally bring to a close their antagonism to the prophetic message.

Our etymological and semantic discussion reveals that the term "shepherd" is used in two broad ways – in its literal and metaphorically/figurative senses. From this we concluded that Ezekiel used the shepherd metaphor in the latter sense. We therefore argued that Ezekiel used the shepherd metaphor metaphorically rather than literally as a rhetoric, emotive, and cognitive device, both to illustrate and demonstrate to the exiles, that the failure of Israel's imperfect human shepherds had a large part in their present predicament. However, appealing to a theological principle, he raised the exiles' hope in their future restoration, assuring that this is to be achieved only by Yahweh, Israel's true Shepherd, based upon his enduring covenant principle.

CHAPTER THREE

The Historical and Literary Contexts for the Shepherd Metaphor in Ezekiel 34

3.1 Introduction

Ezekiel's treatment of the shepherd metaphor emerges from obvious historical and literary contexts. Our understanding of the Old Testament is incomplete apart from its history, whether that of its religious and theological expressions or of its socio-political and anthropological involvement. According to Walter Brueggemann, it is ". . . clear that one cannot understand the literature of the Old Testament or its theological claims without an interest in and awareness of the history of ancient Israel and of its religion."[1] That ". . . the Bible was written in a certain historical, political, social, and cultural context;"[2] that "Biblical literature was written over a period of some one thousand years by many authors, in three languages to differing audiences . . . addressing different people and circumstances;"[3] also that "It was inevitable, among a pastoral community such as the Hebrews, that the vocabulary and occupational habits of the shepherd should colour

---

1. Brueggemann, *An Introduction*, 3. In Richard S. Hess' understanding of the concept "ancient Israel," he notes that "Ancient Israel itself we take to be those people who identified themselves as Israelites and lived between c. 1200 and 586 BC." Hess, *Israelite Religions,* pp.18-21.
2. Bill T. Arnold and Bryan E. Beyer, *Readings from the Ancient Near East: Primary Sources for Old Testament Study* (Grand Rapids, Mich.: Baker, 2002; repr., 2007), 10.
3. Sparks, *Ancient Texts for the Study of the Hebrew Bible,* 1.

their language and help to formulate their way of looking at life,"[4] all suggest the reality of historical and literary contexts for Ezekiel's use of the shepherd metaphor.

We seek to discuss in this chapter the extant historical and literary contexts that aided Ezekiel's successful use of the shepherd metaphor. In this connection, we set out to explore what these extant historical and literary contexts are. We also set out to find out from this query how the shepherd metaphor has been used prior to its employment by Ezekiel and under what contexts. Pursuance to these background queries, this chapter develops in two parts. First, it anchors Ezekiel's use of the shepherd metaphor in its historical foundation both in its ancient Near Eastern and Israelite environments. In this regard, it attempts to discover ancient nomadism specific to the important function of animals and important place of shepherds within these two contexts. It then gives particular attention to the use of the shepherd metaphor in late Babylonian and late Assyrian texts. Lastly, the study briefly considers, within Israelite prophetic tradition, three pre-classical Israelite prophetic texts as the literary context for Ezekiel's use of the shepherd metaphor.

3.2 The Historical Context for the Use of the Shepherd Metaphor in Ezekiel

While the identity of prophet Ezekiel is questioned by critical scholarship, we think it is fair to state that the Ezekiel whose work we are engaging and whose story plays out in the book named after him existed as a literal and historical figure. It will be with some great difficulty therefore to discount his historic reality in view of the "I" and "me" statements[5] replete in his book.

---

4. J. G. S. S. Thomson, "The Shepherd-Ruler Concept in the OT and Its Application in the NT," *SJT* 8 (1955):406.

5. Ezekiel's "I was" statements appear no less than 7 times in the text (1:1; 9:8; 11:13; 12:7; 24:18; 33:22; 27:7) while the personal pronoun "I" appears no less than 775 times. Also, the use of the objective personal pronoun "said to me" statements appear no less than 39 times.

The shepherd metaphor that Ezekiel used also depicts an actual historical reality of animal husbandry in the ancient Near East and in Palestine.[6] Billie Jean Collins concludes from her study of animals in Hittite literature that, ". . . the importance of animals, both wild and domestic . . . provides solid testimony for their central role in all aspects of . . . society."[7] Similarly, Benjamin R. Foster also reports from his study of animals in Mesopotamian literature that sheep, goats, or cattle were considered productive over other domestic animals like dogs and pigs, for their dairy products. He notes also that "animals figure in Mesopotamian mythological narratives both as subjects and as terms of reference or comparison . . . [because of the] belief that animals and humanity belonged to competitive or complementary realms of being."[8] Particularly, Oded Borowski reports that animals play an important role in what is considered as practical and literary documents of Syria-Palestine literature, attesting to "the richness of the animal world in

---

6. Shepherding activities had existed since the time of Abraham. For instance, Vancil reports that "Job had thousands of sheep, camels, oxen, and she-asses (42:12), and Abraham's flocks, herds, camels, and asses were counted among his blessings (Gen 24:35)." Jack W. Vancil, "Sheep, Shepherd," in *The Anchor Bible Dictionary Vol.* 5 (ed. David Noel Freedman; N.Y.: Doubleday, 1992), 1187. This practice continued up to the time of the New Testament. Hence, the idea is not foreign to New Testament writers and to Christian literature. Keener posits that the frequent appearance of the shepherd and sheep imagery in the writings of the NT authors is indeed a reflection of the "broader familiarity with the task of shepherding in ancient Mediterranean culture." Craig S. Keener, "Shepherd, Flock," in *Dictionary of the Later New Testament and Its* Development (eds. Ralph P. Martin and Peter H. Davids; Downers Grove, Ill.: Inter-Varsity, 1997), 1090. He explains that at the time of Jesus however, Pharisees and Roman aristocrats perceived shepherds and the role of shepherding (a hitherto typical Israelite occupation) derogatorily, most likely as a reflection of "a wider view throughout the Roman Empire that shepherds were of lower status than other peasants [more so that] aristocratic ideology toward pastoralists would have especially influenced the thinking of urban dwellers." Keener, "Shepherd, Flock," 1091. Trailing in the line of the prophetic tradition, especially that of Zechariah, the gospel writers present Jesus as the true shepherd who is "God's agent, a royal figure, whose death provides a decisive turning point in redemptive history." David H. Johnson, "Shepherd, Sheep," in *Dictionary of Jesus and the* Gospels (eds. Joel B. Green and Scott McKnight; Downers Grove, Ill.: Inter-Varsity, 1992), 752. Put another way, The NT writers applied the imagery of shepherd to Jesus as "the ultimate shepherd who has come to save the lost sheep" of Israel as its Messiah. Keener, "Shepherd, Flock," 1091.

7. Billie Jean Collins, "Animals in Hittite Literature," in *A History of the Animal World in the Ancient Near East* (ed. Billie Jean Collins; Leiden: Brill, 2002), 237-250.

8. Benjamin R. Foster, "Animals in Mesopotamian Literature," in *A History of the Animal World in the Ancient Near East* (ed. Billie Jean Collins; Leiden: Brill, 2002), 271-288.

ancient Syria-Palestine."[9] In view of the preceding, we are left in no doubt as to the historicity of Ezekiel's use of the shepherd metaphor. As the succeeding discussion will reveal, he drew his animal-human imagery from an already well-established ideology that was not foreign to his audience.

3.2.1 The Shepherd Metaphor in Ancient Nomadic Life

The ideology of human beings co-existing with animals goes back to the biblical story of the first creation (Gen 1:24; 2:19-20a; 3:21). This ideological practice of human-animal cohabitation by way of animal husbandry never goes away since creation as human societies continue to grow. The biblical creation narrative presents the idea that animals were created alongside man for his control and benefit (Gen 2:19-20). This indicates that ancient peoples began existence with nomadic lifestyle before settling to sedentary communal life[10] (cf. Gen 4:2). It would also suggest that the concept of animal husbandry and shepherding were familiar in their daily vocabulary.

The Israelites, having their root in the Mediterranean environment, engaged in nomadic lifestyle as early as the period of their patriarchs (Gen 13:2; 31:17-18). Roland De Vaux observes in this respect that "At the beginning of their history the Israelites, like their ancestors before them, lived as nomads or semi-nomads, and when they came to settle down as a nation, they still retained some characteristics of that earlier way of life. Consequently, any study of Old Testament institutions must begin with an investigation into nomadism."[11] Nomadic lifestyle and language had influenced the vocabularies of Israel so much so that even when the Judeans went into the Babylonian captivity, they could still remember its meaning. As John W. Flight explains, in the history of a people, no event or circumstance of importance ever vanishes without leaving certain traces

---

9. Oded Borowski, "Animals in the Literatures of Syria-Palestine," in *A History of the Animal World in the Ancient Near East* (ed. Billie Jean Collins; Leiden: Brill, 2002), 289-306.

10. Victor Matthews' brief article is helpful in this direction. See Victor H. Matthews, "Pastoralists and Patriarchs," *BA* 4 (1981):215-218.

11. Roland De Vaux, *Ancient Israel: Its Life and Institutions* (English trans. John McHugh; London: Darton, Longman & Todd Ltd, 1961; jointly published by Grand Rapids, Mich.: Eerdmans & Livonia, Mich.: Dore Booksellers, 1997), 3.

for subsequent generational life.[12] This implies that in order to appreciate Ezekiel's usage and development of the language of shepherding, we must trace the idea back into its ANE context. This is critical because the idea of nomadic lifestyle and occupation was characteristic of the Mediterranean and the Palestinian peoples. This contextual understanding is helpful to gain adequate understanding of the meaning of the prophet's shepherd metaphor, especially as it is associated with Yahweh in Hebrew understanding. Hebrew literature, given its understanding, treats Yahweh as Shepherd and king of Israel as early as the emergence of the nation.[13]

The concept of sheep and shepherds had much significance to the common people of biblical times. Their pastoral background accounts for this reasoning. As Thomson rightly states, "It was inevitable, among a pastoral community such as the Hebrews, that the vocabulary and occupational habits of the shepherd should colour their language and help to formulate their way of looking at life."[14] What important place then did sheep occupy in ancient Mediterranean and Israelite societies? Of what importance also was the role of shepherds in these societies since shepherds are needed where sheep and flocks exist?

3.2.1.1 The Function of Sheep in ANE and Israelite Contexts

Generally, the domestication of animals is said to have had tremendous effects upon human society and has become part and parcel of the human

---

12. John W. Flight, "The Nomadic Idea and Ideal in the Old Testament," *JBL* 3/4 (1923): 158-226.
13. Vancil states that the Bible's extensive use of shepherd/flock imagery is attributable to Israel's earliest years of nomadic and seminomadic existence. Vancil, "Sheep, Shepherd," 1188. Jonathan Gan observes that the understanding of the shepherd metaphor in the Hebrew Bible is neglected in its contemporary usage because it carries more of a therapeutic image. He contends that the "usage of the metaphor of shepherd in pastoral ministry has deviated...from the picture of God as shepherd in the Hebrew Bible." Jonathan Gan, *The Metaphor of Shepherd in the Hebrew Bible: A Historical-Literary Reading* (Plymouth, United Kingdom: University Press of America, 2007), 28.
14. Thomson, "The Shepherd-Ruler Concept," 2.

cultural process.[15] Zoology[16] plays a significant role in ANE particularly for domestic animals. G. Ernest Wright observed,

> Considering the fact that "'shepherd'" and "'sheep'" were a most important part of the life of the Ancient East, it is little wonder that no other words in the Bible compare with them in symbolic interest. No other phase of life left a deeper impression than the pastoral among the literary modes of impression, the ideas, and the institutions of every civilization in the Near East.[17]

In this connection, the importance[18] of sheep, for example, is crucial to the ancient Near Eastern and Israelite contexts, not only for their much featured shepherd-sheep imagery, but significantly, for their domestic, economic, cultic, and social functions.[19] To this, B. D. Napier adds,

---

15. Gerald A. Klingbeil, "Agriculture and Animal Husbandry," in *Dictionary of the Old Testament: Historical Books* (eds. Bill T. Arnold and Hugh Godfrey Maturin Williamson; Downers Grove, Ill.: Inter-Varsity, 2005), 7. Regarding matters of ethics as humans relate to the animal world, see Lisa Kemmerer, "Jewish Ethics and Nonhuman Animals," *JCAS* 2 (2007):1-18.

16. Animals such as sheep, goats, cattle and pigs were the most domesticated and most useful to man in ancient Pentateuchal zoological sciences. Paul J. N. Lawrence, "Zoology," in *Dictionary of the Old Testament: Pentateuch* (eds. T. Desmond Alexander and David W. Baker; Downers Grove, Ill.: Inter-Varsity, 2003), 914-918. See also Naomi F. Miller, "Down the Garden Path: How Plant and Animal Husbandry Came Together in the Ancient Near East," *NEA* 1/2 (2001):4-7.

17. G. Ernest Wright, "The Good Shepherd," *BA* 4. (1939):44.

18. Klingbeil states that six main reasons account for the domestication of animals in the ancient period. They are (1) the need for reliable meat provision, (2) the need for significant cultic offering, (3) animals as social indicators, (4) animals as beasts of burden such as camels and horses, (5) as draft animals, and (6) animals as providers of secondary (recyclable) benefits such as fibre, wool, milk and dung. Klingbeil, "Agriculture and Animal Husbandry," 7.

19. Sheep were raised for food and their wool. It is observed that they "were a natural part of life in the arid eastern Mediterranean because they can survive with a minimum of water and grass and can be moved to new grazing and watering areas during dry times." Ryken, Wilhoit, and Longman III, eds., "Sheep, Shepherds," 782. Malone also notes that, "From the time of the banishment of Adam and Eve from the Garden, people all over the world have been engaged in the occupation of raising cattle. Men have needed to be self-sufficient; therefore, they have had to raise their own food, make their own clothes, and find something of material value with which to trade for the things they could not raise or make. Colleen Malone, "Pastoral Images in the Bible" ((Honors Thesis, Ball State

"Sheep represented the chief wealth and the total livelihood of pastoral peoples."[20] In fact, the sheep specie is the most common[21] of all the domesticated animals.

The first notable importance of sheep is its domestic function for the ancient Near Eastern and Israelite societies. Since sheep and goats were raised and grazed together, these are useful for their dairy products. Thomas A. Golding[22] states that milk produced from these animals, more from the latter, were used for drinking, for making yogurt and cheese. Apart from its milk, sheep are also useful for meat[23] as it serves the populace as a source of animal protein.[24] Furthermore, sheep were a source of textile product as P. L. Garber states, apart from its use for food, "sheep were raised principally for wool production"[25] as "Sheep's wool was used for clothing and other products."[26] The chilly weather of Palestine in winter would have naturally necessitated such covering. Additionally, sheepskins and goatskins were highly prized for tent making and other uses in the ancient period. It is to be noted that various leather goods, including clothing, sandals, shields, and in later times, vellum, came from the skins of either animal. Goatskins especially made good containers to hold liquids when sewed up and sealed. Milk, wine, and water were stored in these skin containers.[27] It is reported that the Assyrians even inflated goatskins and used them as flotation devices for crossing rivers.[28] Sheep bones and horns from rams also

---

University, 1986), 17.
20. B. D. Napier, "Sheep," in *The Interpreter's Dictionary of the Bible* (ed. George Arthur Buttrick et al.; Nashville, Tenn.: Abingdon, 1962), 315-316.
21. Klingbeil, "Agriculture and Animal Husbandry," 8. Some of the commonly domesticated species are sheep, goat, cattle, pigs and horses.
22. Golding, "The Imagery of Shepherding in the Bible, Part 2," 162.
23. David W. Baker, "Agriculture," in *Dictionary of the Old Testament: Pentateuch* (eds. T. Desmond Alexander and David W. Baker; Downers Grove, Ill.: Inter-Varsity, 2003), 23.
24. Douglas Brewer, "Hunting, Animal Husbandry and Diet in Ancient Egypt," in *A History of the Animal World in the Ancient Near East* (ed. Billie Jean Collins; Leiden: Brill, 2002), 434.
25. P. L. Garber, "Sheep, Shepherd," *ISBE* 4:463.
26. Golding, "The Imagery of Shepherding in the Bible, Part 2," 162.
27. This function extended to the time of the New Testament as we see Jesus make reference to the need of storing new wine in new wineskin, see Matt 9:17.
28. Golding, "The Imagery of Shepherding in the Bible, Part 2," 304.

had specific usefulness. Garber[29] notes that the horns were used to hold oil and as musical instruments, while needles, scrapers, lances, and arrowheads were gotten from sheep bones.

A second importance for sheep occupying a position of prominence in the ANE and Israelite societies was economical. Andrew Mein explains: "Sheep farming was clearly a fundamental part of the economy of ancient Israel, as it was throughout the ancient Near East . . . on the whole we can be confident that they were kept for their economic benefits rather than for more selfless motives."[30] Given the prominent economic role of animals in ANE societies, Vancil[31] submits that the possession of sheep, goats, cows, asses, camels, and horses was an indication of power and wealth because "Sheep were so valuable that the wealthy man was described as owner" of thousands and ten thousands of sheep.[32] In the ancient period, the list of booty collected after the defeat of an enemy would also include animals such as donkeys, camels, cattle, mules, and sheep, indicating their economic importance. For the ancient peoples, animal husbandry was part and parcel of human subsistence. Borowski points to this when he argues that even the "numerous references to their daily uses demonstrate that they were the mainstay of the economy of ancient Syria-Palestine."[33]

Furthermore, sheep occupied a key place in the ANE and Israelite cultures because of their cultic importance. This cultic function of animals in human society was not a new ideology to the ancients. Even in much later societies in the ancient world, animals played very significant role in cultic sacrifice. For example, a strong tie existed between animals and gods in Egyptian texts.[34] The gods of the ancients usually fed on a high

---

29. Garber, "Sheep, Shepherd," 4:463.

30. Andrew Mein, "Profitable and Unprofitable Shepherds: Economic and Theological Perspectives on Ezekiel 34," *JSOT* 4 (2007):496-7.

31. Vancil, "Sheep, Shepherd," 1187.

32. Garber, "Sheep, Shepherd," 4:463. See also Ps 144:13; Job 42:12; Gen 24:35. Given this understanding, a person's flocks were an extremely valuable commodity because such were one's source of income. See the discussion on this in Golding, "The Imagery of Shepherding in the Bible, Part 2," 161. Also see Prov 27:23-27.

33. Oded Borowski, "Animals in the Literatures of Syria-Palestine," 496-7.

34. See the discussion on this in Emily Teeter, "Animals in Egyptian Literature," in *A History of the Animal World in the Ancient Near East* (ed. Billie Jean Collins; Leiden: Brill, 2002), 251-270.

proportion of a good diet, far beyond those of their worshippers; and the largest amount among the items of religious sacrifice were animals. JoAnn Scurlock[35] reports Nebuchadnezzar II's boast of an increased daily animal offering to Marduk and Sarpanitum who were to receive fine long-fleeced sheep. Nabû and Nanay were also to receive sixteen long-fleeced sheep as a daily sacrifice. An old Akkadian inscription from Elam indicates that one sheep each was offered as a sacrifice in the morning and evening while a total of six sheep were offered as a sacrifice daily to Bel, Nabû, Sikutu and Šarratsamme of the Neo-Assyrian period. Additionally, Scurlock notes that in the Seleucid period, Anu, Antu, Ištar, Nanay and the other gods of the Uruk were fed four times daily, consuming a total of twenty-one barley-fattened sheep, four milk-fed male lambs, and twenty-five grass-fed sheep. Also, in the Neo-Babylonian period, the god Anu of Aruk was offered fine, fattened, ritually pure sheep, which had eaten barley for two years. In ancient Syria-Palestine also, Oded observes that the "... relationship between man and animal ... is manifested most visibly in cultic observance. Animal sacrifice provided the means for expression of devotion and piety."[36]

In Israelite cult practice, certain animals were prohibited while others were not. Included on the list of approved animals for cultic ritual in Israelite society were wild and domestic animals that included sheep.[37] Richard E. Averbeck re-echoes that the lamb was included among the items of sacrifices and offerings stipulated by the Levitical law in Israel.[38] Kings in Israel offered many sheep as an offering. For example, King Solomon sacrificed 22,000 head of cattle and 120,000 sheep and goats (2 Chr 7:5); Asa sacrificed 700 head of cattle and 7000 sheep and goats (2 Chr 15:11); and Hezekiah gave 1000 bulls and 7000 sheep and goats for sacrifice (2 Chr 30:24). Even in the sacrifices of the Rawala Bedouin of Saudi Arabia

---

35. JoAnn Scurlock, "Animal Sacrifice in Ancient Mesopotamian Religion," in *A History of the Animal World in the Ancient Near East* (ed. Billie Jean Collins; Leiden: Brill, 2002), 389-403.
36. Borowski, "Animals in the Literatures of Syria-Palestine," 405.
37. Borowski, "Animals in the Literatures of Syria-Palestine," 411.
38. Richard E. Averbeck, "Sacrifices and Offerings," in *Dictionary of the Old Testament: Pentateuch* (eds. T. Desmond Alexander and David W. Baker; Downers Grove, Ill.: Inter-Varsity, 2003), 706-733.

for various purposes, it is noted, they "prefer sacrificing male sheep six to twelve months old, and no more than two-and-one-half years old."³⁹

Sheep also played an important role in ANE and Israelite societies for their sociological attachment to humans. If, for example, the parable of Prophet Nathan (2 Sam 12:1-6) were to be given literal interpretation, Mein reasons that it would no doubt suggest that ancient Israelites felt genuine affection towards their livestock and treated them as pets because of their closeness to households.⁴⁰ These domesticated animals were quite expressive of affection and trust. One of such animals was the sheep of which it is said, "The sheep's gentleness and loyalty made it a common household pet."⁴¹

3.2.1.2 The Place of Shepherds in ANE and Israelite Contexts

Before we turn our attention to discussing the important functions of shepherds in ANE and Israelite contexts, it is significant to first draw attention to the characteristics of sheep that warrant the need for good shepherding. We have already vividly expressed the idea that among all the domesticated animals, sheep and the figure of a shepherd receive a position of prominence in biblical literature. "This prominence," it is postulated, "grows out of two phenomena – the importance of sheep to the nomadic and agricultural life of the Hebrews, and the qualities of sheep and shepherds that made them apt sources of metaphor for spiritual realities."⁴² The sheep, unlike goats with which they were raised and grazed,⁴³ require "more frequent

---

39. Borowski, "Animals in the Literatures of Syria-Palestine," 415.
40. Mein, "Profitable and Unprofitable Shepherds, 497.
41. Garber, "Sheep, Shepherd," 463. Carnes shares a personal experience from shepherding that it is common to see a herd clustered about their herder seeking food and physical touch only to back away in opposition to a stranger. See Phillip Gene Carnes, "Like Sheep without a Shepherd: The Shepherd Metaphor and Its Primacy for Biblical Leadership," Unpublished Master's thesis (Reformed Theological Seminary, 2007).
42. Ryken, Wilhoit, and Longman III, eds., "Sheep, Shepherds," 782.
43. In ancient animal husbandry sociology, sometimes other animals, especially goats, were included among the flock. In biblical literature for example, Jacob's shepherding experiences with Laban's flocks had sheep mixed with goats (Gen 30-31). Jesus' Olivet Discourse about the final judgement also indicates the mixture of sheep with goats (Matt 25:32-33).

watering . . . are less physically adapted to difficult terrains . . . prefer valleys and more gentle landscapes."⁴⁴ Also, sheep are said to be not only dependent creatures but also ". . . would not survive long without a shepherd . . . [because they are] singularly unintelligent, prone to wandering and unable to find their way to a sheepfold even when it is within sight."⁴⁵ Still, far from being compared with camels, sheep have "to be watered several times daily"⁴⁶ to enhance their survival, especially in hot zones.

Having taken twenty-three trips to Israel and Palestine and having closely observed for close to three hundred hours how the Arab boys tend their sheep in the Arabian and Palestinian deserts, and having directed many documentary films made in those lands, Mal Couch submits this first-hand report about the nature of sheep and their psychology:

> . . . it is true! Sheep are dumb animals! They have been known to die of thirst standing just a few yards from water. They have very poor eyesight. They seem to have little or no personality and have to be led everywhere. When travelling along a hillside, their heads are down and they simply follow the trail right in front of them! In fact the hills of Palestine are scarred with "sheep nuts." They always plot the same old rutty paths! Finally, sheep are beasts of self-imposed habits but appear to be in no way "trainable," as are many of the four-legged creatures of the animal kingdom . . . Helpless, hopeless, and untrainable by nature! Thus, . . . [they] need shepherds.⁴⁷

The nature and psychology of sheep as painted above make them "totally dependent on the shepherds for protection, grazing, watering, shelter and tending to injuries"⁴⁸ without whom they are helpless,⁴⁹ lost, and dead in

---

44. Golding, "The Imagery of Shepherding in the Bible, Part 2," 165.
45. Ryken, Wilhoit, and Longman III, eds., "Sheep, Shepherds," 782.
46. Garber, "Sheep, Shepherd," 464.
47. Mal Couch, ed., *A Biblical Theology of the Church* (Grand Rapids, Mich.: Kregel, 1999), 166.
48. Ryken, Wilhoit, and Longman III, eds., "Sheep, Shepherds," 782.
49. Garber, "Sheep, Shepherd," 464.

some cases.⁵⁰ Given such a complex nature and dependency of sheep, their need of a shepherd is quite obvious.

Shepherding has certain demands and requires certain responsibilities of the shepherd. Douglas Brewer observes that within the Egyptian context, "Good herdsmen were valued and had many and varied responsibilities. They were responsible for the most of the day-to-day care of the animals under their charge. It was their job to see that food for the herd was plentiful and properly balanced."⁵¹ In summary form, Golding captures the functions and duties of a shepherd as "guiding, feeding and watering, protecting and delivering, gathering and returning the scattered or lost, bringing healing, providing security and rest, and culling and promoting productivity."⁵² Basically, the shepherd's functions and responsibilities fall neatly into three categories – provision, protection, and production. The shepherding functions of "leading, feeding, and protecting,"⁵³ are critical; for "shepherds were thus providers, guides, protectors and constant companions of sheep," who also served as "figures of authority and leadership to the animals under their care."⁵⁴ As Vancil notes, "The principal duty of

---

50. Sheep, described to be in a "cast down position," can easily be dead without the quick intervention of a shepherd to attend to them. If they fall over on their side and then onto their back, it is very difficult for them to get up again. They would flail their legs in the air, bleat, and cry in this position. After a few hours on their backs, gas will begin to collect in their stomachs, then the stomach hardens, and the air passage is cut off. This would then cause the sheep to suffocate and eventually die. A careful, watchful, and caring shepherd in this situation would restore any sheep in such dangerous position by his reassuring presence, massaging the legs to restore circulation, then turning the sheep over and lifting it up, and holding it in a standing position so the sheep can regain its equilibrium before letting it join the others. This is what calls for Yahweh's indictment of the bad shepherds of Israel in Ezek 34:3-6 because their bad attitude caused many "cast down" sheep from his flock.

51. Douglas Brewer, "Hunting, Animal Husbandry and Diet in Ancient Egypt," in *A History of the Animal World in the Ancient Near East* (ed. Billie Jean Collins; Leiden: Brill, 2002), 445.

52. Golding, "The Imagery of Shepherding in the Bible, Part 2," 173.

53. Gan, *The Metaphor of Shepherding*, 27.

54. Ryken, Wilhoit, and Longman III, eds., "Sheep, Shepherds," 782. This, no doubt, suggests that "the job of a shepherd becomes one of complex duties, total commitment, and often personal sacrifice on the part of the shepherd." See Colleen Malone, "Pastoral Images in the Bible," 12. Even though a herder, and in case of large herds, hired hands were engaged in the role of shepherding, not everyone qualified as a shepherd except those prepared inherently and physically for the task. This is crucial because shepherding is for the "strong and brave" in view of the terrain and vulnerability of shepherding. Golding,

the shepherd was to see that the animals found enough food and water . . . to keep the flock intact . . . providing a minimum of protection from weather and enemies . . . The good shepherd was especially concerned for the condition of the flock."⁵⁵

The shepherd, whether the flock owner or hired, had the obligation of ensuring adequate provisions for the flock under their care.⁵⁶ G. Wallis⁵⁷ observes that the multiplicity of the Greek translations of shepherd in contrast to the simple Semitic usage illustrates the variety associated with the life and work of a shepherd who must travel with the flock, drive it, and lead it by going before it, and so on. Since the burden of prudent nurturing and management is laid upon the shepherd, they were to ensure good and rich pasture or grazing field by being familiar with both available pastures and their routes. The shepherd had to be timely in leading the flock to watering places and in bringing the flock to the pen for night security. In consonance with this expected shepherding function, a robust flock was a sign of good feeding and security.

The matter of security is not only critical to human society but even in zoological society. One of the causes of leanness in sheep is an atmosphere of insecurity. Hence, the shepherd had to ensure good security for the flock under their care. A good knowledge of the topography of the grazing field is therefore necessary for the achievement of this difficult task. It is said that "Topography was also problematic in the central hill country"⁵⁸ in Israel, requiring a shepherd to guide the flock to place of water and grazing. Topographical and geographical knowledge guarantees safety when the shepherd is aware of safe and dangerous zones. Wallis explains this requirement when he states:

"The Imagery of Shepherding in the Bible, Part 2," 174.

55. Vancil, "Sheep, Shepherd," 1187. The fact that Jesus addressed himself as "the Good Shepherd" presupposes the reality of the presence of bad shepherds. The primary quality of a good shepherd lies in the character trait of care for the flock.

56. Shepherds were not always men. The biblical account reveals, for example, that shepherdesses included Rebekah (Gen 29:9) and the daughters of Jethro the Medianite priest (Exod 2:16).

57. Wallis, "רָעָה," *TDOT* 8: 545.

58. Baker, "Agriculture," 22.

> . . . if he is to lead his flock in time fashion to a safe resting place with pasturage and water . . . He has to be familiar with land forms and soils, as well as with the settlements of a region and their history . . . his close involvement with the natural world gives him outstanding knowledge of meteorology and sharp eye for the early signs of local storms.[59]

This shepherding quality was necessary for the ANE and Palestinian shepherds. In this context, it was "essential that a shepherd be wise"[60] to make up for what the sheep lacked; particularly so that the sheep by its psychology, not being very wise and very intelligent, would require close care as it is totally dependent on the shepherd for its subsistence.

Shepherding within the Middle East and Palestinian environments was quite a sacrificial and dangerous vocation because the shepherd had to "endure life under the harsh conditions of heat by day and cold by night"[61] as they watched over the flock. According to Garber, "That a shepherd might not return alive from his shepherding was well understood . . . Shepherding was [a] serious, demanding, and strenuous work."[62] The apparent dangers of weather and the presence of human and ravaging animal predators such as lions, leopards, cheetahs, hyenas, wild dogs, jackals, and foxes were a present reality in the ANE and Palestine[63] necessitating the need for caring and watchful shepherds. The shepherd would put the sheep in a cave or an enclosure made with stones or a hedge of thorns "to protect them against wild beasts, robbers, and thieves" at night, and "puts himself at their head, leading them to pasture"[64] during the day. Besides, shepherds were away from the natural life in the community all the time into the life of solitude and loneliness as the "lack of rainfall" forced them "to move around during

---

59. Wallis, "רָעָה," *TDOT* 8:547.
60. Golding, "The Imagery of Shepherding in the Bible, Part 2," 174.
61. Wallis, "רָעָה," *TDOT* 8:547.
62. Garber, "Sheep, Shepherd," 464.
63. For the mention of the presence of these animal predators in biblical literature, see some examples in 1 Sam 17:34-37; Amos 3:4, 12; Isa 11:6; 65:25; Jer 5:6; Gen 37:33; 31:39; Exod 22:10-13.
64. John Quasten, "The Parable of the Good Shepherd: John 10:1-21," *CBQ* 1 (1948):6.

the summer months . . . to be away from their base of supplies for days or weeks."⁶⁵

Breeding of the flock, to be engaged with the quality of expertise, was another major responsibility of the shepherd. Given this obligation, the shepherd had to ensure good production of robust animals for their quality products. To this crucial shepherding function, Wallis states that, "The size and quality of a flock is due in large part to breeding and constitutes the wealth of the flock's owner." In this vein, it is the responsibility of the shepherd to use careful "selection to breed robust animals that would provide meat, leather, and wool."⁶⁶ Shepherds who failed in this regard would normally be excluded from shepherding by the flock owner. This is critical on the basis of Mein's argument that a shepherd works ultimately for the benefit of the sheep-owner. This being the case, he asserts that the interest of the latter should always remain paramount.⁶⁷

Another main reason shepherds were important in ancient times is the lack of fences⁶⁸ to hedge the flock as it is the practice in modern husbandry. Because they did not have fences, shepherds moved their flocks to wherever there was suitable food. Apparently also, they did not have trained dogs. For example, in the US and Canada, New Zealand and Australia, and perhaps even Scotland, there are rarely shepherds that keep direct watch over the sheep. In New Zealand, where sheep outnumber people by probably 10 to 1, one never finds or sees a shepherd. Fences are used in the example above to keep sheep in defined fields and trained sheep dogs are used for herding them. Water is provided. This is unlike the nomadic Fulanis of West Africa, the nomadic Masaai of East Africa and the nomadic Bedouins of modern Jordan, Saudi Arabia and other Middle Eastern and North African countries, who still are necessary for the direct care of a flock of sheep.

---

65. Garber, "Sheep, Shepherd," 464.
66. Wallis, "רָעָה," *TDOT* 8:546.
67. Mein, "Profitable and Unprofitable Shepherds, 502.
68. The idea expressed in this whole paragraph is from the editorial suggestions of Dr. Ronald Rice.

3.2.2 Ancient Near Eastern Usage of the Shepherd Metaphor

We indicated previously that animal husbandry and nomadic lifestyle has been an aspect of human society since creation. Gen 2:15, 19-20 alludes to this idea and the narrated case of Abel as a sheep-keeper further confirms the point (Gen 4:2-3). In this regards, we stated that the understanding of the concept of shepherding is very familiar to the peoples of ANE and Palestine because nomadic life and animal husbandry formed part of the lifestyle of both societies.[69] In the literatures of the ANE peoples, the concept of "shepherd" and "shepherding" has several connotations and usage. Apart from the literal aspect, the concept has no less than four other connotations. It is a title for the reigning kings and the gods; it is a functional and descriptive term for the roles of the king and the gods; it is used as a representative term for the king who acts in behalf of the gods or a god; and it is also used with a military import to depict the protective role of the king of his society and subjects.

Apart from the role that other ancient empires played in their relationship with Israel, the Babylonian and Assyrian Empires played particular crucial roles in Old Testament history.[70] For this, we consider below the

---

69. Vancil states: "shepherding was one of man's earlier occupations. Flocks and herds, always a prominent feature in Palestine and other Near Eastern societies, consisted especially of cows, sheep, and goats, but could also include horses, asses, and camels; the principal animal, however, owing to size, abundance, and usefulness, was the sheep." Vancil, "Sheep, Shepherd," 1187. Also, see the article by Mary Beth Gladwell, "The Shepherd Motif in the Old and New Testament," n. p. [cited Tuesday August 21, 2007]. Online:http://scholar.google.com/scholar?q=Imagery+of+Sheperding.

70. It seems almost impossible to discuss the history of Israel without mentioning the roles of the Assyrians and the Babylonians. A wholesale deportation of the covenant people was carried out only by these two great world powers. Bill T. Arnold posits that the Babylonians were notable during the OT period for two main reasons: That from an historical perspective, they were "God's instrument of destruction against Jerusalem;" and more importantly, "they transmitted and in some cases even originated most of the cultural and religious foundations for the Old Testament world." Bill T. Arnold, "Babylonians," in *Peoples of the Old Testament World* (eds. Alfred J. Hoerth, Gerald L. Mattingly, and Edwin M. Yamauchi; 1994; paperback ed., Grand Rapids, Mich.: Baker, 1998), 43. William C. Gwaltney Jr. also notes that "the Bible associates the Israelites with the Assyro-Babylonian world," significantly since the Assyrians are remembered in the history of the Hebrew Scriptures as the ravagers and destroyers of Samaria. William C. Gwaltney Jr., "Assyrians," in *Peoples of the Old Testament World* (eds. Alfred J. Hoerth, Gerald L. Mattingly, and Edwin M. Yamauchi; 1994; paperback ed., Grand Rapids, Mich.: Baker, 1998), 77.

texts of late Babylonian and Assyrian Empires in our search to understand how the shepherd metaphor, used elsewhere other than the Jewish text, serves as background for Ezekiel.

3.2.2.1 The Shepherd Metaphor in Late Babylonian Texts

With the presence of animal husbandry activities in the Mesopotamian context, the term "shepherd" is used in more than one sense. In its literal sense, the term is used to refer to one who grazes flocks. The law of Hammurabi, king of Babylon, for example, confirms this literal usage. Lines 57 and 58 of this law read:

> 57: If a shepherd has not come to an agreement with the owner of a field to pasture sheep on the grass, but has pastured sheep on the field without the consent of the owner of the field, when the owner of the field harvests his field, the shepherd who pastured the sheep on the field without the consent of the owner of the field shall give in addition twenty kur of grain per eighteen iku to the owner of the field. 58: If after the sheep have gone up from the meadow, when the whole flock has been shut up within the city gate, the shepherd drove the sheep into a field and has then pastured the sheep on the field, the shepherd shall look after the field on which he pastured and at harvest-time he shall measure out sixty kur of grain per eighteen iku to the owner of the field.[71]

It is clear from the provision of this law that the term "shepherd" was a day-to-day vocabulary used in its literal sense in Babylon. Nomadic activities in the land would have naturally made this usage possible as almost every family kept some kind of animals.

Also, the term "shepherd" has a titular function assigned to Babylonian deities and humans. According to Erich Beyreuther, the term "shepherd at an early date became a title of honour applied to divinities and rulers

---

71. James B. Pritchard, "The Code of Hammurabi," trans. Theophile J. Meek, in *Ancient Near Eastern Texts Relating to the Old Testament* (3d ed.; ed. James B. Pritchard (1969; 5th print, Princeton, New Jersey: Princeton University Press, 1969; 5th print, 1992), 168-9.

alike . . . [as was] found in a stereotyped form in the Sumerian king-list, in Babylonian courtly style and in the pyramid text."[72] In this king-list, King Hammu-rapi[73] is addressed as shepherd of his people. He is called "the shepherd," appointed by Enlil. As shepherd, it is an aspect of his responsibilities "to promote the welfare of the people . . . to cause justice to prevail in the land . . . [to ensure] that the strong might not oppress the weak."[74] Even the king understands himself as "shepherd." He boasts, "I, Hammu-rapi, mighty king, king of Babylon, king who makes the four quarters be at peace, who achieves the victory of the god Marduk, shepherd who satisfies him."[75]

On the royal inscription of Samsu-iluna, the first son of Hammu-rapi who succeeded the throne is also referred to as "Shepherd to whom the goddess Inanna gave her favourable omen and help."[76] Equally, the term "shepherd" is used as royal title for Nabopolassar the first king who rebuilds Babylon and reigns as founder of the Neo-Babylonian dynasty. He is called "the king of justice, the Shepherd called by Marduk."[77] Not only is his humility and submission as "the worshiper of Nabû and Marduk" acknowledged, but far more, he is "the shepherd who pleases Papnunanki."[78] Even his successor, Nebuchadnezzar, is described as "the loyal shepherd"

---

[72]. Erich Beyreuther, "Shepherd," *NIDNTT* 3:564. This idea also existed in Egypt. Vancil states to this effect that the presence of shepherd imagery in Egypt is evidenced in the "widespread use of the simple shepherd's crook . . . [an instrument that] symbolized the ruler's power and eminence, and especially the nature of his rule, the king's obligation to maintain order and justice (maat) in the land. [In the history of its development], the appearance of the crook-staff in the late pre-dynastic period at first signified princely, and later royal, authority, and in historical times the heket-scepter symbolized rulership." Jack W. Vancil, "Sheep, Shepherd," 1188.

[73]. Hammu-rapi is also spelt as Hammurabi. He was the sixth of eleven kings in the Old Babylonian (Amorite) Dynasty who ruled for 43 years from ca. 1728-1686 BC.

[74]. Pritchard, "The Code of Hammurabi," 164.

[75]. Douglas Frayne, in *The Context of Scripture* Vol. II (ed. William W. Hallo; Leiden: Brill, 2000), 257.

[76]. Frayne, in *The Context of Scripture* Vol. II, 258.

[77]. Paul-Alain Beaulieu in *The Context of Scripture* Vol. II (ed. William W. Hallo; Leiden: Brill, 2000), 307.

[78]. Beaulieu, in *The Context of Scripture* Vol. II, 308. Beaulieu reports that "Papnunanki" is a name of Zarpanîtu, the wife of Marduk, who is also known under the designation Bēltiya "my lady."

because he is "the wise expert who is attentive to the ways of the gods."[79] To assign a shepherd title to the king suggests the recognition and value of the throne as kingship is said to be "probably one of the most enduring forms of government in the history of humankind."[80]

Besides kings, deities also bore the shepherd title in ANE societies. On the cylinder A inscription of Gudea, the Sumerian god, for instance, addressed himself in the temple building text as "shepherd." The phrase, "I, the shepherd," is repeated on cylinder B.[81] Equally, Nanshe, his sister, the goddess of Sirara, addressed him, Gudea, "O my shepherd" in her interpretation of his dream.[82] The god Gudea is referred to as "the faithful shepherd" several times in this text.[83]

Again, in addition to its literal and titular senses, the functions and roles of the kings and the gods are descried in "shepherding" terms. In describing his role to the people of Sumer and Akkad whom the gods, Anum and Enlil gave into his hands to rule, King Hammu-rapi said, in praise of his achievements, that I dug the canal to provide abundant water and "gathered the scattered peoples of the land of Sumer and Akkad (and) provided for them pastures and watering places. In abundance and plenty I shepherded them. I settled them in peaceful abodes."[84] King Cyrus, whom Marduk appointed as a righteous king, is said to have "shepherded with justice and righteousness all the black-headed people, over whom (Marduk) had given him victory."[85] Consequently, as a just and righteous king, he confessed in self-

---

79. Beaulieu, in *The Context of Scripture* Vol. II, 309.
80. Nicole Brisch, ed., *Religion and Power: Divine Kingship in the Ancient World and Beyond*, Oriental Institute Seminar Number 4 (Chicago, Ill.: University of Chicago, 2008), 1.
81. See Richard E. Averbeck in *The Context of Scripture* Vol. II (ed. William W. Hallo; Leiden: Brill, 2000), 429.
82. Averbeck, in *The Context of Scripture* Vol. II, 420.
83. See pp. 421, 423, 425, and 429 of Averbeck in *The Context of Scripture* Vol. II. Averbeck draws attention to the term "shepherd" as a well-known royal epithet in the ANE world. On this basis, reference to the god, Gudea, as "shepherd" and "faithful Shepherd" by himself and by others, becomes obvious in these texts, significantly because he is the shepherd appointed by Nanshe, called in the heart of Ningirsu, as ruler of his people. All those referred to by the title "shepherd," king or god, were expected to demonstrate care, integrity, and skill.
84. Frayne, in *The Context of Scripture* Vol. II, 257.
85. Mordechai Cogan, in *The Context of Scripture* Vol. II (ed. William W. Hallo; Leiden:

praise that "I sought the welfare of the city of Babylon and all its sacred centers . . . [and for those heavily imposed] I relieved their weariness and freed them from their service."[86]

Similarly, the status and the functions of the gods are all described in shepherding terms. For instance, Iahdun-Lim, the king of Mari, ascribed his defeat of a coalition of Amorite tribes to Shamash, the god and lord of Mari. He identified him not only as the "king of heaven and earth, judge of gods and mankind, whose concern is justice," but particularly as "shepherd of the black-headed (people)" who heeds prayers and gives long life to them that revere him.[87]

Furthermore, it is also to be found that the term "shepherd" was used in ANE in a representative sense. Observation from Egyptology reveals that "The king was considered to be the incarnate of the creator god . . . [and] the life of the king was circumscribed and permeated by ritual"[88] as he assumed the duty of the chief spiritualist as a representative of the god/gods. Its representative posture is seen in that it is a designate for the king as the representative of the god or gods, as the case may be. King Nebuchadnezzar of Babylon saw himself as servant of Marduk, the chief and king of the gods of the land, and admittedly confessed that it was he, Marduk, who "gave me the shepherdship of the country and the people."[89] Perceiving themselves as representatives of the god/gods, it is said that the Babylonian and Persian rulers of the sixth, fifth, and fourth centuries BC, instead of deifying themselves, "followed the more traditional Mesopotamian custom of arrogating to themselves, and themselves alone, divine favour."[90] As Vancil

---

Brill, 2000), 315.

86. Cogan, in *The Context of Scripture* Vol. II, 315.

87. Frayne, in *The Context of Scripture* Vol. II, 260.

88. Paul John Frandsen, "Aspects of Kingship in Ancient Egypt," in *Religion and Power: Divine Kingship in the Ancient World and Beyond*, Oriental Institute Seminar Number 4 (ed. Nicole Brisch; Chicago, Ill.: University of Chicago, 2008), 47.

89. Beaulieu, in *The Context of Scripture* Vol. II, 309. Nebuchadnezzar was the son and successor of Nabopolassar. He was considered the real architect of Neo-Babylonian hegemony.

90. Erica Ehrenberg, "Dieu Et Mon Droit: Kingship in Late Babylonian and Early Persian Times," in *Religion and Power: Divine Kingship in the Ancient World and Beyond*, Oriental Institute Seminar Number 4 (ed. Nicole Brisch; Chicago, Ill.: University of Chicago, 2008), 103.

observes, the shepherd image or symbol "suggests the concept of righteous government and often appears in contexts where the subject of justice is prominent. [In such context], the king as a shepherd and as a representative of the gods was expected to rule with justice and to show kindness in counselling, protecting, and guiding the people through every difficulty."[91] This clearly suggests that as a representative of the gods and as a shepherd of his people, it was within the power of the king to create a conducive atmosphere where justice, equity, peace, prosperity, security, and progress flourished in the state.

Apart from kings, lesser gods also performed representative functions on behalf of the appointing higher god. Gudea, for example, appointed by Ningirsu, is said to be "the shepherd of Ningirsu"[92] when the latter took residence in the temple built for him by the former. Ningirsu, himself being a lesser or subordinate god to Nanshe, is described as "the powerful steward of Nanshe, the obedient shepherd of Ningirsu."[93]

We have so far discussed in the preceding pages that kings and the gods in the Babylonian contexts took the title "shepherd." We have also seen that their functions and representative roles are described in shepherding terms in view of the burden of care, guidance, protection, and preservation of the states placed upon them. A military sense is also assigned to the term "shepherd." As shepherd of the land, the king had the responsibility of defending the territorial integrity of the state and to ensure security. In order for the shepherd-king to perform the military role of defending and protecting, he needed to be given such a mandate and might by the god or gods of the land. This sense is seen in the case of King Samsu-iluna who was a devoted and committed conqueror and an empire expansionist. Because of his ambition and quest to expand his empire, "the gods An, Enlil, Marduk, Enki, and goddess Inanna determined his destiny (and) gave to him a mighty weapon that has no rival."[94] With such an impetus,

---

91. Vancil, "Sheep, Shepherd," 1188.
92. Averbeck, in *The Context of Scripture* Vol. II, 431.
93. Averbeck, in *The Context of Scripture* Vol. II, 431.
94. Frayne, in *The Context of Scripture* Vol. II, 258.

the king not only defended his territory but expanded it through the weapon of conquering ideology.

3.2.2.2 The Shepherd Metaphor in Late Assyrian Texts

The shepherd metaphor also appears in the Assyrian texts having different connotations and usage. As it is the case with the late Babylonian texts, the literal sense of the concept "shepherd" is also noticeable in Assyria texts. In the Assyrian laws line 1 of tablet F for example, corporal punishment, the loss of hairs, and hard labour on the king's farm were prescribed for anyone who stole a sheep from his neighbour and then substituted the ownership identification mark with his own.[95] Similarly, in an Assyrian treaty between Ashurnirari[96] V and Mati'-ilu, a literal "spring lamb" is mentioned as a sign "to conclude the treaty of Aššur-nerari, king of Assyria with Mati'-ilu."[97] These instances indicate the presence of animal husbandry activities warranting the literal sense of the usage of the term "shepherd."

The term "shepherd" also connotes a titular import for kings and gods in Assyrian texts. In the law code of King Lipit-Ishtar,[98] he is called "the wise shepherd," and he even addressed himself as "I, Lipit-Ishtar, the humble shepherd of Nippur." The king is appointed shepherd by the Sumero-Babylonian deities, Anu and Enlil, "to the princeship of the land in order to establish justice in the land, to banish complaints, to turn back enmity and rebellion by the force of arms . . . to bring well-being to the Sumerians and Akkadians."[99] Equally, King Ashurnasirpal, king of Assyria, acting as the high priest of the god Ashur, described as "the legitimate king, the king of the world, the king of Assyria, son of Tukulti-Ninurta," is addressed as "the shepherd of all mortals."[100]

The titular sense is applied also in addressing the gods of the land. King Yahdun-Lim addressed Shamash the god of Mari, not only as "the king of

---

95. Pritchard, ed., "The Middle Assyrian Laws," 187.
96. The name Ashurnirari is the same as Aššur-nerari.
97. Arnold and Beyer, eds., *Readings from the Ancient Near East*, 101.
98. King Lipit-Ishtar was the fifth ruler of the Dynasty of Isin, of the Sumerians and the Akkadians.
99. Pritchard, ed., "Lipit-Ishtar Law Code," 159.
100. Pritchard, ed., "The Banquet of Ashurnasirpal II," 560.

the heaven and the nether world" whose role it is to dispense justice and protect what is right, but also as "the shepherd of all the black-headed"[101] people. As shepherd, he was to protect, ensure justice, listen to supplications and vows, accept prayers, and grant long life and happiness to his worshipers. Additionally, King Assurbanipal addressed him as "shepherd of the celestial and earthly region"[102] in his hymn. Closely related to the titular sense is its status usage. This status import is seen in King Assurbanipal's Hymn of Coronation sung to Shamash the god of Assyria. In this hymn, he prayed, "May Shamash . . . raise you, to shepherdship over the four regions!"[103]

Not only was the term "shepherd" used in the Assyrian contexts in the literal, titular and positional senses, but representative and protective senses were also visible. In the Letter-Prayer of King Sin-Iddinam to Nin-Isina, the king prayed to the deity asking for health in the recognition that it was Utu, the god of Sun-god and patron deity of Larsa, who gave to "me the shepherdship over his nation."[104] This king acknowledged that the nation belonged to and was ruled by the deity, Utu, and himself as his human representative. Also, the term serves a protective sense. For instance, the Hittite laws in the series called "if anyone" recognised the status of a "caretaker" in line 35 on tablet I as an overseer or a shepherd. This aspect of the laws recognised the functions of animals, sheep inclusive, by prescribing various laws affecting their welfare.[105] The king is, by implication, to protect the human sheep/animals under his shepherding care as much as to ensure that laws are put in place to protect animals in the land.

---

101. Pritchard, ed., "The Dedication of the Shamash Temple by Yahdun-Lim," 556.
102. Alasdair Livingstone, "Assurbanipal's Coronation Hymn (1:142)," in *The Context of Scripture Vol. I: Canonical Compositions from the Biblical World* (ed. William W. Hallo; Leiden: Brill, 1997), 474.
103. Livingstone, "An Assurbanipal Hymn for Shamash (1: 143)," 473.
104. William W. Hallo, "Letter-Prayer of King Sin-Iddinam to Nin-Isina," in *The Context of Scripture Vol. I: Canonical Compositions from the Biblical World* (ed. William W. Hallo; Leiden: Brill, 1997), 532.
105. Pritchard, "The Hittite Laws," 188-197.

3.3 The Literary Context for the Shepherd Metaphor in Ezekiel

The literature of the Jewish people, though purported to be densely sacred, is none the less, a literary work that follows a particular convention. The shepherd metaphor used within this literary domain reflects the poetic expression of Jewish writing. It is applied to humans, that is, political and religious leaders, as well as to the Jewish deity, Yahweh. In this direction, George Cooke is correct to identify the shepherds of Israel in the context of Ezekiel as the "native kings and rulers"[106] of Israel since this understanding was normative in ancient literature. We see, for instance, in Ezekiel 34:1-10 the presence of ". . . a harsh condemnation of kings in Israel, for whom the metaphor of "shepherd" is used."[107] Charles L. Feinberg extends the list to include "not only kings but all leaders of Judah . . . the civil leaders . . . the spiritual leaders, the prophets and the priests . . . the court officials."[108] Vancil commends that "Israel's leaders were often regarded as shepherds, and even though God was always their principal shepherd, responsible human agents were necessary."[109] Moses had raised the concern before Yahweh, explaining the need for human shepherds so that Israel would not be like sheep without a shepherd (Num 27:16-17).

Ezekiel is not the first on the list of Israelite prophets to employ the term "shepherd" in Israelite prophetic tradition. Other non-writing and writing prophets preceded him years before he came on the scene of Israelite prophetism. We therefore consider the texts of only two pre-classical prophets and that of a close contemporary exilic prophet. This effort seeks the connection between the usages[110] of the "shepherd" concept by preceding prophets in comparison with Ezekiel's.

---

106. George A. Cooke, *A Critical and Exegetical Commentary on the Book of Ezekiel* (Edinburg: T & T Clark, 1936), 373.

107. Brueggemann, *An Introduction*, 199.

108. Charles Lee Feinberg, "Jeremiah," (*EBC* 6; Grand Rapids, Mich.: Zondervan, 1986), 517.

109. Vancil, "Sheep, Shepherd," 1189.

110. The use of the term "shepherd" in the Old Testament has literal, descriptive, and metaphoric senses applied to both humans and the divine. Literally, the term was self-applied by Amos who introduced himself as one of the shepherds of Tekoa in Judah

3.4 The Shepherd Metaphor in Pre-Classical Prophetic Texts

Even though the shepherd image had already been in existence in the Mesopotamian region before Israel became a nation, the Exodus Event particularly served as a major reference point and reinforcing background to its usage in Israelite literature and prophetic tradition. Until the experience of the Egyptian Exodus and wilderness life, the descendants of Jacob had not had a clear understanding of the shepherding role of Yahweh, the God of their patriarchs. Vancil suggests that the origin of the shepherd imagery in Israel's history "may be most attributable to Israel's earliest years of nomadic and seminomadic existence" rooted in her wilderness pilgrimage which gave rise to "the thought of God as their shepherd; for it is during the early period that he alone is viewed as shepherd and protector."[111] This title of "shepherd" attributed to Yahweh acting as the Shepherd of Israel is critical to the nation on the ground of its lingering memory, especially when linked to the Exodus Event in Israel's history, because the first Exodus was an exceptionally unique experience that Israel would not forget in a hurry for many generations to come. Beyreuther submits the opinion in this regard that "the memory of the classical nomadic days of ancient Israel before the occupation, when the people lived as aliens in tents, must

---

(Amos 1:1). That Amos was a literal shepherd or husbandman tending his sheep in Tekoa, is clear in his use of pastoral language (Amos 1:2) and in his response to Amaziah in defence of his call to the prophetic office (Amos 7:10-15). Like in the context of Amos, the same Hebrew is used for King Mesha of Moab who raised sheep (2 Kgs 3:4). Descriptively, Jacob referred to God as his Shepherd (Gen 48:15; 49:24). Also metaphorically, Moses used the term with a leadership import (Num 27:17) in the same way that God used it when referring to the Judges as shepherds (2 Sam 7:7). Prophet Micaiah used the term in a metaphoric sense in reference to King Ahab's death in war (1 Kgs 22:17; cf. Num 27:17). The psalms also fall under this category as the poets assigned the shepherding role of Israel to Yahweh (Pss 23:1; 28:9; 80:1). Similarly, of all the kings that Israel had, only David was clearly depicted as a shepherd-ruler appointed over Israel by Yahweh (2 Sam 5:2; cf. 1 Sam 13:14; 16:1, 11-13; Ps 78:70-72).

111. Vancil, "Sheep, Shepherd," 1189. See Gen 48:15; 49:24; Deut 26:5-8; Jer 13:17; Mic 7:14. Charged with the responsibility of leading and providing for the people, civil and religious leaders are pictured as shepherds and the people as sheep in pastoral literature. In this sense, kings in Israel and foreign nations occupied this status and therefore took on the image of shepherds.

have remained constantly alive, because God's activities in salvation history were bound up with it."[112]

We see Yahweh acting as Israel's Shepherd in the way he displayed his shepherding characteristics in the Exodus Event. When we recall this unique event in Israel's history, we would understand, as Keener observes, that "The image of God as shepherd was an image of leadership and protection moved by caring for and commitment to his people [because] He performed shepherd-like functions for his people"[113] in many respects. The shepherd motif, right from the time of the patriarchs up to the last prophet in Israel, had been in Jewish tradition an ever-fresh concept, picturing Yahweh as the Shepherd of the patriarchs and of Israel. It is for this reason that the prophets used the principle of flashback to remind Israel of her covenant standing with Yahweh, challenging her to do right so she could continually benefit from his shepherding care as was the case in the Exodus experience.

From the preceding, it becomes clear that Ezekiel is not the first prophet in Israel to use the shepherd/sheep metaphor. Other prophets of the 8th century BC like Isaiah (c. 740-680 BC) and Micah (c. 740 BC), his close contemporary, Jeremiah (c. 626-580 BC) of the 7th century BC, and even way into the post-exilic prophets of the 6th century BC like Zechariah[114] (c. 520-518 BC) also used the shepherd metaphor. Our considering the shepherd/sheep metaphor in these three pre-classical prophets is to enhance our understanding of Ezekiel's usage of such metaphor unique to his particular exilic context.

---

112. Erich Beyreuther, "Shepherd," in *NIDNTT* 3:565.
113. Keener, "Shepherd, Flock," 1090.
114. Zechariah's discourse of the shepherd motif appears in the second half of the book (9-14, particularly in 11:4-17 and 13:7-9). The first shepherd text indicates that the prophet himself was commissioned at the command of Yahweh "to assume the role of the shepherd of the flock," serving as the political leader because its present shepherds/political leaders "buy and sell the people with impunity." The setting of 13:7-9 is however considered as "an eschatological oracle of hope and salvation." See comments in Ralph L. Smith, *Micah-Malachi* (WBC 32; Waco, Tex.: Word, 1984), 242-284. For textual discussion on this passage, see articles by Paul L. Redditt, "Israel's Shepherds: Hope and Pessimism in Zechariah 9-14," *CBQ* 51 (1989):631-642, Stephen L. Cook, "The Metamorphosis of a Shepherd: The Tradition History of Zechariah 11:17 + 13:7-9," *CBQ* 55 (1993):453-466.

3.4.1 Its Treatment in Isaiah's and Micah's Texts

Isaiah[115] and Micah are the only Neo-Assyrian and pre-classical or pre-exilic prophets[116] who clearly picked issues with Israel by using the shepherd metaphor. These two prophets used the metaphor under a different historical timeframe[117] when compared to Ezekiel's. While they only foresaw the exile coming upon Judah, Ezekiel experienced it as a direct participant. Robertson reveals that in Isaiah, "the themes of exile and restoration serve as focal points throughout the book." As Isaiah "actually lived through the awesome trauma of the exile of the northern kingdom . . . [he foresaw] that the identical fate awaited the southern kingdom of Judah."[118] Isaiah's mention of the shepherd metaphor appears in 40:11 located within the "comfort" or "hope" section in which Yahweh announces "the coming restoration of Jerusalem and YHWH's return to his city."[119] Gordon Graham notes that this new section in the predictive prophecy "tells how God will deal with Babylon, how He will restore a remnant of His people to the land, and the glory of Christ's millennial kingdom."[120] As one who "witnessed" the

---

115. Robert Chisholm comments that this prophet is best known for his unsurpassed view of the "sovereignty" of God where his presentation of the same is not abstract but oozes out of "a highly personal portrait influenced by his face-to-face encounter with God at the beginning of his ministry." If God is "sovereign," then Isaiah is right in conceiving him as "first and foremost '"the Holy One of Israel'" who possesses absolute sovereign authority over His covenant people and the nations of the earth…[who] personally intervenes in history to accomplish His purposes." Chisholm, Jr., "A Theology of Isaiah," 305. Both dual (chs. 1-39 and 40-66) and a trio (chs. 1-39, 40-55, and 56-66) divisions have been suggested for the book's literary structure.

116. As pre-classical prophets with primary assignment to the North, Robertson states that "Both Isaiah and Micah lived through the traumatic days of the devastation of the northern kingdom and its exile at the brutal hands of the king of Assyria in 722 BC, which is a fact too often overlooked." Robertson, *The Christ of the Prophets*, 210.

117. James Merrill Ward rightly notes that while cultic idolatry is a more prominent concern that provokes in the prophets an ordinary outrage, "The world of Ezekiel was completely different from the world of earlier prophets." His was the world of exile, and its mention evokes the image of a strange setting. James Merrill Ward, *Thus Says the Lord: The Message of the Prophets* (Nashville: Abingdon, 1991), 171.

118. Robertson, *The Christ of the Prophets*, 220. Clements' article gives its readers a general feeling that the entire Isaiah corpus clusters around the events of the dominance of Judah by Babylon. See Clements, "The Prophecies of Isaiah and the Fall of Jerusalem in 587 BC," pp. 421-436.

119. John D. W. Watts, *Isaiah 34-66*: (WBC 25; rev. ed.; Nashville, Dal.: Thomas Nelson, 2005), 606.

120. Gordon Graham, *Isaiah Speaks to the 21st Century* (Drake, U.S.A.: Gordon Graham,

northern deportation, by prophetic inspiration, Isaiah could perceive that the south would experience "the same kind of devastation" in only a matter of time.[121] What Isaiah foretold concerning Judah, Ezekiel explained from both personal and corporate experiences of the Babylonian exile. Although Isaiah saw Judah's deportation still in the future, yet, his use of the shepherd metaphor is emphatic, affirming Yahweh's "deep concern and love for His people," picturing him as a "shepherd who holds His lambs closely to His chest" and leading them back to their land in triumph with his powerful arm.[122] Two opposing principles are operative here – exile is a certainty and restoration is also a certainty.

The shepherd metaphor in Isaiah, as John Watts suggests, has both royal overtones and reference to the towns of Judah. He explains in this vein that, "God's return promises pastoral, royal concern and care for all of them, particularly for the weak and needy."[123] In this connection, he thinks the prophet used the shepherd concept in reference to the first and second advents of Jesus, both as king and as shepherd. He explains that in the first advent, Jesus appeared as,

> . . . a shepherd gathering His lambs into His arms, carrying them nestled against Him, gently leading His flock. . . . offering Himself as a sacrifice. . . . When Jesus returns in the future, He appears as a mighty warrior coming to judge the world and to reign over it as King. . . . [then he will finally] redeem His lost sheep, Israel . . . Like a tender Shepherd, He binds up their wounds and restores them to health."[124]

2000), 391.
121. Robertson, *The Christ of the Prophets*, 226.
122. Chisholm, Jr., "A Theology of Isaiah," 323. Against the popular theory that Isaiah 40-66 was written in the exile, after the eighth century BC prophecy, Chisholm argues "Isaiah's sustained projection of himself into the future, even to the point where he reasons with the exiles as if literally present with them, is unique[ly]" a key element in this prophet, see p. 306.
123. Watts, *Isaiah 34-66*, 612.
124. Watts, *Isaiah 34-66* 395-6.

In essence, Isaiah's use of the metaphor points, first, to the predictive role of Yahweh's restoration of his people, "implied in the exhortation to faith and patience"[125] on their part, and second, to the future kingly shepherding role of Christ as messiah to his sheep, Israel, and by extension, the church.

Focusing more on the gain than on the pain of exile, this good tiding of restoration envisaged by Isaiah is to be proclaimed loudly to the towns of Judah and Jerusalem by the news carrier that God is coming to Jerusalem triumphantly because he is restoring his people back to their land from exile. This envisaged hope is predicated on the fact that the God of Israel, acting as a tender Shepherd, "carefully carries and leads the weak and helpless members of His flock,"[126] thus revealing the pictured would-be condition of the Babylonian exiles following Yahweh's accomplished restorative agenda.

Isaiah's use of the shepherd metaphor is not only predictive but exclusively of the royal reign of Christ. The prophet saw, not only into the period of the exilic experience by Judah, but far beyond, into the post-exilic experience of the returnees where they would be led by a true shepherd. According to Gan, Isaiah proclaimed, in the shepherd metaphor, Yahweh's protective role figuring in his deliverance and redemption of Israel from exile. For this cause, he explains,

> Isaiah urged the nation of Israel to a covenant renewal with her God, Yahweh. This is simply because the sheep will be lost without a shepherd. By not remaining within the covenant relationship, Israel will be devoured and lost forever . . . Only in the covenant relationship, can Israel be saved because they are in their shepherd's arm.[127]

---

125. Joseph Addison Alexander, *Commentary on the Prophecies of Isaiah* (Grand Rapids, Mich.: Zondervan, 1953; repr., 1978), 93.
126. John A. Martins, "Isaiah," in *The Bible Knowledge Commentary, Old Testament Edition* (eds. John F. Walvoord and Roy B. Zuck; America: SP Publications, 1985; repr., 1987), 1092.
127. Gan, *The Metaphor of Shepherd*, 61.

Similarly, like prophet Isaiah, Micah[128] employed the shepherd metaphor (5:2-5; 7:14) also predictively of a "ruler over Israel" from Bethlehem who would "stand and shepherd" the people. Micah's usage is more Christological in import. As Bruce Waltke notes, ". . . pointing to the Messiah, Micah . . . sketch[es] Messiah's remarkable career by a series of successive predictions"[129] of his functions. It seems clear from Micah that the force of his usage is on the functions of a divine rather than a human future shepherd-ruler (5:2). David J. Clark clarifies that the prophet leaves no one in doubt about the Messianic identity of this shepherd because "The terms used are such as to transcend the nature or achievements of any merely human leader, and could be completely fulfilled only in the Messiah."[130] Micah anticipated the "Messiah to come at the end of the Assyrian crisis"[131] as Isaiah had also anticipated. In this connection, following the exile, most likely the Assyrian and Babylonian, the prophet prayed in 7:14-17 "for God to care for his people like a shepherd . . . Israel is God's inheritance as a result of the covenant."[132]

The *care* element expressed by Micah reflects the function of the Messiah-shepherd-ruler who, "as a shepherd, he leads, defends, and cares for his wards," causing them to "live securely."[133] Clark observes that as Micah looked into the dark tunnel of the exile to see what awaits the nation there, and seeing beyond the return from Babylon, he saw the Messiah-shepherd who would not only shepherd his flock, but would do so with the strength and majesty that comes from the LORD whose greatness will

---

128. Micah and Isaiah are described as "prophetic twins" because they "spoke God's word during one of the great crises of Israel's history." Robertson, *The Christ of the Prophets*, 210.

129. Bruce Waltke, "Micah," in *An Exegetical and Expository Commentary on the Minor Prophets* Vol. 2, (ed. Thomas Edward McComiskey; Grand Rapids, Mich.: Baker, 1993; repr., 2006), 707.

130. David J. Clark, "Micah," in *The International Bible Commentary* (2d ed.; ed. F. F. Bruce; Grand Rapids, Mich.: Marshall Morgan & Scott, 1986), 934.

131. Ralph L. Smith, *Micah-Malachi:* WBC 32 (Waco, Tex.: Word, 1984), 45. See Isaiah 10:34-11:1 for a similar anticipatory idea of the future shepherd-ruler. Although scholars disagree on the literary location of Micah 5:4-5/5:5-6, the prophet's use of the shepherd metaphor in reference to the Messianic age lacks ambiguity.

132. Smith, *Micah-Malachi*, 59.

133. Waltke, "Micah," 707.

extend far beyond the boundaries that David's kingdom knew. With no external enemies left unvanquished, his people would at last live securely.[134]

The experience of ultimate peace and security envisaged by Micah would be consequent upon the functions of the Messiah-shepherd-ruler in the envisaged eschatological community. In an expanded function, Martins explains that the Messiah-shepherd-ruler "will reunite and restore the nation" because the idea of the pain of labour "refers not to Mary's giving birth to Jesus, but to Israel's national re-gathering." He also states, "He will care for people and give them security . . . something the nation's leaders in Micah's day were refusing to do." He claims that the experience of security in contrast to the failure of Israel's leaders will be possible on the ground that the Messiah-shepherd-ruler "will destroy Israel's enemies . . . [as] one of Messiah's several accomplishments in bringing peace to Israel."[135] Waltke adds to this submission by arguing that "because Messiah reconciles formerly unreconciled brothers in a new Israel (v. 2) and because his greatness extends to the earth (v. 3), protecting his wards and punishing their oppressors, it follows that he will become '"the one of peace'" [which] means specifically '"wholeness, preservation, [and] salvation.'"[136]

Micah's usage of the metaphor of shepherding leaves his readers with the impression that his shepherd is the Messiah of Israel that is yet to come. His coming is to protect, lead, and feed the flock; yet, he would not do this in his strength as the former shepherds of Israel had done, except in Yahweh's strength. Gan notes that, "the image of shepherd exhibited in the coming shepherd among Israel extends the dimension of shepherding in the strength and in the name of the great shepherd, Yahweh."[137] In Micah's prediction as it is in Isaiah's, is the clear conviction that "beyond the exile will be a restoration, a gathering of dispersed Israel," and at this point, it is clear that "as the kingdom is restored, so the king will be restored, and the paradise will be renewed"[138] under the shepherding of the new ruler.

---

134. Clark, "Micah," 934.
135. Martins, "Isaiah," 1486-7.
136. Waltke, "Micah," 708.
137. Gan, *The Metaphor of Shepherd*, 80.
138. Robertson, *The Christ of the Prophets*, 211.

3.4.2 Its Treatment in Jeremiah's Text

While Jeremiah (c. 626-580 BC) is generally considered a contemporary of Ezekiel (c. 593-570 BC), his prophetic ministry preceded Ezekiel's. Their areas of commonality make some scholars wonder whether Ezekiel's shepherd metaphor is not an elaboration of the former, although James Ward objects to this opinion.[139] A careful reading of the prophecy of Jeremiah however leaves the reader with the impression of his description as "a man of unflinching courage who never, so far as we know, tempered the word that his God had given him by the omission of so much as a syllable."[140] The impetus for such a dogged commitment to a given task certainly can not be "attributed to natural endowments."[141] Roberson captures Jeremiah's courage thus, "his fidelity to the word of the Lord is even more remarkable in view of the varied crises that he faced during his long career as prophet in Israel."[142]

The main theme of chapters 21-24 of Jeremiah is on shepherding failure. His personal ministerial struggles too seem clear here. As Paul House explicates, Jeremiah's fidelity to the divine task "has apparently won few if any converts" to his side. He had to wrestle "with his own relationship to Yahweh," he had to contend with "strong opposition from other priests" with no one standing on his side, and he had "struggles with kings, prophets, priests, nations and common people . . . those he seeks to convince to serve the Lord."[143] Jeremiah 23:1-8 convey the prophet's major treatment

---

139. In his comment on the pre-classical prophets and Jeremiah in connection with Ezekiel's work, Ward explains that "Preexilic prophecy consisted almost entirely of short, poetic oracles developed out of direct, oral confrontation with religious and political leaders. Oracles of this kind are almost entirely lacking in the book of Ezekiel; instead, there are expansive prose discourses, allegories and visionary narratives. The closest literary relations of the writings in this book are the prose discourse in the book of Jeremiah. [Despite the]…marked similarities between the prose writings in these two books, there is a great difference in the overall composition of the two. [For instance, he argues that] in Jeremiah, the prose constitutes roughly half the book and is interspersed with large groups of oracles in traditional poetic form…[while Ezekiel's] is almost entirely prose." Ward, *Thus Says the Lord*, 173.

140. John Bright, *Jeremiah*, as quoted by O. Palmer Robertson, *The Christ of the Prophets*, 267.

141. Robertson, *The Christ of the Prophets*, 267.

142. Robertson, *The Christ of the Prophets*, 267.

143. Paul R. House, *Old Testament Theology* (Downers Grove, Ill.: Inter-Varsity, 1998), 312. If Jeremiah were a Nigerian, living in the present day, he would best be described as

of the shepherd motif. Peter Craigie, Page Kelly, and Joel Drinkard think that Jeremiah's usage of the shepherd metaphor (22:22; 23:1-4) refers to "Judah's leaders, especially her kings."[144] This opinion gains the support of House who asserts that "Jeremiah 21:1-23:8 focuses on Yahweh's expectations for kings."[145] As Vancil also notes, his usage of the shepherd imagery for political leaders of various ranking and authority is indicative that "by the prophet's time it was a well-established and regular portrait for ruling nobility."[146]

Unlike Isaiah and Micah who used the shepherd metaphor predictively in reference to the functions of the Messiah in the messianic age, Jeremiah, like Ezekiel, employed the metaphor with an indicting and repudiating tone in reference to the human shepherds of Israel who failed to care for Yahweh's people under their shepherding obligation.[147] Some even think it "may well also contain a specific message to Zedekiah"[148] the puppet king. Wiseman asserts that following the failures of the kings and leaders that he indicted, Jeremiah's mention of the "Branch" and "the LORD our Righteousness" "clearly looks beyond the immediate history to the time when the Ideal King – the True Shepherd – would reverse the actions which mark all false shepherds."[149]

By using the shepherd metaphor for the Judean human shepherds, the prophet in his indicting and repudiating speech in 23:1-4, charged them for sitting on David's seat without fulfilling the obligations of such status. As House explains, "sitting on David's throne makes kings responsible for administering justice and protecting the weak, the very things God's law,

---

a "suffer head," that is, an unfortunate suffering struggling man. This unpleasant status results because, as the Məship people of Plateau State, Nigeria, would say, "shu jeel buwer," meaning, one who suffers a lot as a result of several factors in life.

144. Peter C. Craigie, Page H. Kelley, and Joel F. Drinkard, Jr., *Jeremiah 1-25* (WBC 26; Nashville, Dal.: Word, 1991), 325.

145. House, *Old Testament Theology*, 312.

146. Vancil, "Sheep, Shepherd," 1189. See Jer 2:8; 3:15; 10:21; 25:34-48.

147. It is observed that "Although the term "shepherd" might refer to any of Judah's leaders, the context seems to refer especially to the kings" whom the prophet accused of leadership irresponsibility. Waltke, "Micah," 326.

148. Donald Wiseman, "Jeremiah," in *The International Bible Commentary* (2d ed.; ed. F. F. Bruce; Grand Rapids, Mich.: Marshall Morgan & Scott, 1986), 778.

149. Wiseman, "Jeremiah," 778.

which they are to apply to daily life, is concerned to do."[150] In this context, "only the law of the covenant could preserve the king from the dangers of his position,"[151] as it is only the ruler's strict observance of "the law and justice" can "divert doom and disaster which follows as a reward for evil."[152] But as was the case, Judah's human shepherds came under the whims of the prophet for their failure to sustain the law and "bestow care" over the people. Against the required ideal, these leaders lived on the grid of "oppression and injustice" because of their "greed and raw power."[153]

3.5 Conclusion

It is clear from the preceding discussion that the shepherd concept is not foreign to the ANE and Jewish environments in view of the long-standing practice of animal husbandry among these peoples. The shepherd metaphor never goes away from the texts of these peoples because of the socio-economic and socio-religious significance of sheep needing the faithful function of shepherds in both ANE and Israelite contexts. By using the shepherd metaphor therefore, Ezekiel drew from a vocabulary that was well known to the surrounding peoples.

While the Babylonians and Assyrians used the shepherd metaphor with literal, titular, descriptive, representative, and militarily/protective connotations, the conceptual understanding of Israelite prophets is based largely on its metaphoric sense. Except in the New Testament where the Gospels employ its literal sense, the shepherd metaphor as used in Jewish literary tradition is always in reference to Yahweh as the Shepherd of Israel. It is also used in reference to Israelite human shepherds as Yahweh's representative shepherds charged with such obligations to his people.

---

150. House, *Old Testament Theology*, 313. Cf. Deut 17:14-20.
151. Peter E. Cousins, "Deuteronomy," in *The International Bible Commentary* (2d ed.; ed. F. F. Bruce; Grand Rapids, Mich.: Marshall Morgan & Scott, 1986), 271.
152. Wiseman, "Jeremiah," 777.
153. House, *Old Testament Theology*, 313.

CHAPTER FOUR

Ezekiel's Shepherd Metaphor and the Norms of Deuteronomic Theology

4.1 Introduction

Ezekiel's treatment of the shepherd metaphor to critique the attitude of human shepherds in the Israelite society is theologically grounded on the basis of Israel's covenant standing with Yahweh their deity. Israel[1] stands as a unique nation in history in many respects. First, she is the only people group and nation that has enjoyed theocentric choice by Yahweh as his personal property. Yahweh initiated this process through covenant principle. Paul R. Williamson[2] expresses the idea that Israel's ancestral covenants and national covenants combine to explain the divine choice of the people. Second, she is the only nation that Yahweh, out of his divine volition, chose

---

1. The nation Israel, takes its name from one of its patriarchs, Jacob. The biblical account describes Jacob's wrestling with a man perceived to be God or his angel, an incident which led to a change in his name from Jacob to Israel (Gen 32:24-32; 35:9-12). From this is speculated that the name "Israel" probably originally meant "El riles," which is here interpreted as "the one who strives with God." When applied to the descendants of this God-wrestler therefore, the community of Israel could be "depicted as a group that successfully strives with God and humans." See the textual commentary on Gen 32:28 by David M. Carr, "Genesis," in *The New Oxford Annotated Bible* (3d ed.; eds. Michael D. Coogan et al.; N.Y., Oxford: Oxford University Press, 2001), 56.
2. Paul R. Williamson, "Covenant," in *Dictionary of the Old Testament: Pentateuch* (eds. T. Desmond Alexander and David W. Baker; Downers Grove, Ill.: Inter-Varsity, 2003), 139-155. For the subject of Israel's covenant choice by Yahweh, see Gen 12:2-3, 7; 17:1-8; 32:27-28; Exod 4:22-23; Hosea 11:1-2; Exod 19:4-6.

to enter into an intimate covenant relationship[3] with through the faith of her patriarchs. Yahweh did this in order that he would achieve his salvific purpose for humanity. Hence, Yahweh's call and choice of Abraham makes the latter become ". . . the focal point of God's dealings with the human race."[4] Lastly, Israel is the only nation with a sacred history and tradition that has not experienced a disruption enough to threaten its continuity. In view of this unique standing, Israel is also the only nation on the face of the earth that has suffered the greatest onslaught of Yahweh's punitive actions for her failure to keep the terms of his covenant.[5] Within this unique covenant status that Israel occupied is located the concept of Deuteronomic theology to which the nation was obligated to observe.

Beginning with the Sinai covenant to the enthronement of the Davidic dynasty stands the birth and nurture of Deuteronomic theology. This follows after Israel's official recognition as a state when Yahweh entered into a lasting relationship with the pilgrim community as his covenant people. This event also marked the birth of Israel's official religion which is rooted in the principle of Yahwism. This Yahwistic religion is largely predicated upon Deuteronomic theology having the Decalogue as its basic ethical-theological frame and national constitution. While Israel's religious conception is basically rooted in Yahwism, her covenant status and relationship with Yahweh is its binding thread. Robin Knauth confirms that Israel's ". . . national conception of what it meant to be 'Israelite'" is vastly

---

3. The Abrahamic covenant (Gen 15:4-7) and Israel's national covenant at Sinai (Exod 19:16-20:26) are here combined. In connection with this covenant relationship, Walter Brueggemann notes that Israel's existence is rooted in Yahweh's inescapable, original commitment to Israel. And as such, he observes on the count of Israel's obedience, that "the initiatory act of love, rescue, and designation is made by a sovereign who in this act of love does not cease to be sovereign. Therefore this relationship, marked by awe and gratitude for its inexplicable generosity, brings with it the expectations and requirements of the sovereign who initiates it. The common rubric for this sovereign expectation is covenant. Yahweh designates Israel as Yahweh's covenant partner, so that Israel is, from the outset, obligated to respond to and meet Yahweh's expectations. As covenant partners of Yahweh, Israel is a people defined by obedience." Brueggemann, *Theology of the Old Testament*, 414-418.

4. House, *Old Testament Theology*, 72.

5. Brueggemann explains that throughout her history, Israel understood and therefore related to Yahweh as a Promise-Maker as well as a Promise-Keeper, basically because he made good all of his promises made to Israel's patriarchs. Brueggemann, *Theology of the Old Testament*, 164-173. See Deut 28:15-68; Num 25; Judg 2:10-15.

overshadowed . . . by the religious conception of Israel as a covenant people bound together by mutual loyalty to a single God – Yahweh – as his special, "'chosen'" inheritance, and by mutual obligations of upholding the covenant law."[6] In effect, Israel's status as a "chosen people and covenant community" and her identity as a "Covenant People" bound in "loyalty to Yahweh and his covenant as his chosen people," and her "mutual worship of the one God Yahweh"[7] separates her from other peoples. It is this "separatist" element of Israel's religion that Ezekiel brings to bear in his treatment of the shepherd motif.

Ezekiel's primary audience, prior to their unfortunate present experience, had lived in the Promised Land as Yahweh's *promised* offspring of the patriarch Abraham (cf. Gen 12:1-2). His prophetic speeches and oracles are therefore primarily to address his audience's concern. What is the warrant for Ezekiel's use of Deuteronomic theology in evaluating the Judean environment in the face of a seemingly failed Israelite state? Our attempt at responding to this question develops progressively as we take into account the significance of Deuteronomic theology for Israel, and the critical concerns of the Babylonian exiles. We also take into account Ezekiel's response to such concerns against the norms of an eschatological motif; and finally, his evaluation and structural critique of the society of Israel as a nation in covenant relationship against the tenets of Deuteronomic theology.

4.2 The Significance of Deuteronomic Theology to Israel

How significant is Deuteronomic theology to the Israelite community? The story began with the Exodus Event and continued right into the book of Deuteronomy, a document considered by some to be a second law and by others as a repetition of the law.[8] Deuteronomy is considered in light of the

---

6. Robin J. DeWitt Knauth, "Israelites," in *Dictionary of the Old Testament: Pentateuch* (eds. T. Desmond Alexander and David W. Baker; Downers Grove, Ill.: Inter-Varsity, 2003), 456.
7. Knauth, "Israelites," 456.
8. We take the position that the book of Deuteronomy is to be understood not as a

Decalogue as Israel's national constitution and as a literary bridge between the Torah and the Former Prophets[9]. Although Duane L. Christensen[10] construes Deuteronomy as a legal document, he thinks it functions essentially as "a national constitution," or as he cites S. D. McBride who understands it as the "Polity of the Covenant People." Christensen argues that Deuteronomy is not so much a law code as it is a "work intended for religious instruction and education in ancient Israel" where all and sundry in its society are obligated, starting with the king as the head of the community to the children. Similarly, Longman III and Dillard argue that, "if Deuteronomy was in fact a treaty-covenant document as well as having features of a law code, it in effect became the "constitution" of ancient Israel." As a constitution, they explain, "It was the written deposit that defined her social order, the codification of her legal principles and juridical procedures, and her self-understanding under the rule of God. As a document, it administered the covenant life of God's people."[11]

The giving of the law to Israel at Mt. Sinai is simultaneously intertwined with a heavy emphasis on Yahweh's self-revelation as "I am Yahweh" or "I am Yahweh your God," the one who is holy and therefore requires the same from the community.[12] If anything, this emphasis suggests that Israel's

---

second law but a repetition of the law. In Christensen's submission, as a repetition of the law of Moses delivered at Mt. Sinai in the books of Exodus, Leviticus, and Numbers, it is also to be understood as a literary bridge between the Torah and the Former Prophets, the latter sometimes called the Deuteronomic history. Duane L. Christensen, *Word Biblical Commentary Volume 6A: Deuteronomy 1:1-21:9* (2d ed.; Nashville: Thomas Nelson, 2001), lvii. As a "faithful" repetition of the law, it is also considered as "a collection of well constructed, brilliantly illustrated sermons" delivered by Moses based on the message God had given him previously. Raymond Brown, *The Message of Deuteronomy* (BST; Leicester, England: Inter-Varsity, 1993; repr., 1993), 14.

9. Brueggemann refers to part of the Jewish literature from Genesis-Kings as "Primary Narrative." This breaks into two subunits, Genesis–Deuteronomy and Joshua – Kings. The first subunit is controlled by the *pre-land* motif and the second is controlled by the *in the land* motif. Brueggemann, *An Introduction to the Old Testament*, 16.

10. Christensen, WBC, lvii.

11. Longman III and Dillard, *An Introduction to the Old Testament*, 2d ed., 112.

12. See the demands on the people to keep the legal requirements in Lev 18:5, 30; 19:2, 4, 10, 12, 14, 16, 18, 25, 28, 30-32, 34, 37; 20:7-8, 24, and 26. Kaiser submits that Yahweh's self-revelation and holiness "was the basis for any and all demands laid on Israel." That as a people chosen by a holy God, she "had no choice in the matter of good or evil if she were to enjoy the constant fellowship of one whose very character did not and would not tolerate evil." Kaiser, Jr., *Toward an Old Testament Theology*, 115.

relationship with Yahweh is expected to be like the maxim, "Like father, like son" because of the nation's covenant standing with him. However, the failure of the people to live up to Yahweh's ethical and theological standards after they had settled in Canaan comes under Ezekiel's examination. Here, Ezekiel is directional in his use of the principles of Deuteronomic theology to draw the people's attention to their failure to live up to the requirements of Yahweh's covenant and of the tenets of Deuteronomic theology as Moses had forewarned in the Deuteronomic Code (Deut 4:9-14, 23-28; 6:12). No sooner did Israel occupy Canaan than the people forsook Yahweh and practiced detestable things in his sight (Deut 8:6) by worshiping idols and even portraying their images in high places in the land (Deut 8:7-18). They worshiped the sun god at the temple area (Deut 8:16-17), idolised their hearts (Deut 14:3-8), and even engaged in human sacrifice (Deut 15:20-22; 20:30-31; 23:37, 39). Additionally, the people forsook the law and turned to violence – they bribed, violated the law and human rights, oppressed the helpless and voiceless in society, and committed murder (Deut 22:9-12). Such unexpected practices, particularly from a people in covenant relationship with Yahweh, consistently flourished in the land unabated. Basic to the flourishing of such acts of disobedience was the absence of credible human shepherds who should have consistently used the norm of Yahwism and the principle of Deuteronomic theology as the main stay of the community's religious, social, economic, and political life in leading and guiding the people.

Israel, as Yahweh's people, had a working constitution that served to regulate her political, ethical, economic, social, agricultural and zoological life; even in her international relations. The Torah, from which Deuteronomic theology grows, is for Israel a defining document that would have enhanced her optimising the Deuteronomistic promises had she followed its provisions to the letter (Deut 26:16-28:68). Putting in retrospect the life of Abraham's descendants as a pilgrim community moving to possess the Promised Land, it could be said that the best was yet to come for them as Yahweh's people, his treasured possession, provided Israel carefully observed his decrees in the Promised Land (Deut 26:16-19). Yahweh's choice of Israel established her covenant status. As such, as Christensen affirms,

"Israel's uniqueness is set over against YHWH's uniqueness"[13] (Deut 4:58, 32-38). The Yahweh who chose Israel into this unique relationship also gave her the Torah as the regulatory agent of the covenant relationship. But Israel's failure, largely described in the literature of the Former and Later Prophets, hampered the anticipated Deuteronomistic benefits from Yahweh. The tragedy of the deportation and Judah's demise which Ezekiel insisted, would occur, was consequent upon the failure on the part of "listening Israel" from intentional and self-conscious acts of discipline[14] in regards to the Torah.

4.2.1 Israel as a Nation Characterised by the Covenant Motif

The Sinai covenant followed on the Abrahamic covenant without which the birth of Israel is unlikely. Yahweh's *promise* of a unique nation and the possession of land was yet anticipated as seen in the use of the phrase ואעשׂך, "I will make you" (Gen 12:1-3). This promise was certified as a covenant (Gen 15:1, 4-5, 17-18) and later ratified by the sign of circumcision (Gen 17:1-8, 10-14). It is from this *promise* that Israel later officially became a nation after the Sinai covenanting event. However, consensus scholarly position on exactly when Israel became a nation is unlikely. While some hold that the nation was borne in the wilderness,[15] others think it was not until the giving of the law at Mt. Sinai.[16] Still, others posit that Israel became a full political entity only after the invasion, conquest and occupation of Canaan.[17] However, it is clear that the Sinai/Mosaic covenant,

---

13. Christensen, WBC, 74.
14. Brueggemann, *An Introduction to the Old Testament*, 24.
15. Bruce K. Waltke holds that "the birth of Israel as a nation" follows the "defining act of salvation" of God in the crossing of the Sea. He sees this act as God's creation of the nation, "…giving the nation birth by dividing the waters of the Red Sea." Waltke, *An Old Testament Theology*, 294-295.
16. John I. Durham posits that the nationhood of Israel began at Sinai when Israel willingly brought herself under the terms of Yahweh's covenant. He asserts, "an affirmative response to Yahweh's '"if"' on the part of the people of Israel will mean the birth of '"Israel"' as Yahweh's people. Without that affirmative response, indeed, there would have been only '"sons of Israel,"' the descendants of Jacob." John I. Durham, *Exodus: Word Biblical Commentary* (WBC 3; Dallas, Tex.: Word, 1987), 262.
17. Knauth holds that "the '"national"' history of the Israelites cannot be said to have begun until the Iron Age, when they gained sovereignty over a territory substantial enough

which represents "the constitution for the nation of Israel that grew out of Abraham's descendants,"[18] was given at Sinai to guide and regulate the socio-political and socio-religious life of this new nation.

Prior to the Sinai covenant, Yahweh's covenants with Israel's individual patriarchs had existed. As Kaiser Jr. points out, "previously, God had appeared to Abraham, Isaac, and Jacob in the character and nature of El Shaddai; but now He would manifest Himself as Yahweh by delivering Israel and leading her into the land He had sworn to give to the patriarchs."[19] Covenant is "one of the most important motifs in biblical theology,"[20] and it also serves "at the core of [divine] self-revelation;" for through it "God both reveals what he is like and obliges himself to a particular course of action."[21] Our understanding of formal national covenant motif in Israel should be rooted on the Abrahamic covenant. It is this covenant that served as the hub on which subsequent covenants stood and around which the entire life of national Israel revolved.

In keeping with this initial groundbreaking and foundational divine initiative, Yahweh "heard" the groaning of Abraham's descendants and delivered them from Egyptian oppression because he "remembered" the Abrahamic covenant (Exod 3:6-10). While we agree with Kaiser that for the author of Exodus, "the Sinaitic covenant was theologically and historically

---

to act as a '"nation.'" However, he acknowledges that Israel's self-acknowledgement of nationhood dates back to the presence of Jacob's family in Egypt. He explains that "the catalyzing event for their emergence into nationhood in this self-conception was the exodus from Egypt when Yahweh their God miraculously freed them from oppressive slavery." Knauth, "Israelites," 456. The Iron Age (1200 BC) falls within the generally accepted period for the exodus.

18. Grisanti, "The Davidic Covenant," 235. Grisanti contends that the Noahic, Abrahamic, Davidic, and the New covenant of Jeremiah are often called a "covenant of promise" or "grant" covenants, while the Mosaic covenant is likened to a "suzerain-vassal" treaty. He differentiates these thus: (1) In a grant, the giver of the covenant makes a commitment to the vassal, but in a treaty, the giver of the covenant imposes an obligation on the vassal; (2) A grant represents an obligation of the master to his vassal, but a treaty represents an obligation of the vassal to his master; (3) A grant primarily protects the rights of the vassal, but a treaty primarily protects the rights of the master; and (4) in a grant, there are no demands made by the superior party, whereas in a treaty, the master promises to reward or punish the vassal for obeying or disobeying the imposed obligations.

19. Kaiser, Jr., *Toward an Old Testament Theology*, 101.

20. Williamson, "Covenant," 419.

21. Hill and Walton, *A Survey of the Old Testament*, 2d ed., 21.

a continuation of the Abrahamic promise,"²² yet, Yahweh's covenanting with Israel at Sinai was a very unique event in its own right. It is crucial to the history of Israel because this is the only event where Yahweh entered into a communal covenant with national Israel, no longer on an individual basis as was the case previously. This experience gave birth to a new nation, the nation of Israel, in fulfilment of Yahweh's promise of "a great nation" to Abraham. Here at Sinai, Yahweh informed Moses he would enter into covenant with Israel that they might become his own possession among all peoples.²³ By this act, Yahweh laid upon the Abrahamic covenant the national covenant because the time was now ripped to fulfil the former.

Yahweh's covenanting with the liberated descendants of Abraham was crucially important to the political, sociological, ethical, and theological wellbeing of Yahweh's chosen people.²⁴ Arthur F. Glasser explains that following Yahweh's display of justice by delivering the Hebrews from their oppressors and his power over Egypt by overcoming them and parting the sea, the people still needed a more comprehensive revelation of God.²⁵ We think that this needed comprehensive self-revelation of Yahweh to the pilgrim community contributed in some sense to the people's experience of Yahweh's self-revelation in the Sinai covenanting event because here at Sinai, the people saw God in his glory and self-revelatory nature through the display of his majestic cosmic power on Sinai (Exod 19:16-19; Deut

---

22. Kaiser, Jr., *Toward an Old Testament Theology*, 101.
23. Lasor, Hubbard, and Bush, *Old Testament Survey*, 72. See Gen 12:1-3; 15:5; 17:6-7 for the Abrahamic covenant.
24. We think that Grisanti's reasoning is on the point when he states that the Sinai covenant functions as a formative background to Deuteronomic theology because it laid the foundation upon which the Davidic covenant would later function. As Grisanti claims, "God's establishment of His covenant with David represents one of the theological high points of the OT Scriptures. This key event builds on the preceding covenants and looks forward to the ultimate establishment of God's reign on the earth." He concludes on this point with the assertion that "the provisions of the Davidic Covenant represent part of the plan God has for His creation. As God set forth the various biblical covenants, each one represented a step forward in the revelation of God's intentions for the world. Rather than operating in distinct orbits or realms, each covenant builds on the preceding covenant or covenants. Each covenant introduces new elements to God's revelation of His plan and these elements become part of the multi-faceted tapestry of biblical covenants." Grisanti, "The Davidic Covenant," 233, 249-250.
25. Arthur F. Glasser, *Announcing the Kingdom: The Story of God's Mission in the Bible* (Grand Rapids, Mich.: Baker Academic, 2003; repr., 2008), 72.

5:23-31). Yahweh "manifested himself in awe-inspiring majesty"[26] to Israel. Such intimate self-disclosure consolidated the power Yahweh had demonstrated in the release from Egypt (Exod 12:29-36) and in the crossing of the Red Sea (Exod 14:13-31) of his redeemed people. This theophanic appearance by Yahweh revealed to Israel his nature of holiness demanding from her total obedience to the tripartite content of the Sinai covenant – the moral, ceremonial, and civil aspects of the law.

Primarily, Israelite society was to be predicated upon the principle of theocracy and its religion upon the principle of Yahwistic monotheism. Israel's national law and theology both operated upon these principles. As such, Geerhardus Vos stresses that the basic requirement for "Israel's retention of the privileges of the *berith* is made dependent on obedience."[27] This means that the Israelites needed to realise that the key condition for their "retention of the land was contingent upon their obedience to Yahweh's law"[28] given at Sinai. The nation's benefiting from Yahweh's blessings was equally contingent upon the same principle of obedience. Israel's obedience in consonance with Yahweh's expressed character qualities was the only ground for her reaping the benefits of blessings in the land. Bruce points to this when he submits that "Yahweh was a God who was not only incomparably powerful, but also incomparably righteous, merciful and true to his promises; and therefore men and women who were holy to him, reserved for him, must reproduce these qualities in their own life and conduct."[29]

In sum, the Sinai covenanting event fundamentally served as formative to the operation of Deuteronomic theology in Israel having Yahweh as its locus. Yahweh, who chose, saved, covenanted, and gave the Decalogue to Israel, also "Sets forth monotheism"[30] as his prescribed pattern of worship for the saved community. He had set total fidelity, loyalty, and unwavering devotion as his prescribed patterns of covenantal and religious obligations.

---

26. Lasor, Hubbard, and Bush, *Old Testament Survey*, 72. See Exod 19:16-18.
27. Geerhardus Vos, *Biblical Theology: Old and New Testaments* (Edinburgh: The Banner of Truth Trust, 1975; repr., 1996), 126-127.
28. Glasser, *Announcing the Kingdom*, 122.
29. Bruce, *Israel and the Nations*, 3.
30. Schultz and Smith, *Exploring the Old Testament*, 33.

4.2.2 Israel as a Nation Characterised by the Blessing Motif

The conceptual understanding of the theology of blessing for Israel is primarily located in the provision of Deuteronomy 28. This builds on the initial provision of the Abrahamic covenant (Gen 12:1-3). Yahweh pursued his *promised* offspring from Abraham through the monarchy, particularly resident in the Davidic tradition. With the Sinai covenant event now over and the Promised Land now conquered and occupied, a paradigm shift in leadership pattern circumstantially occurred in Israel. There was a change from the theocratic form of governance to the monarchical form at the demand of the people during Samuel's epoch (1 Sam 8:1-9). This shift suggests that theocracy is rejected in favour of the monarchy.[31] Given this unique development, the Davidic covenant tradition opened a new chapter in the continued history of Israel. In an affirmative and confirmatory fashion, this tradition emerged in Israel's history with the establishment of the Davidic dynasty and the choice of Zion as a place of divine residence and rule. The Davidic and Zion traditions served to achieve the purpose of the principle of continuity of divine presence, which Israel had experienced in the desert (cf. Exod 3:12; 13:20-21; 14:19-20). Such divine presence presupposes Yahweh's blessings for Israel.

The Davidic-Zion traditions have a fundamental historical background. Going by the Jebusites' theory, the existence and occupation of Zion hill predates Israel's occupation of Canaan. J. J. M. Robertson opines that dating the origin or formation of the "Zion tradition" can be explained most adequately by positing an original *Sitz im Leben* in the era of the Davidic-Solomonic empire.[32] At the formative stage of Israel's monarchy, David captured a small fortified city from the Jebusites called "the fortress of Zion,"[33] and changed the name from "the stronghold of Zion" to the "city

---

[31]. Leadership in Israel continued with the Judges after the Mosaic and Joshua's epochs. As Hess explains, some of the earliest leadership in Israel have been by Judges, a term derived from the West Semitic root *ṭpṭ*. This root is "used of an office of leadership as much as and more than that of a judicial figure. Its usage in the biblical Judges occurs as a charismatically appointed office, that is, one established and controlled by Yahweh rather than one that was hereditary." However, he notes, the people demanded a permanent leader: a king instead of a Judge. Hess, *Israelite Religion*, 226.

[32]. J. J. M. Roberts, "The Davidic Origin of the Zion Tradition," *SBL* (1973): 339-343.

[33]. W. Harold Mare, "Zion," *ABD* 6:1096.

of David."[34] Chad F. Emmett notes that, "once established as the capital of the kingdom of Israel, Jerusalem functioned as a royal capital under David and Solomon."[35] The origin of the Davidic covenant and dynastic tradition[36] is articulated in 2 Samuel 7 where David's intention to build Yahweh a house is set aside by the latter to give way to the establishment of his "lineage as the ruling line over God's chosen people."[37] This motif is replete in what scholars call "royal psalms,"[38] so designated for their sharing a common theme of kingship, both Davidic and Yahwistic.

The location and hill upon which Solomon built the great temple for Yahweh, known as Mt. Zion, has direct bearing on the concept of Zion theology in Israel's tradition. The historical root of this theology is predicated upon Yahweh's choice/election of the temple located in Zion as his abode (2 Chr 7), a choice not unconnected with the choice of the Davidic dynasty.[39] The existence of the temple signified for Israel Yahweh's consist-

---

34. Jon D. Levenson, "Zion Traditions," *ABD* 6:1098. See also 2 Samuel 5:7; 1 Chronicles 11:7-8 for David's conquering and renaming of the fortress called Zion.

35. Chad F. Emmett, "The Capital Cities of Jerusalem," *GR* 2 (April 1996):233-258.

36. David had earnestly desired to build a befitting shrine for the God of Israel that was in no way to be compared to his palace, but his desire was halted by God himself who gave him an established dynasty instead, followed with a covenant to establish his house, kingdom, and throne till eternity (2 Sam 7:1-17). This part of the covenant that concerns an established kingdom forever was perpetuated through Solomon's reign (2 Chr 7:17-20) and finally found its fulfilment in Christ's kingship (Matt 1:1-17; Luke 1:31-33; cf. Acts 2:29-32; 13:33-34; 15:14-17; Heb 1:5; 5:5; Rev 19:16). Disobedience on the part of David's descendants could only attract divine chastisement not annulment of the kingdom because the Davidic covenant is irrevocable.

37. Grisanti, "The Davidic Covenant," 236. See 2 Sam 7:8-16.

38. Royal psalms such as Pss 2; 18; 20; 21; 45; 72; 89; 101; 110; and 144 draw heavily on the idea of a Davidic dynasty. In his discussion of the use of particular Psalms in temple rituals, Kafang notes that each of the Psalms was chosen and sung because of "certain appropriate phrases, words, or for particular occasion." Zamani Buki Kafang, *The Psalms: An Introduction to their Poetry* (Kaduna, Nigeria: Baraka, 2002), 134

39. The choice of the royal seat finds expression in the royal psalms sung by the Israelite society. Levenson argues that "it is probable that the idea in the royal theology that the house of David was chosen for kingship is the mother of the idea of Zion's election." Levenson, "Zion Traditions," 1100. In this connection, William Lee Holladay, in his discussion of the royal psalms and other related psalms that have their origin in the monarchical era, submits that the liturgical use of such psalms evoked Yahweh's blessings and protection on the king as well as affirmed Yahweh's leadership and mighty presence in the city as "Yahweh Sabaoth." He concludes that the theological core of these pre-exilic psalms is Yahweh, Israel's God, who chose David and to dwell in Zion in Jerusalem. William Lee Holladay, *The Psalms Through Three Thousand Years* (Minn.: Augsburg, 1993;

ent presence with both his people and the city. Therefore, basic to the tenets of Zion theology in Jewish tradition is *kingship* and *presence*, all having the city of Jerusalem, the Temple in Jerusalem, and the Davidic kingship in Jerusalem as its focal point. All these are inseparably tied to Israel's theological confession about the city because "Zion is God's city, and Yahweh is God of the city."[40] By implication, continued divine blessings resided in the city for the people's benefit.

Ezekiel calls to mind this significant tradition in Jewish history when he made reference to it in his use of the shepherd motif. Looking into the future of a restored Israel, he reports Yahweh as saying, "I will place over them one shepherd, my servant David, and he will tend them; he will tend them and be their shepherd" (Ezek 34:23 NIV). Ezekiel's use of the phrase, "my servant David" (Ezek 34:23, 24; 37:24), "he will tend them" (Ezek 34:23), and "will be king over them" (Ezek 37:24) is quite significant. Such references allude to David's faithful observance of the Deuteronomic code as Yahweh's faithful human shepherd. This thought is also referred to by the Chronicler when he reports Yahweh as saying to Solomon, "As for you, if you walk before me as David your father did, and do all I command, and observe my decrees and laws, I will establish your royal throne, as I covenanted with David your father when I said, 'You shall never fail to have a man to rule over Israel'" (2 Chr 7:17-18 NIV). Yahweh's election

---

paperback ed., 1996), 17-66. It is on the strength of the legitimisation of the election of David and Zion/Jerusalem that led Kafang to the assertion that the psalmist's "reference to Jerusalem cannot be overlooked." He argues the point further that Jerusalem is the seat of government; it is the political, religious and commercial centre in the land; it became the centre where all sacrifices were offered; and it is from Jerusalem that blessing pours forth, for in it all the members of Israel have their citizenship. "Thus[,] to be able to dwell in Jerusalem, the Temple, Zion where God's glory dwells, deserves the psalmist's thanksgiving and jubilation." Kafang, *The Psalms*, 141.

40. Goldingay, *Psalms Vol. II: Psalm 42-89*, 93. According to Brueggemann, "The Jerusalem temple served as a *magnet* that drew into itself, comprehended, and appropriated all of the antecedent liturgical traditions of Israel...the *engine* that continued to power and structure Israel's liturgical imagination." He holds that it seems clear from the "Songs of Zion" (Pss 46; 48; 76; 84; 87; 122) and the enthronement psalms (Pss 47; 93; 96-99) that Jerusalem worship tradition "reflect the older notion of a sacred mountain that was the residence of God," a place of his divine presence as king; for "the notion of Yahweh as king apparently was central for the Jerusalem temple...the Jerusalem liturgy celebrated the kingship of Yahweh." Brueggemann, *The Theology of the Old Testament*, 654, 655.

of the Davidic dynasty and Zion historically and theologically stand as a prominent motif affirming his promise to Abraham. His presence in the temple has its root in the Exodus Event that culminated finally in the establishment of the Sinai covenant. This reflects Deuteronomic theology, its requirements of which Israel was obligated to keep in order to guarantee her continuous benefiting from Yahweh's blessings of provision and safety.

4.3 The Implications of Deuteronomic Theology for Exilic Israel[41]

The hub of Deuteronomic theology is Yahweh. This suggests that two things are crucial to Israel's existence – Israel's continuous loyalty and obedience to Yahweh and his continuous presence with Israel in the land. The theology of Yahweh's presence goes back to his dealings with the patriarchs. His presence was with Abraham, Isaac, and Jacob. His presence was equally with Joseph in a foreign land. Kaiser explains that the theophany and epiphanies experienced by the patriarchs at different times underscores "The reality of the living God's presence . . . All three patriarchs experienced the impact of God's presence on their lives."[42] This motif of *presence* finds a stronger expression in Jewish tradition following Moses' hesitation to Yahweh's assigning him to be a shepherd when it was time for Yahweh to deliver his oppressed people from Egyptian slavery (Exod 3:7-22; 4:1-17). Moses' hesitation and excuses should be taken to mean the feeling of incompetence and of seeking assurance from Yahweh rather than an act of rebellion. Yahweh's reassuring speech in the assertion that his presence would go with him (Exod 3:12; 33:14-15; 13:21-22) was to dispel his hesitation and fears. A similar reassuring speech was repeated to Joshua who had to take over the leadership of the people on their march to inherit

---

41. Our treatment of Deuteronomic theology, following its historical trend, is exclusive to Judah. While the Northern Kingdom of Israel also went into exile just as the Southern Kingdom did, our treatment stays with Judah where the events of Ezekiel are located. For a treatment of the Assyrian exile as affecting the North, see the article "The Deportations of the Israelites" by K. Lawson Younger, Jr., *JBL* 2 (1998):201-227.
42. Kaiser, Jr., *Toward an Old Testament Theology*, 85. See Gen 12:7; 17:1; 18:1; 26:2-5, 24; 35:1, 7, 9.

the Promised Land after Moses' demise. The narrator of the book of Joshua reports Yahweh as saying, "As I was with Moses, so I will be with you" (Josh 1:5 NIV).

Yahweh's consistent presence with Israel was always in keeping with his promise to Abraham. His presence with Israel was clearly demonstrated during their sojourning in Egypt, particularly in the ten mighty acts that preluded the Exodus Event (Exod 7:8-13:16). Yahweh also demonstrated his continuous presence with the people in their travel through the Sinai Peninsula and the desert until they settled in Canaan. For instance, he went with them in the pillars of cloud and fire (Exod 13:21-22) and in their many wars (Exod 17:8-13). Yahweh's numerous provisions to meet their need of food (Exod 16:13-36), water (Exod 15:22-27), and security (Exod 14:5-31), were also in demonstration of his divine presence. Most significantly was the erection of the tabernacle in the wilderness, an event that signalled that Israel's deity had come to dwell in the midst of the people (Exod 29:43-46). Kaiser affirms that "Yahweh's divine presence was so central and significant in the Mosaic era" that forms such as the "face," "appearance," or "presence" of the Lord, his "glory," the "angel of the Lord," and his "name" are used to speak of it.[43] Because of its crucial role in Israel's history and in biblical theology, the theology of divine presence is extended into the New Testament era.[44]

However, the experience of exile by the people had cast doubts on Israel's traditional understanding of the theology of Yahweh's presence. This event raised a number of concerns in the minds of the Babylonian exiles as to what might have happened with Yahweh. To these concerns we now turn.

---

43. Kaiser, Jr., *Toward an Old Testament Theology*, 120.

44. The theology of presence also finds connection with some key events in the New Testament. The ascended Christ had promised that his presence would be with his disciples. After his resurrection and meeting with them in Galilee (Matt 28:10), he gave the command for global evangelization with a promise as reported by Matthew, "And surely I am with you always, to the very end of the age" (Matt 28:20b NIV; cf. Acts 1:8; John 15:5). Christ's presence was with the early church in its persecution; first, by the Jews (Acts 3-8; 12:1-19; 16:16-40), and second, by the Romans (Rev 1-3). That the church has survived the onslaughts of its enemies throughout its history is a testimony to the theology of Christ's presence in and with his church (cf. Matt 16:17-19).

4.3.1 Exile Questions the Reality of Yahweh's Covenant

Israel understood exile in terms of a total disaster. The event of exile brought to question the reality of Yahweh's covenant with the nation he called his own. In Yahweh's personification of Jerusalem and the drama of Israel's bereavement within the context of pain, Knut Heim aptly captures the agony of the exiles:

> While the basic structure of the community remains intact, the individual can always find help in the religious and social institutions of the nation. But when society as a whole breaks down, nobody is left for the individual to turn to, and the normal structures of social security have disappeared . . . Thus when disaster strikes a whole community, pain is elevated to a different and more complex level.[45]

When we interpret this expressed idea in the light of the Babylonian exile, we readily see that exile posed a great threat to the continued existence of the Abrahamic covenant of an enduring descendant.

In his self-revelatory acts through the events of history, Yahweh chose Abraham to father a family that would become a channel of blessings to all peoples of the earth.[46] And from this point forward, he related with Israel in covenant terms. If Yahweh's covenant with Abraham is the possession of enduring descendants and a land (Gen 12:2-3, 6-7; 15:1, 5-7, 13-14; 17:1-8), what went wrong that Yahweh now supposedly neglected this covenant principle to allow for the painful experience of exile by Abraham's descendants? Ralph Klein describes the loses that Israel suffered as a result of exile thus: "Exilic Israel . . . was a defeated nation that had lost its independence, its land, its monarchy, and its temple . . . Exile meant a host

---

45. Knut M. Heim, "The Personification of Jerusalem and the Drama of Her Bereavement in Lamentations," in *Zion, City of Our God* (eds. Richard S. Hess and Gordon J. Wenham; Grand Rapids, Mich.: Eerdmans, 1999), 130.
46. "The covenant God made with Abraham (Gen 15:12-21) guaranteed him a land, descendants, and blessing. The promises of this covenant were repeated to his descendants at various times." Thomas L. Constable, "1 Kings," in *The Bible Knowledge Commentary: Old Testament Edition* (eds. John F. Walvoord and Roy B. Zuck; America: SP Publications, 1985; repr., 1987), 485.

of physical and socio-economic problems"[47] to Israel. Quite enigmatic and traumatic for Israel was the destruction of the temple, not by natural disaster but worst of all, by Gentiles whom the Jews understood in terms of Godless peoples (cf. Eph 2:1-3, 11-12). Klein explains the ugly scenario of the destruction of the temple thus: ". . . the temple was a tangible symbol of the people's election and a reminder of God's unfailing actions in history on their behalf. [But now the] temple had gone up in flames, and enemies had raced through the sanctuary."[48] Such unimaginable and unexpected disaster would naturally make the exiles reflect on Yahweh's covenant commitment, forcing on them the critical questions, "Is God unjust to Israel?" and "Has God rejected Israel?" (cf. Rom 9-11).

The Israelites interpreted recent events in their history – the demise of the temple with its priesthood, the sacking of the land and lastly the exile – as divine abandonment. Maeeray Shreibe rightly observes that embedded within the concept of exile is the "consequence of a profound severing of the relation between God and the people of Israel," a people torn from the Temple and from the presence of Yahweh in Zion. For "God's absence or perilous distance makes for a condition of chronic loss that becomes the subject of binding song."[49] We can not doubt that "Ezekiel was in fact prophesying of but not to Jerusalem,"[50] for his primary audience was the Judean exiles as he himself was "a prophet to the exiles"[51] who was living among them. Consequent upon the effects of recent events in Judah, the growing apprehension in Ezekiel's audience constituted a reversal of national belief in the Abrahamic covenant and in the provisions of the Mosaic covenant of Yahweh's continued covenant faithfulness.

Both the exiles and the Jerusalem remnants had a dashed hope in the reality of Yahweh's presence and of the survival of the Davidic dynasty. The exiles queried how Yahweh could allow such a tragedy to befall his

---

47. Ralph W. Klein, *Israel in Exile: A Theological Interpretation* (Philadelphia: Fortress, 1979), 3.
48. Klein, *Israel in Exile*, 3.
49. Maeeray Y. Shreibe, "The End of Exile: Jewish Identity and Its Diasporic Poetics," *MLA* 2 (1998):273-287.
50. Ellison, *Ezekiel*, 20.
51. Bruce M. Metzger and Roland E. Murphy1057.

people. In particular, they queried the authenticity of the "hope principle" in Ezekiel's prophecy to a people destitute of their land, Temple, priests, and kings. How convincing was Ezekiel's claim that their momentary pain was to achieve for Israel "a new generation for the return that God had promised when the seventy years had run their course?"[52] This is a situation Isaiah had foreseen, as Robert Chisholm explains, "the exiles were discouraged by their situation and sceptical about their future prospect. Some apparently thought the Lord was no longer interested in their plight, while others even suggested that He had treated them unfairly."[53] On these warrants, exile stood as a threat because it meant, for the exiles, the weakening of Zion theology, and by implication, the demise of the Abrahamic, Sinai, and Davidic covenants. These are issues too difficult to come to terms with for the Babylonian exiles.[54]

The reality of Yahweh's covenant with Israel was brought to question following the exile because Israel had always understood herself in relationship to Yahweh and the theology of the Sinai covenant in terms of his self-revelation. But herein lies the dilemma. If Israel could still experience exile despite divine revelation to the patriarchs, to the nation at Sinai, and to David in his election, then it was unlikely that Yahweh's covenants and promises for the elect nation were still operative. Such concern is predicated on two factors – the loss by Israel of Jerusalem and of the temple, and the loss of Yahweh's presence[55] in the land promised to the patriarchs.

---

52. Ellison, *Ezekiel*, 21.
53. Chisholm, Jr., "A Theology of Isaiah," 323. See Isa 40:27; 41:17; 49:14).
54. Exilic experience not only threatened the existence of Israel but also shook its theological foundation in their covenant relationship with Yahweh. Ellison asserts, for instance, that "true theology…must be based on God's self-revelation" because he disclosed himself to Moses as "I am the God of your father, the God of Abraham, the God of Isaac and the God of Jacob." Yahweh is "I AM WHO I AM" (Exod 3:6, 14). See Ellison, "The Theology of the Old Testament," 55. Robert Gordon also rightly observes that "no event in the later history of Israel can rank with the Exodus deliverance from Egypt or with the making of the Sinaitic covenant. No other book in the OT is so important as Exodus for the understanding of the vocation and destiny of the people of Israel." See Gordon, "Exodus," 149.
55. It is clear that the presence of Yahweh with His people is tied to the temple and the city of Zion/Jerusalem. To lose both, as it were, is crucial because at the crest of Zion theology is markedly Yahweh's presence; for it stands as its nerve centre–Yahweh is in the midst of his people in Jerusalem his city and in the temple his holy shrine.

4.3.2 Exile Questions the Reality of Yahweh's Status

Hitherto, Israel had always understood Yahweh as the most powerful of all deities. But the turn of events in recent times cast doubt on this traditional understanding. That Israel's revered monument, the temple, unbelievably goes up in flames, questions Yahweh's power to protect his people and his shrine. The question for Israel is not so much 'where is God when it hurts?' but 'is Israel's Yahweh now that powerless and a weakling not to defend his holy shrine and to protect his people from the caprice of human assault?' Accordingly, Klein notes that this loathsome and memorable historic event of "... the temple's destruction called God into question: either there were deities stronger than or superior to Yahweh, or for some reason Yahweh had rejected his own people and his place."[56] As a consequence, exile brought to a close the conceptual tradition of the Davidic dynasty. Besides, exile had equally abrogated the promise of land in the patriarchal tradition and caused the decimation of the priesthood and the cessation of sacrifices, thereby clearly indicating the weakness of Yahweh's reign and the erosion of all his promises to Israel. That the temple is no more, the Davidic dynasty and Zion are now an illusion, and the priesthood with its priestly functions are non-existent, would certainly shake the foundation of Israel's conceptual understanding of "covenant theology."[57]

Israel's exilic experience equally called into question the historicity of Yahweh's display of power in behalf of the nation in the Exodus Event and the occupation of land accounts. For instance, the exiles might have called to memory Yahweh's display of power that achieved for Israel her liberation from the caprice of Pharaoh following the death of the first born of Egypt (Exod 14:5-9, 13-14, 23-28; cf. 12:29-30). They also might have called to memory Yahweh's power displayed in the crossing of the Red Sea (Exod 14:15-22) and of the River Jordan (Josh 3). Still, the exiles might have called to memory Yahweh's power displayed in the earth swallowing up Korah and his rebellious party (Num 16), and in the fall of the city of Jericho (Josh 5:13-6:22). Particularly, the victory of Israel in the battle with the Amalekites (Exod 17:8-14) and that won by Joshua over the

---

56. Klein, *Israel in Exile*, 4.
57. Raitt, *A theology of Exile*, 92.

coalition of five Amorite kings (Josh 10:1-28), would have automatic come to memory. In this battle, the sun, against every principle of natural law, stood still. God "stopped the cataclysmic effects that would have naturally occurred . . . [and compelled the] principal deities among the Canaanites . . . to obey."[58] These were some of the historic events that vividly revealed to Israel Yahweh's sovereign power over human might and over cosmic order. But exile forced on Yahweh the question whether the display of such powers was only circumstantial or was to be continuous. If Israel's Yahweh was powerful only to this point, then the experience of exile "at this point of greatest severity," as Raitt observes, raises further questions: "Is the covenant '"broken"' in the sense that it can be said that a covenant relationship no longer exists between God and his people? Is the election of Israel by God reversed so that they become his rejected people, or suspended so that they are, at least for a time, abandoned or forsaken?"[59]

Ironical for the exiles was how their powerful deity, whom they had known in history as great and mighty, would condescend to the level of allowing a Babylonian king to usurp his power, to molest him and abuse his elect people, his elect land, and his elect shrine. As Chisholm observes, "being under the control of the mighty Babylonian Empire, some were tempted to acknowledge the superiority of the Babylonians' gods and to worship their images. Perhaps the God of Israel was only a local deity who, because of geographical limitations, was unable to deliver them from Babylon."[60] To the exiles, they reasoned, how is it possible that human power had successfully dislodged Yahweh, if not for weakness? Does Yahweh still remain a supreme deity above the pantheon of deities of the surrounding nations?

These queries were critical to the exiles. Prior to the Babylonian deportation, Israel had consistently confessed the great power of Yahweh. The Song of the Sea is a clear case in which Israel confessed, "Your right hand, O LORD, was majestic in power. Your right hand, O LORD, shattered the enemy . . . Who among the gods is like you, O LORD? Who is like you

---

58. Donald K. Campbell, "Joshua," in *The Bible Knowledge Commentary: Old Testament Edition* (eds. John F. Walvoord and Roy B. Zuck; America: SP Publications, 1985; repr., 1987), 351.
59. Raitt, *A theology of Exile*, 59.
60. Chisholm, Jr., "A Theology of Isaiah," 323.

– majestic in holiness, awesome in glory, working wonders?"[61] The contest between Yahweh and Baal on Mt. Carmel is yet another display of Yahweh's power where the Israelites also cried, "The LORD – he is God! The LORD – he is God!"[62] Accordingly, the psalmists frequently confessed Yahweh's power exhibited in Israel's history (see for example, Pss 20:6; 66:3; 77:14; 145:6; 147:5; 150:2). Given such great confession of Yahweh's might and greatness, the exile for Israel, was an awful negation and an unfortunate usurpation of the power of her deity. According to Brueggemann, such feeling arose against the backdrop that hitherto, pre-exilic Israel had had a "deep confidence that the God of [their] core testimony, when active in power and fidelity, can prevent and overcome such intolerable life experiences." But as things turned out, exilic "Israel finds that life without the active force of Yahweh is not good," and she is left to fate and therefore wonders "if Yahweh's power and fidelity are operative."[63]

Given Israel's exilic experience, "Ezekiel provided a theological framework for accepting a total disaster with unbroken faith." He sought "to interpret the main outline of historical events in "theological" terms"[64] as he understood it. In Ezekiel's theological thought, it is sometimes good for Israel that Yahweh chooses to allow his divine power to lie low for human power and those of other deities to prevail. Its import is so that perhaps human Israel would acknowledge from historic events, how helpless, vulnerable, and miserable she is without Yahweh. The motivation is so she would learn to always live life according to Yahweh's revealed moral laws. Exilic Israel ought to have learned by now that human decisions, whether made individually or collectively and whether rightly or wrongly, good or bad, always lead to inevitable consequences. People must always reap what they have sown and must live up to what they have done.

---

61. See Exod 14:31-15:20, especially 15:6, 11; cf Hannah's prayer of veneration in 1 Sam 2:1-21.
62. See 1 Kgs 18:30-39. Also compare the experience of King Jehoshaphat where Yahweh fought a crucial battle on Israel's behalf to show the nation the simple principle of trust in their God and of the importance of consistent obedience to him (2 Chr 20:1-30).
63. Brueggemann, *The Theology of the Old Testament*, 321.
64. Raitt, *A Theology of Exile*, 106.

4.3.3 Exile Questions the Traditional Belief in Israel's Existence

The Babylonian exile was obviously an extremely disastrous experience for Judah. With this crucial moment staring exilic Israel in the eye, "Israel asks and wonders about Yahweh's reliability and fidelity"[65] in view of her threatened existence by exile. The Babylonian exile affected every aspect of Israel's national life.[66] As such, the exiles were deeply concerned because of their inherent feeling of nationalism.[67]

When the exiles put recent events in Judah in retrospect, all they could see was only a bleak future for the nation, if any at all. Klein explains this implication for the nation:

> . . . almost all of the old symbolic systems . . . [had been] rendered useless. Almost all of the old institutions no longer functioned. What kind of future was possible for a people which traced its unique election to a God who had just lost a war to other deities? What kind of future was possible for a people who had so alienated their God that categorical rejection was his necessary response? Israel's responses to exile reflect the immensity of the disaster.[68]

---

65. Brueggemann, *The Theology of the Old Testament*, 322.
66. In his review of the book by Oded Lipschits, Rainer Albertz agrees with the author that "Judah lost a lot of people through death, starvation and flight; it lost most of its elite through deportation; and, although its new administrative centre was established in Benjamin, it lost its largest urban centre, Jerusalem." Rainer Albertz, "A Response to Oded Lipschits, The Fall and Rise of Jerusalem: Judah Under Babylonian Rule," *JHS* 2, 6. The reviewed book is: Oded Lipschits, *The Fall and Rise of Jerusalem* (Winona Lake, Ind.: Eisenbrauns, 2005). This book is based on Lipschits' PhD thesis which was presented to the senate of Tel Aviv University in January 1997, under the supervision of Prof. Nadav Na'aman.
67. Deryck C. T. Sheriffs defines the concept of nationalism as an ideology that "consciously attempts to transcend tribalism. It is not the ideology of separate clans, tribes, villages or cities as such, but an ideology which attempts to unify these elements in a greater whole, the nation." He explains in this respect that "The capital city therefore plays a special role in the rituals of nationalism ancient and modern, normally being the place where the ruler is invested and acclaimed." See "'A Tale of Two Cities'–Nationalism in Zion and Babylon," *TB* 39 (1988):21-22.
68. Klein, *Israel in Exile*, 5.

Does the occurrence of recent events in Judah mean therefore that Israel had reached her end and was now disappearing from the scene of history since she had been eclipsed by exile? The question of existence was a crucial part of exilic reflection. The feeling of despair stands as one of the key factors for the exile's apprehension and refusal to give ears to Ezekiel.

Two factors would have naturally triggered the concern and fear of extinction in the Judean exiles. First was Israel's understanding of her possession of the Land. Yahweh had promised the gift of a good Land to Abraham's seed, which he later fulfilled with Israel's occupation of Canaan. The event of ". . . The invasion and inheritance by Israel of the Land promised their forefathers" is said to be an event where ". . . the people and the land were brought together," an act that ". . . recognized the importance of the Land in God's purposes, and its importance to God's people."[69] Such an intimate connection to land shows that an Israelite without land was seen as an outcast, one worst than an alien. The loss of such a treasure on the part of national Israel was therefore tantamount to her death as an ethnic group and as a political entity. This attachment to land indicates that the Promised Land is itself Israel, and Israel is herself the Promised Land; for you cannot divorce the one, yet, have the other. James McKeown explains the importance of land, particularly to Israel: "The acquisition of the Promised Land, while not explicitly described as return to Edenic bliss, gives Israel the rest and security that was endemic to paradise. This rest is not just understood in the negative sense of no longer needing to wander but also denotes security and safety from one's enemies."[70] If such is the case, McKeown points out that for Israel to consistently experience an existing inseparable possession of the land, she needed to sustain "a harmonious relationship" with Yahweh because "The relationship between land and its inhabitants is contingent on good relations between humans and God."[71]

---

69. John Lilley, "Joshua," in *The New International Bible Commentary* (2d ed.; ed. F. F. Bruce (Grand Rapids, Mich.: Marshall Morgan & Scott, 1986), 283.

70. James McKeown, "Land, Fertility, Famine," in *Dictionary of the Old Testament: Pentateuch* (eds. T. Desmond Alexander and David W. Baker; Downers Grove, Ill.: InterVarsity, 2003), 489.

71. McKeown, "Land, Fertility, Famine," 489.

Another factor that moved the exiles to raise the concern of extinction for national Israel lay in their fear of theological and ethical defilement of the Jewish race. Should this fear become a reality, it would result in national disillusion, as had been experienced in the invasion, deportation, and repopulation of the Northern Kingdom in the recent past. After its existence between 931-722 BC, the Northern Kingdom of the formerly united Israel ceased to exist as a national entity following the Assyrian captivity.[72] The demise of Samaria would have naturally raised the question of existence in the historical reflection of the Babylonian exiles as they grappled with the issue whether their captivity now meant a repeat of history for Judah. A high possibility therefore does exist that if all the Judean kings were good shepherds as Yahweh's regents, this anthropological torture on the part of the Babylonian exiles would have been unnecessary. But Judah is now in exile and her deported citizens are being tortured psychologically, ethically, socially, politically, and theologically because of the many losses that Judah had suffered in the recent past. Martin G. Klingbeil explains such traumatic torture caused by exile as a state of being "in the form of a departure from the individual's or people's known environment, their homeland, the shattering of the harmonious relationship between humanity and land, the rupturing of social ties, including humiliation, often violence and always loss of possession."[73]

---

72. Constable reports that the Assyrian policy towards conquered lands was "to deport many of the most influential inhabitants and then import many leading Assyrians to take their places." It is to be noted that "contamination" is a taboo in Israel's religious thought. Constable notes that the historical events in 2 Kgs 17:24-33 shows how the Samaritan people came into being. That being a racially mixed breed of Israelites and various other ANE people, full blooded Jews despised them. One reason perhaps, that accounts for Jesus' several references to the Samaritans in his teachings, was to diffuse this long-standing hostility and rivalry that had existed between the Jews and the Samaritans. Constable supposes that the possibility also exists that the Samaritans were the pure descendants of the Israelites who remained in the land. Constable, "1 Kings," 570-572. The citizens of Samaria were sent to various parts of the Assyrian Empire like the town of Halah and various towns of the Medes northeast of Nineveh. Martin postulates that the purpose of this "…new practice of resettling conquered lands…provided for gradual mixing of race and the erosion of national desire to revolt," and was a practice that led not only to the collapse but also to the extinction of the Northern Kingdom. Martin, "1 and 2 Kings," 434.

73. Klingbeil, "Exile," 248.

The present predicament of Judah forced the exiles to raise the critical questions: Has Judah finally lost her land and city? Has the priesthood gone with the temple and therefore worship of Yahweh is no more? Does the demise of Jerusalem mean the loss of Israel's identity as Yahweh's elect people, and by extension, the extinction of the Jewish race? These were very critical and legitimate concerns that needed urgent attention, and Ezekiel was on hand to address the situation. Against all expectations, his response has eschatological rather than a political motif.

4.4 Ezekiel's Eschatological Response to the Exiles

For those who argue against the reality of the Jewish deportation to Babylon, sufficient internal data confirming this event (Ezek 1:1-3; 2 Kgs 24:10-17; Jer 24:1-10; 52:28) would easily dislodge such thinking. That "Prophetic faith interprets history from a theological perspective"[74] is no doubt a correct assertion. In Jewish prophetism, prophetic oracles moved back and forth between the past and the present events while some project into the future. This is what we see Ezekiel doing in his prophetic speeches to the Judean deportees. It is these deportees that Ezekiel addressed ". . . with his radical pastoral concern."[75]

We readily deduce from the oracular speeches of the book of Ezekiel that nothing happens without a cause. Every cause has an effect. The book reveals that historic events carry lessons and profitable messages when properly decoded. Ezekiel shows that the Babylonian exile holds some very significant theological lessons for Judah and the Judeans, both at home and away from home. As George Barton correctly notes,

> Perhaps no single event in Hebrew history influenced her religion more deeply than the Babylonian exile. Of course the exodus from Egypt and the covenant with Yahweh were more fundamental, but the Babylonian exile helped more

---

74. Raitt, *A Theology of Exile*, 1.
75. Brueggemann, *An Introduction to the Old Testament*, 192.

than any succeeding event to bring these earlier events to their legitimate spiritual fruitage.[76]

If the Egyptian bondage and Yahweh's deliverance earlier experienced by Israel holds significant theological lessons, the Babylonian bondage just opens yet another chapter in Israel's history of theological lessons. With Ezekiel in Babylon, not as a visiting tourist or as a political diplomat, not even as a hired spiritualist to the ruling monarch or monarchy but as a fugitive, how does he see the theological import of exile as he responded to the possibly myriad concerns raised by his fellow Babylonian exiles?

Ezekiel's theological foundation and his use of Deuteronomic theology sprang from his membership and participation in the Zadokite priesthood in Jerusalem (Ezek 1:1-3; 44:15-31). Stephen Cook explains the presupposition of this theology as held by the Zadokites:

> These Jerusalem priests were proponents of "Zion theology," the tradition that emphasized God's choice of Jerusalem as Zion, the holy city, and the protection for Jerusalem that resulted from this choice (2 Sam 7:4-17; Ps 46; 132). These traditions also stressed God's unconditional choice of the Davidic monarchy and of Abraham's descendants.[77]

As one who belonged in this tradition before his forceful ejection into captivity, Ezekiel's critique of Judah, while it is based on the principles of this theology, is eclipsed by the rays of Deuteronomic theology.

It is quite obvious as Klingbeil rightly observes that the basic cause of exile is "the breakage of the covenant relationship as caused by an act of disobedience with regards to the precepts of the law."[78] The Decalogue, the initial legal foundation that brought Israel into her political and theological existence, was abused by her total disregard for the covenant obligations

---

76. George A. Barton, "Influence of the Babylonian Exile on the Religion of Israel," *BW* 6 (1911):378.
77. Stephen L. Cook, "Ezekiel," in *The New Oxford Annotated Bible* (3d ed.; eds. Michael D. Coogan et al.; Oxford, N.Y.: Oxford University Press, 2001), 1181.
78. Klingbeil, "Exile," 246-248.

clearly defined by its legal provisions. As a consequence, she must suffer for this act. Duguid holds that Israel did not simply lose land but she lost the Lord's presence with her. He explains that "the exile was not simply a historical event, however; it had profound theological significance . . . life could not simply return to the way it was before. How could there be joy when all that was sacred and precious had been defiled and destroyed by the invaders."[79] This was quite crucial to the people's political and theological survival. From Ezekiel's perspective, the Babylonian exile held for Israel, though in disguised form, several benefits among which are its punitive, preservative and restorative purposes. The core aim of these benefits was in order to correct the nation's paradigm shift in Yahwism as their religious confession.

4.4.1 Exile Has a Punitive Purpose Preparatory for Eschatological Shepherding

It is clear from the text of Ezekiel that the principle of individual accountability assumes that "the soul who sins is the one who will die" (Ezek 18:4, 20). The reason is as Paul asserts, "the wages of sin is [always] death" (Rom 6:23; 3:23). Ezekiel saw in the experience of exile a punitive purging of Israel's sin of covenant disobedience as well as punishment for her departure from monotheism as required for Yahwistic religion. Consequent upon the nation's persistent infidelity against Yahweh despite his consistent fidelity to Israel on the basis of his covenant, the prophet painstakingly made clear that the basic theological lesson of Judah's present predicament was an indication that covenant infidelity attracts divine retribution. He argued that Yahweh had removed his presence from the people because of their persistent sin[80] and refusal to return to him, an action confirmed by the people's rebellious and obstinate attitude (Ezek 1:2-3; 2:5-8; 3:9, 26-27; 12:2-3, 9, 25; 17:12; 24:3; 44:6). Thomas Renz points to this when he observes that both Israel and the land had been polluted by sin, and "by polluting land and sanctuary, sin jeopardise[d] God's presence." He

---

79. Duguid, "Exile," 475-478.
80. Jerry M. Hullinger, "The Divine Presence, Uncleanness, and Ezekiel's Millennial Sacrifices," BS 163 (2006):406.

makes clear that because of this jeopardy, deportation is not so much the punishment but "death: in the city, in flight, and in exile . . . [because] Rebellion against God leads to death."[81] Ezekiel's effort in this regard was to "convince the people of their utter unworthiness of any consideration from God, in order to shame them into true repentance."[82] He drummed into their ears their need to claim responsibility for the exile instead of blaming it on God who, in fact, had been very patient, compassionate, merciful and considerate with their rebellious attitude. The people's refusal to consent to his message forced on him to employ symbolism, perhaps they would reason and listen to what Yahweh was saying through him.

They seemed to have forgotten that Israel's covenant status was no insulation against divine punitive action for their sin of covenant disloyalty and religious adultery. Against this backdrop, someone had to remind the exiles that the sin of covenant disloyalty was the cause of the Babylonian captivity. The person who best qualified to assume this task of reminding, and in fact, of confronting the exiles with the theological truth is none other than Ezekiel who himself was one of the exiles. Both Ezekiel and Jeremiah his close contemporary confronted Israel's sin of covenant disloyalty headlong. Given such a difficult task, Raitt observes that these two prophets faced a harder theological task. He explains this difficulty:

> Jeremiah and Ezekiel went through the searchings of Job, but they had to make their answer understandable to a whole nation. Jeremiah's and Ezekiel's Oracles of Judgment were more painful to utter than even those of Amos, the most noted "prophet of doom," because Jeremiah and Ezekiel delivered their oracles in the actual existential situation of Judah's demise. Similarly, Jeremiah's and Ezekiel's Oracles of Deliverance required deeper faith and hope in the future than those enunciated by Second Isaiah, the most famous "prophet of salvation," because Jeremiah and Ezekiel promised salvation

---

81. Thomas Renz, "Ezekiel, Book of," in *Dictionary for Theological Interpretation of the Bible* (ed. Kevin J. Vanhoozer et al.; Grand Rapids, Mich.: Baker, 2005; repr., 2006), 218-223.
82. Taylor, *Ezekiel*, 42.

when there was as yet no historical hint that such a turn of events could become an actuality.[83]

The exiled Judeans did not clearly see in the exile what Ezekiel saw, understand what Ezekiel understood, and accept what Ezekiel accepted about their exilic experience. Instead, they were "very sore about it,"[84] refusing even to share with the Babylonians songs they had sung to Yahweh in Zion (Ps 137). It is quite understandable then why apprehension and resistance built up against Ezekiel's message, thereby forcing him to become a "suffering servant" through personal participation in the agony of exile to redirect them to Yahweh.

If the assertion that punishment must follow any act of wrongdoing is to be sustained, then Yahweh must punish Israel's act of covenant disobedience, for discipline is a salient aspect of divine justice, equity, and fairness. Because Yahweh's discipline has a positive side to it, holding a corrective import over against its negative side, the Babylonian exile was a necessary end to serve, as it were, a purgatorial effect on Judah. Raitt explains this thought further in the submission that:

> It was good for Israel to go into exile in 597 and 587. Exile purged the corporate psyche free of the idolatrous connection between God and Zion, God and temple, God and the Davidic dynasty. The exile was a time for the liberation of God, for the awesome power and the holy heat of God's Godness to shatter through all the limiting structures of Israel's religious conceptions and religious institutions.[85]

It is clear from Raitt's claim that the Babylonian exile was to purge Israel of her theological, social, moral and economic sins that were both national and individual in outlook. For it functioned to refocus her religious concentration from mere formalism to its core of pragmatism; to challenge her

---

83. Raitt, *A Theology of Exile*, 4.
84. Kitchen, *On the Reliability of the Old Testament*, 69.
85. Raitt, *A Theology of Exile*, 228.

syncretistic attitude and mark a return to monotheism; and to challenge her outward lifestyle and dependence on mere Zionistic confession. This was to realign such empty confession with the true tenets of Deuteronomic theology that required consistent unwavering obedience to Yahweh as well as covenant loyalty to him as a suzerain lord.

In this connection, Yahweh's punitive action against sinful Israel was quite preparatory not only for the future restoration but much more, to achieve his purpose of eschatological shepherding of the restored community. Raitt sees in the exile a victory for God because "through it he strips Israel, streamlines it, renovates it from inside out"[86] so that a better and more vibrant Israel of Yahweh would be borne. When it is understood in this way, the Babylonian exile can be said to truly hold a punitive purpose for Israel's religious life.

4.4.2 Exile Has a Preservative Purpose to Achieve Eschatological Shepherding

At the confirmation of Yahweh's covenant with Abraham, he said to him, "I am God Almighty, walk before me and be blameless" (Gen 17:1). Also, in the giving of the law at Sinai, he said to the community of Israel, "I am the LORD your God . . . You shall have no other gods before me . . . for I, the LORD your God, am a jealous God" (Exod 20:2-3, 5 NIV). Following Yahweh's "I am God Almighty" and "I am the LORD your God" motifs, Moses, the "I am's" representative, reminded the people in the *shema* regarding their covenant obligation with this specific caution:

> Hear, O Israel: The LORD our God, the LORD is one. Love the LORD your God with all your heart and with all your soul and with all your strength . . . When the LORD your God brings you into the land he swore to your fathers, to Abraham, Isaac and Jacob, to give you – a land with large, flourishing cities you did not build, houses filled with all kinds of good things you did not provide, wells you did not dig, and vineyards and olive groves you did not plant – then when you eat and are

---

86. Raitt, *A Theology of Exile*, 222.

satisfied, be careful that you do not forget the LORD, who brought you out of Egypt, out of the land of slavery. Fear the LORD your God, serve him only and take your oaths in his name. Do not follow other gods, the gods of the peoples around you; for the LORD your God, who is among you, is a jealous God and his anger will burn against you, and he will destroy you from the face of the land. Do not test the LORD your God as you did at Massah."[87]

The Mosaic call upon the pilgrim community to "love" and not "forget" the LORD is crucial. This reveals the point of monotheistic worship contra pantheism in which Israel had been invited by Yahweh himself to participate. According to Peter E. Cousins, the word phrases, "Yahweh," "our God," and "One" in the *shema* are clear emphasis that "Israel's God was not one of a pantheon, but sovereign and the object of entire devotion."[88] This emphasis also reveals Yahweh's jealousy over Israel because the people had the stamp of his ownership.

While the Mosaic warning regarding the spirit of the *shema* reveals that the socio-economic and socio-political systems of the Israelite society were to be theocentric in orientation, its religious life was also to be monotheistic in its expressions and outlook. The religious demands of monotheism laid upon Israel arose against the background that "the constant corollary of the demand for loyalty in ancient suzerainty treaties was the prohibition of allegiance to any and all lords."[89] If Yahweh is a jealous God,[90] as Moses reminded the people, then "He would jealously guard the honour of his name"[91] to hinder Israel, the vassal, from prostituting the devotion of their

---

87. The "shema" was recited daily by the Jewish community as a reminder of their covenant obligation; see Deut 6:4-9; 11:13-21; Num 15:37-41.

88. Peter E. Cousins, "Deuteronomy," in *The International Bible Commentary* (2d ed.; ed., F. F. Bruce; England: Marshall Morgan & Scott, 1986), 263.

89. Meredith G. Kline, "Deuteronomy," in *Wycliffe Bible Commentary* (eds. Charles F. Pfeiffer and Everett F. Harrison; Chicago, Ill.: Moody, 1962), 164.

90. In the national covenant received at Sinai, Yahweh used this motif of jealousy. Moses only reminded the travelling community ahead of the outlook of life in Canaan. See Exod 20:5; 34:14; Deut 4:24; 6:16; 32:21.

91. Kline, "Deuteronomy," 164.

suzerain. The "You shall not" statement in the Sinai covenant reflects the jealousy element of Israel's overlord for the integrity of his holy name, requiring absolute love as "an expression of personal commitment"[92] to monotheistic Yahwism on the part of Israel. However, since the people failed to keep faith with the worship of their One and true Yahweh, choosing instead to go whoring after the gods of Canaan, the experience of exile then was a necessary corrective measure; for it held for Israel a preservative element for Yahwism and monotheistic worship.

As stated earlier, Israel's shift from Yahwism to Baalism recorded a paradigm shift in her religious thought and practice. Since the elect nation chose not to hark to the previous prophetic warnings regarding this shift, exilic experience was therefore necessary to preserve the integrity of Yahweh who is too holy to share his glory with any pantheon god. This principle of Yahweh's holiness and integrity, too precious to be shared with other gods, a principle that Israel failed to uphold and preserve, is clearly enshrined in the Decalogue. Philip Johnson suggests that the prohibition to "have no other gods before me" is "more than just a proclamation of monotheism. It prohibits worshiping or honouring anything but God, in thought or word or deed."[93] And so we could see that "Ezekiel's theology is one in which God is other and acts to preserve the sanctity of his name."[94]

From Ezekiel then, "we get a picture of a holy, transcendent God whose name and glory must be protected."[95] This idea is revealed in the prophet's frequent use of the prophetic recognition formula replete in the book. As Renz points out, "The theocentric message of the book is reinforced by frequent use of the recognition formula."[96] Here, we see that our prophet's "word focuses on the religious shortcomings of the people, singling out idolatry as the greatest of Judah's sins . . . idolatry was undoubtedly symptomatic of Judah's wavering commitment to traditional faith in the Lord as

---

92. Cousins, "Deuteronomy," 263.
93. Philip C. Johnson, "Exodus," in *Wycliffe Bible Commentary* (eds. Charles F. Pfeiffer and Everett F. Harrison; Chicago, Ill.: Moody, 1962), 69; see Exodus 20:37.
94. Petersen, "Ezekiel," 1224.
95. Spiros Zodhiates, Warren Baker, and Joel Kletzing, eds., *Hebrew–Greek Key Word Study Bible* (Chattanooga, TN: AMG, 1990), 1082.
96. Renz, "Ezekiel, Book of," 218-223.

God."[97] By implication, since Judah refused intentionally to acknowledge her God in her worship and commitment to him, she would recognise him when she comes under his wrath. In this connection, the execution of the profaning priests that Ezekiel foresaw in the temple vision is "tantamount to the death of a cult, a city, and a people."[98]

Besides, Ezekiel's presentation of divine abandonment by Yahweh of his people, vividly depicted by the departure of his glory from the temple, is clear indication that Yahweh was protecting his holiness and integrity from incessant assault so it is preserved from further assault. Until now, Ezekiel's theological presentation had centred around a God who was intimately involved with Israel on the ground of Yahweh's covenant commitment to the nation. Such intimate involvement with Israel is a recast of the strength of his promises to Abraham and to Moses. However, we see in Ezekiel that Yahweh's action of his departed glory from Israel had a clear motive: Yahweh was acting out of regard for his own honour and reputation. For instance, in the vision of Israel's detestable act that provoked Yahweh's theological jealousy, he said to Ezekiel, the house of Israel was doing things in the temple that would ". . . drive me far from my sanctuary" (Ezek 8:6). Ward describes the scenes in this vision as a drama. In this "truly amazing drama"[99] which plays out in the four scenes vision of Ezekiel chapter 8, Israel is presented as deflecting theologically from genuine Yahwistic devotion to idolisation right inside Yahweh's shrine. The vision narrative points to the act of the departure of divine presence with a preservative import. For this appears to be the whole focus of Ezekiel 8-11 as "the glory of Yahweh" is a term that "plays a pivotal role in prophecy,"[100] and in this case, Ezekiel's prophecy.

Even in the land that is supposed to be recognised as "holy land" because of the abiding presence of Yahweh, it is seen that what is absent is not only the required reverential worship of Yahweh but that the concept of worship itself had taken the dimension of religious formalism. This played out in

---

97. Clements, *Ezekiel*, 3.
98. James Luther Mays, *Ezekiel, Second Isaiah* (Philadelphia: Fortress, 1978), 34.
99. Ward, *Thus Says the Lord*, 177.
100. Mays, *Ezekiel, Second Isaiah*, 27.

the way the exiles and the few weaklings left in Judah claimed individual righteousness.[101] Worship had become in the land "a deadly affair"[102] entered into only on technical instead of affectionate terms. So, if the maxim, "To be better is to be forewarned," is to become a reality for Yahweh's integrity and future Yahwism to be experienced in the restored community, the temporary departure of the divine glory, signifying the removal of Yahweh's presence from the city of Jerusalem to serve as a preservative methodology, was apparent. This way, the return of Yahweh's glory and worship in the new temple of the restored community would be more glorious than the former.

So, as Brueggemann points out, specifically from what plays out in Ezekiel 40-48:

> The city and the temple that were abandoned are now the place made holy, a suitable habitat for a holy God vindicated before the nations, a welcome habitat for a restored holy people. Thus the great drama of judgment and hope culminates in Ezekiel a powerful theocentric anticipation. The God who judges and terminates is the God who restores and abides permanently and securely in the midst of well-ordered people, now completely at peace.[103]

Yahweh's abandonment of his covenant people, depicted by the departure of his glory from the land of Israel, clearly reveals a preservative theological import for Yahweh's integrity so that Israel "will know that I am the LORD," a jealous deity. This divine action by the true Shepherd of Israel was in preparation to achieving ultimately his purpose of eschatological shepherding with himself as the perfect Shepherd.

---

101. This attitude is captured in Ezekiel's parable of the "sour grapes," giving rise to the prophet's ethical theology of individual responsibility, see Ezek 18:1-29.
102. Ward, *Thus Says the Lord*, 178.
103. Brueggemann, *An Introduction*, 205.

4.4.3 Exile Has a Restorative Motif to Achieve Eschatological Worship

A restorative motif exists in the exilic experience of Judah. Ezekiel who "experienced the exile and tried to make sense of it recognized that it was God's judgment on sin, but that it also opened the way to renewed blessings in the future."[104] For Ezekiel, while admittedly, "Israel was in exile because of her sin . . . the Lord had not abandoned His people . . . the covenantal relationship and promises of God were still intact."[105] Clements states, "Ezekiel asserted the meaningfulness of events, even when so many felt themselves on the edge of despair."[106] In the hope principle offered to the exilic community in Babylon, Ezekiel had the great conviction that Judah's exile experience would have its recourse on a restored worship in Israel in the eschatological community. In an evaluative and contrasting fashion, when citing the prophecy of Isaiah and Jeremiah in this direction, Barton commends:

> In the years of struggle while the exile was impending Jeremiah had under its shadow grasped the great truth that religion is inward in character, that it is a matter of the heart, and that no outward temple or ritual is necessary to its maintenance. This was a great step forward. Little more than a century before Isaiah had declared that Jerusalem was necessary to the worship of Yahweh and that he would defend it (Isa 31:5). Jeremiah on the contrary declared that Yahweh would himself destroy the Holy City (see 22:1-12), and that in the future God's covenant with his people was to be a covenant of the heart, not an outward covenant of stones and ceremonies (Jer 31:33). This great step forward in religious thinking was most timely. In the years to come when the sanctuary was desolate, and when many Jews were exiles in distant lands, it was this faith that religion was a matter of inward attitude rather than

---

104. Robin Routledge, *Old Testament Theology: A Thematic Approach* (England: Apollos, 2008), 621.
105. Chisholm, Jr., "A Theology of Isaiah," 323.
106. Clements, *Ezekiel*, 3.

outward institution that kept Hebrew faith alive. Without it the Judaism of later times could never have been born.[107]

Barton's thought emphasises the fact that one of the major causes of the Babylonian exile was Israel's failure in the worship of Yahweh. National Israel had forsaken Yahweh or YHWH[108] and Yahwism.[109] With the tabernacle erected and the ark placed inside, Yahwism captures the concept of *presence* and *dependence* – Yahweh is in the midst of his people as the ark and tabernacle are representative "vehicles by which he not only meets his people but also reveals himself to them."[110] Israel in turn is dependent on him for subsistence in all spheres of her life. This suggests that any alteration to this Yahweh-Israel bond in any form on Israel's part, as it later turned out to be the case, would spell doom for the nation.

---

107. Barton, "Influence of the Babylonian Exile on the Religion of Israel," 369-378.
108. "Yahweh" or "YHWH" are both God's personal name and his eternal name by which he invites Israel to address him. The word "Yahweh" is the most common designation for God as the most common Hebrew noun for his name. It is made up of the Hebrew consonants *yhwh,* called the Tetragrammaton, a name too holy to be pronounced lest it be profaned. Hence, the MT substitutes it with 'ădōnay by attaching vowels to *yhwh,* resulting in yĕh[ō]wāh. Block notes that "Yahweh was the name most familiar to all Israelites, hence, its 2,019 occurrences out of the 6,828 in the historical writings." Block, "God," 336-355. This name also serves as Yahweh's continued self-introductory formula to Israel (Judg 6:10).
109. The coinage "Yahwism" designates the religious faith of Israel and is nationally recognised as her religious conception. Daniel E. Fleming conceives of religion as "attention to God." Precisely, he says it is every facet of the relationship between God and his creation. Daniel E. Fleming, "Religion," in *Dictionary of the Old Testament: Pentateuch* (eds. T. Desmond Alexander and David W. Baker; Downers Grove, Ill.: InterVarsity, 2003), 670-684. For Israel, Yahwism as a "Religion is not simply what the people bring to God but incorporates everything that relates to the bond itself. Religion here is a fabric of what is said and what is done, what is believed and how it is followed up concretely for maintaining an unbroken life with God." See Fleming as above, p.671. The concept of "Yahwism" officially came into existence with Yahweh's self-disclosure at the Sinai Peninsula, specifically in the giving of the Torah which "defines Israel above all in religious terms, as a people under God." See Fleming p. 672. Within this atmosphere of Israel's first encounter of Yahweh, "God and Israel entered a formal bond," the covenant, where the latter is obligated to obeying the terms stated therein. Soon following is the institution of Israel's religious institution alongside its religious objects and officials. For a brief discussion on the scholarly opinions about the origin of Yahwism and the history of monotheism in Israel, see Bill Arnold's article "Religion in Ancient Israel," in *The Face of Old Testament Studies: A Survey of Contemporary Approaches* (eds. David W. Baker and Bill T. Arnold; Grand Rapids, Mich.: Baker, 1999), 391-420, see especially pp. 400-411.
110. Fleming, "Religion," 672.

However, religious worship in Judah prior to the exile had become defective as the worship of Yahweh, the "I am the God of your father, the God of Abraham, the God of Isaac and the God of Jacob" (Exod 3:3) had now become obsolete in the land. Worship at the time had left Yahweh completely out of the hearts of its adherents. The pendulum of true Yahwism had swung so far to the other end of the religious paradigm, that it was too difficult to be corrected so that the presence of the "I am" would continue in Israel. This abnormal religious paradigm in Judah had to be corrected. It is on this basis that Ezekiel designated about one fourth of his material to eschatological temple worship (chs. 40-48). This signifies a rebirth of Israel at the close of the exile, not as a political community but as a new religious community. Like Apostle John confessed centuries later, it would be the dawn of a new era; everything is made new, "for the old order of things has passed away" (Rev 21:4; cf. 2 Cor 5:17).[111] In line with this spirit, James Ward states, "If the glory of YHWH had withdrawn from the apostate community of Israel during the age of wrath, its return would mark the decisive event in the age of restoration. By coming back to the sanctuary, it would legitimize the public worship of YHWH, making it effective once again."[112]

Judah had always leaned on Zion theology whenever tragedy struck in the land. But the exile of Judah's rulers and the destruction of Jerusalem "directly challenged this theology [as] they called into question God's eternal promises to Zion."[113] Ezekiel used the hope principle to redress the situation. To this Cook states, "Ezekiel answered these challenges with cosmic, eschatological, and apocalyptic visions of a rebuilt Zion that fulfilled the promises of God's eternal protection despite the fall of the earthly Jerusalem" because the prophet optimistically "anticipated much that was

---

111. Contrast Ezek 43-44 with Rev 21-22 for this concept of a new beginning for God's recreation of Israel and of the world. Some points of commonality are "new temple," "new city," "temple and city gates," "measurement," etc. One basic point of connection between these passages of Scripture is the apocalyptic literary type. These two books also share in the common aspect of a highly symbolic style and visions that seem bizarre to some readers. Even the similar context from which these books grow is worth our attention. Both emerged from the background of suffering and agony—Ezekiel grows out of Jewish exile while Revelation grows out of the context of imperial persecution of Christians.
112. Ward, *Thus Says the Lord*, 178.
113. Cook, "Ezekiel," 1181.

yet to come."[114] For Ezekiel, despite the presence of the dark cloud of exile that presently hanged over the nation, the situation still held a hope principle of restoration back to the land of Judah. On this point, Klein states, "... Ezekiel foresaw a new exodus as God's way of remaining faithful to the promise inherent in the first exodus."[115] Ezekiel perceived that no matter how miserable Israel's condition might appear, Yahweh would still choose to act through deliverance to save his reputation. This action would cause a broader and deeper knowledge of his personality in Israel and in the whole earth. Klein clarifies this point further:

> The only reason why exilic Israel can know God is that Yahweh acts for his own name's sake and not according to their own corrupt doings (36:44). That name, or reputation, was slandered when Israel went into captivity among the nations (36:22). Now Yahweh must save his own reputation – that is, he must vindicate his holiness – by rescuing Israel (36:23; cf. 39:25).[116]

In essence, as Clements points out, God's act of ensuring the future restoration and renewal of Israel "... will not be an action dependent on the good behaviour and good intentions of the people but, rather, will be based on the sovereign power of God's holiness to act to uphold the honour and reputation of so great a name."[117]

At the realisation of this anticipated restoration, a new religious institution and worship would emerge in the new Israel to be regulated by the organising principle of professional excellence and purity. Steve Tuell states that the new form of worship will be moderated by the principle of "proper conduct of the sacrificial cult in the Temple . . . the proper priesthood, essential for the conduct of right worship."[118] This way, as Tremper

---

114. Cook, "Ezekiel," 1181. See Ezek 1:22-28; 37:28; 38:12; 43:35.
115. Klein, *Israel in Exile*, 81.
116. Klein, *Israel in Exile*, 82.
117. Clements, *Ezekiel*, 163.
118. Steven Shawn Tuell, *The Law of the Temple in Ezekiel 40-48* (Atlanta, Ga.: Scholars Press, 1992), 103.

and Dillard reason regarding Yahweh's holiness, the exile would have "produce[d] a purged people, a purified remnant ready to live in obedience to a holy God"[119] and to worship him with all the needed commitment and dedication that had long been forgotten. Such a restorative liturgical motif in Ezekiel, emerging from a priestly orientation, is carefully crafted on the ground that, as Brueggemann notes, ". . . the supreme punishment of YHWH, in priestly purview, is *absence*; the supreme resolution of crisis in priestly purview is restored cultic *presence*."[120]

In the prophetic account of Ezekiel, we understand clearly then that with a restored land, restored people, and restored nation, it would naturally follow a restored worship of Yahwism. The divine purpose for allowing the experience of exile by Israel so as to achieve an eschatological worship would then have been achieved in the restoration. When this anticipated rebirth of Israel finally happens, the new state of Israel would be as Kalinda Rose Stevenson explains when she describes Ezekiel's transformed Israel:

> Re-storation refers to re-vival, re-turn, re-building, re-making, re-newing, re-pairing, re-formation – to making something the way it was. However, what the Rhetor sees is not re-storation or re-formation but trans-formation. . . . The goal of the ideology of the Book of Ezekiel is not restoration to what was, but transformation to a new thing.[121]

4.5 Ezekiel Critiques Judah Against the Norms of Deuteronomic Theology

Why did our prophet pass Israel under the plumb line of Deuteronomic theology? From the records of Jewish prophetic tradition, we could see that Israel's prophets were not passive but active participants in the events of

---

119. Longman III and Dillard, *An Introduction to the Old Testament*, 2d ed., 368.
120. Brueggemann, *An Introduction*, 203.
121. As quoted by Walter Brueggemann from her work, *Vision of Transformation: The Territorial Rhetoric of Ezekiel 40-48*. Atlanta: Scholars Press, 1996. Brueggemann, *An Introduction*, 205.

the society of their day. They were not conformists either, but sought to transform the negative events of their time. Ezekiel functioned within this prophetic tradition. Gerhard von Rad describes Ezekiel as a man of unusual intellectual powers of the first rank as a thinker and as a theologian. He sees him as a prophet who was well informed about the context of his day and as one who cannot be seen as a "detached judge of his age and its abuses." Von Rad rightly submits that because Ezekiel found ". . . a place for rational reflection," he was able to "think out problems so thoroughly and to explain them with such complete consistency."[122]

The text of Ezekiel no doubt reveals the ground for the prophet's critique of Judah. The tone suggests that his critique is "sweeping and wholesale."[123] Ezekiel x-rayed the precarious behaviour of the covenant people who, although had pledged covenant loyalty and fidelity of worship to Yahweh, yet failed to keep their pledge. He decried this failure:

> There is a conspiracy of her princes within her like a roaring lion tearing its prey; they devour people, take treasures and precious things and make many widows within her. Her priests do violence to my law and profane my holy things; they do not distinguish between the holy and the common; they teach that there is no difference between the unclean and the clean; and they shut their eyes to the keeping of my Sabbaths, so that I am profaned among them. Her officials within her are like wolves tearing their prey; they shed blood and kill people to make unjust gain. Her prophets whitewash these deeds for them by false visions and lying divinations. They say, 'This is what the Sovereign LORD says' – when the LORD has not spoken. The people of the land practice extortion and commit robbery; they oppress the poor and needy and mistreat the alien, denying them justice. "I looked for a man among them who would build up the wall and stand before me in the

---

122. Gerhard von Rad, *Old Testament Theology Volumes I & II: Volume II* (trans. D. M. G. Stalker; Peabody: Prince, 2005), 222-3.
123. Brueggemann, *An Introduction*, 194.

gap on behalf of the land so I would not have to destroy it, but I found none. So I will pour out my wrath on them and consume them with my fiery anger, bringing down on their own heads all they have done, declares the Sovereign LORD" (Ezek 22:25-31 NIV).

In Ezekiel's response to his audience's questioning the rationale for their being in exile, he confronted them with this scenario as part of the cause for the Babylonian captivity. This ugly situation clearly shows that both "King and people alike have made redemption impossible"[124] by their irreligious attitude and practices.

As a pragmatic and realistic socio-political and socio-religious analyst, Ezekiel's critique arose from what he saw in the many failures[125] in Israel's political and religious past warranting the exile. Arising from his close observation and careful evaluation of her history, Ezekiel pointed out that Israel's relationship with Yahweh had been ". . . a history of failure and obscene violation of trust"[126] (cf. Ezek 16; 20; 23). He concluded that, "Israel's history lacked any period in which righteousness prevailed. From the stay in Egypt until his own day, the prophet sees nothing but abominations, detestable things, and harlotry."[127] Following this, he used the principles of Deuteronomic theology to critique both people and leaders for covenant infidelity and theological adultery. Ezekiel directed his theological searchlights on the Judean environment as his primary target of critique because the events that preceded the exile had occurred in her. Also, his primary audience, the Babylonian fugitives, had come from there.

The theme of *forgetfulness* is a recurrent one in Israel's theological circle. Israel as a covenant nation soon forgot the *shema*[128] to "fear the LORD."

---

124. House, *Old Testament Theology*, 313.

125. Andrew W. Blackwood, Jr., *Ezekiel: Prophecy of Hope* (Grand Rapids, Mich.: Baker, 1965), 206.

126. Brueggemann, *An Introduction*, 194.

127. Klein, *Israel in Exile*, 80.

128. The Hebrew verbs שׁמע (to hear, listen, or hark to) and אהב (to love) are the strength of this instruction. When the nation is able to "hear" and "love" Yahweh consistently, then its benefits would flow unabated (cf. Deut 6:10-12). Of particular note is the form in which these verbs appear in the MT. שׁמע appears in the Qal imperative while אהב

Israel was to remember Yahweh and serve him faithfully so she would enjoy the continuous benefits of the land promised her through Abraham. In this regards, well ahead the occupation of the Promised Land, Moses gave this charge,

> Hear, O Israel, and be careful to obey so that it may go well with you and that you may increase greatly in a land flowing with milk and honey, just as the LORD, the God of your fathers, promised you. Hear, O Israel: The LORD our God, the LORD is one. Love the LORD your God with all your heart and with all your soul and with all your strength" (Deut 6:3-5 NIV).

The observance of the spirit of the *shema*, interpreted in the light of the tenets of Deuteronomic theology, was to become in Israel the confession of faith as was recited daily by the pious. It was to be internalised in the hearts of individuals and not to be held only in form. To "hear" the LORD, "love" the LORD who is One and whose glory is not to be shared because of his covenant jealousy, was especially important in view of the multiplicity of Baals and other gods of Canaan and elsewhere. To this, Vaux commends that the Deuteronomistic code indicates that "the Israelites must suppress all the places of cult in Canaan and must perform their own strictly cultic acts only 'in the place chosen by Yahweh, your God, for his Name to dwell there' . . . Israel has only one God, and it is to have only one sanctuary and one altar."[129]

But it was Israel's deflection from monotheistic Yahwism both in her attitude and practices that attracted Ezekiel's theological critique. For instance, his critique of Israel for her deflection into certain detestable acts is clearly projected in chapters 16, 18, 22 and 23. Although these chapters have received greater attention from scholars with different interpretive methods,[130] we must not let the point slip away that Ezekiel is dealing here

---

appears in the Qal perfect. Both indicate it is the nation at this point, not individual members of the nation, which is addressed.

129. Roland De Vaux, *Ancient Israel: Its Life and Institution* (trans. John MeHugh; Grand Rapids, Mich.: Eerdmans, 1997), 338.

130. For example, Kamionkowski has identified extremes in the interpretation of Ezekiel

with a theological problem. Israel had violated the covenant and by this, had dishonoured Yahweh's name and his holiness before the nations. In his description of Ezekiel 16 as "an Old Testament parable of the prodigal daughter," Clements submits that the people's indictment is apparent for their attitude of ingratitude and forgetting what Yahweh had done for the nation. He argues, ". . . instead of responding with love, loyalty and gratitude to her benefactor and husband, the woman becomes persistently and deeply unfaithful."[131] He concludes that the sins of Ezekiel 16 and 23 which Ezekiel ". . . has been referring to as wrong are not merely superficial religious offenses, such as the breaking of some taboo or the evasion of some ritual duty. They are the most deeply wounding of all human hurts, all the more hurtful because they result from misguided religious zeal."[132] This scenario is, more or less, like biting the finger that feeds one. Walther Zimmerli equally carefully notes that because the people abuse Yahweh's gift freely received, so "Yahweh does in judgement what his covenant partner has done in disloyalty."[133] The guilty in this case is not gracious Yahweh but ungrateful Israel.

---

16 by interpreters who place the understanding of this text on the pedestal of gender/feminist hermeneutic. She argues extensively, "… any reading that treats YHWH and Israel as two distinct, independent characters, representing male and female experience respectively, is at the risk of a fundamental flaw. This text, as a product of male and female writers and readers, does not express female experience, nor can the female point of view be inferred or read into the text. The text does not tell us anything about real women, even if a woman is a central character; it tells us about men's *ideological construction* of gender, and especially masculinity, set within a theological framework. Ezekiel 16 is a witness to a problem: something is wrong in Ezekiel's world. If we try to find fault with either God or Jerusalem, with the husband or wife, we remain trapped within the narrative and we are compelled either to defend the dominant (God-centred) position, elevate it, dislike it, condemn it or reject [it]. Kamionkowski's argument seems to appeal to the use of other methods than a feminist approach as a basis for interpreting this text. To have identified a textual hermeneutical approach that is gender-centred rather than textual-centred as a weakness makes her argument persuasive. Kamionkowski, *Gender Reversal and Cosmic Chaos*, 42.

131. Clements, *Ezekiel*, 69, 71.

132. Clements, *Ezekiel*, 73.

133. Zimmerli, *Ezekiel 1*, 353.

4.5.1 The People Critiqued for False Reliance on Zion Theology

The people's belief in the principle of Zion theology grew from a long-standing tradition. Ezekiel's use of Zion theology hinges on three great circles of traditions – the tradition of the Exodus from Egypt, the election of Zion, and the election of David and his dynasty. This motif of election lays much stress on the city of Jerusalem, a city that also has a long-standing political and religious history. Barton had asserted at the start of the twentieth century that:

> Jerusalem attracts the interest of a larger number of people than any other city in the world. It is a sacred city to all the adherents of three of the great religions – Judaism, Christianity, and Mohammedanism. Millions of people in all parts of the world turn their thoughts to it with feelings of reverence and adoration. It has been the central city of the world's best religious history for three thousand years.[134]

This assertion presupposes the religious significance of the city of Jerusalem to members of the Abrahamic faiths,[135] each of which lays claims to having some connection with it. Jerusalem plays this significant role because for years, the city "has had a special place in the hearts and lives of those who worship the God of Israel."[136] But prior to its capture and being brought under the control of Israel by King David, Jerusalem was a Jebusite city.[137]

---

134. Barton, "The Jerusalem of David and Solomon," 8.
135. Lasor explains that Jerusalem, understood and interpreted as "city of wholeness or peace" (derived from *uru*, "city," and *salim*, "peace," in the Amarna Tablets) was the principal city of ancient Israel, location of the temple, capital of the kingdom Judah, chief city of nascent Judaism, the city where Jesus was tried and crucified, the place visited, according to tradition, by the prophet Muhammad on his way to heaven, and hence the holiest city of Jews and Christians and, after Mecca and Medina, the third holiest city of the Moslems. See his article "Jerusalem," *ISBE* 2:998. Read the whole article on pp. 998-1032 for his skeletal but all-embracing treatment of anything related to Jerusalem.
136. This is the introductory comment of Richard S. Hess and Gordon J. Wenham on the whole idea of "Zion, City of Our God," in *Zion, City of Our God* (eds. Richard S. Hess and Gordon J. Wenham; Grand Rapids, Mich.: Eerdmans, 1999), ix.
137. Hebron is the first location for the capital of the Israelite nation. It predates the Israelite patriarchs and is first mentioned in connection with Abraham when he moved

In this sense, both Jerusalem and Zion[138] are inseparably attached to David himself and the Davidic dynasty. He conquered it, built his palace there "as the original seat of the Davidic dynasty," and made it "the place of YHWH's dwelling"[139] upon which Solomon later built him a residential shrine. Jerusalem became significant to Israel as its cult centre, political capital, and as the nerve centre of the nation. Moshe Weinfeld[140] asserts that "Jerusalem's 'election'" as Israel's capital and as a central temple city represented a profound innovation in Israel's history" which manifested itself in the establishment of a royal dynasty and in the creation of a fixed religious centre.

From the preceding historical briefs, the concept of Zion theology is knit to the origin and the religious and political functions of the city of Jerusalem since located within Jerusalem is Zion the "city of David" and

---

his tents to settle at Mamre in Hebron where he built an altar (Gen 13:18). It is here that his wife Sarah died and was buried on the site acquired as deed by Abraham from Ephron (Gen 23:1-4, 17-20). During the time of Joshua, Hebron was given to Caleb as an inheritance (Josh 14:6-15) and part to the priests as city a of refuge (Josh 21:8-18). David reigned in Hebron for 7½ years before he moved the state capital to Jerusalem (2 Sam 5:5). See the article by Barton, "The Jerusalem of David and Solomon," *BW* 1 (1903): 8-21 for further historical treatment.

138. Zion is first mentioned after its dispossession from the Jebusites by David (2 Sam 5:6-7; 15:8, 63) where their kings had ruled from it as royal seat of power. This geographical area was renamed Zion and made the seat of royal power when David relocated his state capital to Jerusalem (2 Sam 5:6-13). It seems obvious that one of the significant achievements credited to David is the establishment of Jerusalem as his royal city and the nation's capital. Jerusalem/Zion, combined with Israel's cult monument, the Temple, stands both as the political and religious unifying force for the tribes of Israel. The leading understanding of Zion from its etymological and semantic range is its elevation as a tower on top of a mountain and its fortified protective nature as a fortress. A. F. Rainey reports that as a Jebusite fortress conquered by David, Zion became a royal residence as "the city of David" and, after the building of the temple, as the sacred dwelling place of Israel's Lord, the One "who dwells in Zion." A. F. Rainey, "Zion," *ISBE* 4:1198-1200. With the passage of time however, Jerusalem and Zion became synonymous terms, the sense or meaning of which is distinguishable only by the context of its usage. W. Harold Mare points out that "most often Zion refers to parts of the city of Jerusalem and its environs or the country of which the city is the capital. Frequently, Zion even represents the inhabitants of Jerusalem or the whole country. Sometimes physical features connected with Zion are stressed." W. Harold Mare, "Zion," *ABD* 6:1096.

139. Grisanti, "The Davidic Covenant," 172. See 2 Sam 5:11; 6:17; cf. vv. 12, 16.

140. Moshe Weinfeld, "Zion and Jerusalem as Religious and Political Capital: Ideology and Utopia," in *The Poet and the Historian: Essays in Literary and Historical Biblical Criticism* (ed. Richard Elliott Friedman; Chico, Calif.: Scholars Press, 1983), 75.

"of Yahweh."[141] The theology of Zion then is rooted in the basic premise that "Yahweh," the "I AM," had, by his own volition and decree, chosen Zion/Jerusalem as his holy city and throne where he rules as the true King of Israel in particular, and of the cosmos in general. Here, Yahweh resides in his sacred shrine where he makes his permanent residence and rules the people as both his subjects and sheep. By implication then, as Bruce Waltke[142] observes, since Zion is the city of God, the city where the Great King resides and from whence he rules, the Jews had a persistent belief that Zion was invulnerable and inviolable as the Great King makes his residence there. This theological belief is so strong in Jewish tradition because of "three primary emphases: the (connected) election of David and Zion, Yahweh's presence in the city of David (Zion), and Yahweh's covenant with David (which included Zion)."[143]

On the ground that Zion/Jerusalem is a city where both human and divine monarchs abided and exercised their rule, the people's unwavering belief in the city's eternal establishment and its inviolability beclouded their mind. It took precedence over all else, much more, the people's covenant obligation on the warrant of the Davidic covenant and Yahweh's presence. This reveals the exiles' difficulty in reconciling the events of exile with the tenets of this tradition. To this falsity, Jeremiah both indicted and cautioned the people:

> Do not trust in deceptive words and say, "This is the temple of the LORD, the temple of the LORD, the temple of the LORD!" If you really change your ways and your actions and deal with each other justly, if you do not oppress the alien, the fatherless or the widow and do not shed innocent blood in this place, and if you do not follow other gods to your own harm, then I will let you live in this place, in the land I gave your forefathers

---

141. J. J. M. Roberts presents an analysis of the origin and motifs of the Zion tradition. Roberts, "The Davidic Origin of the Zion Tradition," 329-344.
142. Waltke with Charles Yu, *An Old Testament Theology*, 546-7. This belief in the "presence of Yahweh in the midst of his people" in Zion is a basic character of Zion theology. VanGemeren, *Interpreting the Prophetic Word*, 56.
143. Groves, "Zion Traditions," 1020.

for ever and ever. But look, you are trusting in deceptive words that are worthless. Will you steal and murder, commit adultery and perjury, burn incense to Baal and follow other gods you have not known, and then come and stand before me in this house, which bears my Name, and say, "We are safe" – safe to do all these detestable things? Has this house, which bears my Name, become a den of robbers to you? But I have been watching! declares the LORD (Jer 7:4-11 NIV).

Based upon Jeremiah's evaluation of the socio-psychology of the people, the nation had slipped from observing the Deuteronomic code into the falsity of formalistic religious observances in the hope that the city of Yahweh was secured from all harm. Upon this falsity Ezekiel equally built his indictment:

O city that brings on herself doom by shedding blood in her midst and defiles herself by making idols, you have become guilty because of the blood you have shed and have become defiled by the idols you have made. You have brought your days to a close, and the end of your years has come. Therefore I will make you an object of scorn to the nations and a laughingstock to all the countries. Those who are near and those who are far away will mock you, O infamous city, full of turmoil... The people of the land practice extortion and commit robbery; they oppress the poor and needy and mistreat the alien, denying them justice. (Ezek 22:3-5, 29 NIV).

4.5.2 Royal Leadership Critiqued for Official Abuses

The royal leadership[144] in Israel was criticised by Ezekiel in his use of the shepherd metaphor for several official abuses. These "shepherds" had

---

144. Scholars have questioned the appropriate designation of this royal leadership in Israel which Ezekiel critiqued whether what he meant here is a nāśî or a *melek*. Duguid contends that of the 126 entries of the term nāśî in the Old Testament of which 36 occur in Ezekiel, none has anything less than a royal significance because nāśî in the Old Testament always refers to a pre-monarchical figure. He concludes that Ezekiel used nāśî and *melek* as synonymous terms for past and present rulers of his day. He argues, "...the

abused the Deuteronomic code. They had become violent by shedding innocent blood, by using their privileged status and power to oppress the weak and poor (22:6-7), and by despising the law of the Sabbath by becoming loathsome, and in the process, made many widows (22:25-27). D. A. Olubunmo points out that serving as a representative of Yahweh who is the real ruler of his covenant people, the king serves only as a caretaker of Yahweh's people. Given this kingly status as Yahweh's representative, Olubunmo submits that, "the king was expected to be fair to his subjects. If the king was to be fair in his dealings among his people, he could not be an absolute ruler[;] he could not deprive them of their rights."[145] Instead, as a loyal representative, the king, as "an embodiment of national virtue" and as "both the servant of God and of the people . . . was to constantly remind his people of their covenant with Yahweh"[146] so they do not defect from it. If the populace of Israel and Judah became ethically and religiously complacent, it seems most appropriate to charge their human shepherds (their political leaders) for this lapse because of their failure to lead as Yahweh's representatives. If also, as Yahweh's representatives, Israel's human shepherds (royal leaders) had been as upright and godly like Moses, Samuel, David, Hezekiah and Josiah, it is quite unlikely that the people would have failed to follow them as models.

Ezekiel's critique of royal leadership is crucial because Israel's kings abused their custodianship function. The role of kingship in ANE and correspondingly, in Israel, was not only to function as a political fortress but

---

fact that Ezekiel is still able to alternate between melek and nāśî at will and that he also used n ^{e}śî'îm to designate a group of leaders in the past separate from the king suggests that the terminology is not all important. Ezekiel's message concerning the monarchy cannot be determined simply from its use of nāśî in preference to *melek*." Duguid, *Ezekiel and the Leaders of Israel*, 12, 14, and 33. Also see pp. 10-57 for a full discussion on this matter. Vaux observes that it is a common idea among primitive peoples that the king embodies the good estate of his subjects as he is *ipso facto* a saviour. As such, "the country's prosperity depends on him, and he ensures the welfare of his people." By way of contrast then, Vaux notes that just as was the case with the Judges, also "under the monarchy the king delivered the nation from its enemies" as a saviour whom men called to their aid. Vaux, *Ancient Israel*, 110, 111. These presuppositions affirm that the kings are in focus. See Judg 3:9, 15; 2 Sam 19:10; 2 Kgs 13:5; 6:26.

145. D. A. Olubunmo, "Israelite Concept of Ideal King: A Model of Interdependence of Politics and Religion for Nigeria," *AJBS* 2 (1991):59.

146. Olubunmo, "Israelite Concept of Ideal King," 64.

also to serve as the custodian of the religious conscience of the state while the priesthood directed cult worship and service. Moshe Weinfeld notes in this direction by explaining the king's function:

> . . . in his rule, the king was autonomous – the responsibility of managing the government was his and his alone. It is no coincidence that the evil done in the sight of the LORD in the era of the monarchy is reckoned the king's fault . . . The king had it in his power to eliminate apostasy, to remove the "high places," and to bring to an end oppression and injustice . . . it was on his shoulders that responsibility for what was done among the people in the monarchic era was laid.[147]

But despite such role expectation, Israel's national history reveals that only very few Judean kings were able to exhibit the characteristics of a religious custodian monarch. King Josiah of whom it is said that his "reign was a watershed in Judah's spiritual development"[148] following his programme of Temple repairs and religious reformation which led to the discovery of the lost book of the Law, stands out on this point. We think that had the spirit of Josiah's reforms been perpetuated at least by his immediate few successors, the Babylonian exile would have been an unlikely event in Judah's history.

The ethical standing of Judah's kings was also brought to question by Ezekiel. Moral lapses and religious apostasy became prevalent in the land and widespread injustice and exploitation of the poor in the land also became commonplace as a result of the kings' abuse of their ethical function. Quite obviously, the catastrophe that engulfed Israel and Judah, which could have been averted occurred as a result of the kings' religious and moral negligence and complacency as shepherds of Yahweh's people. William J. Dumbrell submits to this effect when pointing out Ezekiel's message that "the message of the book, indeed, is that the prior political leadership has failed and that the future of the people of God will be guaranteed only

---

147. Weinfeld, "Zion and Jerusalem as Religious and Political Capital," 77.
148. Taylor, *Ezekiel*, 29.

by the imposition of divine leadership."[149] Consequent upon this failure on the part of Israel's human shepherds (both royal and religious leaders), Ezekiel therefore used Deuteronomic theology accusatively, in a lawsuit fashion, to critique them for straying from the path of theological and ethical rightness.

Besides the king's military saving role was his theological cult participation. In Israel's monarchical tradition, monarchs were ideally to be adopted and enthroned by Yahweh (Pss 2; 110; 72), though never to be deified, as was the case with ANE peoples. Similar to what obtained in ANE regarding the election and enthronement of monarchs, kings in Israel were elected by Yahweh and anointed by his human representative. Therefore, "It was this election and commissioning by the god(s) of a people or land that provided the basis for the king's authority and power."[150] Cultic rituals were strictly to be under the supervision and assessment of the ruling monarch as the "chief priests [were] officials nominated and dismissed by the king."[151] Vaux states that Yahweh's appointing the king to the throne and anointing him, although this act did not make him a priest in the strict sense, yet, it made the king "a sacred person, with a special relationship to Yahweh, and in solemn circumstances he could act as the religious head of the people."[152] In this connection, an Israelite king "was seen as a channel of God's blessings to the people, which include material prosperity."[153] Given this function, the burden of proof was laid upon the king to ensure the full application of the law of Yahweh to the religious, social, ethical, legal, and political life of the nation (2 Chr 19:5-7; 17:9). By implication, "God was the lawgiver, and the king had responsibility both to uphold and observe covenant law"[154] as he was to watch "over its observance"[155] in the community.

---

149. Dumbrell, *The Faith of Israel*, 2nd ed., 151.
150. Routledge, *Old Testament Theology*, 226.
151. Vaux, *Ancient Israel*, 113. See some biblical examples in the narrative of 2 Sam 8:17; 20:25; and 1 Kgs 2:26-27; 4:2.
152. Vaux, *Ancient Israel*, 114.
153. Routledge, *Old Testament Theology*, 226.
154. Routledge, *Old Testament Theology*, 226.
155. Vaux, *Ancient Israel*, 151. Cf. the narrative of Exod 24:7-8; Josh 24:25-26; and Neh 8.

But if, as Routledge[156] posits, the Israelite settlement and the absence of centralised direction in the pre-monarchical era mainly accounted for the nation's decline in moral and spiritual values, resulting in its sliding into spiritual and moral anarchy, what went wrong now that the nation had the monarchy in place? In his theological evaluation, Ezekiel found past and present royal leadership wanting on several counts. Their covenant failure stood as rebellion against Yahweh. While no doubt Ezekiel certainly had some level of concern with practical politics in Israel, his indictment basically focused on the royal attitude of disobedience in upholding Deuteronomic provisions. This theological lapse was responsible for their gross failure and attitude of greed and oppression, thereby feasting on the covenant people without any sense of remorse. Duguid explains that contained within the imagery of the two lion cubs of Ezekiel 19 "is the possibility of powerful men acting like wild beasts which have the capacity to empty the land" and which in other contexts can "become a figure of fierce cruelty."[157] In this case, Yahweh was to judge the royal leaders (Ezek 17) because they had failed to apply Yahweh's law, thereby committing the moral sin of oppressing the very people they were enthroned by Yahweh to shepherd (cf. Ezek 21:25-27, 30-32). Yahweh's judgement of the royal seat therefore was not out of place as it stands on the point of royal abuse of power. According to Routledge, "The king is dependent upon Yahweh and because his subjects belong to Yahweh, the king is answerable for the right use of his royal power."[158] The kings abused the administration of social justice and regulation of right behaviour in society. They failed to give "special protection to the weak members of society, who also belong to Yahweh."[159]

This socio-judicial lapse became an issue on the ground that it was the royal seat in Israel that had the moral obligation to ensure that shalom permeated every sphere of society. It was the duty of a reigning king to ensure that "the spiritual, moral, social and material well-being that derives from

---

156. Routledge, *Old Testament Theology*, 228-9.
157. Duguid, *Ezekiel and the Leaders of Israel*, 36. Also see 2 Kgs 17:26; Gen 49:9; Deut 33:20; Prov 28:15; Nah 2:12-14.
158. Routledge, *Old Testament Theology*, 237.
159. Routledge, *Old Testament Theology*, 237.

the just and righteous rule of a king who reigns on God's behalf"[160] was enjoyed by all in society. Consequently, since greed beclouded the kings' protective role and their creating a peaceful and secure atmosphere in society as shepherds, "Yahweh is coming in judgement upon his shepherds because of their failure to fulfil this role properly."[161]

Royal officials too came under the prophetic critique as this category of human shepherds served as political advisors, royal guards, scribes, aristocrats, and perhaps, even as financiers of the state. Seeing the crumbling economy of Judah and the potential collapse of Jerusalem, this class of leaders became as greedy as the evil kings. From the catalogue of offenses outlined in Ezekiel 22, Clements guesses that these officials ". . . were seeking to grab what they could for themselves in the fevered years of crisis, seizing every opportunity to take advantage of their positions of authority in frantic bids to rescue something for their own and their family's future."[162] The display of such attitude of greed is an aberration to the tenets of Deuteronomic theology which is inherent in covenant principles. For although these shepherds were aware of the Deuteronomic principle of "Love your neighbour as yourself" (Lev 19:18; cf. Matt 19:19), they not only negated and set it aside but in fact, abused it by their gross exhibition of oppressing the weak and poor of society to achieve their self-aggrandisement.

The kings and these royal officials who had prided in the Zionistic principle of Yahweh's abiding presence with his covenant people should have known that Zion theology meant that Yahweh had chosen Jerusalem and Zion as his city; that Yahweh had chosen the temple in Zion as his abode where he would rule as King over his covenant people; and that Yahweh had chosen the Davidic dynasty as an everlasting kingship over his people. They should have known also that by implication, it should logically follow therefore that the continuity of Yahweh's blessings and protection of the city, the throne and its people was contingent upon the people's consistent loyalty to Yahweh's covenant law and unwavering obedience to Deuteronomic code. In fact, in their status as shepherds of Yahweh's people,

---

160. Routledge, *Old Testament Theology*, 237.
161. Duguid, *Ezekiel and the Leaders of Israel*, 39.
162. Clements, *Ezekiel*, 104.

they ought to have exhibited before the people such ethical behaviour that reflected "the nature and character of God himself" because the "qualities [he] requires of human beings," and in particular from his covenant people, "are the qualities he himself displays in his relationship with them."[163] But since the attitude of the royal leaders stood instead in aberration to what was normative of a covenant people, Ezekiel had to indict them appropriately. They were worthless shepherds who only fed themselves at the expense of the flock (Ezek 34:3-5) even against the norms and enshrined principles of Deuteronomic theology.

4.5.3 Religious Leadership Critiqued for Incompetence

In using the shepherd metaphor to critique dysfunctional royal and religious leadership in the land, Ezekiel was speaking from a theological angle in view of the calamity that had befallen Judah. His indictment of this ugly leadership scenario was to force home the point that leadership failure was among the key reasons responsible for the nation's present repulsive and embarrassing exilic experience. In charging Israel's bad leaders before the Judean exiles, the prophet was reflecting on the principle of Deuteronomic theology from a priestly tradition, which these leaders had abandoned. As a Jerusalemite priest himself and as one among the Babylonian exiles, Ezekiel lived through the agony of his land and his people. The hurtful national and personal experience of exile formed the context for his theological critique of Judah's religious order. This is significant; for a theology that does not emerge from a concrete context is at best a theoretical fantasy, and at worst, a mere academic imaginative postulation. Anyone who engages in theologising of whatever form does so from a particular frame of reference, influenced by a particular context. Theology, to be realistic and effectual, should be planted, nurtured and grown within a particular context. From this presupposition is to be seen the credibility of Ezekiel's theological critique of the Judean religious environment. As McKeating rightly points out, "Theology is never produced in a vacuum. The theology

---

163. Routledge, *Old Testament Theology*, 239.

of the prophetic literature, especially, is a response to a situation in which the literature was shaped."[164]

The religious group in Israelite society consisted of the priesthood[165] and the prophetic guild. This category of leadership was tasked primarily with a theological function, serving as a link between Yahweh and the people. While the priesthood[166] directed cultic activities[167] on behalf[168] of the people, the prophetic[169] guild interpreted Yahweh's mind to the people, serving as vanguards of their contemporary society. The priestly and prophetic functions existed *pari passu* in Israelite society to fulfil Yahweh's cultic requirements and to satisfy the specifics of his expectations of society. Therefore, the priestly and prophetic offices clearly stood out in Ezekiel's critique as he used a combination of Deuteronomic and priestly theologies to achieve this purpose.

The priesthood in Israelite society was expected to perform certain defined cultic functions. Joseph Blenkinsopp submits three such functions:

---

164. Henry McKeating, *Ezekiel* (Sheffield, England: JSOT Press, 1993), 73.

165. Priesthood in Israel consisted of both priests and Levites. This understanding goes back to the institution of this religious function in Israel when Yahweh gave Moses their job description (Num 18). Routledge postulates that the priesthood in Israel was formalised in connection with the tabernacle (Exod 19:22, 24). He states also that the special place of the Levites is linked with their zeal in rallying to Moses after Israel's sin of worshipping the golden calf (Exo 32:26-29; Deut 10:8). Routledge, *Old Testament Theology*, 180-1.

166. Vaux states that official priesthood appeared in Israel only when a considerable social organisation had developed. This development required certain members of the community to be entrusted with the "special tasks of looking after the sanctuaries and of performing rites which were becoming ever more and more complicated." Vaux, *Ancient Israel*, 345.

167. Blenkinsopp suggests that the priests in Israel also "discharged tasks outside the cultic sphere, serving, for example, as scribe and magistrate," Blenkinsopp, *Sage, Priest, Prophet*, 2.

168. Not every member of the Israelite community qualified for the priestly office. During the patriarchal era, priestly functions were performed by the family heads, while from the Mosaic era on, priesthood function took residence in the Aaronic line. This is important, as Vaux notes, for priesthood in Israel was not a vocation but an office. Vaux, *Ancient Israel*, 346.

169. While Blenkinsopp recognises that the prophetic label appears problematic, he submits that "Its contemporary usage in our vernacular is very fluid, covering such things as prediction, emotional preaching, social protest, and, within the sociological community, millenarian movements and their founders." Blenkinsopp, *Sage, Priest, Prophet*, 2. The prophetic office functioned as "a covenant reminder." Gan, *The Metaphor of Shepherding*, 59.

That the priests existed to *facilitate* the carrying out of ritual; to assure survival and material well-being in society by means of sacrifice; and to serve as teachers of the law[170] by interpreting Yahweh's Law, calling the people to its total observance, and redirecting them to Yahweh for forgiveness whenever they strayed from it. The priesthood in Israelite society "represented God before the people" and consulted him to know his will.[171] In addition, the priestly function of delivering divine oracles was achievable by consulting "God by means of the ephod and of the Urim and Thummin."[172] But this function was not too pronounced in Israel and thereby soon eclipsed. The primary duty post of the priests was "to serve in a sanctuary . . . Consequently, it is impossible to imagine a sanctuary without any priest to look after it."[173] In summary, Vaux understands these priestly functions as mediatory because "the priesthood is an institution for mediation."[174]

---

170. Blenkinsopp explains that the carrying out of ritual was due to the "increasing complexity of society and social needs [that] produced a correspondingly more complex and specialized set of cultic acts, thereby rendering the services of priests increasingly indispensable." For the sacrificial function of the priest which required specialisation, he notes that since the role of sacrifice "came to be considered essential for the removal of certain involuntary offenses ("sins") that disqualified one from membership or at least good standing in the cultic-civil community, the exclusive control of sacrifice by the priesthood translated very readily into a fair degree of social control." By implication, this control could become ready ground to breed cultic manipulation and abuses by the priesthood as was the case in Malachi chapters 1-2. Blenkinsopp, *Sage, Priest, Prophet*, 80-83.

171. Routledge, *Old Testament Theology*, 184-187. See Num 27:21; 1 Sam 14:36, 41-42; 28:6; Exod 28:30; Deut 33:8).

172. Vaux explains that the ephod was some kind of linen cloth worn by the priests in performing their offices (cf. 1 Sam 2:18; 22:18; 2 Sam 6:14, 20; Exod 28:6-30; 29:2-21; Lev 8:7). The Urim and Thummim were the sacred lot casting materials, perhaps stones (pebbles or dices) or little sticks stored in the pocket of the priestly ephod (cf. Deut 33:8; 1 Sam 14:18-19, 41-42). Vaux, *Ancient Israel*, 349.

173. The priesthood – the priests, the descendants of Aaron, and the Levites from Levi, Jacob's son, were taken by or given to God instead of the first born of Israel, thereby were set apart for special duties in Israel (see Num 1:50; 3:12; 8:16; Exod 32:25-29; Deut 10:6-9; Josh 13:14, 33; 14:3-4; 18:7). Vaux reports that "One branch within this tribe [the tribe of Levi] received the promise of a perpetual priesthood, as a result of which the other Levites were relegated to a subordinate position and restricted to the less important functions of the cult" (see p. 360). Majorly, the priests performed mediatory roles while the Levites performed service roles to the religious community. The latter also served on the Temple choir like the line of Korah, etc. Vaux, *Ancient Israel*, 348.

174. Vaux holds that "All these various functions have a common basis. When the priest delivered an oracle, he was passing on an answer from God; when he gave an instruction, a *tôrah*, and later when he explained the Law, the Torah, he was passing on and interpreting teaching that came from God; when he took the blood and flesh of victims

Ezekiel used the shepherd metaphor not only to critique royal leadership for their functional failure and official abuses but also included the religious leaders (the priests and false prophets) for the role they had played in the spiritual and political deterioration of the Israelite society. As a case in point, John Skinner describes the ugly scenario stage-managed by the religious leaders thus:

> The priests, whose function was to maintain the outward ordinances of religion and foster the spirit of reverence, by falsification of the Torah, to bring religion into contempt and obliterate the distinction between the holy and the profane . . . the professional prophets . . . who should have been foremost to denounce civil wrong are fit for nothing but to stand by and bolster up with lying oracles in the name of Jehovah."[175]

The religious consciousness in Judah prior to and during the time of Ezekiel was at its lowest ebb, both in its national and global outlook. Against this backdrop, Ezekiel charged the religious leaders as primarily being responsible for the spiritual predicament in Judah; for the priests and prophets left undone what they needed to have done and ironically, did what they should not have done.[176]

In specific terms, first to be criticised on the list of religious leadership in Judah was the priesthood. Though not his primary target, Ezekiel accused the priests and was particularly "critical of the temple priesthood"[177] for professional misconduct and incompetence. They were negligent, complacent, and profanatory in their attitude towards sacrifices. The description

---

to the altar, or burned incense upon the altar, he was presenting to God the prayers and petitions of the faithful. In the first two roles he represented God before men, and in the third he represented men before God; but he is always an intermediary." Vaux, *Ancient Israel*, 357.

175. John Skinner, "The Book of Ezekiel," in *The Expositor's Bible: A Complete Exposition of the Bible in Six Volumes*, Vol. 4 (ed. W. Robertson Nicoll; Grand Rapids, Mich.: Eerdmans, 1943), 272.

176. See Ezek 22:23-29. Their case was a repeat of history as was the case with Eli's sons (1 Sam 2:22-25).

177. Blenkinsopp, *Sage, Priest, Prophet*, 88.

of the sins of the different leadership groups in the land in Ezekiel 22:25-29 includes the priesthood (v. 26; cf. Lev 10:10; 20:4; 26). Duguid comments that though a priest, "Ezekiel is not blind to the sins of his class," and therefore indicted the priesthood for the serious offences of negligence and dishonour of Yahweh.[178] Vaux points out specifically that this attitude of negligence reveals itself in the introduction of "uncircumcised men into the service of the Temple."[179]

Next in the line for critique were the prophets that Ezekiel, one of their very own, confronted. What actions of theirs merited his theological critique and condemnation? The prophetic guild came under the prophet's plumb line of accusation for their sin of deceit and falsehood. The falsity of prophetic activities in Judah at this period of crisis was detrimental to the people. Duguid asserts to this effect that "the battle lines were drawn between on the one hand those who believed that the first exile of 597 BC was sufficient punishment and that Yahweh would soon reverse that captivity, bringing back the exiles, and on the other hand those who saw that Israelite's future held further doom and punishment."[180] The battle to authenticate true prophecy in Israel was not an unknown phenomenon because, right from the time of Moses, prophetic fulfilment was given as a major parameter for measurement. Whose word were the Babylonian exiles and Judean remnants to believe – Ezekiel's which was not unfashionable or that of the false prophets back in Judah? Caught in the web of the need for distinction and validation of the prophetic message, it was an uphill task for Ezekiel as he was confronted by an audience that was unsure if their exile meant the demise of Judah or that they would be restored sooner than anticipated. The exiles' psychology indicates, in Raitt's words, that, ". . . they awaited an uncertain future."[181]

Apart from prophetic deceit and falsehood, the second accusation is premised on their failure to repudiate wrong and declare, "Thus says the LORD" as expected of a prophet of Yahweh. Ezekiel chapter 33; and 22:28

---

178. Duguid, *Ezekiel and the Leaders of Israel*, 75.
179. Vaux, *Ancient Israel*, 365.
180. Duguid, *Ezekiel and the Leaders of Israel*, 91.
181. Raitt, *A Theology of Exile*, 1.

spell out their crime and locates their prophetic illegality. In the Israelite prophetic tradition, prophets were known as serving and acting as vanguards in confronting the evil of their contemporary society. They were also known as protesters who condemned the "syncretic cults and the foreign policy pursued by ruler and court,"[182] calling the people back to observing the tenets of Yahwism. Blenkinsopp notes further that one of the most powerful strands in prophetic preaching is their protest "on behalf of the poor and disadvantaged." They challenge leaders for their act of "disregard for justice and righteousness . . . [calling for] the maintenance of right order, of social structures, and of judicial procedures respectful of the rights of all classes."[183] But contrary to true prophetic function, the false prophets in Judah had become peddlers of the prophetic office along with its function at a very crucial moment that the people needed the truth the most. Duguid[184] explains the scenario when he points out that the origin of their prophecy was from self but made to appear divine; the content of the message lacked substance for it was full of deceit; and the result of their prophesying seductively offered false security against imminent divine judgement.

The third accusation is based on the principle of self-centeredness. Self-interest dominated their prophecy as they prophesied for personal gain. Even their prophesying women anchored their prophetic message on a self-centred source, using magical amulets to entice and trap their undiscerning preys. Accordingly, Duguid points out that the women prophets "are not criticized for dealing with the wrong questions but for giving the wrong answers. They were motivated not by divine calling but by pursuit of personal profit."[185] This scenario obviously had a negative effect. The falsified prophetic functions and cosmetic messages of these false male and female prophets not only had a misleading effect on their innocently preyed upon customers but specifically constituted "a stumbling block to the reception

---

182. Blenkinsopp, *A History of Prophecy in Israel*, 2d ed., 5.
183. Blenkinsopp, *A History of Prophecy in Israel*, 2nd ed., 5.
184. Duguid, *Ezekiel and the Leaders of Israel*, 93-96.
185. Duguid, *Ezekiel and the Leaders of Israel*, 97.

of Ezekiel's message of national judgement" as the exiles stood "opposed to the prophet God has sent [construing him instead] to be a false prophet."[186]

4.5.4 Ezekiel's Watchman Motif as a Model for True Shepherding

Called to be "a sign" to the house of Israel, Ezekiel was to both speak and act out the divine message before the Babylonian exiles (3:1, 4, 11, 15). Yahweh's appointment of Ezekiel as "a watchman" arose against the backdrop of Israel's consistent rebellion against Yahweh their suzerain lord. Yahweh said to Ezekiel, "Son of man, I am sending you to the Israelites, to a rebellious nation that has rebelled against me; they and their fathers have been in revolt against me to this very day. The people to whom I am sending you are obstinate and stubborn" (2:3-4a NIV). Ezekiel 3:16-21 and 33:1-20 treat extensively the "watchman motif" which is centred mainly on the point of the failure of the "house of Israel." Both leaders and people became obstinate and refused to do right and to repent and return to the path of righteousness. The occurring phrases "O house of Israel," "turn," and "watchman," are key indicators that this failure had been persistent. By assuming the role of a "watchman"[187] to the house of Israel, Ezekiel was standing in the Jewish prophetic tradition[188] to serve as Yahweh's mouthpiece, proclaiming judgement to warn and also offering

---

186. Duguid, *Ezekiel and the Leaders of Israel*, 98.
187. For the treatment of the "watchman motif," see Ezek 3:16-21; 33:1-20; cf. Isa 56:10; Jer 6:17; Hos 9:8; and Ezek 18:21-32.
188. The prophetic tradition in this sense is in reference, not to the Former and the Latter Prophets as in the Hebrew Text ordering, but specifically, to the position and roles of the Latter Prophets, comprising of the Major and Minor Prophets. Particularly, "The preexilic prophets supplied insights to divine judgment on Israel and Judah for religious disloyalty and social wrongdoing." Lasor, Hubbard, and Bush, *Old Testament Survey*, 136. For a more elaborate treatment of the Former and Latter Prophets, see pp. 131-137 and 221-230 of this work. Serving as God's mouthpiece, the oracles of the prophets who occupied the prophetic function in Jewish tradition is basically predictive with a retributive contemporary implication. While Israel's prophets spoke about the future, they also addressed the present and referred to the past. See the treatment of prophetic literature, function and prophetic traditions in Petersen, *The Prophetic Literature*, 1-44, 215-238. Given the Jewish tradition, the prophet's task was to "convey a divine view" thereby saying "No to his society, condemning its habits and assumptions, its complacency, waywardness, and syncretism." See the introduction of the work by Heschel, *The Prophets*, vii-26. For an extensive treatment of the prophetic history of Israel, see Blenkinsopp, *A History of Prophecy in Israel*, 2nd. ed.

hope to strengthen the exiles.[189] Walther Zimmerli suggests that here (Ezek 33:7-9), "One could speak of an oracle of appointment, in which Yahweh gives to the prophet his office and the commission included in that office."[190] Ezekiel is assigned a "watchman" responsibility and is therefore to faithfully function in this office.

The main purpose for retelling a story in prose narrative is to reemphasise the point of the story. Earlier on in the narrative of his prophetic tradition, Ezekiel was commissioned (3:16-21) as God's mouthpiece of judgement against a rebellious people so he could warn, as a responsible watchman,[191] the exile community of the impending calamity on Judah. Ezekiel, acting as "a sign," was assigned to perform the very function that Israel's human shepherds should have performed but failed to do.[192] As watchmen of their society, Israel's shepherds, principally royal leaders, were not only to guide the people in political, religious and social affairs, but were also to warn them against covenant disobedience, and in their fallen state, to guide them back to Yahweh in true repentance. Andrew W. Blackwood affirms this thought when he states in regards to Ezekiel's watchman function, "As the prophet is a watchman, so the king is, or ought to be, a shepherd."[193]

---

189. In as much as the prophets were spiritual watchmen, relaying God's word to the people, Ezekiel's function as a watchman was not so much to warn the exiles of the impending doom of Jerusalem as to teach that God holds each one responsible for his own behaviour (Ezek 3:17).

190. Zimmerli, *Ezekiel 2*, 183.

191. Historically, in ancient Near Eastern and Palestinian environments, and elsewhere, "Watchmen were stationed on city walls, hilltops, or specially designed watchtowers. A watchman was to be on the alert for approaching enemies and warn the city's people of any impending attack. This gave city dwellers outside the walls an opportunity to seek protection and gave the people time to secure the gates and man the defenses." Metaphorically, this is the kind of function Ezekiel was called to perform, to be "responsible for sounding the warning of impending judgment to Israel." Dyer, "Ezekiel," 1233. Leslie C. Allen calls the "watchman motif" "lookout." The essential import of the "watchman" or "lookout" man motif was cautionary by means of warning signals and defensive in terms of military warfare. The one so assigned to this responsibility was to warn, using a trumpet signal, those inside and outside the city at the sighting of an enemy. Such alert helped the vulnerable community to take "shelter into the walled city" or some place of safety to escape the sword of the invaders. Allen, *Ezekiel 20-48*, 144.

192. Dyer argues that Israel's failure to obey Yahweh's laws led to her death as a consequence. He explains further that her "homeland [was] gone, her temple destroyed, and her kings dethroned" primarily because "her false leaders within had led the people astray." Dyer, "Ezekiel," 1293.

193. Blackwood, Jr., *Ezekiel*, 207.

But, as Allen notes, Israel's leaders failed in their duty, and became guilty of a capital offense, and woe betide them since they were remiss.[194]

In contrast to Israel's leaders who failed to serve as *watching shepherds* over Yahweh's people under their oversight, Ezekiel's appointment as prophet-watchman over the house of Israel was in order to demonstrate to his audience what being a faithful shepherd-watchman entailed. To achieve this purpose, he was to be "responsible for sounding the warning of impending judgment to Israel,"[195] a role he must not fail to accomplish as the bad shepherds of Israel had done. Herein lies the burden of the principle of blood accountability upon the prophet should he fail to warn the people and the sword of the enemy slew them. His action would be tantamount to him being "responsible for their murder as if he had killed them himself"[196] should he fail to effectively function in this office. VanGemeren notes that as one "responsible to the people as God's priest-prophet watchman," Ezekiel had to "forewarn the people of what Yahweh was about to do in Jerusalem," and "once he had forewarned them, they became individually responsible for their actions,"[197] and this way, he would be exonerated and acquitted.

Consequently, Ezekiel's appointment to this dual function was to serve as model of how Israel's shepherds would have led the covenant community by warning, rebuking, correcting, and guiding as a caring and responsible shepherd would. Such appointment was grounded in the reality that Yahweh himself knew he would be a faithful watchman. His was a radical function with a blunt message, and sometimes blatant too, to his audience. As such, "He must not fail to sound the alarm, warning the people of the coming judgment of the Lord . . . whether they choose to hear or disregard, he must warn them."[198] As Yahweh's model of true shepherding to his covenant people, Ezekiel proved to be faithful. Ralph Alexander attests that "Ezekiel had faithfully performed his responsibility as a watchman for Israel" and had fully accomplished his role as "God's responsible

---

194. Allen, *Ezekiel 20-48*, 145.
195. Dyer, "Ezekiel," 1233.
196. Dyer, "Ezekiel," 1233.
197. VanGemeren, *Interpreting the Prophetic Word*, 324.
198. Robertson, *The Christ of the Prophets*, 80.

watchman"[199] because he was obedient. Ezekiel was faithful in assuming his modelling function because he was fully aware of the obligation "to pass on to his constituency verbal messages of Yahweh's moral judgment in order that they may act as a deterrent."[200] The prophet never relented in his effort to warn the exiles regarding God's anger and impending judgement on Judah, neither did he fail to extend God's second chance to the people for a possibility of divine mercy.

In line with the preceding, Ezekiel charged the Judean exiles to take individual responsibility for their sin and to return to Yahweh in repentance. VanGemeren points out that being a rebellious and a "blame-passing" people who would "become indignant, believing that their suffering was on account of their fathers [sins]," Ezekiel challenged them "that each man was responsible for himself" because "Judah's suffering was because of her long-standing apostasy."[201] To put it another way, if the exiles had previously "blamed their parent's sin for any coming judgment," they should have fully recognised by now that "their own wickedness was causing them to waste away."[202] Ezekiel, as a model, was not to tread softly on these matters but rather to be radical, blunt, and frigid to their negative reaction to his prophetic message of warning.

As Yahweh's messenger, Ezekiel's modelling shepherding role depicted by the watchman motif, would also offer hope within the context of an already bad situation. A true shepherd offers hope to the flock by ensuring security and building confidence by his consistent presence among the flock. The import of the message in Ezekiel's watchman motif looked "to the role of Yahweh as would-be defender of his people and not their destroyer, the preserver and giver of life and not the taker."[203] The setting of chapter 33 invites the reader to understand it "as the beginning of the positive messages of hope" that make up chapters 34-48.[204]

---

199. Alexander, "Ezekiel," 904.
200. Allen, *Ezekiel 20-48*, 145.
201. VanGemeren, *Interpreting the Prophetic Word*, 324.
202. Alexander, "Ezekiel," 905.
203. Allen, *Ezekiel 20-48*, 145.
204. Block, *The Book of Ezekiel: Chapters 25-48*, 234.

4.6 Conclusion

The narrated accounts of the Pentateuch reveal that Yahweh initiated a special relationship with Israel on the basis of a covenant enactment that is fully crystallised in the Abrahamic, Mosaic, and Davidic covenants. But because of Israel's consistent inability to live up to the terms of the covenant, exile had become inevitable as Yahweh's means of purging the nation of her sin. Yahweh had planned to use the pain of exilic experience to purify the people and redirect their religious paradigm to his true worship as the God of their fathers and is now their God. On this basis, Ezekiel used Deuteronomic theology, its tenets which Israel had violated, as recourse to explain that the painful experience of exile was aimed at achieving for the nation a recreation of a new Israel and a purified and reinvigorated new religious worship in the eschatological community of Israel.

Ezekiel contended that both the Northern and Southern Kingdoms had lacked the kind of shepherd leaders with theocentric motivation to give political direction and religious guidance to the people. This absence had plunged the whole nation into covenant infidelity, and finally, into captivity. Ezekiel's theological argumentation and critique brought to the fore the fact that with consistently credible shepherd-like leadership, the nation would not have lost the Temple which stood as its unifying centre and cultic life force. It would not also have lost the land which served as its political identity. Nor would Zion/Jerusalem, the holy abode of Yahweh, have been lost.

CHAPTER FIVE
A Case for Eschatological Shepherding in Ezekiel 34

5.1 Introduction

The language of Ezekiel 34 is undoubtedly metaphorical.[1] This chapter could best be described as the reservoir for the prophetic shepherd metaphor. The shepherd metaphor, not a parable as suggested,[2] is nowhere more graphically presented in the prophets than it is in Ezekiel 34. We think Ezekiel 34 presents a slide show of the massive shepherding failure in Israelite society. Allen describes it as painting the picture of Yahweh's flock "abused by its explosive rulers"[3] for their attitude of brutality, greed, godlessness, negligence and irresponsibility. In Kaiser's postulation, Ezekiel 34 is a passage that "was at the heart of Ezekiel's contribution to the ongoing promise,"[4] serving as a bridge between the old and new order of things in Israel's history.

In this vein, Ezekiel 34 stands at the end of the evil days of what had happened to Judah in the recent past and at the same time stands at the beginning of a new dawn soon to happen to restored Israel. This way, it

---

1. Paul M. Joyce, *Ezekiel: A Commentary*, 199.
2. Ward thinks this chapter is a parable of the shepherds. But this is more a metaphor than a parable when compared with the parable of the vultures or eagles (Ezek 17:1-21) and that of the lion (Ezek 19:1-10). J Ward, *Thus Says the Lord*, 189.
3. Allen, "Ezekiel," 367.
4. Kaiser, Jr., *Toward an Old Testament Theology*, 240.

bridges the theological themes of Israel's period of national anguish through deportation with that of joy in the hope of her future restoration. It also balances the period of a people's gloom with an anticipated future glory. Ezekiel 34 presents an extensive treatment of the theology of shepherding, a theme treated within Jewish perspective. As Vancil points out, "here the prophet uses the evil shepherd theme to illustrate selfish and irresponsible leadership"[5] in Israelite society. Zimmerli summarizes the main thrust of Ezekiel 34 as dealing "with the shepherds of Israel and with the condition of the people of God under good and bad shepherding."[6]

We attempt in this chapter to discuss Ezekiel's motif of eschatological shepherding by probing why he used the shepherd metaphor while an exile at this critical moment in Judah's history. We also probe his methodology as well as the salient theological and eschatological imports in the shepherd metaphor. We argue that Ezekiel employed the shepherd metaphor against the whole sweep of the massive failure of Israelite society under its past and present imperfect human shepherds. He does this with an eschatological undertone to build his hope principle in Yahweh's rescue mission of his flock.

As a matter of procedure, we take a look at the literary and structural context for Ezekiel's use of the shepherding motif in Ezekiel chapter 34. Attention is focused here on the prophet's oracular speeches of indictment of imperfect human shepherds, of Yahweh's sifting of the imperfect flock, of his declaration of a rescue mission, and the promise of a perfect eschatological environment for true shepherding under a perfect shepherd. The chapter concludes with a treatment of the significant role of Ezekiel's recognition formula vis-à-vis the actualisation of Yahweh's eschatological programme in behalf of his flock.

---

5. Vancil, "Sheep, Shepherd," 1190.
6. Zimmerli, *Ezekiel 2*, 212.

5.2 The Literary and Structural Context for Ezekiel 34

Before we focus our attention on the structure of Ezekiel chapter 34, we think that a consideration of the general literary[7] outlook of the book of Ezekiel would yield some dividends to our understanding the chapter. It is difficult to find a consensus among scholarly opinions on the literary structure of the book of Ezekiel. Notably, bipartite, tripartite, and quadruplicate scholarly opinions all exist regarding the book's structure. Firstly, some scholars divide the book of Ezekiel into two broad literary categories. C. F. Keil[8] acknowledged that the prophetic collections placed in the book of Ezekiel to form a complete unity, fall into two main divisions, noting that the first consists of announcements of judgment upon Israel and the heathen nations (Ezek 1-32) while the second consists of announcements of salvation for Israel (Ezek 33-48). He explains, "Each of these main divisions is subdivided into two sections," the first holds judgment prophecies upon Jerusalem and Israel (Ezek 3:22-24) and upon heathen nations (Ezek 25-32). The second holds the predictions of the redemption and restoration of Israel, the downfall of the heathen world power (Ezek 33-39) and the prophetic picture of the re-formation and exaltation of the kingdom of God (Ezek 40-48). The first half (chs. 1-32) covers a gloomy and dark period for both Judah and the foreign nations while the second half (chs. 33-48) covers a bright future for Judah. This means the first half submits condemnation but the second expresses consolation. Along this line of thought, Allen asserts that in the second half, "Darkness was to be followed by the dawn of a new and far better day"[9] for Judah.

Secondly, the majority of scholars hold to the tripartite literary structure of the book of Ezekiel. This is generally patterned along thematic lines.

---

7. As a clear literary work, it is admitted that "Ezekiel more than any other prophet likes to subsume his subjects by a figure or type." This book consists of convergent literary genres. In it exists parables (Ezek 15:1ff), allegories (Ezek 17:1ff; 21:2ff; 24:3ff), laments (19:1-14), types (Ezek 14:12-23), imageries, and so on.
8. C. F. Keil, *Commentary on the Old Testament in Ten Volumes by C. F. Keil and F. Delitzch: Volume Ix-Ezekiel, Daniel* (trans. James Martin; Grand Rapids, Mich.: Eerdmans, n.d.; repr., 1978), 7.
9. Allen, *Ezekiel 1-19*, xxv.

Accordingly, Allen divides the book into three thematic sections, the first covering chapters 1-24, which he says is essentially made up of three collections of messages of judgment. He explains that the literary purpose of this section is to account for the cause of the exile.[10] The second major section covers Ezekiel chapters 25-32, focusing its series of oracles against foreign nations. The third major section covers Ezekiel chapters 33-48, which he notes contains collections of oracles of salvation that celebrate its imminent coming.[11] Allen's submission echoes the structure that older scholars had presented. Walther Eichrodt[12] stated that, "it would not be surprising if Ezekiel had collected his writings and arranged them." He concludes that the book of Ezekiel "was given its final shape by being arranged in three large sections: the pronouncements of judgment upon Israel in chapters 1-24, the prophecies concerning foreign nations in chapters 25-32, and the portrayals of the time of salvation in chapters 33-48, a structure also found in the books of Isaiah and Jeremiah."[13] Christopher Wright[14] submits that the "chronological sequence of the prophecies also works effectively alongside the broader structuring of the book" just as Ezekiel's ministry "itself falls into two clear phases" – the first five years between his call and the fall of Jerusalem and the remaining fifteen years after that event. He notes that chapters 1-24 "are predominantly oracles of judgment, pointing to the coming catastrophe and justifying it on the basis of the accumulated wickedness and rebellion of Israel." Found in this period is the dominant theme of "hope for the future through God's promise of restoration" in chapters

---

10. Allen, *Ezekiel 1-19*, xxvi.

11. Allen, *Ezekiel 1-19*, xxxi.

12. Eichrodt, *Ezekiel*, 18. Equally, in his acknowledging the book's definite chronological arrangement, structural order and harmony, Charles Dyer explains, "the first 24 chapters focus on the judgment of Judah [while] chapters 33-48 focus on the restoration of Judah. [But] These two extremes are balanced by chapters 25-32 which deal with God's judgment on other nations." Dyer, "Ezekiel," 1226. Additionally, John Taylor admitted that "the book of Ezekiel has a basic simplicity and its orderly framework makes it easy to analyse." He notes that the message of chapters 1-24 is destructive and denunciatory, chapters 25-32 are oracles against the nations, and that regarding himself as a watchman, Ezekiel's message of chapters 33-40 deal with individual retribution and responsibility with an encouraging restorative tone. Taylor, *Ezekiel*, 5, 14, 15.

13. Eichrodt, *Ezekiel*, 21.

14. Wright, *The Message of Ezekiel*, 41.

33-48, while in between are Ezekiel's prophecies against foreign nations in chapters 25-32.[15]

Thirdly, the quadruple opinion does not lack proponents though fewer. For example, Ronald E. Clements admits, "it is clear that the book does show an impressive degree of theological homogeneity and a remarkable element of planned literary structure. He states that, "the major divisions of the book between chapters 1-24, 25-32, 33-39, and 40-48 are all undoubtedly the consequence of an attempt to give some literary and theological "form" to the book as a whole."[16] Lamar Cooper[17] also acknowledges a four divisions arrangement of Ezekiel in a slightly different way thus: chapters 1-3 concern the prophet's commission, chapters 4-24 are prophetic judgements concerning the fall of Judah and the destruction of Jerusalem, chapters 25-32 comprise "an interlude of messages of judgment against foreign nations," and chapters 33-48 concern hope. He notes that this hope concerns the restoration of Israel, of the reestablishment of the temple and its sacrificial system, of the redistribution of the land, and of the rebuilding of Jerusalem. In a similar fashion, Daniel Block[18] sides with the quadruple division of the book following its rhetorical agenda. He identifies four major categories of accounts that reflect four of the major sections of the book. In his literary categorisation, the first section holds the prophetic call narrative that involves "an inaugural vision, a verbal commissioning, and a physical binding" (1:1-3:27); the second section holds pronouncements of judgement against Judah and Jerusalem (4:1-24:27; 33:1-34); the third section holds oracles against foreign nations (25:1-32:32); and the fourth holds announcements of salvation and restoration (34:1-48:35). Iain Duguid's outline of a four-division format also follows these preceding scholars in a synergetic fusion. In his order, the first section (1:1-3:27) presents Ezekiel's call and commissioning, the second (4:1-24:27) echoes

---

15. The list of the tripartite opinion seems endless, as it is replete elsewhere. See Bullock, *An Introduction to the Old Testament Prophetic Books*, 239-249; Dillard and Longman III, *An Introduction to the Old Testament*, 320-321; Hill and Walton, *A Survey of the Old Testament,* 2nd ed., 443-444; VanGemeren, *Interpreting the Prophetic Word*, 327-328; Robertson, *The Christ of the Prophets*, 290-293; and Petersen, *The Prophetic Literature*, 18.
16. Clements, *Old Testament Prophecy*, 152.
17. Cooper, *Ezekiel*, 39.
18. Block, *The Book of Ezekiel Chapters 1-24*, 15.

the doom of Yahweh's people, the third (25:1-32:32) reveals the prophetic oracles against the nations, and the last section (33:1-48:35) covers the oracles of good news.[19]

When we carefully put together all the preceding submissions, we have to accept the fact that literally, the book of Ezekiel in its general outlook consists of the following: the prophet's inaugural call (Ezek 1:1-3:15), a prophetic rebuke of Israel for her sin (Ezek 3:16-24:27), a prophetic indictment of the surrounding nations for their crime against the covenant people (Ezek 25-32), and Yahweh's planned restoration of a new united Israel in the eschatological community despite and vis-à-vis the imperfection and failures of her human shepherds (Ezek 33-48).

5.2.1 Ezekiel Chapters 13, 17 and 19 as a Literary Context for the Shepherd Metaphor.[20]

Ezekiel chapters 13, 17 and 19 serve as a good context for his treatment of the shepherd metaphor in chapter 34. Ezekiel 13:5, 10-16 present the metaphor of the builders of the wall overlaid with whitewash. Here, the prophet described the deceptive activities of Judah's rival false prophets who dislodged truth in favour of false visions. By their falsity and deception, Odell says these false prophets consequentially failed to "issue warnings of impending danger and to intercede in order to avert it."[21] Ezekiel described such prophetic falsity as builders of a flimsy wall covered with whitewash. In their masterminded falsehood, these rival prophets led the people astray by promising peace despite the reality of the imminent collapse of Jerusalem (13:10). Blenkinsopp explains that the falsity of these prophets, described as daubing and whitewashing a building wall, "implies the creation of an illusory and specious appearance of truth designed to conceal a fundamental inauthenticity . . . to give it an appearance of solidity."[22] In effect, as Allen states, what the rival prophets had done by the

---

19. Duguid, *Ezekiel*, 40-41.
20. The idea in this subsection was ignited consequent upon Dr. Odell's critical comments to JETS of May 26, 2011 regarding this dissertation.
21. Odell, *Ezekiel*, 147.
22. Blenkinsopp, *Ezekiel*, 70.

superficiality of their action was "tantamount to plastering over such a dry wall, giving the impression of a solid, substantial structure."[23]

In addressing the precarious situation, Ezekiel went beyond the normal prophetic indictment to the declaration of divine vindictive action. He used the imagery of rain, hailstones, and wind to announce divine judgement (13:11, 13-15) soon to come upon these deceivers who had posed as prophets. Blenkinsopp notes that when these whitewashed prophecies finally come under the divine plumb line, then "the prophetic specialist in self-deception is revealed for what he is;"[24] their prophecy would not stand as whitewash can not withstand these storms Yahweh was soon to employ as means of judgement. Also, as Allen and Odell suggest, when Yahweh launched his anger at such prophetic deception, then it would not only be that the "popular hope, so assiduously nurtured by the prophets, would be exposed for the sham it was,"[25] but also such judgement would leave no city or its walls, no prophet, no peace, and no people.[26] The building metaphor suggests that false prophecy within the Judean environment accounted in part for the shepherding failure.[27]

Ezekiel 17:1-24 also presents the metaphor[28] of the cedar and the vine to depict the implication of disobedience to treaty terms and covenant

---

23. Allen, *Ezekiel 1-19*, 202.
24. Blenkinsopp, *Ezekiel*, 70.
25. Allen, *Ezekiel 1-19*, 203.
26. Odell, *Ezekiel*, 150.
27. Not all will concede this statement though, as scholars argue generally regarding Ezekiel's chastisement of male false prophets in Judah and in particular that of female prophets in view of the imminent demise of the city. The argument concludes that such condemnation is sociological and not phenomenological because such a condemning posture is an attempt by Ezekiel and his school to control female prophets for some ideological purpose. Nancy R. Bowen "The Daughters of Your People: Female Prophets in Ezekiel 13:17-23," *JBL* 3 (1999):*417-433*.
28. Some scholars think this passage to be a parable rather than a metaphor. Odell sees it as a parable concerning the respective fates of two Davidic descendants, Jehoiachin and Zedekiah. Odell, *Ezekiel*, 206-7. Block disagrees and sees it rather as a riddle cast in the form of a fable. Block, *The Book of Ezekiel Chapters 1-24*, 530. Duguid sees it as a metaphor that combines both riddle and parable. While a riddle makes a statement that hides the truth it imparts, a parable elucidates the truth that underlies it by putting it in a fresh light. Duguid, *Ezekiel*, 222. Greenberg sees the principle of duality being operative here: a riddle which is "an obscure saying from which something else is to be understood" and a fable which is "a likening of one matter to another." Existent here also is "fable and interpretation, two eagles, two plants, two modes of punishment, two planes of agency

violation. In this metaphor, the act of covenant violation by the last king of Judah, Ezekiel explained, made him a useless and fruitless low vine of a cedar tree that is pressed on both sides by two powerful eagles (17:1-10). The point of the metaphor is located in the king's act of breaking the terms of a treaty (17:14-16, 18-20), and such violation either to a treaty or covenant has dire consequences.

This metaphor expresses the effects of leadership failure in Judah presented by the prophet in terms of covenant violation. Allen observes such monarchical blunder when he states, "Zedekiah, in breaking his vassal oath to Nebuchadnezzar, had invited retribution from Yahweh, in whose name he had made it. So Yahweh had decreed Zedekiah's downfall and masterminded Babylonian reprisals, working out the very curses Zedekiah earlier recited with invocation of his listening God."[29] The explanation for such divine involvement in a politically motivated and executed agenda by a foreign overlord is as expressed in the words of Blenkinsopp, "the political realm does not exist as an independent and autonomous entity; it therefore cannot claim absolute status. No human institution, however well established and powerful, is exempt from divine judgment."[30] Beyond this, it also goes to prove the implication of a lack of dependence on Yahweh on the part of the people of faith. The divided loyalty in the covenant violation of the cedar/vine (17:5-8) reveals such lack of dependence.

Lastly, Ezekiel 19:1-14 takes up a lament for the princes of Judah couched in the metaphor of a lioness and her cubs. Appropriately, it is a "two-part poem that focuses on the fate of a mother and her royal progeny."[31] It appears obvious that this metaphor of a lioness is representative of Jerusalem/Judah, a strong city that had hitherto thrived among nations and her two cubs as a representative of Judah's last two kings.[32] Understood within the

---

(earthly and divine), doom and consolation." Greenberg, *Ezekiel 1-20*, 309, 317.

29. Allen, *Ezekiel 1-19*, 262.

30. Blenkinsopp, *Ezekiel*, 86. He explains further that it is a matter of importance to Ezekiel that "solemn political commitments be honored. Zedekiah's rebellion was not just politically suicidal. It was an irreligious act, a violation of commitments supported by religious sanctions, for the treaty into which he entered with the Babylonian king was guaranteed by an oath in the name of Israel's God" (see p. 81).

31. Odell, *Ezekiel*, 233.

32. Blenkinsopp explains here the identity of these last kings: "The two cubs are Jehoahaz

context of Ezekiel, the metaphor of a lioness that later becomes a vine (19:1, 10) is in reference to none other than Jerusalem and Judah. The strength of the city of Jerusalem, following the overthrow of 587 BC, was reduced to at worst a ruin good only for foxes and jackals (cf. Neh 1:1-3; 2:16-17; 4:1-3).

The three metaphoric examples above all go to make a case for the massive leadership failure and its grave consequences to the nation of Israel. Her prophets, princes, and kings, who ordinarily were to function in society as its shepherds, blatantly neglected their official responsibilities, thereby demonstrating the weakness, evil, and imperfection of human leadership in human society. It is this failure that Ezekiel later expanded upon in his treatment of the shepherd metaphor in chapter 34, to accommodate the expressed crimes of Israel's imperfect human shepherds and the consequential divine indictment. This allowed for the ease of his proclamation of the oracle of a divine eschatological restoration programme in favour of the flock.

5.2.2 The Literary Structure of Ezekiel 34

Although Ezekiel chapter 34 is doubtless a complete literary unit governed by its shepherd metaphor, at least in the final form of the text, its authorship and composition have been questioned by the prophet's critics and responded to as well by those sympathetic to the prophet. For instance, while recognising that a complex compositional history likely underlies Ezekiel 34 as questioned by critics, nonetheless, Katheryn Darr submits

---

and Jehoiachin, among the most tragic and least reprehensible of the kings of Judah in the last period of its existence. Both reigned for only three months. Jehoahaz, son of Josiah, came to the throne after the tragic death of his father at Megiddo in 609 BC but was deported by Pharaoh Neco and died in Egypt (II Kings 23:30-34)....The strongest shoot of the vine is the ruler, and the ruler in question here is undoubtedly Zedekiah, last king of Judah, who reigned from 598 to 586 BC It was his rebellion against the Babylonians that led to the end of independence and the exile." Blenkinsopp, *Ezekiel*, 85. But does the possibility exist that the exile would have been averted and therefore the demise of Judah not to occur had Zedekiah kept his treaty oath? Odell responds in the negative. She says the mother/lioness imagery is an assertion that holds the entire community of Israel morally responsible for the demise of the Davidic dynasty because of her violence. From this she submits, "...if the exiles heed Ezekiel's call to repentance, they must do so knowing that nothing of their rich heritage can be saved, because all of it has nurtured violence." Odell, *Ezekiel*, 241

that "the text invites readers to construe it as a single unit, because its subunits (vv. 2-10; 11-16; 17-31) share shepherd/flock imagery."[33] Similarly, James Muilenburg had conceded that "while the chapter shows signs of unevenness and possibly of composite authorship, it is governed by the common theme of the shepherd and his flock."[34] Block also submits that there is "no a priori reason for considering [it] as inauthentic" since the text "contains no historical anachronisms demanding a later context, no syntactically incoherent elements that cannot be attributed to textual corruption or ancient literary practice, and no blatant internal contradictions."[35] Block contends that Ezekiel 34 should be recognised as "a self-contained literary unit" and as "a deliberate literary composition" despite its literary complexity.[36]

No doubt, Ezekiel 34 is a complete literary unit governed by the shepherd metaphor. When interpreted within its historical context following events in Judah in the recent past, this chapter functions as the historical-literary centre of the entire book. It stands at the end of a series of prophetic indictments full of woe and judgement oracles, thereby concluding a period of gloom and condemnation of Israel and the nations. But it also begins a new section of restoration characterised by salvation oracles, thereby marking a new era of consolation and hope for the exiles and for Israel as a whole. The chapter divides itself literarily into three oracular sections – Yahweh's indictment and judgement oracles against Israel's bad and imperfect shepherds (Ezek 34:1-16), Yahweh's oracle of indictment and sifting of

---

33. Katheryn. Pfisterer Darr, "The Book of Ezekiel," in *The New Interpreter's Bible Vol. VI* (eds. Leander E. Keck et al.; Nashville: Abingdon, 2001), 1461.
34. James Muilenburg, "Ezekiel," in *Peake's Commentary on the Bible* (eds. Matthew Black and H. H. Rowley; London: Thomas Nelson & Sons Ltd., 1962; repr, 1963), 585.
35. Block, *The Book of Ezekiel Chapters 25-48*, 273.
36. Block, *The Book of Ezekiel Chapters 25-48*, 273-5. Block structures this chapter around three deliverance oracular themes which is coordinated by formulaic features with shifts in tone and content thus: (a) the announcement of deliverance (vv. 2-10), (b) the nature of the deliverance (vv. 11-22), and (c) the goal of the deliverance (vv. 23-31). He explains that in the first panel, we find a woe oracle of accusation (vv. 2-6) and a woe oracle of judgement (vv. 7-10) directed at Israel's leaders. The second panel focuses entirely on Yahweh and the salvific activity of his rescue mission on behalf of his flock, first, from external enemies (vv. 11-16) and second, from internal exploiters (vv. 17-22). The third panel (vv. 23-31) captures Yahweh's covenant with His people (vv. 24, 30-31) (see p. 274).

the imperfect flock (Ezek 34:17-22), and Yahweh's oracle of the declaration of a perfect eschatological society for shepherding (Ezek 34:23-31).

When we develop the thought of this chapter along thematic lines, we will notice that broadly, Ezekiel 34 functions along the major themes of human failure (judgement) and divine action (salvation). In this connection, the first 10 verses call attention to the theme of imperfect shepherding (past leadership failure in Israelite society) of a people in covenant relationship. It stresses this shepherding failure as being responsible for bringing upon the nation the Deuteronomic curses with the Babylonian exile, the destruction of the Temple and loss of its priesthood, and the demise of Jerusalem as its major attendant effects. The last 21 verses also draw attention to Yahweh's eschatological rescue mission put in place in behalf of his abandoned flock by these imperfect human shepherds. The duality of human failure (judgement) and divine action (salvation) in this chapter is quite obviously motivated by an eschatological motif. These two visible polls may be explained in summary form as follows: It holds Yahweh's indictment of Israel's weak and imperfect human shepherds for their acts of brutality to his flock on the one hand, and his promised salvation, that is, a refreshing and restful eschatological tranquillity for his wounded flock on the other hand.

We understand Ezekiel to be a literal prophetic figure just as Israel was a literal political entity. The existence of such a self-governed political entity naturally would call for literal human leadership such as kings, princes, administrative bureaucrats, priests, and so on. These are metaphorically designated as "shepherds" as well portrayed by Ezekiel's shepherd metaphor. Our discussion of Ezekiel 34 proceeds with this understanding in mind.

5.3 Indictment of Imperfect Human Shepherds, vv. 1-16

This first major oracle divides itself into three subunits – (1) Yahweh's woe oracle indicting Israel's bad and imperfect human shepherds, vv. 1-6, (2) Yahweh's judgement oracle against Israel's bad and imperfect human shepherds, vv. 7-10, and (3) Yahweh's oracle of eschatological rescue mission of the flock from the caprice of the bad and imperfect human shepherds of Israel, vv. 11-16. The opening verses reveal Ezekiel's reporting of Yahweh's accusation of Israel's bad and imperfect human shepherds for gross shepherding misconduct and acts of leadership irresponsibility. He presents them to be cruel, exploitative and exceptionally greedy at the expense of the sheep (vv. 2-4). Israel's bad shepherds are seen to have exhibited nonchalant attitude toward the plight of the sheep in favour of personal gain, thereby exhibiting "none of the pastoral qualities that were required of them in caring"[37] for the flock's welfare. They had scattered the sheep by their attitude of greed and negligence in failing to keep them together (vv. 5-6). As a consequence, the flock became as sheep without a shepherd in that most pathetic of all states.[38] In sum, Darr notes that Ezekiel's woe oracle metaphorically describes the rulers' sins of commission and omission against Yahweh's people[39] as depicted in vv. 3-4.

5.3.1 "Woe" Oracle Indicting Israel's Bad Shepherd's, vv. 1-6

Vv. 1-2. The first two opening verses are imperative commission statements for the prophet to prophesy. Verse 1 begins with the customary opening word-event or introductory formula ויהי דבר־יהוה אלי לאמר ("Then/and the word of the LORD came to me saying"). Verse 2 is preceded by the address formula בן־אדם ("son of man") uniquely characteristic of Ezekiel's oracular speech pattern. Here, the prophet is commissioned in a directive manner to speak the prophetic word to Israel's imperfect human shepherds. In fact, it is to be against *them*,[40] the imperfect human shepherds as its

---

37. Taylor, *Ezekiel*, 220.

38. Taylor, *Ezekiel*, 220. Cf. Prophet Miciah's statement in 1 Kgs 22:17 and that of Jesus in Matt 9:36 in this respect.

39. Darr, "The Book of Ezekiel," 1461.

40. The word אליהם is absent in the LXX and the Vulgate versions. The NRS translation of the phrase, אליהם לרעים, should be retained as it is an intensive emphatic expression of Yahweh's feeling against the shepherds. Although Block considers Ezek 34-48 as a section that deals with what he calls "the gospel according to Ezekiel" basically for its salvation and restoration motif, he does accept that the theme of judgement persists. In this connection, he is right in observing that "the woe oracle against the leaders of Israel preceding the promise of a restored flock in 34:1-10 is reminiscent of the oracles against the false prophets and prophetesses in ch.13." Block, *The Book of Ezekiel Chapters 25-48*, 270.

direct target. Unmistakably, this "woe" oracle is directed against the bad and imperfect human shepherds of Israel (cf. Jer 23:1f; Ezek 34) as indicated by the preposition עַל, much more as the prophet was initially commissioned to be "a sign" to the house of Israel. The use of הוֹי רֹעֵי־יִשְׂרָאֵל ("woe, shepherds of Israel") lays the ground for the divine accusation of the shepherds that is soon to follow.

One of the key functions of a shepherd is care of pasturage/tending for the flock. But here, there is a reversal of the order of function as the shepherd cares for himself instead. The divine accusation is therefore lodged against shepherds who pasture/tend only themselves. It is quite probable from this accusation that the prophetic word here is trying to say something to the history of Israel as a whole[41] and not just to Judah; for the divine imperative to the prophet is to הִנָּבֵא עַל־רוֹעֵי יִשְׂרָאֵל ("prophesy against the shepherds of Israel").

Vv. 3-4. The use of the לֹא negation in these verses points to the weakness, imperfection, and anti-shepherd character of Israel's shepherds consequent upon their failure to care for Yahweh's flock. It stands in the sense of a negative contrast to the shepherds' action of consuming, clothing, and slaughtering of the flock as a benefit, which was customary of ancient shepherds. In the practice of shepherding in the ANE world, a shepherd benefiting from the products of the flock on certain grounds was something permissive as part of the shepherd's reward (v. 3). Its real intent however was not to operate as an exploitative act[42] on the part of the shepherd but rather as a motivational right. The tone of Ezekiel's accusatory oracle against the attitude of the bad and imperfect shepherds of Israel here suggests that their benefiting from the husbandry goes beyond what is permitted and is therefore a dereliction of the true office of the shepherd.[43]

---

41. While the text does not explicitly express this idea, yet, it is possible to imply it here. While the direct audience of Ezekiel was the Babylonian exiles, the failures of kingship spread across the Northern and Southern kingdoms, serving as the basic cause for the Assyrian and Babylonian captivities. Zimmerli, *Ezekiel 2*, 214.

42. Since the shepherds only cared for their personal needs against those of the flock, they had become exploitative oppressors. See Block's thought in *The Book of Ezekiel Chapters 25-48*, 283.

43. When we put the prophetic charge in historical retrospect and in a reflexive sense, we understand that these bad shepherds of Israel only "tended themselves" at the expense of the flock. See Zimmerli's interpretation in *Ezekiel 2*, 215. See Greenberg's discussion on

While it was not a crime for the shepherds to benefit from the milk,[44] wool, and meat, yet, Yahweh took on a charge lament against them because of their intentional failure, הצאן לא תרעו ("you have not pastured the flock," v. 3). The לא negation occurs six times in vv. 3-4 (once in v. 3 and five times in v. 4) indicating the seriousness of the offense attracting Yahweh's accusation and charge of Israel's imperfect human shepherds. Accordingly, Ezekiel accused the shepherds both for specific crimes of commission and omission. While they *consumed*[45] the products, they failed to care for and *conserve* the flock as required.

Yahweh's accusation in v. 4 links with the reason previously stated in v. 3. But it goes beyond mere benefiting to negligence. The tone of v. 4 suggests that the prophet's accusation of Israel's bad shepherds (its political leaders) is because of their abuse of office and misuse[46] of delegated power. Israel's human shepherds[47], in Ezekiel's view, were nothing more than parasites,[48] sucking the saps of the people for which they were to protect and care for.

---

how to interpret this charge in Greenberg, *Ezekiel 21-37*, 695-6.

44. The LXX and Vulgate versions translate חלב as milk instead of fat. The LXX's use of γάλα is preferred. The usage is within the context of a shepherd benefiting from the husbandry and not in the context of offering burnt sacrifice, fellowship meal or one feeding oneself, in which case the former reading would have been most appropriate. The idea of leadership failure caused by greed and negligence should always be kept in view when translating Ezekiel 34.

45. The verb *consume* seems a preferred reading over *eat* when connected with milk. This also follows the reading אכלין of the Palestinian Syriac Tragum. Consequent upon the failure of the shepherds to care for the flock, "the flock has been jeopardised because of gross malpractice by the leaders." Block, *The Book of Ezekiel Chapters 25-48*, 283.

46. The shepherds' acts of brutality and harsh handling of the flock reveals their misuse of political power. Cooke suggests that the shepherds' cruelty to the flock, as Ezekiel charged in 34:4, may be an allusion to the harsh treatment of slaves, as Israel had experienced in Egypt (Exod 1:13-14). Cooke, *A Critical and Exegetical Commentary*, 374. But according to Eichrodt, this abuse reveals itself in the shepherds' right of consuming the milk and meat produced by the flock and the use of its wool for clothing which, in the case of Israel's shepherds, did not go side by side with the duty of caring for the flock and faithfully providing for its pasture. Hence, that "right becomes a crying injustice." Eichrodt, *Ezekiel*, 470.

47. While in specific terms Ezekiel used "shepherds" metaphorically as designation for the kings, the term "shepherds" is also generally identified with the political rulers, the powerful, and the religious leaders of the society of his day (cf. 34:2-6; 22:6-7, 25-28).

48. This is a descriptive word used for the shepherds by Bruce Vawter and Leslie J. Hoppe. Bruce Vawter and Leslie J. Hoppe *A New Heart: A Commentary on the Book of Ezekiel* (Grand Rapids, Mich.: Eerdmans, 1991), 154.

The shepherds are repudiated for their negligent attitude towards the needs of the flock even though they enjoyed benefiting from the produce. In five strong verbs, each used in reference to a specific category of needy sheep, the prophet repudiated the shepherds for their inability to חזקתם (to make strong the weak, used in the Piel pf 2nd per. mp), רפאתם (to heal the sick, used in the Piel pf 2nd per. mp), חבשתם (to bind up the broken/injured, used in the Qal pf 2nd per. mp), השבתם (to bring back the strayed, used in the Hiphil pf 2nd mp), and בקשתם (to seek the lost, used in the Piel pf 2nd per. mp). The לא negation captures the negligent attitude of Israel's bad shepherds towards the flock because they failed to do any of the required functions of a good shepherd described by these strong verbs above.

Vv. 5-6. Following the shepherd's failure and act of irresponsibility to the flock, the sheep strayed away and wandered helplessly over the mountains and every hill and over the face of the whole earth for lack of proper shepherding. What aggravated matters here is the shepherds' insensitivity because the prophet charged them for ruling the flock harshly and brutally (v. 4b). In this regard, Ezekiel used the feminine noun חזקה to express the idea of force and violence and the masculine noun פרך to express the idea of harshness and severity. As a consequence of such a brute-like action, the flock's reaction of פוץ ("scattering" or "wandering") resulting in their becoming אכלה ("food" or "a prey") to חיהשדה (the "wild beasts of the field") is because of the absence of a רעה ("shepherd") to care for them (v. 5). A high probability exists here that this scenario might well echo the reality of Israel's exile[49] to Assyria and Judah's to Babylonia as a consequence of bad leadership. Even when the flock had scattered and wandered, no רעה bothered to seek or search[50] for them (v. 6).

Here, the "watchman" motif assumes its clarity. The *shepherds* of Israel had been assigned a shepherding responsibility to lead and take care of the *sheep* on behalf of Yahweh. By this, they were expected to have assumed, metaphorically, the role of a watchman over the sheep pen. But they had

---

49. See Zimmerli's thought on this in *Ezekiel 2*, 215.
50. Ezekiel used the verbs דרש (a word expressing the idea to resort to or to seek in the Qal) and בקש (to seek, in the Piel) following each other. The latter word expresses the strong idea of not only seeking but a thorough and careful examination of something. Its tone is more intensive, hence, the Piel stem.

failed. The watchman motif in Ezekiel expresses two implications: First, it reveals the aspect of responsibility to an assigned task. The one so assigned must *warn* so the person or people being warned could *turn* from evil and escape imminent danger. Second, it also expresses the point of accountability for either failure on the part of the person occupying a position of responsibility to *warn*, or failure on the part of the person being warned to heed the warning of imminent danger. In this case, Israel's bad and imperfect human shepherds failed the test of being "watchmen" over Yahweh's flock. By implication, to have worthless shepherds like Israel had is worse than being a shepherdless community.[51] For as it turned out in Israel's history, the exile can be said to be the bitter fruit of the leader's bad shepherding[52] of Yahweh's flock entrusted to their care because it is their actions that had precipitated the crisis[53] the flock experienced.

5.3.2 Judgement Oracle Against Israel's Bad Shepherds, vv. 7-10

This subunit opens with the particle adverb לכן ("therefore"), which stands in a consequential position to the words that follow in this section. The position of לכן in this construction, having the shepherds as its direct object, stresses the certainty of the divine action soon to follow. The "therefore" here links the shepherds' actions in vv. 2b-5 and its resultant effects on the flock in vv. 5-6. The oath signature formula חי־אני ("As surely as I live," v. 8) has embedded in it the announcement of judgement against the bad rulers of Israel and a message of salvation for Yahweh's neglected flock. Here, the one is removed from office and the other is rescued from official abuses. The oracle of Yahweh's judgement comes immediately following after a repeated accusation oracle (vv. 8; cf. vv. 3-4). The invitation phrase שמעו את־דבר יהוה ("You [shepherds], hear the word of the Lord"), is directed at the irresponsible shepherds. Its repetition (twice here in vv. 7, 9) calls attention to the action Yahweh is about to take on the shepherds for the sake of

---

51. See the idea as expressed in Block, *The Book of Ezekiel Chapters 25-48*, 284.
52. See the idea in Zimmerli, *Ezekiel 2*, 215.
53. Block charges Israel's bad shepherds as being responsible for the crises of the exiles in Israel's history. Block, *The Book of Ezekiel Chapters 25-48*, 283.

his flock. In a judicial courtroom fashion then, the phrase gives "summons to approach" the bench in view of Yahweh's action against the shepherds.[54]

The position of the particle adverb יַעַן ("because of," "on account of") in v. 8 when linked with the second לָכֵן in v. 9 suggests that on account of the shepherds' fatal failure to be true shepherds of Yahweh's flock, Yahweh now stands against them (v. 10) in judgement to depose them from office and rescue his helpless sheep from their voracious grasp[55] and caprice. This is explained by the הִנְנִי אֶל־הָרֹעִים ("Behold, I am against the shepherds") construction in v. 10 which indicates Yahweh's opposition to the shepherds' action. The actual owner of the flock, on whose behalf the shepherds are entrusted shepherding responsibility, now intervenes by cashiering the shepherds[56] to rescue the molested sheep out of the shepherd's greedy hands. Holding the guilty imperfect human shepherds accountable for their act of official irresponsibility, Yahweh discharges them from his service in order to save his flock from continuous oppression.

By implication, this action by Yahweh would halt further disaster on the flock as Yahweh's appointed "shepherd-watchmen" of his flock "not only neglected their duty but turned into ravenous wolves themselves."[57] Since Yahweh's under-shepherds showed themselves to be incapable, "The divine shepherd will care for precisely those who have no one else to care

---

54. As Yahweh's human co-regents, delegated to shepherd his flock as watchmen, Israel's bad leaders preyed instead on the very flock they were to care for, and as a consequence, sent them into the traps and nests of waiting predators. Yet, these shepherds put up a nonchalant attitude, paying deaf ears and turning blind eyes to the plight of the people because they cared less. Also see Zimmerli, *Ezekiel 2*, 215. The expression וְאֶת־צֹאנִי לֹא רָעוּ ("For you do not shepherd my flock," v. 8) literally bemoans the crisis of Yahweh's flock. Therefore, since these bad shepherds, proving themselves not capable and responsible co-regents, logically, the "responsibility for this state of affairs is placed squarely on the shoulders of the shepherds." See Block's interpretation in *The Book of Ezekiel Chapters 25-48*, 285. Like Yahweh saved Abraham's descendants from the Egyptian slavery, so in like manner, he is saving his flock from internal taskmasters, their shepherds.

55. Taylor, *Ezekiel*, 220.

56. Eichrodt, *Ezekiel*, 470. In Muilenburg's opinion, Ezekiel delivered a severe indictment of the past rulers of Israel, condemning in a very harsh tone, specifically "Israel's former kings for exploiting their subjects to their own advantage, for neglecting their elemental obligations as rulers, and for allowing them to be scattered" and devoured by various predators. Muilenburg, "Ezekiel," 585. Since the shepherds chose to "feed themselves at the flock's expense," the owner of the flock has now resolved to discharge them from his service. Duguid, *Ezekiel*, 394.

57. Block, *The Book of Ezekiel Chapters 25-48*, 286.

for them."[58] This divine action is couched by the use of the phrase והצלתי
צאני מפיהם ("And I will snatch[59] my flock from their mouth").

5.3.3 Oracle of Yahweh's Eschatological Rescue Mission, vv. 11-16

The oracle in vv. 11-16 reveals Yahweh's action of stepping on the scene in a rescue mission to do for his flock what the bad and imperfect human shepherds of the house of Israel had failed to do. It opens with an emphatic phrase of personal action in v. 11 הנני־אני ("Behold, I myself," repeated in vv. 12, 15), with Yahweh's promise to נצל ("rescue") his flock, an intention earlier expressed in v. 10c. Yahweh declares, והצלתי אתהם מכל־המקומת אשר נפצו שם ביום ענן וערפל ("I will rescue them from all the places[60] that they were scattered there on a day of clouds and heavy darkness," v. 12b).

Diversity of interpretation exits regarding the phrase "a day of clouds and heavy darkness." Some understand the idea as Yahweh's day of judgement, interpreted as presenting features portraying cosmic disaster.[61] Others see it as possessing eschatological overtones that suggest deliverance for Israel in the day of the Lord when he acts in salvation and judgement to usher in a new age of his righteous rule on earth.[62] Yet, another school of thought thinks it is referring "to the recent destruction of Jerusalem, which Ezekiel understands to be Yahweh's just punishment for Israel's long-lived history

---

58. Cooke, *A Critical and Exegetical Commentary*, 374-376. By their status, the shepherds should have been responsible to Yahweh as they ruled the people by his sanction. But since they became oppressors themselves, acting as ravenous beasts to the flock, Yahweh now acts against them to snatch and deliver his sheep from their caprice.

59. The verb נצל is used in the Hiphil perfect because the action to follow is causative. While the action is to rescue from danger, the basic textual idea of the verb, used within a shepherding context, refers to snatching away with force an animal from the mouth of a predator to save it. This is clear indication that "Yahweh was compelled to intervene and rescue his sheep from their jaws." Block, *The Book of Ezekiel Chapters 25-48*, 286.

60. We think the idea of "all the places" refers to the dispersion of the covenant people. The deportation of Samaria in 722 BC was to different nations while that of Judah in 605, 597 and 587 BC was to Babylonia. While some citizens, including Prophet Jeremiah, escaped in self-exile to Egypt, it is highly possible that others sought refuge elsewhere. Cooke suggests that the idea of "all the places" in Ezekiel 34:12 goes beyond Babylonia to include Egypt, Phoenicia, and S. Arabia. Cooke, *A Critical and Exegetical Commentary*, 375.

61. Eichrodt, *Ezekiel*, 471.

62. Taylor, *Ezekiel*, 221.

of sin."⁶³ This expression is to be understood against its historical context, else the point is missed. Its meaning is appropriately located in the context of exile. The Assyrian and Babylonian captivities of the covenant and once united Israel can rightly be pictured as the scattered and strayed sheep of Israel becoming prey to every wild beast. The experience of the loss by Israel of land and Temple following the final siege, is expressed by Ezekiel in the poetic language of the day of "clouds" and "darkness".

Located in vv. 13-14 is the salvation oracle of Yahweh's rescue mission in behalf of his flock. The heavy presence of the perfects in the Qal (vv. 11, 13b, 14), Hiphil (vv. 10c, 12b, 13a), and Piel (12a, 13a) used in the divine speech is clear indication of the salvific element in his rescue mission. The whole of this sub-unit reveals two streams of Yahweh's action of his rescue mission – to search for and to pasture the flock he brings back. The declarative plan of action by Yahweh, וּרְתִיםהִנְנִי־אָנִי וְדָרַשְׁתִּי אֶת־צֹאנִי ("Behold, I myself will search for my flock and seek them out" v. 11), is for the rescuing of the flock, after which he will pasture them in a secured place, that is אֶל־הָרֵי יִשְׂרָאֵל ("on the mountains of Israel," v. 13). Ezekiel depicts Yahweh's rescue of his scattered and ravaged sheep in terms of an exodus motif that is apparently more glorious than the first. Yahweh will seek them out, find them, gather them, and lead them out, taking them back to their homeland, designating an atmosphere of tranquillity, safety and of bliss (vv. 14-16).⁶⁴

The theological import of this divine action is eschatologically motivated. Verses 11-16 do not leave Ezekiel's readers in doubt regarding his eschatological motif. The content of these verses obviously reverses the bad treatment that the flock had experienced from the manhandling of Israel's

---

63. Darr, "The Book of Ezekiel," 1466. Similar to Darr's opinion, Allen thinks this poetic phrase as summing up the horror of the fall of Jerusalem and its tragic consequences in 587. Allen, *Ezekiel 20-48*, 162.

64. Under his direct care, victims of the Assyrian and Babylonian exiles "will undertake a new exodus" mightier than the first; for they are being gathered and led out from the four corners of the earth by Yahweh himself. In this operation, the very category of the lost sheep neglected by the bad shepherds, Yahweh himself will seek (vv. 4, 16)." Darr, "The Book of Ezekiel," 1466. "Here," it is observed, "God himself appears in the role of the faithful shepherd, taking over the duties neglected by the faithless shepherds he has been forced to dispossess." Herbert G. May and E. L. Allen, "Ezekiel," in *The Interpreter's Bible Vol. VI*, eds., George Arthur Buttrick et al (Nashville: Abingdon Press, 1956), 252.

bad and negligent human shepherds in v. 4. Putting the unfortunate catastrophe that had plagued the flock behind, Ezekiel now speaks of the new thing[65] that Yahweh would do for his people as he himself declared he would personally take over the shepherding of his flock. The long chain of verbs used in vv. 11-16, all having Yahweh as subject and his flock as object of the salvific action, highlights every event in them as an act of Yahweh himself[66] towards his flock. As much as material cosmic salvation belongs to the LORD, so also the flock's salvation should be expected to come from the LORD, the only true shepherd of Israel in whose hands "shepherdly duties would be capably discharged."[67]

5.4 Indictment and Sifting of Israel's Imperfect Flock, vv. 17-22

This second major oracular section divides into two subunits. The first is Yahweh's indictment and judgement oracle against Israel's evil sheep (vv. 17-21) and the second concerns his justice for the helpless sheep (v. 22). From this point on, a shift in focus occurs as the bad and evil shepherds disappear from the scene to now give full view of the flock. Yahweh's operational justice on Israel's imperfect shepherds (v. 10) shifts to the flock (v. 16). The phrase ואתנה צאני ("As for you, my flock," v. 17) serves as

---

65. The idea of the concept of "new thing" is from Zimmerli, *Ezekiel 2*, 216. Also, the idea of Yahweh's take over is from Allen, *Ezekiel 20-48*, 162. Eichrodt reasons that Yahweh's rescue action here transcends the shepherd imagery in that his verdict is on the history of the nation. In this historical perspective, it is to be seen that "Yahweh's endeavour to build up a people of God has broken down through human failure." However, in Ezekiel's rehearsal of Israel's history, he sees specifically Yahweh's retribution coming down heavily at the moment on its leadership as only the leaders responsible for this failure are worthy of divine condemnation and rejection. In this rescue operation, "what is all-important is that Yahweh's original plan should be successfully carried out: man's betrayals only make his faithfulness shine out more brightly, and serve to display how his personal intervention is the sole means by which deliverance is effected." Eichrodt, *Ezekiel*, 472.

66. The idea of "act of Yahweh" is from Block, *The Book of Ezekiel Chapters 25-48*, 289.

67. Allen, *Ezekiel 20-48*, 162. In Allen's understanding, such divine operation clearly explains one key point–that "the derelictions of the pre-exilic monarchy (v. 4) would be no more. Now, in keeping with the exilic context, the retrieval of the lost and strayed is set at the head of the list. Justice–ever an ideal royal virtue, but denied by the overbearingness of v. 4–was to be the hallmark of Israel's divine shepherd and king."

the dividing marker here. Also, the phrase ארענה במשפט ("I will pasture with justice," v. 16) serves as a "neat carry-over,"[68] a transitional link from Yahweh's dealing with the bad shepherds to his dealing with the evil members of his flock in the next subunit (vv. 17-22).

This section presents Yahweh as the God of justice, equity, and fairness. It is expected, in respect to the spirit of Yahweh's universal laws, that the rights of all humans be respected. But where violation of rights does occur, his punitive action takes its course. Here in Ezekiel 34:17-22, Yahweh's justice "dominates the oracle at beginning, middle and end,"[69] where he "sift[s]"[70] members of the flock, and in particular, the wicked and humanely insensitive ones. Two sub-oracles, "retribution for the guilty and vindication for their victims"[71] do exist here. The eschatological separation of the sheep from the goats[72] by Jesus Christ in Matthew re-echoes the action occurring here in Ezekiel, indicating that Yahweh deals with men and women according to the principle of his divine justice. On this basis, Yahweh will pasture the rescued flock on the principle of his justice just as he had previously done with the bad and imperfect human shepherds of Israel.

5.4.1 Yahweh's Indictment and Judgement of the Evil Sheep, vv. 17-21

V. 17. Here is found the divine declaration of an intended action on the flock captured in the opening phrase ואתנה צאני ("As for you, my flock"). This construction clearly indicates Yahweh's ownership of the flock. Justice is the dominant theme in this verse since the controlling key word in this

---

68. Allen, *Ezekiel 20-48*, 162.
69. Allen, *Ezekiel 20-48*, 162.
70. Keil, *Commentary on the Old Testament*, 86.
71. Allen, *Ezekiel 20-48*, 162. Eichrodt notes that in this sub oracle, Ezekiel was not searching for a scapegoat to bear all the blame for the disaster, but shifting focus from shepherds to sheep, as here "each of the details refers to the people." He particularly emphasises the *strong sheep* who had "become guilty of unbrotherly behaviour" to the other sheep. Like Amos and other prophets, Ezekiel clamped down on anti-social guilt in society as he recognised the lack of social righteousness as a cancerous sore of Israel. Eichrodt, *Ezekiel*, 473.
72. Matthew reports (Matt 25:31-46) Jesus as saying that when he comes in his glory for judgement with all nations gathered before him, he will separate the peoples "as a shepherd separates the sheep from the goats." The key word is *separation*, to reward the righteous and judge the unrighteous unto condemnation.

section is שׁפט "to judge." V. 16 had already signalled Yahweh's justice in the phrase ארענה במשׁפט ("I will pasture [them] with justice"). The divine judgement is to be executed between one sheep and another. Specifically, the judgement is to be between rams and goats (v. 17) and between the fat sheep and lean sheep (v. 20). The fat and strong sheep among the flock are described as [73]אילים and [74]עתודים ("rams and male goats," v. 17; cf. Jer 50:8).

A close socio-anthropological observation will lead to the conclusion that within the context of an imperfect, evil, wicked, and unjust human society, the downtrodden, poor, weak, voiceless and helpless of every society always suffer oppression, domination, manipulation, coercion, and brutality at the caprice of the rapacious members of its society.[75] The rams and goats and the fat and strong sheep who were guilty of these expressed crimes of greed, brutality, wickedness and oppression are considered to be the oppressive nobles or the bulling merchant-classes[76] of the Israelite society. These terms "designate individuals within the flock at the top of the butting order."[77] This class consists of those who were "the most powerful members" of the flock[78] in the Judean community "who enriched

---

73. The word איל can mean a leader, chief or a ram. A ram with its horns and robust body, being the male sheep who naturally serves as the chief leader of the flock, physically looks stronger than the female sheep. It is possible for the ram to use its horns and strength to its own advantage. Ezekiel's figurative usage of this word is therefore in reference to the rich, the politically and economically powerful in Israelite society who used their privileged status in society to oppress the lowly, weak, voiceless, poor, and disadvantaged.

74. The word עתוד refers to the male goat, that is, the he-goat. Like the ram, the male goat appears stronger than the she-goat and is always ready to use its physique and horns to intimidate and fight the others. Its figurative usage by Ezekiel refers to the princes and chief men in Israel who participated in the rulership and leadership of the nation. Ezekiel's employment of איל and עתוד fits the translation of צאן as flock, because this word group ordinarily is inclusive of both animals.

75. The description of this category of sheep is an Ezekielian expression that identifies the males of the respective species. Block, *The Book of Ezekiel Chapters 25-48*, 292. Duguid also identifies this category of sheep as the broader class of "rapacious and self-serving leaders of the community" who were accused of "general social misconduct of oppressing the weak with violence and grasping the limited resources to the detriment of those without influence or power." Duguid, *Ezekiel and the Leaders of Israel*, 122.

76. Taylor, *Ezekiel*, 221.

77. Block, *The Book of Ezekiel Chapters 25-48*, 293.

78. Darr, "The Book of Ezekiel," 1461.

themselves at the expense of their fellows, robbing them of all that makes life worthwhile."[79]

The weak political will to administer justice and to punish wrong by Israel's kings and the greedy attitude of those who served in other leadership positions in the Israelite society became a fertile breeding soil for the strong sheep to brutalise the weak and defenceless sheep. Cooke rightly points out that this class in society perpetrated evil because "kings and princes give place to powerful, oppressive members of the community... The common rights of humanity are invaded by these selfish oppressors."[80] Acts of evil and injustice always thrive where a society is under weak leadership.

Vv. 18-19. Following the declarative intention is the divine accusations of the sleek and strong rams and goats. The prevalent use of the 2nd person masculine suffix in these verses naturally places the robust rams and goats in the objective position of the divine accusation. The misconduct of the fat rams and he-goats shows itself in their lack of consideration for the weak and powerless among the flock, depriving them of the little means of subsistence. Such misconduct is captured in the verbs רפס (to "trample," v. 18b) and מרפש (to "muddy," v. 18d). Yahweh accused this class of sheep for their greed, insensitivity, brutality, wickedness, lack of compassion and evil done to the remaining helpless sheep because such acts were against the principle of brotherhood in Israel. Their act of "trampling" the pasture under foot of even the little that is left is evil. Such action reveals that it went beyond ordinary greed to a gross violation of the Deuteronomic code.[81]

In Ezekiel's moral ethics and theology, right is rewarded but wrong must be repudiated and punished. As was the case with the bad, evil and worthless shepherds of Israel, so also the evil sheep of Israel – the leaders at the lower ranks and the evil members of the Israelite community – must

---

79. May and Allen, "Ezekiel," 254.
80. Cooke, *A Critical and Exegetical Commentary*, 376-7.
81. The powerful and wealthy of the Israelite society showed themselves to have lost every sensitivity and human feeling towards their fellow needy and disadvantaged citizens. "Not satisfied with filling their own stomachs, they trample[d] the grass that remain[ed] and foul[ed] [muddied] the drinking water with their feet, denying their colleagues this nourishment." Block, *The Book of Ezekiel Chapters 25-48*, 293. Put differently, "not content with exhibiting their power by cornering the best pasturage and clearest water and leaving the inferior pasturage and the partly settled water for the rest of the flock, they wilfully foul[ed] what they do not consume themselves." Greenberg, *Ezekiel 21-37*, 701.

equally come under Yahweh's retributive justice for their role in the "great injustices that were the product of Judah's stratified society."[82] Therefore, since "the powerful and prosperous citizens, who had been greedily taking for themselves all the good things of the land and denying the benefit of them to their fellows"[83] are by this act guilty of both civil and covenantal offenses, they also would surely stand up to Yahweh's judgement for abusing their privileged status and failure to contribute to the good of society.

Vv. 20-21. The לכן used in v. 20 links the evil actions of the robust rams and he-goats in vv. 18-19 with Yahweh's rescue action soon to come for the oppressed helpless sheep in v. 22. Yahweh's rescue mission here indicates that such compassionless victimisation and "bullying calls for a response"[84] from Yahweh, the sheep owner. Therefore, in a judicial fashion, Yahweh accuses the strong evil sheep (v. 18), beginning with a declarative messenger formula כה אמר אדני יהוה ("Thus says the Lord God") in v. 17. This is followed by the submission of the causation of the offenses with exhibits (v. 19), then finally the verdict is passed, also with a declarative and emphatic messenger formula כה אמר אדני יהוה אליהם ("Thus says the Lord Yahweh to them," vv. 20-21). The basis for the divine justice in v. 21 introduces yet two additional accusations. The fat rams and goats הדף ("thrust, drive") with their side and shoulder and נגח ("gore") all the weak sheep with their horns, consequentially putting their victims at the disadvantage position of פוץ (scattering or dispersing). Their inhumane depriving behaviour had "driven" the weak sheep away outside of the sheep pen in search of safety, peace, food and water.

Just as Yahweh had earlier stood in opposition to Israel's bad and imperfect human shepherds for their greed, negligence, and acts of irresponsibility to his sheep, here also, he stands in opposition to the strong and privileged members among the flock. The expressions הנני־אני ("Behold, I myself") following the messenger formula כה אמר אדני יהוה אליהם ("Thus says the Lord Yahweh to them") suggests it is Yahweh himself who is to judge the evil members of the flock and not any human agent. So cruel and

---

82. Vawter and Hoppe, *A New Heart*, 155.
83. Taylor, *Ezekiel*, 222.
84. Block, *The Book of Ezekiel Chapters 25-48*, 293.

inhumane was the violent brutality of the fat and strong against the powerless sheep that the latter were deprived of even that which the former has no need.[85] Hence, Yahweh announced his rescue mission in behalf of the violated sheep in the purpose statement ולא־תהיינה עוד לבז ("So they will not continue to be robbed," v. 22). The preceding reveals that the act "of brutality within the flock when the strong animal displace[d] the weak," rendering them helpless in the absence of the expected "protection exercised by the shepherd who sees that justice prevails,"[86] would not escape Yahweh's judgement (Ps 46:1, cf. v. 10).

As he sat among the exiles in Babylon, Ezekiel reflected on the prevailing injustices of Israel's society and blamed it primarily on the inhumane and unpatriotic behaviour of its national leadership. But apart from his heavy indictment of "the rapacious rulers of Israel, who must bear responsibility for the plight of the people" (Ezek 34:1-10), the lesser officials and the wealthy of the Jewish community had also tyrannised "over their fellow-countrymen."[87] These *strong* members of Yahweh's flock are found by Ezekiel to be equally guilty of contributing to the hurts of the poor whom they delighted in oppressing and sapping to their advantage. Therefore, their oppressive and evil usurpation was soon to be overturned and overrun by Yahweh's justice. When this happened, his oppressed helpless sheep would gain their freedom at last.

5.4.2 Yahweh's Justice for the Helpless Sheep, v. 22

Technically, vv. 20-22 form a unit but with focus on v. 22. The particle adverb לכן ("Therefore") in v. 20 separates the previous sub-oracle of Yahweh's judgement against the evil sheep and his justice for the helplessly oppressed sheep. Characteristic of Ezekiel's literary style in this chapter, the idea in vv. 18-19 is restated in vv. 20-21 preparatory for the execution of the divine

---

85. Of the inherent evil of the powerful sheep (the fat rams and goats), it is said "…even what they did not need for themselves they spoiled, thus denying it to others. [They] abandoned the traditional responsibility of the upper class for the social well-being of the other classes." Duguid, *Ezekiel*, 395. Zimmerli describes this brutality as thoughtless since they trampled and muddied what was still to serve as food and water for others, after they had satisfied themselves. Zimmerli, *Ezekiel 2*, 217.
86. Zimmerli, *Ezekiel 2*, 217.
87. Beasley-Murray, "Ezekiel,", 680.

judgement. The oracle in this subunit indicates that Yahweh will soon come to the defence of these helpless weak and lean sheep that Israel's bad shepherds, in alliance with the strong, evil, and powerful rams, male goats and fat sheep had taken undue advantage of. The helpless and oppressed sheep have now become the object of Yahweh's salvation oracle, for he says, והושעתי לצאני ("And I will save my flock," in the Hiphil perfect, v. 22). Here, the thought of Yahweh's action of vv. 10-16 is re-echoed in a slightly different context.

The helpless sheep who had been pushed around by the robust rams and he-goats had suffered double tragedy. They suffered molestation and various abuses from their fellow countrymen – their political leaders and fellow citizens, and secondly and worst of all, by their foreign captors, "the powerful expropriator."[88] Here is a case of the deprivation of one's human rights. These brutalised and molested sheep were neither free and protected at home, nor were they safe outside of home. Consequently, Yahweh rescuing them had become inevitable.

It is an empirical fact that in every human society, people are not the same on the basis of class structure. Besides the ruling class, there are the rich and powerful in society on the one hand, and the weak, poor, voiceless and helpless on the other. The latter class always suffers various abuses from the former class such as oppression, domination, molestation, slavery and assaults, because of their disadvantaged status in society. However, the God of all flesh (Gen 1:1; Jer 32:27; Num 16:22) who also is the God of justice (Ps 33:5; 2 Chr 9:8; Amos 5:24) always rises to the defence of the oppressed and downtrodden in society. Like the case of the oppressed sheep in Ezekiel, Yahweh "offers hope to the oppressed by taking his stand on their side,"[89] establishing his justice by punishing the wicked oppressors and proclaiming his salvation for the oppressed. Here, Yahweh serves as their deliverer just as the Judges in Israel who rose to the nation's defence from continuous foreign incursion and oppression.

---

88. Greenberg, *Ezekiel 21-37*, 702.
89. Block, *The Book of Ezekiel Chapters 25-48*, 293.

5.5 The Declaration of a Perfect Eschatological Society for Shepherding, vv. 23-31

The third and final major category of the prophetic oracle divides into two oracular subunits. In the first is Yahweh's revisitation of the Davidic tradition of shepherding (vv. 23-24) and the second presents the disclosure of Yahweh's covenant of a future tranquillity for his restored and re-gathered flock in their Land (vv. 25-31). This second subunit presents Yahweh not as acting as an avenger any more as was the case previously (Ezek chs. 3-24), but rather acting as one on a rescuing mission and as a Messiah. In order to actualise his salvific declaration to his oppressed sheep, Yahweh presented his eschatological plan to compensate his abused flock.

Against the backdrop of the massive failure earlier experienced in Israelite society of every aspect of its systems, and against the leadership impotents of its imperfect human shepherds, Yahweh now takes over to demonstrate the perfectness of what an ideal shepherding activity ought to have been. The evilness, weakness, wickedness, oppressiveness, failure, and imperfection of a human Israelite society necessitated the declaration of divine action by Yahweh. Therefore, his rescue mission requires setting aside the old order of things to allow for his putting in place a new pattern of eschatological shepherding for the restored community of new Israel in the new society. As scholars observe, "the expected change in Israel's governance will be accomplished not so much through a change in the nature of the *office* but through a change in the nature of the *occupant*."[90] This links naturally to the Davidic tradition of shepherding. Here then, Yahweh unveils the programme of the eschatological hope for the scattered and lost sheep of the house of Israel. The core of this 'hope unit' covering from vv. 23-31 is located in Yahweh's promise earlier declared in vv. 11-16.

---

90. Duguid, *Ezekiel and the Leaders of Israel*, 47. As revealed by Ezekiel, the future shepherd will not merely be "an ad hoc solution to the necessities of governing the restored people [but] nothing less than the fulfilment of the covenant with David." Duguid, *Ezekiel*, 396.

5.5.1 An Eschatological Experience of a Davidic Tradition of Shepherding, vv. 23-24

V. 23. The bad shepherds along with their evil accomplices who had existed in an imperfect Israelite society as longstanding obstacles to true shepherding now being removed, Yahweh now קוּם ("raises over" or "sets up over") his flock[91] another trustworthy shepherd to shepherd them.[92] The phrase עבדי דויד הוא ירעה אתם ("My servant David who will shepherd them") not only reveals a revisitation to the once cherished Davidic tradition of shepherding in the history of Israel as Yahweh's nation, but also suggests the past political leaders of Israel to be unfaithful in the discharge of their official functions. The mention of David as Yahweh's servant who would shepherd the restored Israel is unlikely to be taken literally but to be understood rather in terms of its prototype. The name David, despite his exhibited failures as a human, epitomises the principal qualities and duties of a good king – piety towards Yahweh, justice towards his subjects, and care of the public welfare. Flavius Josephus describes these qualities inherent in David thus:

> This man was of an excellent character, and was endowed with all the virtues that were desirable in a king, and in one that had the preservation of so many tribes committed to him; for he was a man of valor in a very extraordinary degree, and went readily and first of all into danger, when he was to fight for his subjects . . . He was prudent and moderate, and kind to such as were under any calamities; he was righteous and humane, which are good qualities peculiarly fit for kings; nor was he guilty of any offense in the exercise of so great an authority, but in the business of the wife of Uriah. He also left behind him greater wealth than any other king, either of the Hebrews or of other nations, ever did.[93]

---

91. The word עליהם to be translated "over them" is omitted in the Targum but the LXX and the Vulgate use עליהן instead.

92. The whole of the phrase הוא ירעה אתם ("who will pasture them") is absent in the LXX.

93. Flavius Josephus, *Josephus: The Complete Works* (trans. William Whiston A. M.;

A recall of the Davidic dynasty is therefore very significant for the new shepherding leadership to be put in place in the restored Israelite community. The bad and imperfect human shepherds serving as political leaders of Israel had failed to imitate and exemplify in their leadership, those three major shepherding qualities required of a king, which David had exhibited in his kingship over Israel as Yahweh's flock.

Verse 23 indicates that David, the עבד of Yahweh, is the only true and good shepherd who is suitable and who alone qualifies to shepherd Yahweh's flock in the eschatological society. But Vawter and Hoppe query, "Is the text looking forward to the restoration of the Davidic dynasty or the rise of an ideal Davidic figure in the future?"[94] This query raises an interpretive question. In response, while Taylor objects to the suggestion of the Davidic figure being the historical David to be resurrected, nor a human king of the Davidic lineage to favour him rather being "the servant of the Lord, represented as an idealized David,"[95] Muilenburg thinks in terms of "the perpetuation of the Davidic dynasty."[96] It seems persuasive rather to side with Darr who proposes that "here, Ezekiel speaks not of the resurrection of Israel's second king, but of the reestablishment of the Davidic dynasty."[97] Whatever interpretation is to be assigned to this verse, its understanding must focus on the character-role rather than on the identity of the *one or another shepherd*. Ezekiel's main concern in pointing to David as the עבד of Yahweh lies not in the concept of resurrection, restoration, and ascension, but pointing to a true and perfect shepherding role to be assumed as this eschatological David will "discharge the duties of the good shepherd"[98] who cares, seeks, heals, binds up, and leads the sheep to a good pasturage and a secured place.

V. 24. Here, Yahweh affirms his consistent position as one who has always been the chief Shepherd of Israel. The phrase ואני יהוה אהיה להם לאלהים ("Then I Yahweh, will be their God") follows his action of placing

---

Nashville, Tenn.: Thomas Nelson, 1998), 251.
94. Vawter and Hoppe, *A New Heart*, 156.
95. Taylor, *Ezekiel*, 223.
96. Muilenburg, "Ezekiel," 585.
97. Darr, "The Book of Ezekiel," 1462.
98. May and Allen, "Ezekiel," 255.

another shepherd over his flock (v. 23). Now with a faithful David serving as his servant-shepherd, his flock will now benefit from the true shepherding they had not experienced in a very long time in an imperfect society. This is in particular as the Davidic servant-shepherd of the eschatological community will function as a "prince." This signifies that the Davidic servant-shepherd is to function as a נשיא בתוכם ("prince among them") and not as an overlord as the former imperfect human shepherds had done. This construction suggests a contrast between the old order of abusive and oppressive shepherding (vv. 3-6) with the new one presented by this motif. Significantly, the eschatological shepherding will take on a new pattern of shepherding, new community of flock, new shepherding environment, and new benefits from true and perfect shepherding. Here, everything and every activity will be characterised by the ideology of "newness." As Donald E. Gowan notes, in Ezekiel's eschatology, three basic transformation of the present world by Yahweh is required for its actualisation. He explains that,

> God must transform the human person; give a new heart and new spirit (Ezek 36:25-27). God must transform human society; restore Israel to the promised land, rebuild cities, and make Israel's new status a witness to the nations (36:24, 28, 33-36). And God must transform nature itself, to make the produce of the land abundant and to banish hunger forever (36:30, 35).[99]

We find here in the eschatological society a reversal of the scheme of things as the eschatological servant-shepherd who is identified as a *nāsî*,[100]

---

99. Donald E. Gowan, *Eschatology in the Old Testament* (2d ed.; Edinburg, Scotland: T & T Clark, 2000), 2. Gowan understands Old Testament eschatology as rooted basically in the "destiny of peoples and of the world in which they live," p. viii.

100. The עבד ("servant") of Yahweh who will shepherd his flock in the restored community of Israel is described as a נשיא (a "prince"). Why does Ezekiel use the term "prince" for this future shepherd? Eichrodt submits that the term *melek* is Ezekiel's special reserve for the king of Babylon, a term that holds strong prejudice for Israel's prophets for its associations with despotism and absolute rule. As such, he argues that Ezekiel employed the word נשיא (*nāsî*) as a descriptive term in reference to "the king of salvation" who is "the prince" in order to avoid using the abhorred title *melek*. Eichrodt, *Ezekiel*, 477. Additionally, Vawter and Hoppe suggest that Ezekiel's preference for *nāsî'* over *melek* gives

and who will serve as an עֶבֶד of Yahweh, will shepherd instead of rule the flock; he will give instead of take from the flock; he will gather instead of scatter the flock; and he will attend to the weak and heal the bruised instead of neglect them. As one who is Yahweh's servant, appointed to serve as his representative, this *nāśî'* shepherd will function in this capacity as a sacrificial and as the righteous ruler of the saved community of Israel.[101] By his righteous rule and shepherding characteristics, Judah's future will eclipse its past.[102] With his perfect rule then, shall come to pass for the regathered nation of Israel the declaration expressed by the Apostle Paul, "Where, O death, is your victory? Where, O death, is your sting?" (1 Cor 15:55). The sting and power over Israel has been the experience of exile, but the victory of a restored Israel is located in the righteous rule of David the prince, who will be Yahweh's faithful shepherd-servant.

The role of David in this section is very particular in the repetition of the phrase וְעַבְדִּי דָוִד ("My servant David," vv. 23a, 24a). Scholars submit three reasons for the use of the name David in connection with the eschatological shepherding: David is the great ancestor of the royal house in Jerusalem; the mention of David's name as king most fully recalls the time when Israel was united; and David's name recalls Yahweh's promise of continuing permanence for his royal house.[103] James Mays notes, "the Davidic kingship assumed a crucial role as the agency through which God provided protection, prosperity, and justice for his people."[104] The signature formula אֲנִי יהוה דִּבַּרְתִּי ("I, Yahweh, have spoken") at the end of this verse is critical. Its Piel perfect form suggests that the appearance of David is not only affirmative of Yahweh's action for the good of his flock, but is also a stamp authenticating this reality of a perfect eschatological shepherding in the new age.

---

insight into the role to be played by the future David. That perceiving himself as Yahweh's loyal servant, he is committed to obedience and to ensuring Israel's fidelity to Yahweh, contrary to what their bad shepherds had done. Vawter and Hoppe, *A New Heart*, 157.

101. See further discussion in Taylor, *Ezekiel*, 223.
102. See further stress in Vawter and Hoppe, *A New Heart*, 155.
103. Zimmerli, *Ezekiel 2*, 218. Cf. 2 Sam 7.
104. Mays, *Ezekiel*, 11.

5.5.2 Yahweh's Covenant of a Tranquil Society for Eschatological Shepherding, vv. 25-31

As an aspect of the "newness" of the expression of the eschatological shepherding community, Yahweh here makes a covenant of lasting peace with his flock, also guaranteeing their safety in the new shepherding environment. This section (Ezek 34:25-31) lays heavy emphasis on a new covenant that is combined with a land-based theology[105] earlier stated by Jeremiah (Jer 30:3; cf. Ezek 34:27b, 29). While Jeremiah speaks of a covenant of a new heart (Jer 31:31-34), Ezekiel speaks of a new covenant that is characterised and precipitated by the theme of peace, prosperity, security, and freedom in the land. This new experience is to be permeated by the presence of Yahweh, and heavily characterised by the proof and final realisation of the enduring bond between Yahweh the true Shepherd and the people as his sheep. This is obviously reflected in the heavy presence of the imperfects ("I will") in this last section undoubtedly affirming its eschatological motif.

In v. 25, Yahweh undertakes to make a covenant of peace and security with the restored community. In this new covenant where Yahweh is its main initiator and actor, there would be no any need for the traditional suzerain-vassal covenant terms or for any mention of its violation because it has a new form and a new tone. For the experience of life in this new heaven and new earth (cf. Rev 21:1-7, 22-25) will not necessitate such covenantal requirements. The image of "wild beasts," "desert" and "forests" are here imported to guarantee the experience of perfect safety for the flock in the eschatological experience. In this new era with Yahweh now in full charge of the new system, he will have rid the land of all the causes of previously experienced acts of oppression and insecurity under the old order of things.

Verses 26-29. This new covenant also includes the experience of bountiful blessings on the land. The divine blessing will transcend from human to land to enhance its fruition (vv. 26-27). The waw consecutive perfect conjunction in the word וְיָשְׁבוּ ("And they will dwell/live") in v. 25 functions as a purpose clause with direct focus on the new exodus in v. 27. When the flock of the regathered and reunited Israel finally settles in their new abode,

---

105. The expression "land-based theology" is from Allen, *Ezekiel 20-48*, 164.

and when Yahweh, the chief Shepherd, the true Shepherd, and the perfect Shepherd of his people Israel, has dealt a final blow to their internal oppressors, וידעו כי־אני יהוה ("Then they will know that I am Yahweh"). This recognition formula is critical to Yahweh's liberating prowess as Israel's true Shepherd in contrast to the former bad and imperfect human shepherds the nation had.

Still, the divine covenant extends to the experience of absolute freedom on the part of the restored community (vv. 28-29). Yahweh's rescue operation of liberation in the new exodus is to put a stop to the continuous plunder of his flock by internal sappers as seen previously. In particular, as is the case here, it is to end their peril at the hand of their foreign captors as well, that is, from the tyranny and clutches of the גוים (v. 28). This operation will also put an end to the flock's being perpetual victims of famine in a hitherto devastated and unproductive land as well as from national disgrace (v. 29). A reconfiguration of land and people will be the experience in this new community.

Verses 30-31. The final recognition formula climaxes Yahweh's grand purpose for his rescue operation at the establishment of the new state in the eschatological age. V. 30 clarifies this purpose: ישראל נאם אדני יהוהויד־ עו כי אני יהוה אלהיהם אתם והמה עמי בית ("Then they will know that I am Yahweh their God, and the house of Israel are my people, declares the LORD Yahweh"). After all has been done by Yahweh for the sake of his neglected, oppressed, and dispersed flock, then,[106] under Yahweh's eschatological shepherding, the scattered flock of Israel will know unprecedented, lasting peace and security on Yahweh's mountains in a blossomed blissful land.

The declarative concluding signature in vv. 30 and 31 affirms the certainty of this recognition of the divine action. Such recognition motif points to Yahweh's faithful commitment to his covenant with the people and to reveal as well his ownership of the people. Yahweh's claim ואתן צאני צאן מרעיתי ("And you my flock are the flock of my pasture") indicates such ownership and אני אלהיכם ("I am your God") affirms his covenantal

---

106. The idea expressed in these last few lines, though heavily modified, is rooted in Dr. Margaret Sinclair Odell's critical comments to Jos ECWA Theological Seminary (JETS) on this dissertation of May 26, 2011.

relationship with the flock (v. 31). This therefore clearly articulates Ezekiel's use of the shepherd metaphor within a covenantal context with a decidedly fixed eschatological motif.

5.6 The Eschatological Role of Ezekiel's Recognition Formula

Prophetic recognition formula[107] always plays out within the domain of divine speeches. Divine speeches in prophetic literature, prose narrative or prose-poetry, play out in what the prophets report Yahweh to have said or commanded them to say and or to do. The recognition formulae found scattered all over Ezekiel's material[108] are embedded in the divine speeches. Such speeches are clearly marked out, in the case of Ezekiel's shepherd metaphor, by statements such as בן־אדם הנבא על־רועי ישראל ("Son of man," "mortal one" or "human one," prophesy against the shepherds of Israel"), הוֹי ("Woe"), ("I am the LORD"), and so on. In Ezekiel's text, the function of recognition formula serves to achieve an awesome recognition and admission of the greatness, power, and supreme authority of Yahweh on the part of the targeted recipients of the prophetic message. Also, it functions to achieve the purpose of clarification in perception of the unique personhood and acts of the divine as the latter are seen displayed in the cosmic order or historic events. In this regard, recognition formula functions as an enhancer to achieve a deepened understanding of Yahweh in all the embodiment of his glory, dignity, and majesty.

In Ezekiel, a unique pattern of such divine recognition unfolds: Yahweh reveals his intended action to the messenger, discloses the effects of the

---

107. One of the basic unique characteristics of prophetic literature is the presence of its many formulae. Among these are the messenger, introductory, judgement/denunciatory, concluding, signature, recognition, speech/oracle, accusatory, law suit, annunciation, divine speech, and other formulae. The address formula "son of man" is uniquely Ezekielian.

108. Such divine speech formulae are found in Ezekiel thus: (1) "Prophesy and say to them," 34:2; 37:12; (2) "Prophesy," 11:4; 13:2; 21:14, 19, 33; 30:2; 34:2; 36:1, 3; 37:4, 9, 12; 38:14; 39:1; (3) "Woe," 13:3, 18; 34:2; (4) "I am the LORD,"5:13, 15; 17:21, 24; 21:22, 37; 22:14; 24:14; 26:14; 30:12; 34:24; 36:36; 37:17; (5) "As long as I live, declares the LORD," 5:11; 14:16, 18, 20; 16:48; 17:16; 18:3; 20:31, 33; 33:11; 34:8; 35:6, 11.

A Case for Eschatological Shepherding in Ezekiel 34

action on its intended target, then follows with its purpose clause statement in the recognition formula. Ezekiel's account appears consistent in this pattern. This pattern points to the account of what Israel and the heathen nations always experienced following a divinely initiated dramatic event in their history, whether pleasant or unpleasant. The reality of such recognition of the divine by Israel and the nations would normally surface only after Yahweh had accomplished his purpose through an event. The pattern of prophetic recognition formula in Ezekiel is marked out by direct divine statements such as וידעתם כי־אני יהוה ("Then/And you will know that I am Yahweh"), and וידעו כי אני יהוה ("Then/And they will know that I am Yahweh").

It appears quite obvious that the use of the recognition formula is nowhere as pronounced in Jewish prophecy as it is in Ezekiel. This formula occurs no less than 21 times in the second person masculine plural form with wav consecutive וידעתם ("Then/And you will know") and no less than 42 times in the third person common plural form with wav consecutive וידעו ("Then/And they will know"). When it occurs in the first instance, it is exclusive to exilic Israel, but when it occurs in the second instance, it is in reference to both Israel and the nations. Divine speeches with such tone are more dominant in Ezekiel than in any other prophet. Zimmerli clearly asserts in this regard that the recognition formula is "a particularly characteristic element of the book of Ezekiel."[109]

The major motivation of such unique Ezekielian pattern of using the recognition formula in divine speeches is to cause a sorrowful repentance and achieve in Israel a "return" to Yahweh her faithful Shepherd. In most cases in Ezekiel, the recognition formula is always preceded by the divine speech oracle of judgement or of punishment. In this sequential order, Yahweh would declare or pronounce an event to be assumed personally or by his directed instrument. After the accomplishment of the event, its intended effect leads to a greater awareness and knowledge of him as well as an admission of his incomparably great power on the part of the intended beneficiaries. In the case of Israel, adequate recognition and unreserved acknowledgement of Yahweh's person, power, rule, authority, dignity, and

---

109. Zimmerli, *Ezekiel 1, Chapters 1-24*, 37.

sovereignty on her part was necessary. This was to propel her return to Yahweh so she could perform her function as the channel through which Yahweh would bless the nations.

This intended purpose plays out very vividly in Ezekiel's eschatological treatment of the shepherd metaphor specific to Yahweh's rescue mission, having his perfect eschatological shepherding in view. At the end of the second exodus, following the ultimate liberation of his flock from foreign oppression, perfect security will be guaranteed with every physical blessing on the land, then the eschatological community of a regathered united Israel will *know* that Yahweh is Lord (Ezek 34:27). Also, when Yahweh finally removes all the causes of social injustice such as dehumanisation, cruelty, slavery, and insecurity hitherto suffered by his people, the house of Israel will unequivocally *know* that Yahweh is their God and Shepherd and that they are indeed his sheep (Ezek 34:30). The final divine signature formula נאם אדני יהוה ("declares the Lord Yahweh," v. 31) is to seal such total recognition of Yahweh by the new Israel and therefore certify the long existing covenant relationship between Israel and Yahweh. Israel is Yahweh's people, the sheep of his pasture, and Yahweh is truly Israel's God and true Shepherd. Here, both Ezekiel's theological import of the shepherd metaphor and its eschatological motif come to a climatic fruition.

5.7 Conclusion

We have argued in this chapter that the bad and imperfect human shepherds of Israel are seen to be rapacious by their ravaging anti-shepherd attitude characterised by their failure to assume a caring responsibility for the flock as Yahweh's co-regents. We have also argued that even the evil sheep among the flock, that is, the strong and powerful of the Israelite society, were also capricious and brutal to the less privileged, the economically and politically weak, and the helpless members of their society. We have pointed out that such acts stood against the principle of Deuteronomic theology. On this ground, their oppressive behaviour must be met with Yahweh's justice as he overturned their nefarious activities.

Even though evil and wickedness pervaded Israelite society for lack of a shepherd, a new dawn would greet the restored community with the arrival of the "prince" as Yahweh's "servant" and faithful shepherd. At the conclusion of Yahweh's missional rescue operation, existence in a good land and the experience of ultimate peace, prosperity, security, and freedom would have been achieved by the eschatological experience. When everything is in place, then Yahweh would have vindicated himself theologically as Israel's perfect Shepherd. The eschatological motif of Ezekiel's purpose of the shepherd metaphor would also have been achieved.

CHAPTER SIX

Ezekiel's Theology of an Eschatological Shepherd and the New Society

6.1 Introduction

Like other prophets in the Israel's prophetic tradition,[1] Ezekiel also "condemns the Judean people and their leaders for religious idolatry and moral corruption, and prophesies national destruction as YHWH'S punishment for their wickedness."[2] As a priest and prophet, forced out of Jerusalem to spend "his life among the exiles in Mesopotamia . . . Ezekiel was particularly concerned with matters of Temple and cultus as expressions of Israel's epical relationship with Yahweh."[3] But beyond this, he distinctly charged Israel's human shepherds for acting in negation to the principle of divine shepherding. This enabled him to construct a theology of eschatological shepherding as he looked into the future of a new Israelite society where Yahweh will take over shepherding in this community.

---

1. To be "prophet" is to have a word from the divine for a community. It was normative within the prophetic traditions of Israel and the surrounding nations that prophets always have a message from the deity whom they serve as representatives. True prophets only deliver the word they have been given without addition, subtraction, or even modification. The context of the time of a particular prophetic function in Israel determined the nature of the prophetic message.
2. Ward, *Thus Says the Lord*, 173.
3. Eugene H. Merrill, "A Theology of Ezekiel and Daniel," in *A Biblical Theology of The Old Testament* (ed. Roy B. Zuck; Chicago, Ill.: Moody, 1991), 365.

We have already argued that an evil, weak, and imperfect Israelite society with imperfect human shepherds was responsible for the Babylonian exile and the final demise of Jerusalem. We proceed in this chapter by examining the theological framework[4] of eschatological shepherding that Ezekiel constructed with which he evaluated and critiqued Israel's imperfect human shepherds (both its royal and religious leadership). We cannot doubt the radical theocentricity[5] of Ezekiel's theological motivation. What we discuss below therefore is Ezekiel's knowledge of Yahweh as the basic foundation for his theological construct and submissions regarding the eschatological shepherding motif. We note that in Ezekiel's theological understanding, a return to Yahweh by exilic Israel is required for participation in Yahweh's eschatological shepherding. Also, we consider Ezekiel's contrast of Yahweh's shepherding attributes with the negative shepherding attitudes exhibited by Israel's worthless imperfect human shepherds. This served as a basis for the prophetic indictment and disqualification of these shepherds from eschatological shepherding in the restored Israelite community. We consider lastly Ezekiel's theological concept of "I AM YAHWEH" as cardinal for eschatological shepherding of Yahweh's regathered flock.

---

4. The question is posed whether the phrase "theology of Ezekiel" means the theology of Ezekiel the man or the theology of the book of Ezekiel. Henry McKeating opines that we must begin by speaking of the theology of the book because it is an existing artefact, about whose theology we can make firm and checkable statements, and it does offer us a theology which is, in the main, coherent and consistent, and which makes sense in the historical context to which it ostensibly relates. In his own judgement, McKeating posits that "the coherence of the book's theology is such that it is likely, at least in its main outlines, to reflect the single mind of an original prophet." McKeating, *Ezekiel*, 73. Our discussion of Ezekiel's theological framework of shepherding is based upon the conviction that the theology that emerges from the book is a reflection of the original mind of the prophet that the book is named after. As such, the theological framework is the firsthand thinking of Ezekiel as a person. The content of the book is a reflection of his theological thought.

5. Paul M. Joyce, *Ezekiel: A Commentary*, 199.

6.2 Ezekiel's Theology of Eschatological Shepherding Is Yahwistic in Outlook

Prophets in Israel were among the most intelligent of their society. The literary works that they left behind clearly reveal their knowledge of history, politics, anthropology, sociology, psychology, cosmology, geography, agriculture, ethics, religion, international relations and commerce, military intelligence, and so on. With such vast knowledge, Israelite prophets addressed issues from rational and theological perspectives. Within this rational class stands Ezekiel of whom Petersen says "Ezekiel was among the most creative theological thinkers of all Israel's prophets."[6]

The theological framework, which Ezekiel constructed regarding the eschatological shepherd and the new Israelite community, is classically grounded in Yahwistic outlook and motivation. This means his theologising is anchored in Yahweh the covenant God and the God of Israel's patriarchs. The idea of Yahweh dominates Ezekiel's theological core because the import of his literary piece rises and falls on his deepened knowledge of the Person and acts of Yahweh in history. On this basis, the presence of the recognition formula in his work "may well be the central theological theme of the book."[7] Walther Zimmerli states that the concept of Yahweh is a great central theme in Ezekiel. He explains that, "the frequent use of the recognition formula of the proof-saying shows that this preaching of the prophet has to do above all with Yahweh's great self-revelation."[8] The whole of his book is everywhere spiced with the presence of Yahweh in relation to his covenant people. The predominant use of the personal name יהוה, אלהים and אדני, and the personal pronoun אני used for Yahweh's divine speeches in the book sustains the claim.

Israelite prophets always stressed the adequate knowledge and appropriate worship of Yahweh. This has been the bedrock for the prophetic ministry of all the prophets who ever emerged in the history of Israel's prophetic tradition. Theirs was a ministry of calling the covenant people

---

6. Petersen, *The Prophetic Literature*, 158.
7. Merrill, "A Theology of Ezekiel and Daniel," 367.
8. Zimmerli, *Ezekiel 1*, 52.

back to Yahweh and to his unitary worship. It was a call to the people to remember their earlier commitment to covenant loyalty and obedience under Joshua when they responded to him in unison:

> Far be it from us to forsake the LORD to serve other gods! It was the LORD our God himself who brought us and our fathers up out of Egypt, from that land of slavery, and performed those great signs before our eyes. He protected us on our entire journey and among all the nations through which we traveled. And the LORD drove out before us all the nations, including the Amorites, who lived in the land. We too will serve the LORD, because he is our God (Josh 24:16-18 NIV).

Ezekiel stands in this prophetic tradition of calling Israel back to her covenant obligations to Yahweh. In his theology, he not only stays with the themes of disobedience, sin, individual responsibility, judgement, hope and restoration, idolatry, and the like, but far more, with much emphasis on the theology of Yahweh and Israel's return to undivided loyalty to him in their relationship and worship of him. Ward contrasts Israel's unfaithfulness to Yahweh's faithfulness when he comments that the message of Ezekiel points to Israel's history in that it reveals unequivocally that:

> Throughout their history, YHWH lavished blessings upon the people of Israel and showed unflagging compassion and forbearance toward them; but they responded, from the first moment to the last, with unrelieved ingratitude, infidelity, and iniquity. Their wickedness was absolute and unqualified. There was nothing at all in their entire history that deserved approbation or mitigated the prophet's condemnation.[9]

Ezekiel and his colleagues within Israel's prophetic guild should be understood to be theologising against the backdrop of Israel's covenant disloyalty and disobedience.

---

9. Ward, *Thus Says the Lord*, 175.

The Israelites, though a rarely privileged people in covenant relationship, chose to rebel against Yahweh their king and suzerain lord. Their worthless imperfect human shepherds were clearly in the lead in this rebellion. Ezekiel took notice of this act of disrespect for Yahweh. Duguid puts it aptly that the overarching theme of the entire prophecy of Ezekiel is *the sovereignty and glory of God*.[10] Against this backdrop, Ezekiel's theological proposals are in response to a paradigm shift in Israel's covenant relationship and worship of Yahweh, an unfortunate shift that climaxed in the exile. To Ezekiel, "from Moses until the day of the ruin of Jerusalem, the covenant people had refused to submit to their Lord"[11] choosing instead the worship of foreign gods. Therefore, for a people who held to the knowledge of Yahweh only in form, Ezekiel's developing a theology of the proper knowledge of Yahweh and a return to him as a redress for this shift was unavoidable.

6.2.1 His Shepherding Theology Has a Visionary Undertone

As we pointed out above, Ezekiel's knowledge of Yahweh became the theological nucleus of his prophetic oracles and speeches. While the knowledge of Yahweh, alongside all that is embedded in it, is the theological core of Ezekiel, his theophanic visionary experience of Yahweh is the primordial bedrock of Ezekiel's prophetic ministry. The voice of this prophetic narrator is heard to be reporting Ezekiel as saying וָאֶרְאֶה מַרְאוֹת אֱלֹהִים ("and/then I saw visions of God," Ezek 1:1). The phrase "and I saw" or "I saw," used in relation to visionary activity is a recurrent phrase in Ezekiel occurring no less than 14 times, always appearing as a particle conjunction in the first person masculine singular. One other phrase that is critical to Ezekiel's visionary experience is הָיְתָה עָלַי יַד־יְהוָה ("the hand of Yahweh was upon me"), occurring four times (Ezek 1:3; 3:22; 37:1; 40:1). In Ezekiel, the vision or what the prophet sees is always linked to a voice speaking to him. The purpose of this theophanic encounter by the prophet is as suggested by Merrill – "to introduce the living God of Israel and to magnify

---

10. Duguid, *Ezekiel*, 35.
11. Merrill, "A Theology of Ezekiel and Daniel," 369.

His terrifying glory" to the exiles in the hope that his sinning people now languishing in exile are convinced to now "encounter this One whose trust they have violated and learn from Him what remedial steps to restoration must be taken."[12] Also, Cooke submits that the vision of God in his glory and holiness through which God reveals himself to Ezekiel outside the land of Israel serves not only as a call to prophecy, but "it determined the substance of his message."[13] The whole book is a reflection of what Ezekiel had seen and heard, an encounter he could hardly forget in a hurry for its magnanimous nature and impact. This is quite significant to him and to his prophetic ministry in that it is when he was בְּתוֹךְ־הַגּוֹלָה ("among the exiles") in Babylon as a fellow exile that he claims וָאֶרְאֶה מַרְאוֹת אֱלֹהִים ("and/then I saw visions of God").

More significant is the likelihood that Ezekiel possibly never had such theophanic experience when serving as priest[14] in Jerusalem until now. This would further strengthen his theological perspective about the *knowledge* of Yahweh as a sovereign deity who is not restricted by time and space. While Yahweh reveals himself in the shrine in Jerusalem, his mobility as the God of the cosmos equally allows for the same self-revelation elsewhere outside

---

12. Merrill, "A Theology of Ezekiel and Daniel," 368.
13. Cooke, *A Critical and Exegetical Commentary*, xvii.
14. We should never lose sight that Ezekiel's prophetic call that came through vision, following which his commission to the prophetic function was given, succeeded his priestly experience in Judah. As Wilson puts it, "to be sure, Ezekiel's vision was shaped by motifs from Israelite tradition and was deeply rooted in his own priestly background. Fire, storm, and wind are often said to accompany God's appearance (cf. Exod 19; Deut 33:2; Judg 5:4-5; Pss 18:7-15; 68:7-10), and the prophet's knowledge of the Temple cherubim helped him to recognize what he was seeing in his vision.... The visionary combination of vague, evocative images with concrete but fantastic objects helps the prophet to describe the divine reality that he saw." The *image, likeness, and glowing human form* that Ezekiel saw seated upon a throne required no need for interpretation for the prophet to know that he was encountering the appearance of the likeness of the glory of the God of Israel. Ezekiel's knowledge of the cherubim should not be construed as a new experience as he should have been familiar with such imageries. Consequently, at the realisation of what he saw, Ezekiel fell to the ground with his face down (1:28c). Robert R. Wilson, "Ezekiel," in *The Harper Collins Bible Commentary* (2d ed.; eds. James Luther Mays et al.; San Francisco, N.Y.: Harper Collins, 2000), 592. Two opposing views about Ezekiel's priestly engagement prior to the second deportation are suggested. One contends that Ezekiel was about to enter full priestly function in Jerusalem when in 597 BC he was whisked to Babylonia and that dream was short-lived. The other holds that he had already been engaged in full priestly order. Whichever is the case, his literary work indicates a nice sandwich of the priestly and prophetic elements.

Zion. The force of the vision therefore is not so much what Ezekiel sees as it is *the glory of Yahweh* revealed in what he sees. As Wilson observes, in such a theophanic experience of visionary revelation, Ezekiel "came face to face with God's glory, the overwhelming radiance that surrounds the deity."[15] This experience is crucial because it is what would revolutionise the prophet's ministry. Mays[16] aptly points out in this respect that it is this revealed glory that "plays a pivotal role in his prophecy." He stresses that this suggests the disclosure of the majesty of God's personal presence, the invisible made visible outside the temple in an unclean land to "address the predicament of prophet and people." Mays explains further that the import of such revelation is significant to the prophet's ministry as "God appears in his identity as the lord of Israel's history and worship, the one who intervened in their affairs to save and punish;" the one who rules over cosmic order, and therefore is "free of all limits, sovereign over all of history." Since the entire cosmic order is Yahweh's domain, when he acts, nothing else will be vindicated, and since he moves in historic events, nothing is capable of standing in his way.

The prophetic phenomenon of seeing a vision or visions in Jewish prophetic tradition began way back with the pre-classical prophets who preceded Ezekiel's era. Isaiah had given a similar report about his prophetic commission. In his case, the Lord whom he saw sat upon an exalted throne (cf. Isa 6:1-7 with Ezek 1:1-28). Isaiah declares, ואראה את־אדני ישב על־כסא רם ("And/then I saw the Lord sitting upon a high throne"). Daniel and Jeremiah had similarly received revelatory messages from Yahweh through visions (Dan 1:17; 8:1; 9:24; 10:14; 11:14; Jer 14:14; 23:16.) In the book of Ezekiel, the phrase מראות אלהים ("visions of God") appears as a special term, always in the plural and always occurring with the word "God" instead of with the more personal name "Lord." As Mays submits, such expressions "are ways of insisting that the experience happened solely at divine initiative . . . The vision was not a wilful dream, neither was the report an invention of Ezekiel [but] an action which God took from his side."[17]

---

15. Wilson, "Ezekiel," 592.
16. Mays, *Ezekiel*, 26.
17. Mays, *Ezekiel*, 26. Prophetic visionary experience, especially the one Ezekiel encountered, is quite critical to the prophetic function as such visionary revelatory

What sets apart Ezekiel's visionary experience as unique from those of other prophets[18] within the prophetic tradition is the element of its mobility. It should not escape our memory that "the world of Ezekiel was completely different from the world of earlier prophets. It was, of course, the world of exile. We need only mention the word to evoke the image of a strange new setting."[19] Until Ezekiel's time, Israel had always understood divine revelation as a localised phenomenon. Yahweh was traditionally resident among his people in Zion and there he revealed himself to them. Commenting on the concept of divine mobility, Keith Carley says "the vision of Yahweh's glory in the plain and of its departing from Jerusalem must have involved for the prophet himself a radical reassessment of his former beliefs. For the location of the [glory] at the Jerusalem sanctuary formed part of the traditions with which he was familiar"[20] as one from the Zadokite priestly order. His theophanic experience of the manifestation of the glory of God, a theological theme "very prominent in the priestly tradition,"[21] and Yahweh's personal presence outside Jerusalem in Babylonia, a foreign and unclean land, was not only perplexing but revolutionary for Ezekiel as it altered and reordered his theology of Yahweh's presence and residence hitherto held. As an aspect of a revolutionised theology, this theophanic experience both raises and answers the arching question, "How is it possible for the God of Israel to reveal the divine self with such majesty outside of God's temple and land? . . . the God of Ezekiel is not

---

experience always precedes divine auditory speech declaration. Like lightning and thunder are intertwined, so are these two a combination of prophetic experience of seeing and hearing an accompanying voice, either directly that of Yahweh or of his representative.

18. Vawter and Hoppe note that we must acknowledge that there is a considerable difference in visionary experience between those of the prophets before and after exile–or, in Ezekiel's case, during exile. Herein lies the difference–before the exile, the visions of the prophets tend to be parabolic: they are suggestive rather than descriptive (see for example, Amos 8:1-2; Jer. 1:11-12). That these parabolic visions usually involve ordinary things that, viewed without prophetic insight, would attract no remark at all. But the vision, which is now of strange things, no longer suggests the message but is the message itself, because every detail of it is corresponding with some revealed reality. Such are the visions of Ezekiel, allegorical in all and on the verge of apocalyptic, distinct in literary forms. Vawter and Hoppe, *A New Heart*, 7.

19. Ward, *Thus Says the Lord*, 171.

20. Keith C. Carley, *Ezekiel Among the Prophets: A Study of Ezekiel's Place in Prophetic Tradition* (London: SCM, 1975), 75.

21. Ruiz, "Ezekiel," 1057.

the God of a temple or a land, but the God of a people."[22] Despite the fact that the walls of Zion, the city within which Yahweh reigns as its King, is destroyed; despite the fact that Yahweh's shrine, the holy Temple in which he dwells among his people, now lies in pitiable ruins; the people for whose sake Yahweh chose Zion and the Temple, though momentarily living in exile, are not destroyed.

With this given, Jerusalem will yet blossom and the city will again burble with life to the envy of the nations. Ezekiel's vision of a new sacrificial system instituted in chapters 40-48 makes this connection between the old and new order. As Niditch notes in her conclusion, "This vision is cosmogony and deals with the creation and ordering of a world. . . . [hence,] Ezekiel 40-48 now stands in an especially appropriate place in the complete Book of Ezekiel, culminating a larger pattern of creation."[23] Thus, the theophanic experience of Yahweh in Babylonia is reaffirming to Ezekiel, consolidating his theological understanding of the Being, Personhood, and power of Yahweh.

6.2.2 Yahweh's Shepherding Exhibits His Covenant Fidelity

In Israelite religious ideology and theology, Israel's God has always proved himself to be a faithful covenant-keeping deity. The basis of Yahweh's covenant fidelity with Israel is not because the latter merits it, but rather because of reverence for his holy name in consonance with his divine character. Ezekiel captures such fidelity vis-à-vis Israel's infidelity in specific terms in chapters 16, 23, and 37. Each of the first two chapters begins with the introductory messenger formula, וַיְהִי דְבַר־יְהוָה אֵלַי לֵאמֹר ("And/then the word of Yahweh came to me saying") while the last begins with הָיְתָה עָלַי יַד־יְהוָה ("The hand of Yahweh was/came upon me"). In chapter 16, Yahweh charged Israel for her adulterous attitude and lifestyle. As his wife, she does not *remember* her covenant standing and obligations (Ezek 16:22,

---

22. Ruiz, "Ezekiel,", 1057.
23. Susan Niditch, "Ezekiel 40-48 in a Visionary Context," *CBQ* 48 (1986):224. See also Parunak's discussion on the interrelatedness of Ezekiel's vision to the prophetic vocation (1:1-3:15), of judgement upon Jerusalem (8:1-11:25), and of a restored community (40:1-48:25) in H. Van Dyke Parunak, "The Literary Architecture of Ezekiel's Marot Elohim," *JBL* 1 (1980):61-74.

43) with her husband, preferring instead to be in romance with strangers rather than to her own faithful and caring husband (Ezek 16:32). This act is both a covenant violation and an aberration on the part of a people in covenant relationship with Yahweh. Merrill explains that Ezekiel describes Israel's incessant attitude of covenant disobedience against her deity under three rubrics: "violation as harlotry, violation as idolatry or apostasy, and violation as the breaking of law or stipulation. He reminded his people that from the beginning their history had been one of unfaithfulness to their God. . . . In language filled with covenant overtones, the prophet rehearsed that dismal account."[24] In spite of such continuous covenant violation by Israel, yet, Yahweh was making atonement for her and re-establishing his covenant with her. This, as Ezekiel pointed out, clearly authenticates the fact of his covenant fidelity with his people (Ezek 16:62-63).

Chapter 23 continues with the theme of the people's covenant violation,[25] specific to Israel's socio-religious and socio-political prostitution begun in chapter 16. Israel, represented as Oholah, and Judah, represented as Oholibah, were both charged for perpetrating a perpetual promiscuous lifestyle characteristic of the covenant people's refusal "to submit to their Lord."[26] Such a rebellious attitude as presented in ch. 23 reveals the people's theological myopia to the extent that instead of loyalty to Yahweh, they were so impressed by Egypt's highly organised state and power, that the people "doubted Jehovah's ability to triumph without human order and power to succour Him."[27] This shift in loyalty was not only disbelief but a clear act of disobedience by Israel. Conceiving Israel's apostate state as fundamentally a defection from truth, Merrill posits that "as a result of idolatry and apostasy . . . Covenant rapture occurred"[28] when the nation went into political and religious alliances with pagan peoples. The effects

---

24. Merrill, "A Theology of Ezekiel and Daniel," 369.
25. Ellison argues that the main thought in the two chapters is dissimilar. He thinks chapter 23 is "merely a variant of the theme" in chapter 16. Chapter 16 unearths the enormity of Israel's sin but chapter 23 reveals the condemnation of Israel's unfaithfulness of relationship to other nations. Ellison, *Ezekiel*, 92. We see the theme of covenant violation in both chapters.
26. Merrill, "A Theology of Ezekiel and Daniel," 369.
27. Ellison, *Ezekiel*, 92.
28. Merrill, "A Theology of Ezekiel and Daniel," 370.

of such rapture shows clearly that self-estrangement from Yahweh always deprives one of the source of life-force, of clear focus and wisdom, and of life's true shalom.

More fundamental to Israel's act of infidelity apparent in her persistent disobedience to the principles of the Torah and violation of covenant provisions is her expressed attitude of forgetfulness and ingratitude. Severally in the Deuteronomic code, the covenant people are called upon to *remember* the goodness of Yahweh to Israel (Deut 5:15; 8:2-4; 24:18) and not *forget* his covenant (Deut 4:23; 6:12; 8:11-14, 19). The motif of *remembrance* was meant to function as the main grid of Israel's relationship with Yahweh in view of the covenant. This is what was to propel Israel to keep Yahweh's law. Christensen agrees in the submission that "one of the great lessons we can learn from the experience of ancient Israel in the religious life is that memory serves to lead to the continuing experience of the presence and activity of God. It is forgetfulness that opens the door to tragic failure on the part of the community of faith."[29] The idea of *remembrance* is crucial to Deuteronomic theology in Israelite tradition as its effects traversed both present and future generations.[30] But since leaders and subjects of the covenant community failed to remember their very unique relationship with Yahweh so they are able to keep the provisions of the Torah which they also forgot, Ezekiel's acted symbolism and the shepherd metaphor both functioned to serve as a recall of Israel's amnesia.

Closely knit to the preceding is the idea of Israel's ingratitude for all of Yahweh's goodness to her. This act naturally led to the nation's forgetting his covenant provisions. The covenant community not only failed to *remember* Yahweh's legal requirements but showed herself out to be an ingrate for all he had done in history for her sake. In what scholars consider to be the "centre of Deuteronomic theological interpretation"[31] (Deut 5:1-28:68),

---

29. Christensen, *Word Biblical Commentary*, 82.
30. In the stipulation of ancient treaties, exclusive allegiance to the covenant suzerain lord was demanded from the vassal. In God's covenant with Israel, however, the force seems to tilt towards the future (Deut 31:9-22). As Tremper and Dillard state, "the treaties included provisions for future public readings of the covenant document in order to remind both suzerain and vassal of their duties under its provisions." Longman III and Dillard, *An Introduction to the Old Testament*, 2nd ed., 110.
31. Brueggemann, *An Introduction*, 87.

Moses is heard rehearsing Yahweh's dealings and goodness to Israel in his speech. Yet, that Israel goes whoring again and again after foreign gods in total disregard to the legal code (Deut 12-25), and to the mutuality of oath in the Sinai covenant ". . . whereby YHWH, the God of the covenant, and Israel, the people of the covenant, commit themselves to each other in an exclusive, mutual loyalty"[32] (Deut 26:16-19), is a clear display of ungratefulness on Israel's part. Expectedly, Israel should have always perceived her national identity and self-expression in covenantal terms as Yahweh's chosen people. Everything about her is supposed to have been Yahwistic in its import and expression, serving as baseline for the operation of the Deuteronomic theological tradition. This is very significant for the people's relationship with Yahweh and with other peoples. Brueggemann explains this point further: "The purpose of that theological intentionality is to provide interpretive ground whereby Israel, as an intentional community of covenant, may contrast itself in its daily life with any indigenous alternative in the land of Canaan and with any temptation to submit to Assyrian cultural hegemony."[33] But that part of her ungratefulness incapacitated her ability to measure up to such expectation as pointed out by Ezekiel (Ezek 16, 23).

In spite of the act of disobedience and covenant violation which the covenant people put up against their suzerain lord however, Yahweh did not give up on his stubborn and rebellious people (Ezek 23:2-4) as he had put in place certain corrective measures with which to achieve his covenant purpose. In this regard, Yahweh was to direct his jealous anger against his chosen, yet shamelessly sinning people (Ezek 23:25) by using the same lovers with whom they had prostituted to punish them in their lewdness (Ezek 23:22-24, 46-49). Since Israel chose to discredit Yahweh's name and worship, it is only proper that rebels should "feel the weight of his chastisement"[34] to stay alive. According to Ezekiel, chastisement becomes evident because as "a God who tolerates no rival . . . covenant violation is,

---

32. Brueggemann, *An Introduction*, 89.
33. Brueggemann, *An Introduction*, 90.
34. Ellison, *Ezekiel*, 86.

first and foremost, disloyalty to the sovereign God who alone has legitimate claim to worship."[35]

By this retributive act, Yahweh is not only acting in judgement against his ungrateful people to chastise them but particularly acting as a responsible father who disciplines his child to correct his dislocated personal ethics, habits, attitudes, behaviour and disloyalty (cf. Heb 12:7-11). Like McKeating observes, two foci exist in the theology of the book of Ezekiel: "the inevitability and irrevocability of judgment, and the awful totality of judgment, on the one hand, and yet on the other, the conviction that judgment was survivable, and that God *meant* his people to survive"[36] so a lost relationship is restored. Merrill[37] supports this idea in the assertion that Israel's judgement then is not only retributive but also redemptive since its purpose is not to destroy but to bring her back into harmony with Yahweh's purposes for choosing her. Yahweh's dual opposing actions of retributive punishment and redemptive restoration is in keeping with the principle of his covenant fidelity with Israel whom he addresses as "my people" (Ezek 13:21, 23; 34:31; 36:28; 37:11-13, 23, 27). This point of covenant fidelity is graphically captured in Ezekiel's vision of the revived dry bones (Ezek 37) symbolising the restoration of Israel. Yahweh's forgiving character re-echoes an earlier motif when he relented from his anger against the people following the golden calf[38] saga (Exod 32:1-14).

The account of Israel's relationship with Yahweh in the Hebrew Scripture has not been favourably presented consequent to the nation's whoring attitude that always plunged her into a disadvantaged condition. In Ezekiel's thought, the exiles needed a reminder regarding their longstanding history of rebelliousness against faithful Yahweh. His theological presentation of Yahweh's covenant fidelity despite Israel's persistent infidelity is an

---

35. Merrill, "A Theology of Ezekiel and Daniel,", 371.
36. McKeating, *Ezekiel*, 77.
37. Merrill, "A Theology of Ezekiel and Daniel," 372.
38. In this ugly scenario, Aaron had aided the people in making a gold-cast idol soon after their commitment at Sinai to serve no other god except Yahweh (Exod 32:1-8; cf. Josh 24:14-24). Israel's idolatrous behaviour while still in transit so stirred up Yahweh's anger that he threatened to eliminate the nation and perpetrate his promise to Abraham through Moses. But Moses' objection and his reminding Yahweh of his covenant with the patriarchs reversed Yahweh's intended action (Exod 32:9-14).

indictment on his fellow exiles. Its import was to make Israel realise that she had perpetually sought after her personal interest against Yahweh's through covenant disobedience, thereby inviting his fury upon herself in judgement in spite of his resistance to do so. Ezekiel also presented Yahweh's covenant fidelity expressed in his use of the shepherd metaphor with the intention that it would draw the exiles to the realisation that their bad human shepherds (both royal and religious leaders in Israel) had not sought after the flock's good but only after their personal gains. This act is an aberration of the principle of leadership in general, and of godly leadership in particular.

Ezekiel therefore insisted on the point of divine faithfulness to Israel despite her cultic misbehaviour. To him, that Yahweh did not consume both people and leaders in his judgement through total elimination was an act of grace in keeping with the covenant he made with Israel's patriarchs. Such covenant fidelity is a clear exhibition of Yahweh's shepherding character. It is therefore on this warrant that restored Israel was to be shepherded by Yahweh himself as its perfect shepherd.

6.3 Eschatological Shepherding Requires a Return to Yahweh

The prophetic message over and over is replete with a *return* motif. Israel was urged repeatedly by the prophets to *seek* the LORD and live (Isa 55:6; Jer 50:4; Hos 10:12; Amos 5:6; Zeph 2:3; Zech 8:21, 22. She was equally called upon to return or come back to the LORD to find his salvation in the time of need (Isa 44:22; Jer 3:14, 22; 31:21-22; Hos 14:1).

As the undergirding understanding of Israel's restoration to Judah is expressed in a *return* motif, the nation and her individual citizens were required to return to Yahweh in heart. The prophetic call for an inward rather than an outward return by Israel to her deity, Yahweh, is preparatory for an eschatological shepherding under Yahweh himself. This is crucial because there would be no place for the old order in the scheme of things in the new community of Israel.

6.3.1 Eschatological Shepherding Demonstrates Yahweh's Grace

The element of Yahweh's graciousness both in his election and preservation of Israel plays out in Ezekiel's theology. The Yahweh who gravely punishes is the same Yahweh who graciously saves and restores his dissident people. From this premise, it is not in error therefore to assert that, "Ezekiel is the great prophet of the grace of God." This is because he presents "The God whose transcendent majesty is almost ineffable yet condescends to his utterly undeserving people" who, though they suffered the pains of exile, do not think it expedient to repent, but "continued to profane Yahweh's holy name among the nations."[39] The choice of Israel into nationhood and into covenant standing with Yahweh, a rare privilege and honour not appreciated by those so chosen as painted by Ezekiel's allegory[40] of the unfaithful wife in chapter 16, is an act of divine grace particularly that Israel was a nonentity when Yahweh found her (Ezek 16:4-7). Her nonentity is captured in that the girl's "chances at birth for a happy life would have been reckoned at zero"[41] and this shows her complete "weak and unwanted position, and her positive and negative ignorance of God"[42] also at birth. But her capricious attitude towards gracious Yahweh equates with that of an ingrate who turns round to bite the very finger that feeds him. Against all logic, "instead of responding with love, loyalty, and gratitude to her benefactor and husband, [Israel rather] becomes persistently and deeply unfaithful"[43] to Yahweh, not minding what he ever suffered or lost in the course of her choice and sustenance.

---

39. David Muir Gibson Stalker, *Ezekiel: Introduction and Commentary* (2d impres.; London: SCM, 1971), 40.
40. Reading the context of Ezekiel 16, Ellison notes that herein lies Ezekiel's most elaborate allegory. He recommends that its "ill accords with modern taste is no ground for passing over it quickly, for it stresses some of his basic concepts." Conceding that the imagery is ugly and unattractive, yet, he submits that "it only matches the even more ugly sin it represents." Ellison, *Ezekiel*, 60-61. Ronald E. Clements also observes that while the language of Ezekiel 16 is strong and sounds coarse to the modern Bible reader, it is worth careful attention because "it was intended to sound coarse and shocking to those who heard Ezekiel speak in such a manner…[so] important to its power to communicate a divine message." Clements, *Ezekiel*, 68.
41. Clements, *Ezekiel*, 70.
42. Ellison, *Ezekiel*, 61.
43. Clements, *Ezekiel*, 71.

To risk the purpose of emphasis, the demise of Jerusalem/Judah insisted upon by Ezekiel, an event that finally occurred in 587 BC, was consequent upon Israel's persistent sin. This event would have marked the exit and end of the nation from the scene of history, as Blenkinsopp correctly observes:

> In the normal course of events the extinction of dynasty and national cult would have meant the end of the nation and its religion, as had happened when the kingdom of Samaria became part of the Assyrian empire a century and a half earlier. That this did not happen after the fall of Jerusalem and destruction of the national sanctuary is one of the more interesting circumstances of ancient history, the effects of which are still very much with us.[44]

This extraordinary divine preservation of Judah at such a critical point in her history is, undoubtedly, predicated upon Yahweh's gracious handling of the covenant nation. The interpretation of Israel's reversal of extinction by her existence in the restoration and eschatological community as Ezekiel envisioned is only traceable in retrospect to the Abrahamic, Sinaitic and Davidic covenants than it is to Israel's good. The nation throughout her history had done nothing to attract Yahweh's compassion except his unrelenting foaming wrath against her. Yet, he chose to be gracious in consonance with his divine character as a merciful, compassionate, and forgiving gracious Yahweh.

The picture we see in Ezekiel's presentation of Yahweh's character as a gracious and compassionate Yahweh shows a seemingly contradictory dualism. Yahweh hates, yet, he loves what he hates. Yahweh destroys, yet he rebuilds what has been destroyed. Yahweh kills, yet, he revives and makes alive again what was dead. Yahweh causes the absence of his presence from the sinning community, yet he returns his presence to the restored community. Joel Drinkard explains this ironic dealing with Israel further:

---

44. Blenkinsopp, A *History of Prophecy in Israel*, 149.

> Ezekiel's theology centers around a God who is intimately involved with the people. The prophet declares God's judgment on the people due to their sins, and that judgment is devastating – the total destruction of the nation and its religious institutions. But this God also offers restoration if the people will repent. And in that glorious restored community God will be ever-present with them. . . . The fall of the nation and the destruction of the Temple were the direct result of the people's rebelliousness [which] . . . was especially abhorrent to God . . . Nevertheless, judgment was not the last word to Israel-Judah. The prophet also issues a call to repentance. This call if heeded could not avert the judgment that was pronounced. But it could lead to a restoration.[45]

This act of divine grace plays out in Ezekiel's vision of a throne surrounded by a rainbow where seated upon it is a Being (Ezek 1:28). In Ezekiel, the grace emanating from Yahweh is represented not only by the symbols of the few hairs tucked away (Ezek 5:3), the promise to spare some hairs (Ezek 6:8), the marking of the faithful (Ezek 9:4), and so on, but significantly in the historical understanding of the rainbow, indicating for Israel "the covenant sign that judgment against sin will never obliterate the remnant of God's true people."[46] To this, Merrill observes,

> The picture of God that emerges from [his] stupendous self-disclosures . . . to Ezekiel in theophanic splendour and glory almost unrivalled in the Old Testament . . . is sufficient to demonstrate that He is the Creator, the omnipotent One, who can and will alter the whole course of events to effect the redemption of His own chosen ones."[47]

---

[45]. Joel F. Drinkard, Jr., "Ezekiel," in *The Prophets: Mercer Commentary on the Bible Vol. 4* (eds. Watson E. Mills et al.; Macon: Mercer University Press, 1996), 163.
[46]. Duguid, *Ezekiel*, 37. The rainbow motif is always connected with the Noahic covenant following the destructive downpour (see Gen 9:8-17).
[47]. Merrill, "A Theology of Ezekiel and Daniel," 386.

He explains that although Yahweh punished his people with exile because they had "broken His covenant by their apostate and idolatrous behaviour . . . God also will not be capricious in salvation, for He has made an everlasting covenant with the people of Israel."[48] Nothing else can explain the exhibition of such gracious action apart from divine grace freely expressed for the sake of preserving Yahweh's own name and glory. Herein lies one of the key imports of Ezekiel's recognition formula, that both Israel and the nations may know the sovereignty of the creation God who cannot be equated with any pantheon deity.

The imagery of dry bones captures this divine grace in Ezekiel quite vividly. To this point, whether the lifeless, tasteless, odourless and extremely dry bones in the vision would have the capacity to live in view of their present state, Ezekiel's response to the question posed to him by Yahweh acknowledges Yahweh's sovereignty. Ezekiel said, "O Sovereign LORD, you alone know" (Ezek 37:1-14). The statement, אדני יהוה אתה ידעת, reveals without any ambiguity, that no one else and nothing else could *know* the future state of the lifeless bones except Yahweh himself. Greenberg points out that such response about the bones' "improbability" to live, no doubt, transfers the certainty of *knowledge* to "their creator" who alone "has the expertise to tell."[49]

Through his presentation of the grace side of Yahweh in this dry bones imagery, Ezekiel is here stimulating the exiles to now appreciate what Yahweh had done, was doing, and will still do in behalf of his covenant people. This ordinarily would have motivated the exiles to prepare their hearts and to return to Yahweh as prospective participants in his eschatological shepherding of the reborn and renewed flock in the new community of shepherding.

6.3.2 Eschatological Shepherding Demands Honour for Yahweh's Name

Overfamiliarity has a way of downplaying the respect, dignity, and honour that people in close relationship should be expressing for one another. This

---

48. Merrill, "A Theology of Ezekiel and Daniel," 386.
49. Greenberg, *Ezekiel 21-37*, 743.

ideology seems in consonance with the maxim that "one never values what one has until one loses it." This fact is apparent by the expressed character of Israel. The account of Ezekiel indicates that the covenant nation had disrespected and treated Yahweh her God, shepherd and King, and who graciously chose her among all peoples, as a mundane being and with every disdain, both by her attitude and action.

Ezekiel is not alone in the fight to protect the reverence for Yahweh's honour. Ironically, even in the postexilic era, the restored community did not think it right to accord her deity the respect he deserves. Even if for nothing else, but for the fact that Yahweh had graciously restored them back to Judah, he should have been revered and the provision of his law observed. But Israel's continued covenant violation forced Yahweh himself to contend with Israel through Malachi in defence of the honour due his name:

> "'A son honours his father, and a servant his master. If I am a father, where is the honour due me? If I am a master, where is the respect due me?" says the LORD Almighty. "It is you, O priests, who show contempt for my name." But you ask, 'How have we shown contempt for your name?' "You place defiled food on my altar." But you ask, 'How have we defiled you?' "By saying that the LORD's table is contemptible. When you bring blind animals for sacrifice, is that not wrong? When you sacrifice crippled or diseased animals, is that not wrong? Try offering them to your governor! Would he be pleased with you? Would he accept you?" says the LORD Almighty. My name will be great among the nations, from the rising to the setting of the sun. In every place incense and pure offerings will be brought to my name, because my name will be great among the nations,'" says the LORD Almighty" (Mal 1:6-8, 11 NIV).

The gods of the heathen nations were highly venerated by their worshippers as the human leaders were also respected by their citizens. In keeping with this tradition, Israel should have accorded higher honour and respect to Yahweh as her deity. But unfortunately, the reverse turned out to be the case as the nation again and again went whoring after the gods of the nations, bowing the knee to them in place of Yahweh. By this act, Israel gave nothing in return to Yahweh who had shown himself to be everything to her. The nation accorded not even the least dime or kobo of respect to Yahweh's name.

Yahweh's self-revelation to Moses in a covenant name suggests the need for its respect. It is because of the dignity, power and honour synonymous with his name that Yahweh disclosed himself to Moses simply as "I AM WHO I AM" (Exod 3:14). With this he instructed him, "Say to the Israelites, 'The LORD, the God of your fathers – the God of Abraham, the God of Isaac and the God of Jacob – has sent me to you.' This is my name forever, the name by which I am to be remembered from generation to generation" (Exod 3:15 NIV). The concept of honour and shame expressed by Ezekiel captures this picture. As Alex Luc asserts, God's name plays a more important role in Ezekiel's thought because for him, "Yahweh's name was more important than his glory;" and much more because, "to Ezekiel the whole history of Israel was intimately tied to God's concern for his name."[50] Yahweh's revealed glory and name primarily points to its need to attract honour. For this, it is asserted, that we get from Ezekiel "a picture of a holy, transcendent God whose name and glory must be protected"[51] by all means and by whatever way possible. But the people in covenant relationship with him did not recognise the "awe-inspiring presence of God"[52] let alone to give glory to him and reverence for the honour of his name. This is one reason why Ezekiel, like his prophetic counterpart, Malachi, accused particularly the priesthood for misleading the people into despising Yahweh's name before the Gentiles.

Following the need for Israel to accord respect to and reverence for Yahweh's name, the recognition formula used by Ezekiel was intended to achieve two effects in this connection. First, it was to discipline dissident and rebellious Israel in order to bring her back to covenant loyalty and to the worship of Yahweh. The expectation is that the humiliation of exile

---

50. Alex Luc, "A Theology of Ezekiel" God's Name and Israel's History," in *JETS* 26/2 (1983):137-8.

51. Zodhiates, Baker, and Kletzing, eds., *Hebrew-Greek Key Word Study Bible*, 1082.

52. Ralph L. Smith, *Micah-Malachi* (*WBC 32*; Waco, Tex.: Word, 1984), 311.

would cause self-awareness and the knowledge of Yahweh in Israel, that is, to make Israel realise her wrong and seek for Yahweh, the God of her fathers. Hence, the expression, "And they will know that I am the Lord" and "Then you will know that I am the Lord."[53] As Odell explains, the recognition formula in Ezekiel, always at the conclusion of an oracle, functioning as a proof-saying, indicates that, "the goal of the judgment is for Israel to see that Yahweh has been disclosed in the event . . . [causing] an acceptance of Yahweh's claim on their lives."[54]

The second effect was to display Yahweh's cosmic power via the instrument of punishment of the nations for their sins because they had, as pointed out by Merrill, "maligned God's own chosen people, thus cursing them"[55] by their molestation. Acting through other cosmic events also, Yahweh would make these nations acknowledge that there is a God in heaven more powerful than their pantheon of national gods. The oracles against the nations "had a particular purpose,"[56] to cause these nations to turn to Yahweh's worship, having Israel in the lead. It is well stated in this connection that the messages of the oracles addressed to the nations surrounding Israel "reveal the concern of the Lord not only for His own covenant people but also for the whole world. The God of Israel is also the God of the nations . . . the selection of Israel was for the express purpose of providing through it a servant people who would mediate the salvation of the Lord to all mankind."[57] Sadly though, Israel failed in carrying out this divine salvific purpose to the nations.

This, notwithstanding, Ezekiel revealed that Yahweh would still restore Israel back to Judah for his name's sake. This presupposes that as perfect shepherding activity is restored in the eschatological community with

---

53. In Ezekiel alone, the phrase "And they will know that I am the LORD" occurs 27 times (Ezek 6:10, 13, 14; 7:27; 12:15, 16; 24:27; 25:11, 17; 26:6; 28:22, 23, 26; 29:9, 21; 30:8, 19, 25, 26; 32:15; 33:29; 34:27; 35:15; 36:38; 38:23; 39:6, 28), and "And you will know that I am the LORD" occurs 19 times (Ezek 6:14; 7:27; 12:16; 25:11, 17; 26:6; 28:23, 26; 29:9, 21; 30:8, 25, 26; 32:15; 33:29; 35:15; 36:38; 38:23; 39:28). Also, the phrase "Then you will know" occurs no less than 19 times (Ezek 7:4, 9; 11:10; 12:20; 13:9, 21, 23; 14:8; 17:21; 20:20, 38, 42; 23:49; 25:5; 35:4, 9, 12; 36:11; 37:6, 14).
54. Odell, *Ezekiel*, 81.
55. Merrill, "A Theology of Ezekiel and Daniel," 385.
56. Luc, "A Theology of Ezekiel, God's Name and Israel's History," 141.
57. Merrill, "A Theology of Ezekiel and Daniel," 383.

Yahweh as its only perfect shepherd, this act proves only one fact – reverence for the honour of Yahweh's name must be restored in the sight of both Israel and the nations.

6.4 Ezekiel's Theological Basis for Disqualifying Israel's Shepherds from Eschatological Shepherding

Ezekiel's theological *knowledge* of the Person and acts of Yahweh, observably displayed in historical events for the sake of Israel, lays a concrete foundation for his critique of royal leadership in Israel's society. The primary theological hub on which his critique revolves is the charge that Israel, and particularly her bad human shepherds, forgot Yahweh. Ezekiel charged that Israel's successive bad human shepherds since after Solomon's day did not follow Yahweh's undergirding principles of true shepherding of the flock. Instead, they had abused the rights of their office and became brutes because of greed. He also charged that Israel's bad human shepherds had equally failed to pattern their shepherding after that laid down by Yahweh himself by caring and sacrificing for the flock. As a consequence, such leadership failures reveal themselves in the disrespectful treatment of Yahweh's name by the evil shepherding attitude and behaviour of these bad human shepherds. Against this backdrop, Ezekiel's critique of Israel's imperfect human shepherds is full of indictment and repudiation.

The primary principle upon which Israel's royal shepherds were to lead the flock is reverence for Yahweh. They were to administer state affairs according to the rules and principles regulated by the Deuteronomic Code. But since Israel's human shepherds lost sight of the dignity of Yahweh and the regulatory principles of this theology, they immersed themselves in gross leadership misconduct of the highest degree. Charles Feinberg explains such a misnomer:

> The leaders were guilty of gross dereliction of duty. By oppression and shedding innocent blood, they destroyed the flock; those who were not destroyed were scattered to wander without protection. So the leaders were guilty of the very

things the shepherds are charged with preventing. By leading the nation into idolatry and so into the Babylonian captivity, the leaders had scattered the people. Moreover, contrary to the duty of shepherds to lead and feed the flock, they had driven the flock away.[58]

In addition, Marvin Sweeney lends support in the submission that Ezekiel's "basic charge is that the nation's leaders have failed in their responsibility to care for the people as they served their own interests. In keeping with Davidic ideology, Ezekiel argues that YHWH will function as the true shepherd for his people."[59] On this basis, the prophet made clear his argumentation by contrasting Yahweh's approach to shepherding with those of Israel's imperfect human shepherds.

6.4.1 A Contrast of Yahweh's Shepherding Attributes with Israel's Imperfect Human Shepherds

Ezekiel's contrasting Yahweh's shepherding attributes as Israel's true Shepherd-King with her bad and imperfect human shepherds in his critique becomes necessary because the latter had glaringly failed both Yahweh and the people they had the duty to lead and care for. As Paul Joyce asserts:

> The primary task of the prophet Ezekiel . . . was to provide a theological interpretation of the disaster which was engulfing his nation . . . standing in the tradition of the eighth-century classical prophets, Ezekiel affirms that the catastrophic events of his own day are not merely chaotic and meaningless, but are rather the powerful and just actions of the God of Israel, who is acting righteously to punish the present generation of Israelites for their sins.[60]

---

58. Charles Lee Feinberg, "Jeremiah," in *The Expositor's Bible Commentary Volume 6* (ed. Frank E. Gaebelein; Grand Rapids, Mich.: Zondervan, 1986), 517.

59. Sweeney, *The Prophetic Literature*, 156.

60. Paul M. Joyce, "King and Messiah in Ezekiel," in *King and Messiah in Israel and the Ancient Near East: Proceedings of the Oxford Old Testament Seminar* (JSOTSup. 270) (ed. J. Day; Sheffield, England: Sheffield Academic Press, 1998), 323.

The larger share of the blame for Israel's sin is particularly put on the nation's imperfect human shepherds. Theo Clements explains that it is because of leadership failures that "Ezekiel 34 is entirely devoted to God's shepherding . . . God is acting here instead of the failing kings of Israel, who are also represented as shepherds."[61] Here, Yahweh is seen "pronouncing woe upon oppressive leaders" to save his downtrodden flock that were in despair from the grip of "internal captivity."[62]

Ezekiel charged that both past and present monarchs[63] in Israel had not been good shepherds of Yahweh's flock as Yahweh himself has been to his people. This charge is quite particular because Yahweh had already put in place a particular leadership paradigm that was to be operative in Israel since the time of Moses. Such leadership paradigm was intended initially to function as the main grid of leadership in Israelite society. Tracing the failures of these kings in retrospect, Trent Butler[64] states that in presenting the narrative history of the events of the book of Joshua, the Israelite historian added a theological element to it located in "the paradigm of Israelite leadership." By contrast, he explains that Israel's history of leadership presents Moses as its outstanding human leader who is conceptualised as "the prophet without parallel" as an icon. As such, "all leadership in Israel occurs in the shadow of Moses." He explains further that following in this tradition, the other leaders of Israel who came after Moses, such as the "great leaders of Israel – Joshua, Samuel, David, Solomon, Hezekiah, Josiah, and so on," and in particular, those who followed after these leaders, must have had to stand on the instructions of Deut 17:14-20 which "gave a legal standard by which to measure Israel's leaders."

---

61. Theo Clements, "Searching for the Good Shepherd," *Netherlands archiefs voor kerkgeschiedenis* 1 (2003):18.

62. Block, *The Book of Ezekiel Chapters 25-48*, 277.

63. The identity of these monarchs is still a contentious issue in scholarship. See for example, Odell's thinking in *Ezekiel*, 423, and that of Daniel I. Block in Block, *The Book of Ezekiel Chapters 25-48*, 277 in this regard. This work however, proceeds with the understanding that the indicted "shepherds of Israel" incorporates all past royal, political and religious leaders of both Northern and Southern kingdoms of Israel, even the last king of Judah. The list includes the last three kings of Judah as those described as "present leaders" because of their role in the final demise of Judah.

64. Trent C. Butler, *Joshua* (*WBC 7*; Waco, Tex.: Word, 1983), 13.

Taking his measurement against this main leadership grid in Israel's history and against Yahweh's standard of good leadership for his people, Ezekiel found the subsequent leaders of Israel grossly wanting. For example, Ralph Klein states that Ezekiel observed, above all, that "ruling violently, they turned their flock over to wild beasts. The unrighteous rulers, in short, are responsible for Israel's falling prey to the nations."[65] What follows below is the prophet's careful examination of the attitudes of Israel's bad and imperfect human shepherds vis-à-vis those of Yahweh, Israel's true Shepherd-King.

6.4.1.1 Yahweh's Qualities as Israel's Ideal Shepherd-King

Our theological analysis of Ezekiel 34:7-16 in the previous chapter reveals, not only Yahweh's rescue mission in behalf of his bruised, brutalised, and abused flock, but also presents his inherent qualities as Israel's true Shepherd-King captured by his concern for the flock. These qualities are represented in his action of rescuing and gathering the scattered sheep, feeding them, making them lie down in rich pastures, ministering to the injured and weak, and ensuring equal justice for both the strong and the weak. In Ezekiel, the qualities of true shepherding, as Yahweh's attitude towards his flock demonstrates, involves three pillars of shepherding which are *care* for the flock, *provision* for the flock, and *protection* of the flock.

The Hebrew particle adverb לכן "therefore," repeated thrice in Ezekiel 34:7, 9, and 20 is significant to the shepherding pillar of *care* for the flock. Standing in antithesis to Yahweh, Israel's bad and imperfect human shepherds "had left off caring for the flock and were concerned only with their own well-being"[66] at the detriment of the flock. This means "the shepherds' sinful self-interest"[67] jettisoned their shepherding character and responsibility of care for the flock. Following such failure, Yahweh, the true Shepherd-King, now assumes the shepherding of his flock to make available for them the care that they have been robbed of when their bad and imperfect human shepherds could not provide. In the Israelite society for

---

65. Klein, *Israel in Exile*, 83.
66. Merrill, "A Theology of Ezekiel and Daniel," 376.
67. Dugid, *Ezekiel*, 394.

instance, Cooper explains that "The king was to be the under-shepherd and God the true King and Shepherd." But since these under-shepherds failed in performing their shepherding roles, "Ezekiel contrasted the exploitation of the corrupt shepherds with the diligent care [Yahweh] himself would exercise on behalf of his flock."[68] Such character of diligent shepherding care from Yahweh for his flock plays out in David's experience of him both as a shepherd boy and as the king of Israel (see Ps 23).

A true shepherd does not only empathise with the agony but also identifies with the need of the sheep without discrimination. In accomplishing their leadership task, Israel's human shepherds needed to have aimed at achieving the "perfect balance of comforting the afflicted and afflicting the comfortable"[69] among the flock. Ezekiel portrays Yahweh as demonstrating this shepherding quality of indiscriminate empathy and impartial identification with the plight of the flock (34:16). All this is captured by the use of the first person personal pronoun (the Qal imperfect "I will") in Yahweh's promises of acting in behalf of his flock. Cooper commends further in this respect that "the proliferation of "'I wills'" in 34:10-29 suggests Yahweh's determination personally to be involved in the lives and destinies of his people."[70]

The second shepherding pillar of *provision* is revealed by Yahweh's action of shepherding the flock in rich pasture (Ezek 34:13-15). The verb[71] רעה used only here in v. 13 having Yahweh as its subject, denotes his action of providing for his neglected, yet, sapped flock by the greedy, worthless, and bad human shepherds of Israel. Ezekiel is forced to subject the whole monarchy to condemnation in the wake of their failure in their "royal duty of enforcing social justice"[72] in society. This lax of proper shepherding of the

---

68. Cooper, Jr., *Ezekiel*, 300.
69. Dugid, *Ezekiel*, 400.
70. Cooper, Jr., *Ezekiel*, 301. The failure of Israel's shepherds left great effects on the nation. Ellison observes that Israel was incapacitated by the lack of a king who was "living out the will of Jehovah" since one effect of fallen man is "his very great difficulty, if not incapability, in picturing the ideal and perfect" because of the imperfection of things. Such situation therefore makes it very obvious that Yahweh should do what is left undone for his flock. Ellison, *Ezekiel*, 119.
71. The Qal verb form וּרְעִיתִים appears only once in Ezekiel (Ezek 34:13). Its imperfect form אֶרְעֶה, also in the Qal, appears only twice in Ezekiel (Ezek 34:34, 35).
72. Ellison, *Ezekiel*, 120.

flock by the royal chair in Israel made them "responsible for their fate"[73] as Yahweh deposed them from shepherding.

In contradistinction to the shepherds providing only for themselves, Yahweh now feeds his rescued flock in the rich pasturage on the mountain of Israel, denoting safety and tranquillity for the scattered flock now restored. That Yahweh would at last literally care for the flock as "a loving shepherd," scholars reason this, no doubt, implies that "individual needs would finally be met" because it is the Lord himself that "would care for every need of his flock"[74] by making every adequate provision available for them in an eschatological atmosphere conducive for shepherding.

Lastly, Ezekiel reflects Yahweh's attribute of true shepherding in the shepherding pillar of *protection* as he himself rescues the flock from the caprice of their external and internal predators, gathers them, and brings them back to their homeland to live and graze in total tranquillity and safety (Ezek 34:10-13, 16). As a mother is naturally emotionally attached to her child, so Yahweh will exhibit his compassion by ensuring protection for his defenceless and vulnerable flock. Greenberg[75] suggests, on the basis of hermeneutics, that the threefold mention of "the mountains of Israel" in vv. 13-14 in the plural means "the entire land." If this is accurate, it then follows that Yahweh's flock will always dwell in safety only inside the land of Israel and nowhere else. This explains one major reason why the idea of land is so crucial to the national life of Israel because land is tied to the people's national identity and existence.

If the character quality of care, protection, and provision for the flock is what qualifies one to shepherd Yahweh's flock, the bad and imperfect human shepherds of Ezekiel were neither suitable nor qualified for the job. It is only in Yahweh that these true shepherd qualities reside. The prophet's evaluative contrast is therefore to drive home the point to reveal that in an evil and imperfect human society, human shepherds are ordinarily prone to be wicked, evil, loathsome and imperfect. Only Yahweh has shown himself

---

73. Greenberg, *Ezekiel 21-37*, 695.
74. Alexander, "Ezekiel," 913.
75. Greenberg, *Ezekiel 21-37*, 700.

to be a perfect shepherd who will create a perfect shepherding environment in the eschatological community.

6.4.1.2 The Characteristics of Israel's Worthless Shepherds

In Ezekiel's use of the shepherd metaphor to depict the leadership lapses in Israelite society, a picture of Israel's royal and religious leaders is painted to show them to be care-less, self-centred, cruel, abusive, and negligent leaders. According to Cooper, Ezekiel carefully "employed the metaphor of a flock and its selfish and corrupt shepherds"[76] to show the harm unleashed on the flock. What these bad and imperfect human shepherds of Israel had done to the flock is simply this: as shepherds, they enjoyed feeding on the sheep but did not feed them. Also, they carted away from the sheepfold but did not care for them. Still, they sucked milk out of the sheep but did not supply for the need of the flock nor sought out the lost, sick and weak sheep. Further still, these bad and imperfect human shepherds fed on the sheep but failed to pasture and protect them (Ezek 34:1-6). In Ezekiel's shepherding theology, this is not only evil but it is an action that negates the characteristics of good shepherding as Yahweh himself had demonstrated in his dealings with Israel throughout her history.

The negative leadership characteristics exhibited by Israel's bad and imperfect human shepherds not only show them out to be brute-like but far more, they put on a "care-free" attitude to the concerns of the sheep provided their own personal means were met. The shepherd metaphor of Ezekiel in reality reveals that Israel's bad leaders were actually "sheep dispersers" and destroyers of the sheep pen rather than being "sheep keepers," keeping watch over the sheep placed under their care by the chief shepherd.[77]

The characteristic behaviours exhibited by Israel's human under-shepherds qualify their description as bad, insensitive, and worthless shepherds

---

76. Cooper, Jr., *Ezekiel*, 298.
77. As Alexander observes, Israel's imperfect human shepherds "had been selfish, insensitive leaders who had plundered the flock for personal gain and had allowed the people to become prey for other nations.... [they] thought only of themselves and material gain.... They did not care what happened to the people as long as they as leaders had all their own personal needs met." Alexander, "Ezekiel," 911-913. Since Israel's bad and imperfect human shepherds lost every sense of humaneness as it were, they would not show concern for the flock they took pleasure in feasting upon.

when compared with the shepherding qualities observable in Yahweh. It is inescapable that the various classes of the shepherds of Israel (the political rulers as well as the religious leaders, and more specifically, the royal leaders of the land; see Jer 23; 1 Kgs 22:11), were responsible for the fate of Israel[78] In specific terms, Greenberg is assertive in his submission that the shepherds of Israel are the "political leaders responsible for the disaster that befell Israel."[79] The image of a shepherd used in the context of leadership within the Israelite society appropriately depicts the quality of care, provision, protection, nurture, and an inherent quality of selflessness and every sense of leadership responsibility expected of the rulers. But because such qualities were glaringly lacking in the leadership of Yahweh's people, Drinkard observes:

> Ezekiel decries the violence of these shepherd-rulers [who had] fed on the sheep rather than caring for them . . . Because the shepherds abandoned their responsibility . . . [and] have not protected the flock nor cared for it, [Yahweh himself would] rescue the sheep from their false shepherds. The vivid image of rescuing the sheep from the mouth of the shepherds shows the shepherds as they actually are: ravening animals who feed on the flock.[80]

Bad shepherding always has negative affects on the sheepfold; but an affected sheepfold also will always attract the urgent attention and action of the sheep owner. The attendant repercussion of bad shepherding therefore is the removal from shepherding such unqualified bad, wicked and imperfect human shepherds to allow for the appointment of a truly qualified one.

---

78. Wilson, "Ezekiel," 618. Ellison explains that "Throughout the Bible lands monarchy was a divine institution; the king was the gods' supreme representative, himself a god in Egypt, a man capable of achieving deity elsewhere–chief ruler, chief priest, chief prophet." Ellison, *Ezekiel*, 119.
79. Greenberg, *Ezekiel 21-37*, 694.
80. Drinkard, Jr., "Ezekiel," 201.

6.4.2 Theological Indictment of Israel's Worthless Shepherds

Leadership failure exhibited through the abuse of rights on the part of Israel's imperfect human shepherds, forced on Ezekiel a theological critique and indictment of their negative attitude towards Yahweh's flock. Although Merrill's assertion that "fundamentally the theology of Ezekiel revolves around the bipolar themes of judgment and restoration"[81] may hardly gain acceptance by all scholars, the judgement of Yahweh on people and leaders occupies the mind of the prophet. Ezekiel is very particular; perhaps more particular than other prophets, about the sin of Israel's bad and imperfect human shepherds and Yahweh's judgement in response as this plays out in his theological indictment. Duguid points out that, "All of the prophets preached against the sin and idolatry of their own day, but perhaps none was quite as comprehensive or as sweeping in their indictments as Ezekiel."[82] What Israel's bad and imperfect human shepherds had done to the flock necessitated Yahweh's sharp indictment and retributive actions upon them through the prophetic word. Judgement on account of sin is clearly a major component of the theology of Ezekiel. Yahweh's judgement upon leadership failure, as presented by his prophet, is apparent because "Israel's leaders, both religious and political authorities, carried a particularly heavy responsibility, for by their initiatives and example they set the course for the life of the nation."[83] It is impossible for a just and vindictive Yahweh, to turn the eye against such leadership failure when it willingly and intentionally failed in its mandated functions to society.

In Ezekiel's theological evaluation and critique of the leadership environment in Israelite society, our prophet discovered that the kings, prophets, priests, and any other person who engaged in leadership function of some sort, were all equally guilty severally of abuse of their office (Ezek

---

81. Merrill, "A Theology of Ezekiel and Daniel," 386.
82. Duguid, *Ezekiel*, 36.
83. Merrill, "A Theology of Ezekiel and Daniel," 376. Israel's bad and imperfect human shepherds were judged because of their brutality and the failure to keep watch over the people, thereby violating the very covenant terms they had pledged to uphold. For their greed, self-centredness, unleashed self-aggrandisement, and for their act of insensitivity, negligence and irresponsibility to Yahweh's flock, these worthless shepherds would not escape Yahweh's judgement of reprobation and repudiation.

22:6, 25-27; 34:3-6, 18-19). Ezekiel revealed that such guilt plays out in the leadership failure and sets the pace for covenant disloyalty to flourish in the land. For instance, while stressing Israel's relationship to Yahweh as a people under covenant obligations, Olubunmo opines that "the king [is] the guardian of the covenant . . . The king and his people were covenant people."[84] But the failure of Israel's kings to measure up to this covenant obligation was detrimental to its society as the sin of covenant disloyalty was seen to have "affected kings, priests, bureaucrats, prophets, the elite families of Jerusalem, elders, women,"[85] and even the land itself.[86]

Following the kings' failure to live up to covenant terms, Ezekiel couched the divine action of judgement by means of an oracle of indictment. In Ezekiel's theology, Yahweh's judgement on the shepherds is an action that was imminent and irreversible because leadership is assuming the status and function of public responsibility, a task that goes with accountability.

6.4.2.1 Israel's Shepherds Do Not Possess a Shepherd Heart

As a very familiar concept and as a very normative vocabulary in Jewish society, shepherd imagery and shepherding functions are replete all over the Jewish Scripture because the Jews had engaged in animal husbandry. To enter the shepherding guild in this society was to assume great responsibility both to the flock and to its owner. Vancil states in this direction that "the principal duty of the shepherd was to see that the animals found enough food and water . . . that he guard the sheep . . . The good shepherd was especially concerned for the condition of the flock . . . essentially to keep the flock intact."[87] Primarily, it was the duty of the good shepherd, not a

---

84. Olubunmo, "Israelite Concept of Ideal King," 59.
85. Duguid, *Ezekiel*, 36. Duguid explains that since God is not man nor is he any respecter of man, "sin cannot be swept under the carpet. It cannot be prettified, excused, or ignored. It is ugly, dirty, and offensive and cannot coexist with the presence of a holy God."
86. Moses had warned the travelling community long ago against the effects of covenant disloyalty when Israel finally inherited the Promised Land, because when the land was defiled, it would have a way of rejecting its inhabitants by vomiting them out (see Lev 18:25, 28; 20:22). However, the effect of covenant failure led by the Israelite kings was obvious such that sin stretched throughout the length and breadth of Israelite society, affecting every layer of life in the land.
87. Vancil, "Sheep, Shepherd," 1187.

hireling nor the one filled with greed, to provide food and safety, to ensure absolute tranquillity, and to ensure comfort and calm for the flock. The task was to attend to the weak and the sick and to protect the flock from weather and enemies. Such qualities of good shepherding were to be attitudinal and exhibited as a lifestyle by the shepherd because the profession carries along with it great responsibility. But as Ezekiel reveals the negative attitudes of the bad and imperfect human shepherds of Israel towards the flock in his evaluation, Greenberg claims they are shown to have "taken all the perquisites attached to their job – and more – without doing their job . . . [hence] they stand accused of exploiting it rather than caring for it."[88]

The duty of shepherding in ancient times was quite tasking in that it entailed giving unwavering attention, taking great risks, and making huge sacrifices, all for the benefit of the flock. As scholars observe, this given obviously shows the enormous expectation of the shepherd and any aide to "show caution, patient care and honesty." This is particularly critical because the helpless nature of sheep and the poor topography and grazing terrain of ancient Palestine, especially in summer, required that "the shepherd had to care tirelessly for the helpless beast."[89] In addition to the nature of sheep and shepherding terrain, the presence of animal predators such as wolves, lions, leopards, hyenas, bears, and other ravenous animals, and human predators like robbers and thieves, all demanded dogged determination and great sacrifice on the part of the shepherd. The quality of care and sacrifice were unavoidable in such contexts because these predators posed great risks to both sheep and shepherd.

Very sadly however, the bad and imperfect human shepherds of Israel did not possess the requisite shepherd character, and as such, failed in assuming these shepherding functions. As an effect, this failure caused the sheep under their care to stray into the domain of their enemies. Failure becomes obvious in the case of Israel's bad and imperfect human shepherds because they lacked the shepherd spirit and shepherd character in their leadership.[90] As Walther Eichrodt has observed,

---

88. Greenberg, *Ezekiel 21-37*, 696.
89. Beyreuther, "Shepherd," 564.
90. These greedy shepherds of Israel failed to trail the Davidic model of shepherding so as to lead Yahweh's flock under their care skilfully and honestly (Ps 78:70-72). Moses and

> ... the office of a shepherd is represented to us as a very onerous and responsible vocation, requiring unwavering vigilance and readiness for sacrifice. Yet the shepherds of Israel have not only failed to show self-sacrifice in protecting and providing for those in need of their care, but have violently trodden down the stronger sheep, which would otherwise be the pride of the flock.[91]

Israel's imperfect human shepherds were disobedient to the application of the provisions of the Decalogue and Deuteronomic code. Beyreuther notes in this regard that "the prophets in their denunciations spoke of the political and military shepherds in unquestionably negative terms; these had all failed because of their arrogance and disobedience to God."[92] The shepherd's disregard for the stipulations of the Decalogue and Deuteronomic code, and much more, their outright disrespect for Yahweh who appointed them as his under-shepherds made possible for Ezekiel's theology to gain ground.

Learning from such past leadership failure to live up to the expectation of the office, Paul (Acts 20:17-36) and Peter (1 Pet 5:1-4) cautioned and counselled church leaders of their day to lead according to shepherding specifications. Their premise suggests that hurting Yahweh's flock, no matter how minute, is tantamount to hurting Yahweh himself.

6.4.2.2 Israel's Shepherds Are Negligent and Irresponsible

The prophetic indictment of the negligent attitude and acts of irresponsibility on the part of Israel's bad and imperfect human shepherds is clear from 34:4-5. This is obvious in the prophetic use of the לֹא particle negation used

---

David were highly acclaimed in Israelite tradition of leadership history for the quality of their leadership. It seems highly likely to us that these icons of good shepherding became successful leaders by the exhibition of their credible leadership qualities in leading Israel because they had been literal shepherds. Their shepherding experience under the guidance of Yahweh would have taught them what it means to shepherd, and in particular, to be shepherd of a covenant community.

91. Eichrodt, *Ezekiel*, 470.
92. Beyreuther, "Shepherd," 565. See Jer 2:8; 3:15; 10:21; 22:22; 23:1-5; 25:34; 50:6; Ezek 34:2-10; Isa 56:11; Zech 10:3; 11:5f.

in reference to the failure of these shepherds to appropriately function in their office. The shepherds' attitude of negligence and acts of irresponsibility in the discharge of their primary function plays out in Ezekiel's submission in which Yahweh charges, "you do not feed the flock. You have not strengthened the weak, you have not healed the sick, you have not bound up the injured. You have not brought back the strayed; you have not sought for the lost" (Ezek 34 3-4). The לֹא particle negation used once in v. 3 and five times in v. 4 displays the manner of this shepherding dislocation. That the bad and imperfect human shepherds of Israel tolerate these negative leadership threats is a denial of the trust and responsibility of public office.

Ezekiel indicted the self-centred shepherds of Israel because they had no account of their stewardship to render to their assignor, Yahweh, the chief shepherd. The prophet's theological analysis of the leadership performance of these shepherds indicated they had not passed the test of leadership accountability and integrity on the ground of their negligence. Viewed in retrospect, the history of Israel reveals that the period of the Judges saw to their primary function as military-saviour Judges. Every Judge that Yahweh raised at this critical period in Israel's history led the nation to war against their encroaching and invading enemies, and thereby saved the nation from foreign incursions, oppressions, molestations and disgrace. By comparison, these bad and imperfect human shepherds were to do far more than what the Judges had done as Israel's leaders. Cooper asserts that the roles of Israel's shepherds "were more than military-political leaders. They bore a primary responsibility for the moral and spiritual direction of the nation."[93] But their failure plunged Israel into ruin more than their relief from crises situations and national disgrace.

Theocratic and monarchical systems of governance have inherent characteristics that are quite distinct. The latter has always shown itself to possess weaknesses in contrast to the former. The prophetic indictment of the attitudes of the operators of the latter system, arising from a historical-theological evaluation, appears to suggest that Ezekiel favours the former pattern of governance. Cooke argues that Ezekiel's cherishing of the ideal of a theocracy, following such massive failure, "arose out of the unhappy

---

93. Cooper, Jr., *Ezekiel*, 298.

experiences of the people under the monarchy . . . The kings were felt to be responsible for most of the evils in the national life, even for the destruction of the state."[94] Blenkinsopp[95] equally submits that Ezekiel charged the bad shepherds of Israel with "dereliction of duty" and indicted them on the counts of "venality, self-interest, and the exploitation of those for whom they were responsible." He argues, that the sheep were scattered and became prey for every wild beast means that, "Israel's rulers bear responsibility for the exile." Blenkinsopp's point of argument, simply put, centres on the fact that the purpose of "public office of any kind is a pastoral responsibility, an opportunity for service, not for personal gain and glory."[96]

6.4.2.3 The Shepherds' Exclusion from Eschatological Shepherding

Following the failed leadership of Israel's shepherds, they unavoidably had to come under Yahweh's heavy repudiation because bad shepherding demands recompense. Yahweh charges, "because my flock lacks a shepherd and so has been plundered and has become food for all the wild animals, and because my shepherds did not search for my flock but cared for themselves rather than for my flock" (Ezek 34:8), he declares, "Behold, I am against the shepherds and will require my flock from their hand. I will remove them from pasturing my flock so that the shepherds can not continue to feed themselves" on my flock (34:10). As stated previously, every leadership responsibility goes with accountability and recompense. Since judgement is clearly a major component of the theology of Ezekiel, consequently, Israel's "worthless shepherds would not go unpunished . . . They

---

94. Cooke, *A Critical and Exegetical Commentary*, 375.
95. Blenkinsopp, *Ezekiel*, 157. "Uneasy lies the head that wears the crown" is a prevailing maxim that relates well to leadership function in every age. In view of the perils, responsibility, and accountability that go with leadership, one would postulate that a person should never seek to occupy a leadership position or accept one if such a person feels not capable to perform the functions of the office.
96. Blenkinsopp, *Ezekiel*, 157. The modern scenario of leadership experience reveals that some people go into leadership position with dignity but leave office with much disdain and more enemies than friends. This results either because of a lack of performance in view of a performance evaluation from divine and human perspectives, or for some ills that trap such people into dancing to the tune of the music of corruption, bad leadership, bad companions, bad advisors, and bad opinions. Arrogance and greed on the part of such leaders is equally a major contributory factor.

would be held accountable for failing to care for God's flock and would lose their privilege as His under-shepherds."[97] Consequent upon "their irresponsible and selfish lack of leadership the Lord counted them guilty of violating his trust and announced their removal"[98] without any hesitation. Since public office has recompense, Yahweh would hold each false shepherd "accountable for his shepherding."[99]

This divine action connects with the Gospels' report of Jesus' parable of the talents (Matt 25:14-30; Luke 19:11-27). Yahweh's action of removal, put *pari passu* with this parable, reveals the need for faithfulness and good stewardship on the part of people who are assigned to leadership responsibility of whatever magnitude. Particularly, it is intended to reveal that a person's attitude towards leadership and actions in office, whether good or bad, is favourably or unpleasantly rewarded because divine recompense always stands at the end of leadership responsibility. As Andrew W. Blackwood argues, "if Israel stands in a special relationship with God, then clearly those who bear responsibility for Israel bear a special responsibility to God. Since the shepherds have abused their privilege,"[100] they have failed in executing such responsibility to Israel and to God. As a consequence, their exclusion from shepherding the flock becomes irreversible and unquestionable.

6.5 Ezekiel's Theology of "I AM YAHWEH" for Eschatological Shepherding

The prophet's treatment of the theology of "I AM YAHWEH" revolves on the principle of the divine shepherding motif. Yahweh's deliverance of exilic Israel in the second exodus is to the glory of the honour of his name before both Israel and the nations. Andrew Mein rightly asserts in this connection that "nowhere else in the Bible is it made so clear that YHWH restores

---

97. Merrill, "A Theology of Ezekiel and Daniel," 376.
98. Cooper, Jr., *Ezekiel*, 300.
99. Alexander, "Ezekiel," 913.
100. Blackwood, Jr., *Ezekiel*, 207.

Israel not out of love, duty or forgiveness, but solely for the sake of his own name."[101] Yahweh's declaration using the phrase "I AM YAHWEH" in divine speeches, a phrase which Ezekiel uses to develop his theology of eschatological shepherding, presupposes the theological concept of divine presence, power, supremacy and sovereignty. This concept takes its root from the idea of בראשית ברא אלהים which opens the gate to biblical narratives in Genesis 1:1. If the One who marks the origin of all beginnings and existence declares, "I AM YAHWEH," then it means that he never abandons his covenant people even if his actions at the moment seem to indicate that. It also means he alone is all-powerful to both protect and defend his covenant people from harm. Again, it means that the character of his supremacy warrants him to act in behalf of his covenant people. It means lastly, that no historic event ever escapes his notice or takes him unawares because he is not only the God of history but he himself controls and directs the course of history.

Coming from this theological angle of divine presence, power, supremacy, and sovereignty, Ezekiel presents the theology of "I AM YAHWEH" on three cardinal points: Yahweh's annunciation of restoration for his flock because He Is; Yahweh's affirmation of the realisation of a future Messianic Leader for his flock because He Is; and Yahweh's confirmation of true rest for his flock because He Is. When the dark cloud of despondency which now hangs over the exiles clears and when the storm of exile is over, Yahweh will restore the remnants of his physically and emotionally mutilated covenant people, by both internal and external enemies, to their land. The basis for this hope principle as announced by Ezekiel lies in the fact of Yahweh's ownership of the people. Blackwood affirms that "The people whom earthly shepherds have buffeted about are God's people . . . Political institutions have failed to save Israel . . . God has not forgotten [because] The people of the covenant are still"[102] Yahweh's sheep. Ezekiel's final vision of the returned כבוד יהוה, "glory of Yahweh" into the future temple reinforces such a theological claim (cf. Ezek 43:1-6). As Duguid states, this vision, being the high point of chapters 43-46, "reverses the abandonment of the temple

---

101. Mein, "Profitable and Unprofitable Shepherds," 494.
102. Blackwood, Jr., *Ezekiel*, 207.

and its destruction" and now acts as "the fulfillment of the central promise of restoration: the Lord dwelling in the midst of his people forever."[103]

The possibility of a regathered future Israel is rooted in Yahweh's intervention in behalf of the nation. His rescuing mission will cause Israel to have a deepened knowledge and admission of Yahweh's power, shepherding care and sovereignty. He says, "They will know that I am the LORD, when I break the bars of their yoke and rescue them from the hands of those who enslaved them" (Ezek 34:27 NIV). In the eschatological state of a restored Israel, the new community of the covenant people will now experience absolute freedom and tranquillity from any form of oppressive leadership. When this divine agenda is finally realised, Yahweh himself, the Sovereign LORD declares, "Then they will know that I, the LORD their God, am with them and that they, the house of Israel, are my people" (Ezek 34:30 NIV). The acknowledgement of this divine presence, power, supremacy, and sovereignty is affirmative of the Psalmist's declaration: "God is our refuge and strength, an ever-present help in trouble . . . Be still, and know that I am God; I will be exalted among the nations, I will be exalted in the earth" (Ps 46:1, 10 NIV). Yahweh's self-exaltation in the earth follows at the foot of his accomplished rescue mission in behalf of his covenant people, an action that will cause the implantation of a new heart and new spirit in the restored eschatological community of a new Israel.

Ezekiel's theology of "I AM YAHWEH" presupposes that with Yahweh at the nerve centre of eschatological shepherding activities in favour of his flock in the restored community, the bruised, wounded, and broken among the flock will find healing. It presupposes also that the lost and hopeless will be found and have a new hope restored. It presupposes again that the oppressed and sapped will find lasting relief. It presupposes lastly, that the strayed and those preyed upon by internal and external predators will now find guidance and safety. At this point, the restored remnants of the covenant people will breathe a sigh of relief, proclaiming, "Free at last!" It is noted to this effect that their restoration would have become "the occasion for a demonstration of the sovereign might and faithfulness of Israel's

---

103. Duguid, *Ezekiel*, 489.

God"[104] to his holy name and to his covenant people. It is quite correct then to state, as Block articulates, that "the book of Ezekiel concludes on a glorious note, with a vision of Yahweh returning to his temple and establishing his residence in his city in the midst of his people."[105] The return of the divine glory to the land by taking its residence again in the new eschatological temple, Duguid[106] asserts, is the heart of this vision.

Consequently, we find the idea of the theme of the return – the return of the King, the restoration of the people to their land, and the return of the remnants to a state of blessing dominating the remainder of Ezekiel's book (Ezek 27-48). In the eschatologically structured society where Yahweh is shepherd of his flock, shepherding activities will be carried on around the ideological concept of *newness* – a new community, new shepherding environment, and a new shepherd.

6.6 Conclusion

This chapter has argued that Ezekiel's theological grid for the evaluation and critique of Israel and its imperfect human shepherds is his knowledge of Yahweh. Upon this grand theological framework of shepherding, the prophet centred his theological critique of shepherding responsibility and accountability. We have also argued that in Ezekiel's theological postulation, a responsible shepherding attitude is rewarded but acts of a negligent attitude and irresponsible shepherding are repudiated. Ezekiel leaves no one in doubt as to the effects of imperfect human shepherding as he holds leadership in Israelite society to account for the pain of exile. To this, Ruiz submits, "the rulers of Israel are responsible for the exile in Babylonia. The shepherds have sought their personal profit instead of that of the sheep, abandoning the flock and leaving it unprotected from destruction. The political and religious catastrophes are proof of this neglect."[107]

---

104. Merrill, "A Theology of Ezekiel and Daniel," 378.
105. Block, *The Book of Ezekiel Chapters 25-48*, 494.
106. Duguid, *Ezekiel*, 38.
107. Ruiz, "Ezekiel," 1075.

Ezekiel's theological argument, anchored in his use of the shepherd metaphor, presupposes that Yahweh's relationship with Israel demonstrates that leadership must be motivated by a shepherd heart characterised by love, care, compassion, selflessness, provision, and protection for the populace.[108] As Alexander points out, Israel's history reveals that, "lack of leadership always leads to the disintegration of God's people and personal and corporate heartache and injury."[109] Israel's weak and imperfect human shepherds demonstrated and proved their irresponsibility of good shepherding in their abuse of the rights of the shepherding position for greed, in their failure to call the people back to Yahweh as the prophets had done, and to lead the way as role models of moral wholeness and theological uprightness in society.

Consequently, if the people sinned against Yahweh, it is because their leaders who were to function as their watchmen allowed and led them to. If the people were disloyal to covenant terms, it is because their leaders were themselves disloyal to it and to Yahweh as well. If the people were disobedient to Yahweh, it is because their leaders became disobedient to him. And if the people were morally bankrupt and socio-politically, socio-economically and socio-religiously impoverished, it is because their leaders proved themselves to be irresponsible, greedy and self-centred, since they feasted on the flock under their care as predators would instead of sacrificing for the flock's wellbeing.

---

108. Of a truth, every human society, community or nation, stands or falls on the quality of its leadership. As scripture asserts, "when the righteous thrive, the people rejoice; when the wicked rule, the people groan" (Prov 29:2 NIV).

109. Alexander, "Ezekiel," 912. It could be argued in this regard therefore that the Assyrian and Babylonian captivities befell Yahweh's covenant people for lack of shepherd leadership in Israel and Judah. Jewish history reveals that the Israelite nation did not consistently enjoy good governance, a kind that should characterise an ideal human government, which should always foster security, posterity, peace, and moral wholeness for any people and any nation. The Assyrian and Babylonian captivities very well capture this point.

CHAPTER SEVEN

Summary and Conclusions

7.1 *Summary of the Study*

This chapter marks the end of the long journey begun in chapter one. All is well that ends well. As to whether this maxim is true of this present work depends on the judgement of its individual readers. We have pointed out that the undergirding motivation for Ezekiel's use of symbolic sign-acts and the shepherd metaphor within an exilic context lies at the point of the massive failure of Israel's imperfect human shepherds in her long history. Because Israel's shepherds showed themselves to be weak and self-seeking in the discharge of the shepherding functions of their office, prevalent covenant disloyalty, massive abuse of human rights in disregard for Deuteronomic code, and finally exile to Babylonia unavoidably became some major attendant effects on the people of Israelite.

Chapter one observed the neglect and bypass by older and modern scholars on Ezekiel's theological-eschatological treatment of the shepherd motif as a lacuna. On this ground, it calls the attention of Ezekiel's students to this missing element because it presupposes the eschatological shepherding motif to be playing a more critical function in the book of Ezekiel than other themes. Chapter two discussed Ezekiel's use of symbolism and the shepherd metaphor. Given the exilic experience of Judah as the context for the prophet's use of symbolic sign-acts and the shepherd metaphor, this chapter argued that symbolic sign-acts function prominently in Ezekiel as a literary device. Our prophet employed these to defuse the apprehension of his fellow Babylonian exiles so he could gain their attention as he offered explanations to help them come to terms with the reality of the Babylonian exile and of Jerusalem's demise. It also argued that Ezekiel employed the shepherd metaphor to show his audience that the massive failure and various abuses committed by Israel's bad and imperfect human shepherds, both past and present, were fundamentally responsible for the exile.

Chapter three focused attention on the historical and literary contexts for the shepherd metaphor in Ezekiel chapter 34. It pointed out that the shepherd metaphor that Ezekiel used here was an already familiar vocabulary in the shepherding tradition of both ANE and in Israel. Hence, it argued that given the socio-anthropological, economic and cultic functions of the sheep, shepherding was indispensable in these two societies. It also argued that the unique characteristics of sheep necessitated the importance of shepherds in the scheme of animal husbandry in both ANE and Israelite societies. This chapter also considered the various nuances of the shepherd metaphor in some ANE and Israelite prophetic texts in order to supply the literary context for Ezekiel's usage of the metaphor. The fourth chapter took a look at Ezekiel's use of the shepherd metaphor against the norms of Deuteronomic theology. It noted that this theological grid was significant to Israel as a nation characterised by covenant and blessings motifs, the latter which was to be enjoyed only on the ground of loyalty to covenantal terms. It argued that because Deuteronomic theology held some threatening implications for the Judean exiles, Ezekiel had to respond to their concerns in eschatological terms by the use of this theology. We insisted here that Ezekiel took on the use of Deuteronomic theology to evaluate and critique both the Judean people and their imperfect human shepherds on the point of covenant disobedience and disloyalty.

Chapter five is our major contribution to this research as it makes a case for eschatological shepherding in Ezekiel chapter 34. Here, we argued that Ezekiel used the shepherd metaphor against the whole sweep of massive shepherding failure in Israelite society. In this chapter, we posited that the indictment with which Ezekiel addressed the imperfect human shepherds and the evil sheep among the flock is obvious evidence substantiating this claim. The main thrust of our argument is that against the backdrop of the massive failure of an oppressive Israelite society, and against the whole sweep of an imperfect shepherding environment with bad, wicked, oppressive, and self-seeking human shepherds in charge, true shepherding activities could not flourish. Consequently, Ezekiel used the shepherd metaphor with a theological-eschatological motif to point to a perfect future pasturage when Yahweh himself will be shepherd of his flock. We contended that when this eschatological hope principle becomes operative in the future regathered community of Israel, then Ezekiel's recognition formula will have been perfectly realised and come into full effect.

Following is chapter six where an attempt is made to present Ezekiel's theology of an eschatological shepherding and the new society. We stated that the construct of Ezekiel's theological framework, which he used as the basis upon which he hinged his theology of shepherding, is totally Yahwistic in undertone. We argued that the prophet's comparative analysis of the shepherding attributes of Yahweh in contrast to those of Israel's bad and imperfect human shepherds showed up the latter as not possessing a shepherd character. Israel's shepherds were found to be weak-will, greedy, negligent, irresponsible, care-less, and professionally incapable of shepherding Yahweh's flock placed under their oversight. On this warrant, they were disqualified from eschatological shepherding in the new community. Such disqualification now allows for Ezekiel's development of "I AM YAHWEH" theology of eschatological shepherding in the regathered community of Israel. The research effort drew its conclusion with some specific implications for contemporary leadership in both sacred[1] and secular domains. It stroke the note that when godless, heartless, care-less, greedy, and self-seeking leaders occupy leadership positions in any human society, the attendant effects will be bad governance and enslavement of the populace.

---

1. The term "sacred" refers to the type of leadership that has a religious connotation. Specifically, it is used in this work to refer to the religious leadership within the church. As such, the word "sacred" and "ecclesiastical" are used interchangeably in reference to church leadership. "Secular," on the other hand, is used in reference to the type of leadership being exercised outside religious domain. Specific to our contextual usage is political leadership.

7.2 Some Observations from the Study

Acting as a road construction worker, Ezekiel was compelled to use symbolic sign-acts as dynamite to break through to the ears and hearts of his apprehensive and hardened audience. We have shown in this study that our prophet discovered, through his prophetic experience, the reality of the Yahwistic statement to him during his commission that he was sent to a stubborn people and a "rebellious nation" (Ezek 2:3-4). We have explained that because of false prophets, the exiles had false reliance on the principle of Zion theology by holding to the inviolability of Jerusalem as Yahweh's city. Consequently, they discounted Ezekiel's warning concerning the city's imminent demise. However, the people's question, "Won't you tell us what these things have to do with us?" (Ezek 24:19), is clear indication that Ezekiel's use of the literary device of symbolic sign-acts to gain attention had achieved its purpose. If the eardrums of his audience were resistant to the sound of Yahweh's warnings through Ezekiel, their eyes would not fail to see, neither would their minds fail to reason out the interpretation of the prophetic sign-acts as they unfolded in dramatic fashion.

We noted also in our study that Ezekiel employed the shepherd metaphor first, to address the massive failure of Israel's bad and imperfect human shepherds, pointing out as well the negative effects of such failure on the Israelite society. Against the backdrop of this sweep of massive failure of shepherding, we argued that Ezekiel employed the shepherd metaphor with a theological-eschatological motif as a corrective of this shepherding dislocation. We therefore posited from this that every society stands or falls on the quality of its leadership because the success or failure of every government, society, community, organisation, group, and family, depends largely on the quality of its leadership. D. J. Human agrees when he asserts that "The quality of leadership determines the well-being of and prosperity in society."[2] It is in line with this thinking that Joseph Blenkinsopp suggests that for the sake of understanding, the theme of shepherding or the shepherd metaphor "be restated as *pastoral responsibility*, allowing the adjective

---

2. D. J. Human, "An ideal for leadership-Psalm 72: The (wise) king–Royal mediation of God's universal reign," VERBUM ET ECCLESIA JRG 23 (3) (2002):658-677.

the broader connotation of public office of any kind involving responsibility for people."³ When leadership is perceived as a position of responsibility that goes along with accountability and recompense, such understanding will witness the demise of the attitude of greed, selfishness, self-aggrandisement, and negligence which are some characteristics of persistent nagging leadership problems, better described in Ralph Klein's words as "today's "'exilic'" challenges"⁴ of contemporary leadership.

From our study, it is quite obvious that Ezekiel used the shepherd metaphor to accuse and hold Israel's bad and imperfect human shepherds accountable for causing losses and heartaches for the covenant community through their bad governance. Quite observably, such bad and imperfect human shepherds that Israel had failed to make all the necessary sacrifices that the functions of the shepherding office requires, so they were able to save the people from harm. This failure is largely because they had become consumed by the spirit of greed and robbery for what was meant for the flock, and this way, they became abusive of the rights and privileges of their office as Yahweh's under-shepherds. They had taken pleasure in feasting on the flock while neglecting their primary responsibility of feeding and caring for the sheep. By this act, the shepherds missed out on the most significant point of shepherding. Zimmerli points out this missing element when he notes that "the nobility and dignity of the office of shepherd reside in the fact that the shepherd works wholeheartedly for the flock"⁵ as it is seen demonstrated by Jesus' statement in John 10:11. It means therefore that the office and attitude of shepherding is to be wholly regulated by the character of sheep-centredness against self-centredness. Yahweh himself demonstrated this character of sheep-centredness by "his caring activity towards the people" of Israel as his sheep (Ps 77:21; 23; Isa 40:11).

But as Zimmerli further observes, "The shepherds of Israel have denied this nobility by thinking of themselves while busy with the flock. They thought of what benefit they could derive from the flock, but not of the

---

3. Blenkinsopp, *Ezekiel*, 155.
4. Klein, *Israel in Exile*, 8.
5. Zimmerli, *Ezekiel 1*, 214.

well-being of the flock itself"[6] as the accusation pattern in Ezekiel 34:3-7 reveals. In this respect, their attitude to shepherding is both flawed and fraught. Since Israel's imperfect human shepherds showed themselves incapable of performing their duty to *care* for his flock,[7] Yahweh, the true Shepherd-King of Israel, indicted and dismissed them from office. We imply from this then that the key import of the shepherd motif for contemporary leadership in both sacred and secular domains entails possessing an inherent attitude and character of *care* and *sacrifice* for the people being led.[8]

From our study, we observed that a cursory tour of the book of Ezekiel would readily reveal that among its several themes, the book revolves around the key theme of the honour for Yahweh's name and glory. For instance, Yahweh took up issues with his covenant people in regards to their covenant violation because their sinful behaviour stood in aberration to the honour due his name. Secondly, he turned his judgement on the foreign nations because their cruel treatment of his people discredited the honour due his holy name. Lastly, he undertook to restore the remnant of his covenant people and to return his glory to the new eschatological temple of the restored community because of the honour due his name. The shepherd metaphor must be seen as revolving around this theme of honour as well. This, Ezekiel clearly exhibited in his theological-eschatological treatment of the shepherd motif. Yahweh's indictment and therefore, setting aside the services of the bad and imperfect human shepherds of Israel who had failed in their shepherding functions was because they had shown themselves to

---

6. Zimmerli, *Ezekiel 1*, 214.

7. Keener observes by way of contrast that "if most Christological shepherd texts draw on biblical imagery associated with God, most shepherd texts applying to the church draw on biblical images of shepherds as human leaders of God's people [just as] The leaders God assigned to care for his flock for him" were in the Old Testament. Keener, "Shepherd, Flock," 1091-1092.

8. As Johnson notes in connection with the Johannine discourse of the idea of good shepherding when John presents Jesus as the good shepherd who is not a hireling, he says "the main thrust…is soteriological and ecclesiastical, highlighting the sacrifice of Jesus for his sheep." He observes further in this respect that "the true nature of ministry [is that] Adversity tests the true motivation of the shepherds of the church [because] the good shepherd lays down his life for the sheep." This, no doubt, presupposes the character of self-sacrifice for good leadership to be achieved in any domain of leadership. David H. Johnson, "Shepherd, Sheep," in *Dictionary of Jesus and the Gospels* (eds. Joel B. Green and Scot McKnight; Downers Grove, Ill.: Inter-Varsity, 1992), 753. Cf. John 10:1-18 for the Apostle's presentation of Jesus as the good shepherd.

be irreligious and therefore unable to reverence his name to preserve the honour due him. If Yahweh himself is concerned about the honour and glory due his holy name, leadership must show reverence for the name and glory of Yahweh. This is the warrant by which both Israel and the nations were to know that Yahweh is LORD.

7.2.1 Its Implications for Contemporary Ecclesiastical Leadership

It is assumed that spiritual leadership should be morally and theologically motivated as a pacesetter for ideal leadership in society. But unfortunately, leadership in the sacred domain is not insulated from leadership vices such as corruption, greed, self-centredness, pride, a negligent attitude to official and sacred responsibilities, and the like. Comparatively, the shepherding concept in Ezekiel finds connection with the concept of contemporary ecclesiastical leadership as they are also figuratively perceived as shepherds. In William B. Oglesby's understanding, the shepherd or shepherding concept is to be seen as "a pastoral care metaphor which attempts to integrate the notions of healing, sustaining, and guiding, as well as other characteristics of the ancient shepherd of Old and New Testament."[9] While he acknowledges the difficulty in relating this concept to contemporary ecclesiastical leadership, he thinks that despite the obscurity of the concept in contemporary understanding, "the concept is nonetheless of primary importance in the work of pastoral care and counselling . . . [for] the terms "pastor" and "pastoral" reflect the shepherding dimension of ministry."[10] He therefore contends that contemporary shepherding represents the "incarnational model" of ministry where, out of true concern and love for the care-receiver, the pastoral caregiver identifies with human hurt and suffering.

Ezekiel's indictment of Israel's imperfect human shepherds for their failure to faithfully function as *shepherds* of the flock under their care is quite significant when contrasted with the leadership of the church in modern Africa. Many of those who occupy church leadership positions today, taking

---

9. William B. Oglesby Jr., "Shepherd/Shepherding," in *Dictionary of Pastoral Care and Counseling* (2d ed.; eds. Rodney J. Hunter and Nancy J. Ramsey; Nashville: Abingdon, 2005), 1164.
10. Oglesby Jr., "Shepherd/Shepherding," 1164.

the Nigerian experience as a case in point, are there not really to shepherd God's flock but rather to benefit from their position like the shepherds of Israel had done. They "milk" the office and the people for their personal benefits but fail to give spiritual nourishment to the people so they could become robust spiritually. In Paul's theology, the church belongs to God and therefore, requires proper care, nurture, and oversight by its leadership. In clear imperative tone, he charged the leadership of the Ephesian church to "keep watch over yourselves and all the flock of which the Holy Spirit has made you overseers. Be shepherds of the church of God, which he bought with his own blood" (Acts 20:28 NIV). It is clear from Paul's caution that any act of shepherding irresponsibility and abnormality on the part of the leadership of the church is detrimental to the redeemed community of faith. In this connection therefore, just as Ezekiel revealed that the massive failures of Israel's bad and imperfect human shepherds had effects on both sheep and shepherds, the Nigerian experience has also shown that the Christian community has suffered assaults and sometimes great casualty where godly leadership with a shepherd character is lacking. The ungodly lifestyle, unwarranted actions and character exhibitions, and the obnoxious speech of some of the church leaders have sent quite a sizeable number of Christians into the nest of the predators of the church. The situation is even worsened when ecclesiastical leadership becomes ethno-tribalistic, sentimental, discriminatory, greedy and self-seeking in the performance of its functions and in its attitude towards members. For instance, in his discussion on divisive ethnicity, Barje Maigadi[11] holds that this unwelcomed stranger has had great effects on the church in Africa. Citing the case of the Evangelical Church Winning All (ECWA) in particular, he contends that the presence of divisive ethnicity in the church that is a transformed community and a visible manifestation of the reconciliatory power of the gospel is a misnomer. In view of the enormous effects that abnormal leadership characteristics have on the flock, Yahweh's retributive action on the shepherds in Ezekiel should serve as a caution to contemporary church leadership regarding their responsibility to God's people under their care.

---

11. Barje Sulmane Maigadi, *Divisive Ethnicity in the Church in Africa* (Kaduna, Nigeria: Baraka, 2006), 235.

We submit that contemporary ecclesiastical leadership is to blame for the low level of Christian spirituality being experienced by the church today in Africa at large and in Nigeria in particular. For example, it would be quite obvious even to a visitor to the Nigerian society, to discover that there is a prevailing spirit of ministerial greed, a competitive quest for materialism, rivalry, subtle but salient exhibition of ethno-tribalism and sectionalism, pride, corruption and so on among ministers of the gospel in both traditional missionary and Pentecostal circles. These vices are now characterising a sizeable number of pastors serving in the parishes and those serving in leadership positions at the denominational headquarters, in Christian Association of Nigeria (CAN),[12] and even those serving in the corridor of political power where chapels[13] exist at the seat of power.

Although those in church leadership are aware (hopefully so) that Jesus says the leaders of his church should not lord it over the people (Mark 10:35-45), yet some force their way into leadership to be venerated and idolised because they are power-drunk. Still, others seek leadership in the church as an opportunity to unleash their self-aggrandizement. Such leaders blatantly exhibit their immaturity, greed, self-centredness, and domineering attitude when occupying office. With the exhibition of such negative leadership characters, it is quite obvious that the leadership of the church would no longer function as shepherds but as its predators. One

---

12. The acronym CAN is uniquely Nigerian. It means Christian Association of Nigeria. Its primary aim is to represent and defend before the Nigerian state, the interest of the church or Christian community in Nigeria. The incessant ethno-religious and politico-religious violence and discrimination in the country saw to the emergence of CAN. For the role of the Muslim Ulama of Nigeria, see the work by Olufemi Olayinka Oluniyi, *The Council of Ulama and Peaceful Co-Existence in Nigeria* (Lagos, Nigeria: Frontier, 2006).

13. In Nigeria, some States that are predominantly Christian have chapels erected by their Christian governors at the State headquarters. This recent development is in reaction to the presence of elegant mosques built in strategic government offices by Muslim leaders. These chapels serve the purpose of prayers and Sunday worship services. When General Olusegun Aremu Matthew Obasanjo was the civilian President of Nigeria (May 1999-2007), he built a chapel at the seat of power in Aso Rock Villa, Abuja, Nigeria, for the first time in the country's national history. These State chapels and the one in Aso Rock Villa have chaplains/pastors in charge as royal ministers. Not just any clergy qualifies as chaplain here except the one the serving Governor or President chooses, either by his personal judgement/volition or by some political influence. Given the prestige and benefits that go along with such position, politicking on the part of desiring ministers to occupy it is certainly not lacking.

wonders why such leadership failure should prevail in the twenty-first century church given the effort of contextualising Christian theology in Africa in the hope that it would positively increase the level of biblical literacy and achieve quality spirituality. We stand with Tite Tiénou[14] when he rightly argues that the theological task in Africa goes beyond evangelical reaction to an already set theological agenda. We propose that in view of the numerous theological issues plaguing the church in modern Africa, there is a need to set another theological agenda unique in its own right to address these challenges. We do think that bad clerical leadership is a major issue deserving attention in the theological discourse on the church in Africa because it stands as an "internal theological threat"[15] to the existence and growth of the church itself. Like an automobile with a malfunction engine, so is the church in modern Africa with bad and immature leadership.

Furthermore, it is not uncommon to find in modern Africa, and particularly in Nigeria, that very many who occupy leadership positions within Christian communities, Christian organizations, and local churches do not in fact qualify for the office and for the task to be assumed, if such people were to pass under the plumb line of Scripture (see 1 Tim 3; Acts 7:1-6; 20:17-28). People get elected and or appointed to leadership positions in the Christian environment not on merit but on the basis of tribal and ethnic affiliation, nepotism, favouritism, godfatherism, and so on. We think that more of the leadership positions within Christian circles are being occupied by amateurs who are not motivated by the spirit of godliness and service, but rather by the gains and glamour of such positions. It is no wonder that those envious of such positions campaign, politic, coerce, manipulate, and even blackmail in some cases, those who stand as a threat to their getting into office. What is most worrisome and quite unfortunate is the situation where the righteous and right candidates are not given leadership positions. Such qualified and capable people are sometimes not only deprived of the chance to occupy the office and render quality service to God's flock, but their voice is not always heeded even when they cry

---

14. Tite Tiénou, *The Theological Task of the Church in Africa*, 2nd ed., (Achimota, Ghana: Africa Christian Press, 1990), 19.
15. Tiénou, *The Theological Task*, 35.

fault to the processes and practices of electing and or appointing people to leadership positions. It seems almost impossible therefore for such people to become leaders as they are frequently in the minority.

In addition to the factors responsible for leadership malfunction within the sacred domain as we pointed out earlier, we think that the lack of proper and adequate biblical theology and Christian ethics are some other causes of such church leadership abnormality. Bad church leadership in modern Africa is caused by what Byang Kato had described as "theological anaemia." He asserted at his time that biblical Christianity was being threatened, and as such, "the spiritual battle for Africa . . . will be fought, therefore, largely on theological ground. But the church is generally unprepared for the challenge."[16] Since some in the leadership of the church in modern Africa still behave as weaklings in their response to theological and ethical issues plaguing the church, this prophetic-like statement is a very present reality. As is rightly argued, the church requires faithful, effective, and visionary leaders who will work for the good of the whole church, resolutely checkmating secular infiltrations into the church.[17]

Samuel Kunhiyop asserts that "African Christians [are] struggling with their own problems in their own situations."[18] Some of such struggles are old enough to have been resolved and long forgotten, but they are still obvious in the church because some of its leaders have a very poor knowledge of biblical and Christian ethics. Such poverty affects their sense of leadership values and sense of right judgement. As a result, they are unaware of proper Christian conviction and standards as well as proper leadership focus. In comparing the dislocated leadership attitude of Ezekiel's shepherds

---

16. Byang Henry Kato, *Biblical Christianity in Africa* (Achimota, Ghana: Africa Christian Press, 1985), 11.

17. R. Robert Cueni, "Facing the Disciples Leadership Challenge on the Front Edge of the 21st Century," *LTQ* 3 &4 (2006):224. He notes that "unfortunately, the task of even the most faithful, effective, visionary Disciple leadership is significantly complicated by a plethora of intensifying and interrelated issues that result from the peculiarities of our governance structure, that emanate from the ethos particular to Disciples and that leak into the church from the wider culture. In order for leadership to challenge the church to face its problems and to learn new ways to deal with them, each of these intensifying and interrelated factors must be acknowledged and addressed. Leadership ignores these factors at peril."

18. Samuel Waje Kunhiyop, *African Christian Ethics* (Kaduna, Nigeria: Baraka, 2004), xv.

with today's church shepherds, Odell observes that such a negative picture of leadership is a reminder to the church that "the world is overrun with bad shepherds and greedy goats and rams, whose claims to govern in behalf of their constituents often mask other, less altruistic interests." Given this base experience from Israel's shepherds, she states that "God's resolve to rescue the sheep from such as these constitutes a repudiation of those powerful entities that consume the resources of the earth only to enhance their own strength, while cloaking their aims in the rhetoric of stewardship and service."[19] We think that Jesus will have to bear with the current situation of bad church leadership in modern Africa, and in particular, forgive the prevailing negative attitudes and sinful practices by some of these church leaders. Otherwise, where he cannot temper justice with mercy, then, like the shepherds of Ezekiel's day, these leaders of his church in modern Africa would face banishment from office or outright execution.

7.2.2 Its Implications for Contemporary Political Leadership

Leadership in the political arena in modern Africa at large and in Nigeria in particular finds points of connection with the leadership we find represented by the shepherd metaphor in Ezekiel. Put in retrospect, Margaret Odell[20] claims that the shepherds in Ezekiel were indicted by Yahweh for leadership failure because "the shepherd metaphor was closely associated with the king's responsibility for the welfare of his people." She explains that the shepherd metaphor clearly "illustrates its connotations of care and nurturing" which the shepherds of Ezekiel's day failed to offer because of "their determination to dominate with violence harshness." While we cannot doubt that bad leadership and its abuses in all domains is a global challenge, we think that the African continent in particular seems to be in the forefront of the onslaught of various epidemiological feasting on its peoples as a result of this very menace. Human rightly observes in this regard:

---

19. Odell, *Ezekiel*, 433.
20. Odell, *Ezekiel*, 432.

> The current reality of poverty, starvation and epidemics, abuse and exploitation of political and military power, mass manslaughter, and oppression, violation of human rights and always-existing regional conflicts or inter-continental wars are merely symptoms of imbalances in leadership. Selfish and power driven leaders in all spheres of life corrupt their environments and societies to the deepest roots of life."[21]

From the foregoing, it is quite obvious that the inherent negative leadership character of greed, which consequentially produces poor governance, is clearly responsible for bad leadership on the African continent. This vice is a vicious plague on the continent. The Hebrew Sage's drawn conclusion on this matter when he asserted, "What has been will be again, what has been done will be done again; there is nothing new under the sun" (Eccl 1:9; 3:15), may well explain the point. The persistent nagging leadership trait of greed, selfishness, corruption, failure, imbalance, and imperfection in Africa is not new. What should be considered as new and always seen to be so, which should serve as the catalyst that should break these negative leadership traits, is the exhibition by those in political leadership of a shepherding character. They should be seen to possess the character quality of godliness, righteousness, and moral uprightness. They should, in clear terms, be seen to uphold the rule of law, justice, fairness, equity, good governance, the attitude of care and compassion for the people being governed, and the provision of goods and services for the electorates.

As crucial as the need for good governance is, the world is having its fair share of pains and losses as a result of bad leadership. E. O. Usue submits that the entire world and the African continent in particular, is faced with leadership crises due to the challenge of the lack of good leadership in the context of politics, business, education, religion, and family. He insists that the lack of good leadership "is a major factor in the prevalence of the various political, economic, ethnic, family and religious violence, wars and conflicts that have ravaged/ransacked the Continent in the last fifteen

---

21. Human, "An ideal for leadership,"658-677.

years."²² The contemporary bad political leadership climate that now hangs over Africa is heavily characterised by the spirit of ethno-tribalism, socio-religious sentiments, greed, self-centredness, and the profuse unleashing of self-aggrandisement on the people. Some quite obvious examples of this leadership behavioural dysfunction and character dislocation in recent times are the case of Rwanda,²³ Democratic Republic of Congo,²⁴ Sudan,²⁵ Zimbabwe,²⁶ and very recently, the post-election crisis that has wrecked Côte D'Ivoire.²⁷

---

22. E. O. Usue, "Leadership in Africa and in the Old Testament: A Transcendental Perspective," HTS 2 (2006):635-656.

23. Massive genocide was experienced in Rwanda in recent times following leadership greed and enmity against citizens who reserve every right to life and to their motherland. The monster of ethnicity incubated particularly by the Hutu majority and Tutsi minority fuelled such genocide. See Gérard Prunier, "Rwanda: The Social, Political and Economic Situation June 1997," published by WRITENET, a network of researchers on human rights, forced migration and ethnic and political conflict, a subsidiary of Practical Management (UK). While scholars have associated this massive genocide of over 800,000 Tutsi civilians between April and June 1994 alone to a number of factors, one may certainly not shy away from its political element, masterminded and manipulated by the Hutu northern elites for some interior personal and ethnic gains for the control of political and economic power. See the article by Moise Jean, "The Rwandan Genocide: The True Motivations for Mass Killings."

24. Until recently, war and violence had ravaged unceasingly the Democratic Republic of Congo, formerly Zaire, unabated. This has led scholars to describe the country variously as the "heart of darkness," an "epitome of African state collapse," "a forsaken black hole characterized by calamity, chaos, and confusion," a "shadow of its former self," etc. See the article by Raeymaekers, "Sharing the Spoils: The Reinvigoration of Congo's Political System." The Congolese civil war of 1996-1997 and 1998-2003 is not unconnected with local politics and political power for control. See article by Koen Vlassenroot & Timothy Raeymaeker, "New Political Order in the DR Congo? The Transformation of Regulation," Afrika Focus 2 (2008):39-52.

25. President Omer al-Bashir of Sudan is accused of being cruel to the ethnic southern Sudanese. The international community has charged him as being responsible for the deaths of millions in Sudan. The International Court of Justice (ICJ) had ordered his arrest on this ground. His oppressive leadership led to the freedom of the ethnic southern Sudanese as a sovereign nation state on July 9, 2011.

26. Robert Mugabe is one of Africa's first nationalists like President Kenneth Kaunda of Zambia, the late Dr. Kwame Nkrumah of Ghana, the late Jomo Kenyata of Kenya, the late Dr. Nnamdi Azikwe (the Zik of Onisha) of Nigeria, to mention just few. However, since then, President Mugabe has refused to leave the presidency even when his comrades listed above had relinquished power to subsequent generation of political leaders. He has single-handedly almost destroyed Zimbabwe.

27. The political situation that had prevailed in Côte D'Ivoire, former Ivory Coast, was quite interesting and alarming. Côte D'Ivoire has been under the cloud of likely dangers of ethnic and xenophobic identity politics that has developed for a dozen years

Summary and Conclusions

The political terrain in Africa certainly leaves observers with the obvious conclusion that most politicians in Africa seek to gain political power essentially not to render public service by leading with justice and prudence but instead to rule, dominate, and oppress the people for their own self-interest. The embedded aim of such a quest for political leadership by majority politicians is for the perpetration of personal dynasties and the building of enclaves and empires for themselves and their lineal generations. Taking the case of Nigeria for instance, it is common place for politicians to ask for votes from the electorates with the claim that they would serve the populace only to service themselves at the expense of the electorates soon after they assume office. Instead of serving the people who gave such political leaders their mandate and improve their socio-economic conditions, these leaders amass ill-gotten wealth through corruption and looting of the national treasury, whether at the Federal, State, or Local Government levels. This is one of the reasons that saw the emergence of the Economic and Financial Crime Commission (EFCC) and the Independent Corrupt Practices Commission (ICPC) in the nation. In Nigerian politics, it is now normative to find some political leaders frustrating the efforts of any opposing voice. Such bad leaders even go to the extent of employing both physical and diabolical means to threaten and even to eliminate through murder via the agent of hired assassins, the life of any person or group of persons who dare to contend with them or question their decisions and actions of governance. Olubunmo asserts in this direction that in the Nigerian

---

during the Ivorian economic crisis. See Press release by Prevention Genocides, Brussels, 3 October, 2002 & the article by Dele Ogunmola, "Managing Paradoxes: The Political Economy of Côte D'Ivoire Crisis," *Journal of Social Science* 15, no. 2 (2007), 117-119. The attempted coup of 19 September, 2002 has aggravated the already boiling political context. The former President Laurent Gbagbo had refused to cede office to political rival Alassane Ouattara, despite preponderant evidence that the latter won the November 28 presidential runoff election. After the Independent Electoral Commission announced a 54 to 46 percent outcome in favour of Ouattara, the country's Constitutional Council, at the behest of Gbagbo, overruled the commission, annulling results in nine northern precincts and giving Gbagbo a 51 to 49 percent victory. Both men had subsequently sworn themselves in as president in separate ceremonies, and each appointed his cabinet members. This is one clear case of African politics and its presumed democracy. Not even the sanctions and threats of forceful removal from office by both the African Union (AU) and the United Nations (UN) could shake or make the former president consider ceding power to the president elect. Of course, many suffered unjustified loses as a result of the faceoff.

case, most Nigerian politicians join "politics in an attempt to make quick money." As such, they introduce "thuggery into politics in order to subdue their opponents" against the principle of "fair play, respect of the rights of the people, selfless service, honesty and the fear of God."[28] The principal cause of this endemic attitude is greed and self-centredness.

These embedded negative socio-political characteristics apparent in African leadership are a tragedy that appears to be an irreparable orthopaedic dislocation of leadership in the African societies, particularly, in the Nigerian society. The ideal, as Human[29] insists regarding political leadership, is that it is the responsibility of modern leaders in Africa to be reliable and trustworthy, to reorder social and cosmic disorder, to establish justice and peace in their societies, and to especially ensure that the poor, the oppressed and the afflicted of the society who are the core objects of their leadership enterprise enjoy good governance. But this is a far cry from reality. Like the case with the bad and imperfect human shepherds of Ezekiel's day, greedy leaders in modern Africa lack the moral value of justice and compassion for the people they lead. In contradistinction to providing quality leadership and service to the people, they are full of self and wanton spirit. James was right in his indictment of the rich of his day, and by implication in our own case, the rich African political overlords, when he asserted:

> What causes fights and quarrels among you? Don't they come from your desires that battle within you? You want something but don't get it. You kill and covet, but you cannot have what you want. You quarrel and fight. You do not have, because you do not ask God. When you ask, you do not receive, because you ask with wrong motives, that you may spend what you get on your pleasures. You adulterous people, don't you know that friendship with the world is hatred toward God? Anyone

---

28. Olubunmo, "Israelite Concept of Ideal King," 66.
29. Human, "An ideal for leadership," 674. Also, Alexander notes rightly that a leader's primary "responsibility [is] to care for those he leads, even at the sacrifice of his own desires," and not himself or his kin and kindred. However, because of the obvious lack of such desirable leadership quality, he laments, "would that political and spiritual leaders both then and now would recognize this heart attitude of leadership!" Alexander, "Ezekiel," 912.

who chooses to be a friend of the world becomes an enemy of God (Jas 4:1-4 NIV).

There is the need to have a fearless, radical, realist and pragmatic prophet in our time to submit a similar indictment and declaration to all greedy political leaders in modern Africa, and Nigeria in particular.

It is as a result of bad leadership that cases of incessant clan and tribal conflicts, crises, wars, violence, poverty, epidemics, industrial strikes, and many more appear synonymous with the African continent in modern day. Yusuf Turaki conceives the prevalence of ethnic, racial, tribal and cultural tensions, violence and conflicts in Africa as the "Tribal Gods of Africa." He charges African leadership as being responsible for the presence and growth of these tribal gods. He asserts:

> African leadership is impotent in the face of Africa's contemporary problems . . . African leadership has failed to stop the dearth and stem the tide of social crisis and chaos. It has also failed to grant man his historical freedom, peace and justice, and sustainable societies and stable governments. There is something which is fundamentally wrong with leadership in Africa.[30]

Certainly, that which is fundamentally wrong with leadership in Africa is the weak moral will on the part of political leaders to do what is right and just. Also, it is the weak political will of those in political power to enforce the rule of law for a just society to flourish for the common good. Such failure is basically caused by greed and egoistic quest to hold on to power by political leaders. Again, like was the case with the weak shepherds of Ezekiel's day, since many of those past and present leaders want to please the few greedy rich and powerful in society, they are unable to confront acts of violence and injustice for the general good of society. The situation even

---

30. Yusuf Turaki, *Tribal Gods of Africa: Ethnicity, Racism, Tribalism and the Gospel of Christ* (Nairobi, Kenya: Ethics, Peace and Justice Commission of AEA, 1997), 1. AEA stands for The Association of Evangelicals in Africa.

more becomes complex when some of those buzzards are the godfathers and financiers of those in power.

It is fast becoming a norm in African politics for political leaders not to feel any sense of moral guilt or sense of responsibility for their unethical lifestyle, corruption, oppressive evils, bad actions and wrong decisions in governance. While some claim to have interacted with their political counterparts in civilised societies, yet, it beats one's imagination that such modern African leaders still fail to learn and apply accepted moral values to public office. Although bad governance threatens the peace and existence of a nation, lack of remorse and nonchalant attitude still exists in African leadership. As was the case in Ezekiel's time, the effects of leadership failure in Nigeria for instance, has threatened the experience of true civil society for the common good.[31] Such threat can be observed in the eclipsed spirit and the inculcation of the sense of patriotic nationalism in the hearts of most citizens, particularly, in the present growing 21st century generation. Onah Augustine Odey rightly points out some other effects of bad governance on the Nigerian society when he says, "there are places in Nigeria where people have suffered, or are suffering, as a result of dishonest politicians or even ancestors. The evil deeds of an evil ruler could affect the lives of the people long after the ruler had left the scene."[32] Such bad leaders themselves behave as selfish thieves because service is not and cannot be the watchword of wicked and evil rulers. They love to parade their unleashed self-aggrandisement devoid of all sensitivity to moral conscience.

To be able to change the paradigm of bad leadership ethics and attitude in Africa as is being championed by the Re-branding Nigeria project, a total overhaul of the mindset of all Nigerians is critical. It is this that would achieve for the nation, according to Iyede Matthew Ogheneochuko, a "Rediscovery of the place of integrity and [the] principle of [the] rule of law in democratic governance."[33] We posit that the problem of Africa is never

---

31. For further discussion on this area of concern, see Matthew Hassan Kukah, *Democracy and Civil Society in Nigeria* (1999; repr., Ibadan, Nigeria: Spectrum, 2000).

32. Onah Augustine Odey, "Prophet Ezekiel's Concept of Individuality: Guidelines for Nigeria," *AJBS* 2 (1991):77.

33. Iyede Matthew Ogheneochuko, "Josiah's Reform As A Model for Religious Political Re-Branding in Nigeria," *AJBS* 1 (2010):111.

poverty, ethno-tribal conflicts, or violence and wars. It is not even disease and HIV/AIDS, though these are life threatening. The problem of Africa is the Africans; and the problem of the Africans is bad African leadership. The fundamental problem of Africa has ever been that of leadership greed, the vacuum of the spirit of patriotism, the lack of national consciousness, focus and vision since the demise of African nationalists. To risk integrity seems not a problem to some African leaders provided that their interior motives and personal ambitions are gratified.

To many African and Nigerian political leaders in our time, the ethical maxim which states that "the means justifies the end," has been redefined and neatly repackaged to state, on the contrary, that it is "the end that justifies the means," provided one gets what one wants through whatever means and ways. With this given, an emerging maxim which states that "Use what you have to get what you want" is fast gaining ground in the Nigerian nation. This is an unfortunate dislocated egocentric philosophy that has replaced ethical rightness in the Nigerian society. So, like the Babylonian exiles in Ezekiel's time who resisted the prophetic message following the demise of Jerusalem, positive apprehension has ever been flowing in the hearts, spirits, and blood of the right-thinking Africans against the negative attitudes and actions of their bad, evil, and wicked leaders, consequent upon which the Continent appears to be the most backward of all continents. Some have even asked if Africa is cursed. Others have queried what sin or offense it is that Africa has committed if the continent is indeed under any curse or a spell. There is no reason why African leadership cannot get it right if it begins to do things right. The nations that get things right never use magic. They just apply the principle of universal law as well as the appropriate principle of selflessness, patriotism, nationalism, people-centredness, focused leadership, and good governance.

The type of leadership one has observed in the Nigerian society over time could better be described in the words of Ebenezer Ola Adeogun as an "embarrassing behavioural milieu."[34] The Nigerian case is mind-boggling and quite perplexing. As Adeogun notes, "with all the parading of many

---

34. Ebenezer Ola Adeogun, "Jeremiah 31:31-34 and its Theological Implications for Rebranding," AJBS 1 (2010):1.

religions with their paraphernalia, pomp and pageantry, and ceremonies, many have gotten their consciences drowned."[35] To liberate personal and national consciences from the prison of self and greed, the majority of Nigerian politicians and leaders, even those occupying various professional leadership positions, require careful but drastic ethical and theological re-branding of their psyche, thoughts, attitudes, and behaviours. When this long expected re-servicing is achieved, it is assumed, as Olatundun Abosede Oderinde postulates, it would cause the political authority in Nigeria "to turn away from the evil of greed, self-centeredness and corruption, [and] become more considerate of the masses and live a life of sharing"[36] as exemplified by Nehemiah when he was governor in Judah (Neh 5:1-18).

It is quite obvious that nagging leadership issues and challenges are timeless and global. Much of the issues of leadership malfunction with which Ezekiel had to confront the leadership of his day are a present reality, if not far more when we consult the archive of contemporary leadership. Similar to Ezekiel's time, leadership failure leaves negative effects on the populace, causing society unnecessary loses and heartaches that good governance could have averted.

7.3 Recommendations for Further Research

We observe from our study that scholars have concentrated energy discussing the identity of the shepherd-prince in Ezek 34:23-24. The aspect of his functionality seems to have been left unattended. We need to probe whether Ezekiel's reference to the shepherd-prince has its focus in the identity of the personality of the future leader, on his functionality, or if in fact the possibility of both does exist.

Secondly, the identity of the shepherds that Ezekiel referred to is not quite resolved by scholarship. While some think that the shepherds in question were the past evil kings who led Israel (both the Northern and

---

35. Adeogun, "Jeremiah 31:31-34," 27.
36. Olatundun Abosede Oderinde, "John the Baptist's Message of Repentance and the Re-Branding Nigeria Project: A Re-Reading of Luke 3:7-14," *AJBS* 1 (2010):80.

Southern kingdoms), others suggest that Ezekiel was referring rather to the present leadership in Judah whose bad leadership brought calamity upon the city and temple in Jerusalem, probably the last three kings of Judah. Still, a third opinion construes or limits the understanding of these shepherds only to all past and present kings, except for Hezekiah and Josiah who had served in Judah. Others even suggest that it may well be that these shepherds were foreign intruders that is, foreign overlords. This tension warrants a further careful research that would interpret the available data against the historical context of the time of Ezekiel, taking into account the period of the three deportations that Judah suffered, alongside that of the Northern kingdom.

Bibliography

Allen, Leslie C. *Ezekiel 20-46.* Word Biblical Commentary 29. Dal.: Word, 1990.

_____. *Ezekiel 1-19.* Word Biblical Commentary 28. Dal.: Word, 1994.

_____. "Ezekiel." Pages 356-369 in *Old Testament Survey: The Message, Form and Background of the Old Testament.* Rev. ed. Edited by William Sanford Lasor, David Allan Hubbard, and Frederic William Bush. Grand Rapids, Mich.: Eerdmans, 1996.

Aaron, David. H. *Biblical Ambiguities: Metaphor, Semantics and Divine Imagery.* Leiden: Brill, 2001.

Arnold, Bill T., and Bryan E. Beyer. *Readings from the Ancient Near East: Primary Sources for Old Testament Study.* Grand Rapids, Mich.: Baker, 2002. Repr., 2007.

_____. *Encountering the Old Testament: EBS.* 2d ed. Grand Rapids, Mich.: Baker, 2008.

Arnold, Bill T. "Babylonians." Pages 43-75 in *Peoples of the Old Testament World.* Edited by Alfred J. Hoerth, Gerald L. Mattingly, and Edwin M. Yamauchi. Grand Rapids, Mich.: Baker, 1994. Paperback ed., 1998.

Alexander, Ralph H. "Ezekiel." Pages 737-917 in *The Expositor's Bible Commentary 6.* Edited by Frank E. Gaebelein. Grand Rapids, Mich.: Zondervan, 1986.

Alexander, Joseph Addison. *Commentary on the Prophecies of Isaiah.* Grand Rapids, Mich.: Zondervan, 1953. Repr., 1978.

Andrew, Maurice E. *Responsibility and Restoration: The Course of the Book of Ezekiel.* Dunedin: The University of Otago Press, 1985.

Albertz, Rainer. *A History of Israelite Religion in the Old Testament Period I: From the Beginnings to the End of the Monarchy.* Louisville, Ky.: Westminster John Knox Press, 1994.

Adeogun, Ebenezer Ola. "Jeremiah 31:31-34 and its Theological Implications for Rebranding." *African Journal of Biblical Studies* 1 (2010):1-28.

_____. *A History of Israelite Religion in the Old Testament Period II: From the Exile to the Maccabees*. London: SCM Press, 1994.

_____. "A Response to Oded Lipschits, The Fall and Rise of Jerusalem: Judah Under Babylonian Rule." *The Journal of Hebrew Scriptures 7*, Article 2, p6.

Averbeck, Richard E. Pages 417-433 in *The Context of Scripture II*. Edited by William W. Hallo. Leiden: Brill, 2000.

_____. "Sacrifices and Offerings." Pages 706-733 in *Dictionary of the Old Testament: Pentateuch*. Edited by T. Desmond Alexander, and David W. Baker. Downers Grove, Ill.: Inter-Varsity, 2003.

Adams, Jay Edward. *Shepherding God's Flock: A Handbook on Pastoral Ministry, Counselling, and Leadership*. Grand Rapids, Mich.: Zondervan, 1980. Repr., Nnewi, Nigeria: Life Care Ministry, 1986.

Barr, James. "Etymology and the Old Testament." In *Language and Meaning: Studies in Hebrew Language and Exegesis*. Edited by A. J. van der Woude. OTS 19; Leiden: Brill, 1974.

Baker, Warren, and Eugene Carpenter. *The Complete Word Study Dictionary: Old Testament*. Chattanooga, Tenn.: AMG, 2003.

Baker, David L. *Two Testaments, One Bible: The Theological Relationship Between the Old and New Testaments*. 3d ed. Downers Grove, Ill.: Inter-Varsity, 2010.

Boadt, Lawrence. "Rhetorical Strategies in Ezekiel's Oracles of Judgment." Pages 182-200 in *Ezekiel and his Book: Textual and Literary Criticism and their Interpretation*. Edited by Johan Lust. Leuven: Leuven University Press, 1986.

Block, Daniel Isaac. Ezekiel 1-24. *New International Commentary on the Old Testament*. Grand Rapids, Mich.: Eerdmans, 1997.

_____. Ezekiel 25-48. *New International Commentary on the Old Testament*. Grand Rapids, Mich.: Eerdmans, 1998.

_____. "God." Pages 336-355 in *Dictionary of the Old Testament: Historical Books*. Edited by Bill T. Arnold, and Hugh Godfrey Maturin Williamson. Downers Grove, Ill.: Inter-Varsity, 2005.

Brownlee, William H. "Ezekiel." Pages 250-261 in vol. 2 of *The International Standard Encyclopaedia*. Edited by Geoffrey W. Bromiley, Everett F. Harrison, Roland K. Harrison, and William Sanford Lasor. Grand Rapids, Mich.: Eerdmans, 1982. Repr., 1987.

Black, David Alan. *Linguistics for Students of New Testament Greek: A Survey of Basic Concepts and Applications*. Grand Rapids, Mich.: Baker, 1988.

Bruce, Fredrick Fyvie. "Ezekiel." Pages 807-846 in *The International Bible Commentary*. Rev. ed. Edited by F. F. Bruce. England: Marshall Morgan & Scott, 1986.

_____. *Israel and the Nations: The History of Israel from the Exodus to the Fall of the Second Temple.* Revised by David F. Payne. Downers Grove, Ill.: Inter-Varsity, 1997.

Beasley-Murray, George R. "Ezekiel." Pages 664-687 in *The New Bible Commentary*. 3d ed. Edited by Donald Guthrie, J. A. Motyer, A. M. Stibbs, and D. J. Wiseman. Grand Rapids, Mich.: Eerdmans, 1970. Repr., 1981.

_____. John: *Word Biblical Commentary* 36. 2d ed. Dal.: Thomas Nelson, 1999.

Baumann, Gerlinde. *Love and Violence: Marriage as Metaphor for the Relationship between YHWH and Israel in the Prophetic Books.* Translated by Linda M. Maloney. College Ville, Minn.: Liturgical, 2003.

Brown, Francis, S. R. Driver, and Charles A. Briggs. *The Brown-Driver-Briggs Hebrew and English Lexicon.* Boston: Houghton, Mifflin & Company, 1906. Repr., Peabody, Mass.: Hendrickson, 2005.

Baker, David W. "Agriculture." Pages 21-26 in *Dictionary of the Old Testament: Pentateuch.* Edited by T. Desmond Alexander, and David W. Baker. Downers Grove, Ill.: Inter-Varsity, 2003.

Blenkinsopp, Joseph. *Ezekiel: Interpretation.* Louisville, Ky.: Westminster John Knox, 1990.

_____. *Sages, Priest, Prophet: Religious and Intellectual Leadership in Ancient Israel.* Louisville, Ky.: Westminster John Knox, 1995.

_____. *A History of Prophecy in Israel.* Rev. and enl. ed. Minn.: Fortress, 1996.

Brueggemann, Walter. *An Introduction to the Old Testament: The Canon and Christian Imagination.* Louisville, Ky.: Westminster John Knox, 2003.

_____. *Theology of the Old Testament: Testimony, Dispute, Advocacy.* Minn.: Fortress, 1997. Paperback CD-ROM ed., 2005.

Bullock, C. Hassell. *An Introduction to the Old Testament Prophetic Books.* Chicago, Ill.: Moody, 1986.

Brewer, Douglas. "Hunting, Animal Husbandry and Diet in Ancient Egypt." Page 427-456 in *A History of the Animal World in the Ancient Near East.* Edited by Billie Jean Collins. Leiden: Brill, 2002.

Borowski, Oded. "Animals in the Literatures of Syria-Palestine." Pages 289-306 in *A History of the Animal World in the Ancient Near East.* Edited by Billie Jean Collins. Leiden: Brill, 2002.

Beyreuther, Erich. "Shepherd (ποιμήν)". Pages 564-569 in *The New Internal Dictionary of New Testament Theology Vol. III.* Edited by Colin Brown. Translated, with additions and revisions, from the German Theologisches

Begrisffslexikon Zum Neuen Testament. Edited by Lohar Coenen, Erich Beyreuther, and Hans Bietenhard. Grand Rapids, Mich.: Zondervan, 1978. Repr., Devon.: Paternoster, 1979.

Beaulieu, Paul-Alain. Pages 306-314 in vol. II of *The Context of Scripture*. Edited by William W. Hallo. Leiden: Brill, 2000.

Brisch, Nicole. *Introduction to Religion and Power: Divine Kingship in the Ancient World and Beyond, Oriental Institute Seminar Number 4*. Edited by Nichole Brisch. Chicago, Ill.: University of Chicago Press, 2008.

Blackwood, Andrew W. Jr. *Ezekiel: Prophecy of Hope*. Grand Rapids, Mich.: Baker, 1965.

Barton, George A. "The Jerusalem of David and Solomon." *The Biblical World* 1 (1903):8-21.

_____. "Influence of the Babylonian Exile on the Religion of Israel." *The Biblical World* 6 (1911):

Butler, Trent C. Joshua: *Word Biblical Commentary* 7. Edited by David A. Hubbard, and Glenn W. Baker. Waco, Tex.: Word, 1983.

Clements, Ronald Ernest. *Old Testament Prophecy: From Oracles to Canon*. Louisville, Ky.: Westminster John Knox, 1996.

_____. *Ezekiel*. Louisville, Ky.: Westminster John Knox, 1996.

Clements, Theo. "Searching for the Good Shepherd." *Netherlands archiefs voor kerkgeschiedenis* 1 (2003):11-54.

Couch, Mal, ed. *A Biblical Theology of the Church*. Grand Rapids, Michi.: Kregel, 1999.

Cogan, Mordechai. Pages 302-303 in vol. II of *The Context of Scripture*. Edited by William W. Hallo. Leiden: Brill, 2000.

Cooper, Lamar Eugene. *The New American Commentary on Ezekiel 17*. Clendenen: Broadman & Holman, 1994.

Christensen, Duane L. *Word Biblical Commentary 6A: Deuteronomy 1:1-21:9*. 2d ed. Nashville: Thomas Nelson, 2001.

Cooke, George A. *A Critical and Exegetical Commentary on the Book of Ezekiel*. Edinburg: T & T Clark, 1936.

Cook, Stephen L. "Ezekiel." Pages 1180-1252 in *The New Oxford Annotated Bible: The Revised Standard Version with the Apocrypha*. 3d ed. Edited by Michael D. Coogan, and Marc Z. Brettler. Associate editors, Coral A. Newsom, and Pheme Perkins. Oxford: Oxford University Press, 2001.

Cueni, R. Robert. "Facing the Disciples Leadership Challenge on the Front Edge of the 21st Century." *Lexington Theological Quarterly* 3 &4 (2006):223-233.

Craigie, Peter C., and Marvin E. Tate. *Psalm 1-50: Word Biblical Commentary 19*. 2d ed. Columbia: Thomas Nelson, 2004.

Craigie, Peter C., Page H. Kelly, and Joel F. Drinkard, Jr. *Jeremiah 1-25: Word Biblical Commentary 26*. Nashville: Word, 1991.

Cotterell, Peter. "Linguistics, Meaning, Semantics, and Discourse Analysis." Pages 131-157 in *A Guide to Old Testament Theology and Exegesis*. Edited by Willem A. VanGemeren. Grand Rapids, Mich.: Zondervan, 1999.

Chisholm, Robert B. Jr. *From Exegesis to Exposition: A Practical Guide to Using Biblical Hebrew*. Grand Rapids, Mich.: Baker, 1998.

Collins, Billie Jean. "Animals in Hittite Literature." Pages 237-250 in *A History of the Animal World in the Ancient Near East*. Edited by Billie Jean Collins. Leiden: Brill, 2002.

Carnes, Phillip Gene. "Like Sheep without a Shepherd: The Shepherd Metaphor and Its Primacy for Biblical Leadership." Master's Thesis, Reformed Theological Seminary, 2007.

Constable, Thomas L. "1 Kings." Pages 483-537 in *The Bible Knowledge Commentary: Old Testament*. Edited by John F. Walvoord, and Roy B. Zuck. America: Scripture Press, 1985. Repr., 1987.

Campbell, Donald K. "Joshua." Pages 325-371 in *The Bible Knowledge Commentary: Old Testament*. Edited by John F. Walvoord and Roy B. Zuck. America: Scripture Press, 1985. Repr., 1987.

Cousins, Peter E. "Deuteronomy." Pages 256-282 in *The International Bible Commentary*. Rev. ed. Edited by Frederick Fyvie Bruce. England: Marshall Morgan & Scott, 1986.

Carley, Keith C. *Ezekiel Among the Prophets: A Study of Ezekiel's Place in Prophetic Tradition*. London: SCM, 1975.

Darr, Katheryn Pfisterer. "Ezekiel Among the Critics". *Currents in Research* 2 (1994):9-24.

_____. "The Book of Ezekiel." Pages 1075-1473 in vol. VI of *The New Interpreter's Bible*. Edited by Leander Keck. Nashville, Tenn.: Abingdon, 2001.

Day, Linda. "Rhetoric and Domestic Violence in Ezekiel 16." *Interpretation* 3. (2000):205-230.

Day, Peggy L. "Adulterous Jerusalem's Imagined Demise: Death of a Metaphor in Ezekiel XVI." *Vetus Testamentum* 3 (2000):285-309.

De Vaux, Roland. *Ancient Israel: Its Life and Institutions*. Translated by John McHugh. Grand Rapids, Mich.: Eerdmans, 1997.

Duguid, Iain M. *Ezekiel and the Leaders of Israel*. Leiden: Brill, 1994.

_____. Ezekiel: *The NIV Application Commentary*. Grand Rapids, Mich.: Zondervan, 1999.

_____. "Exile." Pages 475-478 in *New Dictionary of Biblical Theology*. Edited by T. Desmond Alexander, Brian S. Rosner, Donald Anderson Carson, and Greame Goldsworthy. Downers Grove, Ill.: Inter-Varsity, 2000.

Dillard, Raymond B. and Tremper Longman III. *An Introduction to the Old Testament*. Leicester, England: Apollos, 1995.

Davis, Ellen F. *Swallowing the Scroll: Textuality and the Dynamics of Discourse in Ezekiel's Prophecy*. Almond, 1989.

Dille, Sarah J. *Mixing Metaphor: God as Father and Mother in Deutero-Isaiah*. London: T & T Clark, 2004.

Drinkard, Joel F. Jr. "Ezekiel." Pages 159-203 in vol.4 of *The Prophets: Mercer Commentary on the Bible*. Edited by Watson E. Mills, and Richard F. Wilson. Associate eds. Roger A. Bullard, Walter Harrelson, and Edgar V-McKnight. Macon: Mercer University Press, 1996.

Durham, John I. *Exodus: Word Biblical Commentary 3*. Tex.: Word, 1987.

Dumbrell, William J. *The Faith of Israel*. Rev. ed. Leicester: Apollos, 2002.

Dyer, Charles H. "Ezekiel." Pages 1225-1316 in *The Bible Knowledge Commentary: Old Testament*. Edited by John F. Walvoord, and Roy B. Zuck. America: Scripture Press, 1985. Repr., 1987.

Ellison, Henry Leupold. *Ezekiel: The Man and His Message*. Grand Rapids, Mich.: Eerdmans, 1956.

_____. "The Theology of the Old Testament." Pages 55-66 in *The International Bible Commentary*. Rev. ed. Edited Frederick Fyvie Bruce. Grand Rapids, Mich.: Marshall Morgan & Scott, 1986.

Eichrodt, Walther. *Ezekiel: A Commentary*. London: SCM, 1970.

Ehrenberg, Erica. "Dieu Et Mon Droit: Kingship in Late Babylonian and Early Persian Times." Pages 103-131 in *Religion and Power: Divine Kingship in the Ancient World and Beyond, Oriental Institute Seminar Number 4*. Edited by Nicole Brisch. Chicago, Ill.: University of Chicago Press, 2008.

Emmett, Chad F. "The Capital Cities of Jerusalem." *Geographical Review* 2 (1996):233-258.

Freedman, David Noel. "The Book of Ezekiel." *Interpretation: A Journal of Bible and Theology* 4 (1954):446-471.

Fleming, Daniel E. "Religion." Pages 670-684 in *Dictionary of the Old Testament: Pentateuch*. Edited T. Desmond Alexander, and David W. Baker. Downers Grove, Ill.: Inter-Varsity, 2003.

Flight, John W. "The Nomadic Idea and Ideal in the Old Testament." *Journal of Biblical Literature* 3/4 (1923):158-226.

Fohrer, Georg. *Introduction to the Old Testament*. Translated by David E. Green. Nashville, Tenn.: Abingdon, 1968.

Foster, Benjamin R. "Animals in Mesopotamian Literature." Pages 271-288 in *A History of the Animal World in the Ancient Near East*. Edited by Billie Jean Collins. Leiden: Brill, 2002.

Frayne, Douglas. Pages 256-302 in vol. II of *The Context of Scripture*. Edited by William W. Hallo. Leiden: Brill, 2000.

Frandsen, Paul John. "Aspects of Kingship in Ancient Egypt." Pages 47-73 in *Religion and Power: Divine Kingship in the Ancient World and Beyond, Oriental Institute Seminar Number 4*. Edited by Nicole Brisch. Ill.: University of Chicago Press, 2008.

Feinberg, Charles Lee. "Jeremiah." Pages 517-529 in vol. 6 of *The Expositor's Bible Commentary*. Edited by Frank E. Gaebelein. Grand Rapids, Mich.: Zondervan, 1986.

Gabel, John B., and Charles B. Wheeler. *The Bible As Literature: An Introduction*. New York: Oxford University Press, 1986.

Groves, J. Alan. "Zion Traditions." Pages 1019-1025 in *Dictionary of the Old Testament: Historical Books*. Edited by Bill T. Arnold, and Hugh Godfrey Maturin Williamson. Downers Grove, Ill.: Inter-Varsity, 2005.

Grisanti, Michael A. "The Davidic Covenant." *The Master's Seminary Journal* 10/2 (1999):233-250.

Greidanus, Sidney. *Preaching Christ from the Old Testament: A Contemporary Hermeneutical Method*. Grand Rapids, Mich.: Eerdmans, 1999.

Greenberg, Moshe. *Ezekiel 1-20: Anchor Bible 22B*. Garden City, New York: Doubleday, 1983.

_____. *Ezekiel 21-37: Anchor Bible 22A*. 1997. Garden City, New York: Doubleday, 2004.

Gordon, Robert P. "Exodus." Pages 149-187 in *The International Bible Commentary*. Rev. ed. Edited by Frederick Fyvie Bruce. Grand Rapids, Mich.: Marshall Morgan & Scott, 1986.

Galambush, Julie. *Jerusalem in the Book of Ezekiel: The City as Yahweh's Wife*. SBLDS 130. Atlanta, Ga.: Scholars Press, 1992.

Golding, Thomas A. "The Imagery of Shepherding in the Bible, Part I." *Bibliotheca Sacra* 163 (2006):18-28.

_____. "The Imagery of Shepherding in the Bible, Part II." *Bibliotheca Sacra* 163 (2006):158-175.

Garber, P. L. "Sheep; Shepherd." Pages 463-465 in vol. 4 of *The International Standard Bible Encyclopaedia*. Edited by Geoffrey W. Bromiley. Grand Rapids, Mich.: Eerdmans, 1988.

Gowan, Donald E. *Eschatology in the Old Testament*. 2d ed. Edinburg: T & T Clark, 2000.

Goldingay, John A. "Ezekiel." Pages 623-657 in *Eerdmans Commentary on the Bible*. Edited by James D. G. Dunn, and John W. Rogerson. Grand Rapids, Mich.: Eerdmans, 2003.

_____. *Psalms Vol. II: Psalm 42-89*. Grand Rapids, Mich.: Baker, 2007.

Gan, Jonathan. *The Metaphor of Shepherd in the Hebrew Bible: A Historical-Literary Reading*. Plymouth: University Press of America, 2007.

Gladwell, Mary Beth. "The Shepherd Motif in the Old and New Testament." No Pages. Cited 21 August 2007. Online: http://scholar.google.com/scholar?q=Imagery+of+Sheperding+in+the+new+Testament&hl=en&um=1&oi=scholart.

Gwaltney, William C. Jr. "Assyrians." Pages 77-106 in *Peoples of the Old Testament World*. Edited by Alfred J. Hoerth, Gerald L. Mattingly, and Edwin M. Yamauchi. Grand Rapids, Mich.: Baker, 1994. Paperback ed., 1998.

Graham, Gordon. *Isaiah Speaks to the 21st Century*. Drake, U.S.A.: Gordon Graham, 2000.

Glasser, Arthur F. *Announcing the Kingdom: The Story of God's Mission in the Bible*. Grand Rapids, Mich.: Baker, 2003. Repr., 2008.

Heschel, Abraham Joshua. *The Prophets: Two Volumes in One*. Peabody, Mass.: Hendrickson, 2007.

Hals, Ronald M. *Ezekiel*. Grand Rapids, Mich.: Eerdmans, 1989.

House, Paul R. *Old Testament Theology*. Downers Grove, Ill.: Inter-Varsity, 1998.

Hess, Richard S., and Gordon J. Wenham, eds. *Zion, City of Our God*. Grand Rapids, Mich.: Eerdmans, 1999.

Hess, Richard S. *Israelite Religion: An Archaeological and Biblical Survey*. Grand Rapids, Mich.: Baker, 2007.

Hullinger, Jerry M. "The Divine Presence, Uncleanness, and Ezekiel's Millennial Sacrifices." *Bibliotheca Sacra* 163 (2006):405-22.

Hill, Andrew E., and John H. Walton. *A Survey of the Old Testament*. 2d ed. Grand Rapids, Mich.: Zondervan, 2000.

Holladay, William Lee. *The Psalms Through Three Thousand Years*. Minn.: 1993. Paperback ed., Fortress, 1996.

Heim, Knut M. Heim. "The Personification of Jerusalem and the Drama of Her Bereavement in Lamentations." *In Zion, City of Our God*. Edited by Richard S. Hess and Gordon J. Wenham. Grand Rapids, Mich.: Eerdmans, 1999.

Harrison, Ronald Kenneth. *Introduction to the Old Testament*. Grand Rapids, Mich.: Eerdmans, 1969. Repr., 1979.

Human, D. J. "An ideal for leadership-Psalm 72: The (wise) king–Royal mediation of God's universal reign." *Verbum et Ecclesia JRG* 23 (3) (2002):658-677.

Irvin, William A. "Ezekiel Research Since 1943." *Vestus Testamentum* 1 (1953):54-66.

Jonker, Louis. "רעה". Pages 1138-1143 in vol. 3 of *The New International Dictionary of Old Testament Theology and Exegesis*. Edited by Willem A. VanGemeren. Grand Rapids, Mich.: Zondervan, 1997.

Jeremias, J. "ποιμήν". Pages in vol. VI of *Theological Dictionary of the New Testament*. Translated by Geoffrey W. Bromiley. Edited by Gerhard Friedrich. Grand Rapids, Mich.: Eerdmans, 1968. Repr., 1980.

Josephus, Flavius. *Josephus: The Complete Works*. Translated by William Whiston, A. M. Tenn.: Thomas Nelson, 1998.

Joyce, Paul M. "King and Messiah." Pages 323-37 in *King and Messiah in Israel and the Ancient Near East: Proceedings of the Oxford Old Testament Seminar, JSOTSup. 270*. Edited by John Day. Sheffield: Sheffield Academic Press 1998.

———. *Ezekiel: A Commentary*. New York and London, T & T Clark, 2007.

Joyce, Paul M., and Andrew Mein, eds. *After Ezekiel: Essays on the Reception of a Difficult Prophet*. London: T & T Clark, 2011.

Johnson, David H. "Shepherd, Sheep." Pages 751-754 in *Dictionary of Jesus and the Gospels*. Edited by Joel B. Green and Scott McKnight. Downers Grove, Ill.: Inter-Varsity, 1992.

Johnson, Philip C. "Exodus." Pages 51-86 in *Wycliffe Bible Commentary*. Edited by Charles F. Pfeiffer, and Everett F. Harrison. Chicago, Ill.: Moody, 1962.

Kohn, Risa Levitt. "Ezekiel At the Turn of the Century." *Currents in Biblical Research* 9 (2003):9-31.

Kistemaker, Simon J. *New Testament Commentary: Exposition of the Acts of the Apostles*. Grand Rapids, Mich.: Baker, 1990. Repr., 2004.

Kukah, Matthew Hassan. *Democracy and Civil Society in Nigeria*. Ibadan, Nigeria: Spectrum, 1999. Repr., 2000.

Keil, C. F., and F. Delitzch. *Commentary on the Old Testament in Ten Volumes*: Volume Ix-Ezekiel, Daniel. Translated by James Martin. Grand Rapids, Mich.: Eerdmans, n.d. Repr., 1978.

Klingbeil, Gerald A. "Agriculture an Animal Husbandry." Pages 1-20 in *Dictionary of the Old Testament: Historical Books*. Edited by Bill T. Arnold, and Hugh Godfrey Maturin Williamson. Downers Grove, Ill.: Inter-Varsity, 2005.

Klingbeil, Martin G. "Exile." Pages 246-248 in *Dictionary of the Old Testament: Pentateuch*. Edited by T. Desmond Alexander, and David W. Baker. Downers Grove, Ill.: Inter-Varsity, 2003.

Kato, Byang Henry. *Biblical Christianity in Africa*. Achimota, Ghana: Africa Christian Press, 1985.

Karin, Schöpflin "The Composition of Metaphorical Oracles within the Book of Ezekiel." *Vestus Testamentum* 1 (2005):101-120.

Koehler, Ludwig and Walter Baumgartner. *The Hebrew and Aramaic Lexicon of the Old Testament*. Revised by Walter Baumgartner and Johann Jakob Stamm. Translated and edited by M. E. J. Richardson. Leiden: Brill, 1996.

Kafang, Zamani Buki. *The Psalms: An Introduction to their Poetry*. Jos, Nigeria: Author, 2002.

Kövecses, Zoltán. *Metaphor: A Practical Introduction*. New York: Oxford University Press, 2002.

Klein, Ralph W. *Israel in Exile: A Theological Interpretation*. Philadelphia: Fortress, 1979.

_____. "Introduction: Ezekiel at the Dawn of the Twenty-First Century." Pages 1-11 in *The Book of Ezekiel: Theological and Anthropological Perspectives*. Edited by Margaret Sinclair Odell and John T. Strong. Atlanta, Ga.: Society of Biblical Literature, 2000.

Kline, Meredith G. "Deuteronomy." Pages 155-204 in *Wycliffe Bible Commentary*. Edited by Charles F. Pfeiffer, and Everett F. Harrison. Chicago, Ill.: Moody, 1962.

Kamionkowski, S. Tamar. *Gender Reversal and Cosmic Chaos: A Study on the Book of Ezekiel*. JSOTSup. 368. Sheffield, London: Sheffield Academic Press, 2003.

Kunhiyop, Samuel Waje. *African Christian Ethics*. Kaduna, Nigeria: Baraka, 2004.

Keener, Craig S. "Shepherd, Flock." Pages 1090-1093 in *Dictionary of the Later New Testament and Its Development*. Edited by Ralph P. Martin, and Peter H. Davids. Downers Grove, Ill.: Inter-Varsity, 1997.

Knauth, Robin J. DeWitt. "Israelites." Pages 452-458 in *Dictionary of the Old Testament: Pentateuch*. Edited by T. Desmond Alexander, and David W. Baker. Downers Grove, Ill.: Inter-Varsity, 2003.

Kaiser, Walter C. Jr. *Toward an Old Testament Theology*. Grand Rapids, Mich.: Zondervan, 1978. Repr., 1991.

_____. *Preaching and Teaching from the Old Testament: A Guide for the Church*. Grand Rapids, Mich.: Baker, 2003.

Keel, Othmar. *The Symbolism of the Biblical World: Ancient Near Eastern Iconography and the Book of Psalms*. Translated by Timothy J. Hallett. New York: Seabury, 1978. Repr., Winona Lake, Ind.: Eisenbrauns, 1997.

Kitchen, Kenneth Anderson. *On the Reliability of the Old Testament*. Grand Rapids, Mich.: Eerdmans, 2003.

Kittay, Eva Feder. *Metaphor: Its Cognitive Force and Linguistic Structure*. Oxford, New York: Oxford University Press, 1987.

Lust, Johan. *Introduction to Ezekiel and His Book: Textual and Literary Criticism and their Interpretation*. Edited by Johan Lust. Leuven, Belgium: Leuven University Press, 1986.

Levenson, Jon D. "Zion Traditions." Pages 1098-1102 in vol. 6 of *The Anchor Bible Dictionary*. Edited by David Noel Freedman. New York: Doubleday, 1992.

Luc, Alex. "A Theology of Ezekiel: God's Name and Israel's History." *Journal of the Evangelical Theological Society* 2 (1983):137-143.

Longman, Tremper III, and Raymond B. Dillard. *An Introduction to the Old Testament*. 2d ed. England: Inter-Varsity, 2007.

Laniak, Timothy S. *Shepherds after My own Heart: Pastoral Traditions and Leadership in the Bible*. Downers Grove, Ill.: Inter-Varsity, 2006. Repr., 2007.

Lasor, William Sanford. "Jerusalem." Pages 998-1032 in vol. 2 of *The International Standard Bible Encyclopaedia*. Edited by Geoffrey W. Bromiley, Everett F. Harrison, Roland K. Harrison, and William Sanford Lasor. Grand Rapids, Mich.: Eerdmans, 1982. Repr., 1987.

Lasor, William Sanford, David Allan Hubbard, and Frederic William Bush. *Old Testament Survey: The Message, Form, and Background of the Old Testament*. 2d ed. Grand Rapids, Mich.: Eerdmans, 1996.

Lilley, John. "Joshua." Pages 823-308 in *The New International Bible Commentary*. Rev ed. Edited by Frederick Fyvie Bruce. Grand Rapids, Mich.: Marshall Morgan & Scott, 1986.

Mare, W. Harold. "Zion." Pages 1096-1097 in vol. 6 of *The Anchor Bible Dictionary.* Edited by David Noel Freedman. New York: Doubleday, 1992.

Maigadi, Barje Sulmane. *Divisive Ethnicity in the Church in Africa.* Kaduna, Nigeria: Baraka, 2006.

McKeown, James. "Land, Fertility, Famine." Pages 487-491 in *Dictionary of the Old Testament: Pentateuch.* Edited by T. Desmond Alexander, and David W. Baker. Downers Grove, Ill.: Inter-Varsity, 2003.

May, Herbert G. and E. L. Allen. "Ezekiel." Pages 41-257 in vol. VI of *The Interpreter's Bible.* Edited by George Buttrick Arthur. Nashville: Abingdon, 1956.

Mays, James Luther. *Ezekiel, Second Isaiah.* Philadelphia: Fortress, 1978.

Merrill, Eugene H. "A Theology of Ezekiel and Daniel." Pages 365-395 in *A Biblical Theology of the Old Testament.* Edited by Roy B. Zuck. Chicago, Illinois: Moody, 1991.

McKeating, Henry. *Ezekiel.* JSOT, Sheffield, England: Sheffield Academic Press, 1993.

Mein, Andrew. *Ezekiel and the Ethics of Exile.* Oxford, New York: Oxford University Press, 2001.

_____. "Profitable and Unprofitable Shepherds: Economic and Theological Perspectives on Ezekiel 34." *Journal for the Study of the Old Testament* 493 (2007):493-504.

Mayo, Jim. "Covenant Theology in Ezekiel." *Restoration Quarterly* 1 (1973):23-31.

Muilenburg, James. "Ezekiel." Pages 563-585 in *Peake's Commentary on the Bible.* Edited by Matthew Black, and H. H. Rowley. London: Thomas Nelson, 1962. Repr., 1963.

MacRae, Allan A. "The Key to Ezekiel's First Thirty Chapters." *Bibliotheca Sacra* (1965):227-233.

Malone, Colleen. "Pastoral Images in the Bible." Honors Thesis, Muncie, Ind.: Ball State University, 1986.

Moore, F. C. T. "On Taking Metaphor Literally." *In Metaphor: Problems and Prospects.* Edited by David S. Miall. Sussex, Britain: The Harvest Press, 1982.

Martins, John A. "Isaiah." Pages 1029-1121 in *The Bible Knowledge Commentary, Old Testament Edition.* Edited by John F. Walvoord and Roy B. Zuck,. America: Scripture Press, 1985. Repr.,1987.

Martin, Charles G. "1 and 2 Kings." Pages 393-440 in *The New International Bible Commentary.* Rev. ed. Edited by Frederick Fyvie Bruce. Grand Rapids, Mich.: Marshall Morgan & Scott, 1986.

Metzger, Bruce M., and Roland E. Murphy, eds. *The New Oxford Annotated Bible*. New York: Oxford University Press, 1994.

Moore, Michael S., and Michael L. Brown. "צאן." Pages 727-732 in vol. 3 of *The New International Dictionary of Old Testament Theology and Exegesis*. Edited by Willem A. VanGemeren. Grand Rapids, Mich.: Zondervan, 1997.

McQuilkin, J. Robertson. *Understanding and Applying the Bible*. Chicago: Moody, 1983.

Newsom, Carol A. "A Maker of Metaphor–Ezekiel's Oracles Against Tyre." *Interpretation* 38 (1984):151-164.

Napier, B. D. "Sheep." Pages 315-316 in *The Interpreter's Dictionary of the Bible*. Edited by George Arthur Buttrick, and Thomas Samuel Kepler. Associate eds., John Knox, Herbert Gordon May, and Samuel Terrien. Nashville, Tenn.: Abingdon, 1962.

Niditch, Susan. "Ezekiel 40-48 in a Visionary Context." *The Catholic Biblical Quarterly* (1986):208-224.

Odell, Margaret Sinclair. *Ezekiel: Smyth and Helwys Bible Commentary*. Macon, Ga.: Smyth & Helwys, 2005.

Osborne, Grant R. *The Hermeneutical Spiral: A Comprehensive Introduction to Biblical Interpretation*. Downers Grove, Ill.: Inter-Varsity, 1991.

Olsen, Stein Haugom. "Understanding Literary Metaphor." Pages 36-54 in *Metaphor: Problems and Perspectives*. Edited by David S. Miall. Sussex, Britain: The Harvester Press, 1982.

Oglesby, William B. Jr. "Shepherd/Shepherding." *In Dictionary of Pastoral Care and Counseling*. Edited by Rodney J. Hunter. 2d ed. Edited by Nancy J. Ramsay. Nashville: Abingdon, 2005.

Olubunmo, D. A. "Israelite Concept of Ideal King: A Model of Interdependence of Politics and Religion for Nigeria." *African Journal of Biblical Studies* 2 (1991):59-67.

Odey, Onah Augustine. "Prophet Ezekiel's Concept of Individuality: Guidelines for Nigeria." *African Journal of Biblical Studies* 2 (1991):68-77.

Ogheneochuko, Iyede Matthew. "Josiah's Reform As A Model for Religious Political Re-Branding in Nigeria." *African Journal of Biblical Studies* 1 (2010):102-114.

Oderinde, Olatundun Abosede. "John the Baptist's Message of Repentance and the Re-Branding Nigeria Project: A Re-Reading of Luke 3:7-14." *African Journal of Biblical Studies* 1 (2010):72-83.

Petersen, David L. "Ezekiel." Pages 1222-1227 in *The Harper Collins Study Bible*. Edited by Wayne A. Meeks. New York, London: Harper Collins, 1993.

_____. *The Prophetic Literature: An Introduction.* Louisville, Ky.: Westminster John Knox, 2002.

Pearson, Anton T. "Ezekiel." Pages 703-767 in *The Wycliffe Bible Commentary.* Edited by Charles F. Pfeiffer, and Everett F. Harrison. Chicago, Ill.: Moody, 1962.

Pritchard, James B., ed. *Ancient Near Eastern Texts Relating to the Old Testament.* 3d ed. with Supplement. Princeton, N.J.: Princeton University Press, 1969. Repr., 1992.

Pritchard, James B. "The Code of Hammurabi." Pages 168-9 in *In Ancient Near Eastern Texts Relating to the Old Testament.* 3d ed. Translated by. Theophile J. Meek. Edited by James B. Pritchard. Princeton, N. J.: Princeton University Press, 1969. Repr., 1992.

Pfeiffer, Robert H. *Introduction to the Old Testament.* London: Adam & Charles Black, 1952.

Quasten, John. "The Parable of the Good Shepherd: Jn 10:1-21." *Catholic Biblical Quarterly* 1 (1948):1-169.

Routledge, Robin. *Old Testament Theology: A Thematic Approach.* England: Apollos, 2008.

Ruiz, Jesús Asurmendi. "Ezekiel." Pages 1050-1075 in *The International Bible Commentary: A Catholic and Ecumenical Commentary for the Twenty-First Century.* Edited by William R. Farmer. Collegeville, Minn.: Liturgical, 1998.

Robertson, O. Palmer. *The Christ of the Prophets.* Phillipsburg, N. J.: P&R, 2004.

Roberts, J. J. M. "The Davidic Origin of the Zion Tradition." *Society of Biblical Literature* (1973):329-344.

Ryken, Leland, James C. Wilhoit, and Tremper Longman III, eds. *Dictionary of Biblical Imagery.* Downers Grove, Ill.: Inter-Varsity, 1998.

Ryken, Leland. *Words of Delight: A Literary Introduction to the Bible.* Rev. ed. Grand Rapids, Mich.: Baker, 1992. Sixth pri., 2001.

Raitt, Thomas M. *A Theology of Exile: Judgment/Deliverance in Jeremiah and Ezekiel.* Philadelphia: Fortress, 1977.

Rainey, A. F. "Zion." Pages 1198-1200 in vol. 4 of *The International Standard Bible Encyclopaedia.* Edited by Geoffrey W. Bromiley, Everett F. Harrison, Roland Kenneth Harrison, and William Sanford Lasor. Grand Rapids, Mich.: Eerdmans, 1988.

Renz, Thomas. "Ezekiel, Book of." Pages 218-223 in *Dictionary for Theological Interpretation of the Bible.* Edited by Kevin J. Vanhoozer, and Craig G. Bartholomew. Associate eds., Daniel J. Treier, and Nicholas Thomas Wright. Grand Rapids, Mich.: Baker, 2005. Repr., 2006.

Schöpflin Karin, "The Composition of Metaphorical Oracles within the Book of Ezekiel." *Vestus Testamentum* 1 (2005):101-120.

Soulen, Richard N. and R. Kendall. *Handbook of Biblical Criticism*. 3d ed. Louisville, Ky.: Westminster John Knox, 2001.

Sommer, Benjamin D. "Revelation at Sinai in the Hebrew Bible and in Jewish Theology." *The Journal of Religion* 3 (1999):422-451.

Schultz, Samuel J. and Gary V. Smith. *Exploring the Old Testament*. Wheaton, Ill.: Crossway, 2001.

Shields, Mary E. "Multiple Exposures: Body Rhetoric and Gender Characterization in Ezekiel 16." *Journal of Feminist Studies in Religion* 1 (1998):5-18.

Soskice, Janet Martin. *Metaphor and Religious Language*. Oxford, New York: Oxford University Press, 1985. Paperback, 1989.

Stienstra, Nelly. *YHWH is the Husband of His People*. Kampen: Kok Pharos, 1993.

Silva, Moisés. *Biblical Words and Their Meaning: An Introduction to Lexical Semantics*. Rev. ed. Grand Rapids, Mich.: Zondervan, 1994.

Sparks, Kenton L. *Ancient Texts for the Study of the Hebrew Bible: A Guide to the Background Literature*. 2d ed. Peabody, Mass.: Hendrickson, 2006.

Stitzinger, James F. "Pastoral Ministry in History." Pages 34-63 in *Rediscovering Pastoral Ministry: Shaping Contemporary Ministry with Biblical Mandates*. Edited by John McArthur. Nashville, Tenn.: W. Publication Group, 1995.

Soggin, J. Alberto. *Introduction to the Old Testament*. 2d. ed. Translated by John Bowden. London: SCM, 1980.

Sweeney, Marvin Alan. *The Prophetic Literature: Interpreting Biblical Texts*. Nashville, Tenn.: Abingdon, 2005.

Shreibe, Maeeray Y. "The End of Exile: Jewish Identity and Its Diasporic Poetics." *In Modern Language Association* 2 (1998):273-287.

Stalker, David Muir Gibson. *Ezekiel: Introduction and Commentary*. 1968. 2d impression. London: SCM, 1971.

Skinner, John. "The Book of Ezekiel." Pages 220-303 in vol. 4 of *The Expositor's Bible: A Complete Exposition of the Bible in Six Volumes*. Edited by Robertson W. Nicoll. Grand Rapids, Mich.: Eerdmans, 1943.

Scurlock, JoAnn. "Animal Sacrifice in Ancient Mesopotamian Religion." Pages 389-403 in *A History of the Animal World in the Ancient Near East*. Edited by Billie Jean Collins. Leiden: Brill, 2002.

Smith, Ralph L. *Micah-Malachi: Word Biblical Commentary 32*. Waco, Tex.: Word, 1984.

Seitz, Christopher R. *Prophecy and Hermeneutics: Toward a New Introduction to the Prophets.* Grand Rapids, Mich.: Baker, 2007.

Sheriffs, Deryck C. T. "'A Tale of Two Cities'–Nationalism in Zion and Babylon." *Tyndale Bulletin* 39 (1988):21-22.

Taylor, John Bunn. *Ezekiel: An Introduction and Commentary.* London: Tyndale, 1969.

_____. "Ezekiel." Pages 223-337 in vol. 6 of *The Broadman Bible Commentary (Jeremiah-Daniel).* Edited by Clifton J. Allen. Nashville, Tenn.: Broadman, 1971.

Thomson, J. G. S. S. "The Shepherd-Ruler Concept in the OT and Its Application in the NT." *Scottish Journal of Theology* 8 (1955):406-18.

Tiénou, Tite. *The Theological Task of the Church in Africa.* 2d ed. Achimota, Ghana: Africa Christian Press, 1990.

Turaki, Yusuf. *Tribal Gods of Africa: Ethnicity, Racism, Tribalism and the Gospel of Christ.* Nairobi, Kenya: Ethics, Peace and Justice Commission of AEA, 1997.

Tuell, Steven Shawn. *The Law of the Temple in Ezekiel 40-48.* Atlanta, Ga.: Scholars Press, 1992.

Tromp, Nicholas J. "The Paradox of Ezekiel's Prophetic Mission: Towards a Semiotic Approach of Ezekiel 3, 22-27." Pages 200-213 in *Ezekiel and His Book: Textual and Literary Criticism and their Interpretation.* Edited by Johan Lust. Leuven, Belgium: Leuven University Press, 1986.

Travers, Michael E. "The Use of Figures of Speech in the Bible." *Bibliotheca Sacra* 164 (2007):277-290.

Usue, E. O. "Leadership in Africa and in the Old Testament: A Transcendental Perspective." *HTS* 62, 2 (2006):635-656.

VanGemeren, Willem A. *Interpreting the Prophetic Word: An Introduction to the Prophetic Literature of the Old Testament.* Grand Rapids, Mich.: Zondervan, 1990.

Vawter, Bruce and Leslie J. Hoppe. *A New Heart: A Commentary on the Book of Ezekiel.* Grand Rapids, Mich.: Eerdmans, 1991.

Vancil, Jack W. "Sheep, Shepherd." Pages 1187-1190 in vol. 5 of *The Anchor Bible Dictionary.* Edited by David Freedman Noel. New York: Doubleday, 1992.

Vaux, Roland De. *Ancient Israel: Its Life and Institutions.* English translation by John McHugh. London: Darton, Longman & Todd, 1961. Jointly published by Grand Rapids, Mich.: Eerdmans & Livonia: Dore Booksellers, 1997.

Vos, Geerhardus. *Biblical Theology: Old and New Testaments*. Edinburgh: The Banner of Truth Trust, 1975. Repr., 1996.

Wevers, John W. "Ezekiel." Pages x-265 in *The Century Bible: New Series*. Edited by John W. Wevers. London: Thomas Nelson, 1969.

Wilson, Robert R. "Prophecy in Crisis: The Call of Ezekiel." *Interpretation: A Journal of Bible and Theology* 2 (1984):117-130.

_____. "Ezekiel." In *The Harper Collins Bible Commentary*. Rev. ed. Edited by James Luther Hays, and Joseph Blenkinsopp. New York: Harper Collins, 2000.

Wright, Christopher J. H. *The Message of Ezekiel: A New Heart and a New Spirit*. Leicester, England: Inter-Varsity, 2002.

Wood, Leon James. *A Survey Israel's History*. Rev. ed. Revised by David O'Brien. Grand Rapids, Mich.: Zondervan, 1986.

Wright, G. Ernest. "The Good Shepherd." *The Biblical Archaeologist* 4. (1939):44-48.

Walton, John H. "Principles for Productive Word Study." Pages 158-168 in *A Guide to Old Testament Theology and Exegesis*. Edited by Willem A. VanGemeren. Grand Rapids, Mich.: Zondervan, 1999.

_____. *Ancient Near Eastern Thought and the Old Testament: Introducing the Conceptual World of the Hebrew Bible*. Grand Rapids, Mich.: Baker, 2006.

Waltke, Bruce K. "Micah." Pages 591-764 in vol. 2 of *An Exegetical and Expository Commentary on the Minor Prophets*. Edited by Thomas Edward McComiskey. Grand Rapids, Mich.: Baker, 1993. Repr., 2006.

_____. *An Old Testament Theology: An exegetical, Canonical, and Thematic Approach*. Grand Rapids, Mich.: Zondervan, 2007.

Weinfeld, Moshe. "Zion and Jerusalem as Religious and Political Capital: Ideology and Utopia." Pages 75-115 in *The Poet and the Historian: Essays in Literary and Historical Biblical Criticism*. Edited by Friedman Richard Elliot. Chico, Calif.: Scholars Press, 1983.

Ward, James Merrill. *Thus Says the Lord: The Message of the Prophets*. Nashville, Tenn.: Abingdon, 1991.

Wood, W. Carleton. "The Religion of Canaan: From the Earliest Times to the Hebrew Conquest." *Journal of Biblical Literature* 1/2 (1916):18-22.

Wiseman, Donald. "Jeremiah." Pages 764-799 in *The International Bible Commentary*. Rev. ed. Edited by Frederick Fyvie Bruce. Grand Rapids, Mich.: Zondervan, 1986.

White, Roger M. *The Structure of Metaphor: The Way the Language of Metaphor Works*. Oxford, U. K.: Blackwell, 1996.

Weiss, Andrea L. *Figurative Language in Biblical Prose Narrative: Metaphor in the Book of Samuel*. Leiden: Brill, 2006.

Wallis, G. "רָעָה". Pages 544-553 in vol. XIII of *Theological Dictionary of the Old Testament*. Edited by G. Johannes Botterweck, Helmer Ringgren, and Heinz-Yosef Fabry. Translated by David E. Green. Grand Rapids, Mich.: Eerdmans, 2004.

Watts, John D. W. *Isaiah 34-66: Word Biblical Commentary 25*. Rev. ed. Nashville, Dal.: Thomas Nelson, 2005.

Williamson, Paul R. "Covenant." Pages 139-155 in *Dictionary of the Old Testament: Pentateuch*. Edited by T. Desmond Alexander, and David W. Baker. Downers Grove, Ill.: Inter-Varsity, 2003.

Zimmerli, Walter. *Ezekiel 1: A Commentary on the Book of the Prophet Ezekiel, Chapters 1-24*. Translated by Ronald Ernest Clements. Hermeneia, Philadelphia: Fortress, 1979.

_____. *Ezekiel 2: A Commentary on the Book of the Prophet Ezekiel, Chapters 25-48*. Translated by J. D. Martin. Hermeneia, Philadelphia: Fortress, 1983.

Zodhiates, Spiros, ed. Assistant eds., Warren Baker, and Joel Kletzing. *Hebrew-Greek Key Word Study Bible*. Chattanooga, Tenn.: AMG, 1990.

Langham Literature and its imprints are a ministry of Langham Partnership.

Langham Partnership is a global fellowship working in pursuit of the vision God entrusted to its founder John Stott -

> *to facilitate the growth of the church in maturity and Christ-likeness through raising the standards of biblical preaching and teaching.*

Our vision is to see churches equipped for mission and growing to maturity in Christ through the ministry of pastors and leaders who believe, teach and live by the Word of God.

Our mission is to strengthen the ministry of the Word of God through:
- nurturing national movements for training in biblical preaching
- multiplying the creation and distribution of evangelical literature
- strengthening the theological training of pastors and leaders by qualified evangelical teachers

Our ministry

Langham Preaching partners with national leaders to nurture indigenous biblical preaching movements for pastors and lay preachers all around the world. With the support of a team of trainers from many countries, a multi-level programme of seminars provides practical training, and is followed by a programme for training local facilitators. Local preachers' groups and national and regional networks ensure continuity and ongoing development, seeking to build vigorous movements committed to Bible exposition.

Langham Literature provides majority world pastors, scholars and seminary libraries with evangelical books and electronic resources through grants, discounts and distribution. The programme also fosters the creation of indigenous evangelical books for pastors in many languages, through training workshops for writers and editors, sponsored writing, translation, strengthening local evangelical publishing houses, and investment in major regional literature projects, such as one volume Bible commentaries like *The Africa Bible Commentary*.

Langham Scholars provides financial support for evangelical doctoral students from the majority world so that, when they return home, they may train pastors and other Christian leaders with sound, biblical and theological teaching. This programme equips those who equip others. Langham Scholars also works in partnership with majority world seminaries in strengthening evangelical theological education. A growing number of Langham Scholars study in high quality doctoral programmes in the majority world itself. As well as teaching the next generation of pastors, graduated Langham Scholars exercise significant influence through their writing and leadership.

To learn more about Langham Partnership and the work we do visit **langham.org**

www.ingramcontent.com/pod-product-compliance
Lightning Source LLC
Chambersburg PA
CBHW070233240426
43673CB00044B/1780